Distant Justice

The Impact of the International Criminal Court on African Politics

There are a number of controversies surrounding the International Criminal Court (ICC) in Africa. Critics have charged it with neo-colonial meddling in African affairs, accusing it of undermining national sovereignty and domestic attempts to resolve armed conflict. Here, based on 650 interviews over eleven years, Phil Clark critically assesses the politics of the ICC in Uganda and the Democratic Republic of Congo, focusing on the Court's multi-level impact on national politics and the lives of everyday citizens. He explores the ICC's effects on peace negotiations, national elections, domestic judicial reform, amnesty processes, combatant demobilisation and community-level accountability and reconciliation. Clark also reveals that, in attempting to distance itself from African conflict zones geographically, philosophically and procedurally, the ICC has become more politicised and damaging to African polities. This necessitates a substantial rethink of the ideas and approaches that underpin the ICC's practice of distant justice.

PHIL CLARK is a Reader in Comparative and International Politics at SOAS, University of London. He specialises in conflict and post-conflict issues in Africa, including transitional justice, peacebuilding and reconciliation. He is also a senior research fellow at the School of Leadership at the University of Johannesburg. Previously, Dr Clark was the co-founder and convenor of Oxford Transitional Justice Research and established the Research, Policy and Higher Education programme at the Aegis Trust Rwanda. His articles have featured in the *Guardian*, the *New York Times*, the BBC and CNN websites, *Foreign Affairs*, *Times Higher Education Supplement*, *Prospect*, *Dissent*, *The East African*, the *Australian* and the Huffington Post. His last book was *The Gacaca Courts, Post-Genocide Justice and Reconciliation in Rwanda: Justice without Lawyers* (Cambridge, 2010). He holds a doctorate in Politics from the University of Oxford, where he studied as a Rhodes Scholar.

Distant Justice

The Impact of the International Criminal Court on African Politics

PHIL CLARK
School of Oriental and African Studies, University of London

CAMBRIDGE
UNIVERSITY PRESS

CAMBRIDGE
UNIVERSITY PRESS

University Printing House, Cambridge CB2 8BS, United Kingdom

One Liberty Plaza, 20th Floor, New York, NY 10006, USA

477 Williamstown Road, Port Melbourne, VIC 3207, Australia

314–321, 3rd Floor, Plot 3, Splendor Forum, Jasola District Centre,
New Delhi – 110025, India

79 Anson Road, #06–04/06, Singapore 079906

Cambridge University Press is part of the University of Cambridge.

It furthers the University's mission by disseminating knowledge in the pursuit of
education, learning, and research at the highest international levels of excellence.

www.cambridge.org
Information on this title: www.cambridge.org/9781108474092
DOI: 10.1017/9781108576260

First published 2018

Printed and bound in Great Britain by Clays Ltd, Elcograf S.p.A.

A catalogue record for this publication is available from the British Library.

Library of Congress Cataloging-in-Publication Data
Names: Clark, Philip, 1979- author.
Title: Distant justice : the impact of the International Criminal Court on African politics /
    Phil Clark.
Description: New York, NY : Cambridge University Press, 2018. |
    Includes bibliographical references and index.
Identifiers: LCCN 2018024262 | ISBN 9781108474092 (hardback : alk. paper) |
    ISBN 9781108463379 (pbk. : alk. paper)
Subjects: LCSH: International Criminal Court–Influence. | Complementarity
    (International law) | International Criminal Court–Political aspects–Africa, Eastern. |
    Criminal justice, Administration of–Africa, Eastern. | International crimes–Law and
    legislation–Africa, Eastern.
Classification: LCC KZ7312 .C53 2018 | DDC 345.01–dc23
LC record available at https://lccn.loc.gov/2018024262

ISBN 978-1-108-47409-2 Hardback
ISBN 978-1-108-46337-9 Paperback

Contents

Acknowledgements

A book based on eleven years of research is only possible with the sustained support of many people around the world. I am particularly grateful to the three university departments where I worked between 2006 and 2017 – the Transitional Justice Institute, University of Ulster; the Centre for Socio-Legal Studies, University of Oxford; and the Department of Politics and International Studies, SOAS, University of London – for giving me the necessary time and resources to conduct field research and to write. The vibrant network of staff and students at Oxford Transitional Justice Research (OTJR) has also been an invaluable source of debate, critique and encouragement throughout the writing of this book.

This project began as a report for the Open Society Justice Initiative (OSJI) but rapidly developed into something much larger. I am grateful to the OSJI for the funding that kick-started the project and to Kelly Askin and Tracey Gurd for their advice, enthusiasm and patience during the early stages, even when I missed the thirteenth deadline. I have also received generous funding for the field research that underpins this book from the Fetzer Institute, the Planethood Foundation, the REDRESS Trust, the Aegis Trust and the Royal African Society.

Some superb Ugandan and Congolese friends and colleagues have been indispensable research partners at every stage of this project. In particular, I am indebted to Jacob Candano, Stephen Oola, Babra Atim, Henry Komakech, Ketty Anyeko, Lyandro Komakech, Lino Ogora, Richard Kica, Stephen Okello, Marcel Wetsh'okonda, Joel Bisubu, Brigitte Mapendo and Olivier Kambala.

Many other people have graciously shared their contacts, commented on my draft chapters and public seminars and provided constant support, especially Alison Cole, Maria Warren, Nicholas Waddell, Ron Atkinson, Denise Dunovant, Holly and Ben Porter, Anna Macdonald, Beau Hopkins, Mareike Schomerus, Katherine Liao, Katherine Southwick, Clare McRae, Dick Munyeshuli, Kirk

Simpson, Michael Hamilton, Kirsten McConnachie, Jérémie Gilbert, Shane Darcy, Kieran McEvoy, Louise Mallinder, Sara Templer, Maria Varaki, David Anderson, Henry Shue, Leigh Payne, Francesca Lessa, Leila Ullrich, Carolyn Hoyle, Denis Galligan, Matilde Gawronksi, Lydiah Bosire, Lionel Nichols, Briony Jones, Julia Paulson, Par Engstrom, Harry Verhoeven, Phil Roessler, Zachary Kaufman, Adam Branch, Sarah Nouwen, Sharath Srinivasan, Iavor Rangelov, Miles Jackson, Felix Ndahinda, Leslie Vinjamuri, Stephen Hopgood, Fiona Adamson, Tom Young, Stephen Chan, Marco Jowell, Chandra Sriram, George Crowder, Sara Kendall, Christian De Vos, Carsten Stahn, Mark Drumbl, Stephan Parmentier, Tim Murithi and Fanie du Toit. This book also benefited substantially from Richie Howarth's research assistance, the constant backing of Maria Marsh at CUP and the insightful comments by three anonymous CUP reviewers.

Close friends have helped keep this project on track when the finishing line seemed unreachable, particularly Clinton Free, Ian MacAuslan, Steve Allender, Megan Claringbold, Charlie Foster, Gill Cowburn, Mark Bahlin, Matt Skopal, Phil Gregory, Robyn George, Ali Millard, Matt Lucas, Anamitra Deb, Polly Haste, Bill and Sue Bonney, Kym, Dianne, Elizabeth and Amanda Boxall, David, Cheryl and Matthew Turnbull, Niall Maclean, Len Epp, James Hickling, Jan Strugnell, John and Jo Pickhaver, Chloe Lamb, Ben Hooper, Denis Bikesha, Aimable Twahirwa, Kate Orkin, Jonny Steinberg, Lomin Saayman, Trav McLeod, Julia Mathieson, Neil Kruger, Jess Purcell-Jones, Nick Gallus, Tony Buti, Steve Daley, Luke Jones, Matt Baker, Gareth Morgan, Alex Wyatt, James Watson, Dave Close, Debbie and Daniel Matthee, Ty Graham, Hannah Clayton and Troy Utz.

In Belfast and Adelaide, Lis and Norm Porter have provided endless intellectual and emotional sustenance. The first drafts of this book were written under their roof in North Belfast and the final drafts were debated with them over late night whiskey in North London. Meanwhile, in Grahamstown and Kenton, my parents-in-law Tony and Tally have provided abundant hospitality and coastal escapes from the writing grind.

The timespan of this project has witnessed upheaval in my family – deaths, a marriage and a birth. My maternal grandparents Gwenda and Harrold, both energetic writers and readers, died in 2012 and 2015, respectively. For the bulk of the time I was writing this book, my dad Peter was undergoing chemotherapy after being diagnosed with lymphoma in 2009. I regret that he never got to see this published, not least because he spent a decade inquiring with increasing exasperation, 'So have you finished it yet?' All the while, my mum Miriam, my brothers, Dan, Dave and Steve, and sister-in-law Bek have responded to Dad's death with characteristic grace and have been a constant source of love and strength.

   In 2014, I married Nikki Palmer, whose love, encouragement and incisive comments on the final manuscript have carried me through this project. This book draws heavily on our debates over the last decade – most of them in crammed minibuses across central Africa – as well as the ideas expressed in her book, *Courts in Conflict: Interpreting the Layers of Justice in Post-Genocide Rwanda* (OUP). In 2015, soon after Nikki's book was published, our son Angus was born. His scribbles on the manuscript – literal and metaphorical – mark every page here. This book is dedicated to Dad, whose influence resonates, and to Angus, who brings us such joy.

Abbreviations

ABA/ROLI	American Bar Association/Rule of Law Initiative
ADF	Allied Defence Forces
AFDL	Alliance des Forces Démocratiques pour la Libération du Congo/Zaire
AI	Amnesty International
ARLPI	Acholi Religious Leaders Peace Initiative
ASP	Assembly of States Parties
AU	African Union
BBC	British Broadcasting Corporation
CAR	Central African Republic
CNDP	Congrès National pour la Défense du Peuple
CoR	Council of Representatives
CPA	Comprehensive Peace Agreement
DDR	disarmament, demobilisation and reintegration
DRC	Democratic Republic of Congo
ECOWAS	Economic Community of West African States
EC	European Commission
EU	European Union
FARDC	Forces Armées de la République Démocratique du Congo
FDC	Forum for Democratic Change
FDLR	Forces Démocratiques de Libération du Rwanda
FIB	Force Intervention Brigade
FIDH	Fédération Internationale des Ligues des Droits de l'Homme
FN	Forces Nouvelles
FNI	Front des Nationalistes et Intégrationnistes

FRPI	Forces de Résistance Patriotiques en Ituri
GNC	General National Congress
HRW	Human Rights Watch
IBA	International Bar Association
ICC	International Criminal Court
ICD	International Crimes Division
ICJ	International Court of Justice
ICTJ	International Center for Transitional Justice
ICTR	International Criminal Tribunal for Rwanda
ICTY	International Criminal Tribunal for the former Yugoslavia
IDP	internally displaced person
IHRLG	International Human Rights Law Group
ILP	initiatives locales de paix
IRC	International Rescue Committee
IS	Islamic State
IWPR	Institute for War and Peace Reporting
JCCD	Jurisdiction, Complementarity and Cooperation Division
JLOS	Justice, Law and Order Sector
JRP	Justice and Reconciliation Project
KKA	Ker Kwaro Acholi
LC	Local Council
LRA	Lord's Resistance Army
M23	March 23 Movement
MLC	Mouvement pour la Libération du Congo
MoD	Ministry of Defence
MONUC	Mission de l'Organisation des Nations Unies en République Démocratique du Congo
MONUSCO	Mission de l'Organisation des Nations Unies pour la Stabilisation en République Démocratique du Congo
MSF	Médecins sans Frontières
NATO	North Atlantic Treaty Organisation
NGO	non-governmental organisation
NRC	Norwegian Refugee Council

NRM	National Resistance Movement
NTC	National Transitional Council
NUPI	Northern Ugandan Peace Initiative
ODM	Orange Democratic Movement
OHCHR	United Nations Office of the High Commissioner for Human Rights
OSISA	Open Society Initiative for Southern Africa
OSJI	Open Society Justice Initiative
OTJR	Oxford Transitional Justice Research
OTP	Office of the Prosecutor
PC	Presidential Council
PDA	People's Democratic Army
PNU	Party of National Unity
PPRD	Parti du Peuple pour la Reconstruction et la Démocratie
PTC	Pre-Trial Chamber
PUSIC	Parti pour l'Unité et la Sauvegarde de l'Intégrité du Congo
R2P	responsibility to protect
RC	Resistance Council
RCD	Rassemblement Congolais pour la Démocratie
RCN	Réseau des Citoyens-Citizens' Network
REJUSCO	Restoration of Justice in the East of the DRC
RHA	Réseau Haki na Amani
RPA	Rwandan Patriotic Army
RPF	Rwandan Patriotic Front
SPLM/A	Sudan People's Liberation Movement/Army
SSR	security sector reform
TFV	Trust Fund for Victims
TJRC	Truth, Justice and Reconciliation Commission
TJWG	Transitional Justice Working Group
TRC	Truth and Reconciliation Commission
UK	United Kingdom
UN	United Nations
UNICEF	United Nations Children's Fund

Map of Key ICC-Related Locations in Central Africa

Map of Key ICC-Related Locations in Central Africa

1 | *Introduction*
The Warlord in the Forecourt

Introduction

On the morning of Monday, 18 March 2013, a white taxi pulled up outside the United States (US) embassy in the Rwandan capital, Kigali.[1] A broad-shouldered man wearing a dark blue jacket and a black baseball cap stepped out of the vehicle and walked into the security office to the left of the main gates. At the front desk, he demanded to speak to the US ambassador. The security official asked whether he had an appointment, to which he replied, 'When you tell the ambassador who I am, I'm sure he'll want to see me.' The official asked the man to take a seat while she made a telephone call. He remained there for one hour before being motioned through the metal detectors and told to wait in the paved forecourt, dotted with green ferns, between the office and the white-columned doors of the embassy. Pacing back and forth, he waited another hour before an embassy official emerged and whisked him inside.

The man in question was the Congolese rebel leader, Bosco Ntaganda. In 2006 and 2012, the International Criminal Court (ICC) issued warrants for his arrest on eighteen counts of war crimes and crimes against humanity committed in the Ituri district of north-eastern Democratic Republic of Congo (DRC) in 2002 and 2003.[2] Once Ntaganda was safely inside the embassy, he informed US officials that he wanted to hand himself over to the ICC. For two hours one of the world's most wanted fugitives – dubbed 'The Terminator' by much

---

[1] The account that follows here is based on the author's interviews with US embassy staff and other foreign diplomats, 4–10 April 2013, Kigali.
[2] International Criminal Court, 'The Prosecutor *v.* Bosco Ntaganda', ICC-01/04-02/06, www.icc-cpi.int/drc/ntaganda.

1

of the international press[3] – had waited outside the embassy, unsure if he would be allowed to surrender himself to justice.

By the end of that Monday, word had reached the global media that Ntaganda was in US custody.[4] A rumour, almost certainly false, spread through Kigali that the taxi driver who delivered Ntaganda to the embassy, upon discovering the identity of his passenger, contacted the US authorities to claim the $5 million legislated two months earlier under the US War Crimes Reward Program for anyone providing information leading to the arrest, transfer or conviction of a suspected perpetrator of international crimes.[5] Baffled US and Rwandan officials meanwhile debated what to do with Ntaganda. Neither state is a signatory to the Rome Statute governing the ICC, and both have often been openly hostile toward the Court. Neither government wanted to be seen to aid the ICC by handing over Ntaganda, and both wanted to extract vital intelligence from him before deciding their next moves.

For Rwanda in particular, Ntaganda was potentially a political timebomb. The Rwandan government had trained, armed and supported Ntaganda – a Congolese citizen but born in Kinigi, a small border town in north-western Rwanda in the foothills of the Virunga mountain range – as he led various rebel groups in eastern DRC before being integrated into the Congolese national army and rising to the rank of colonel. Rwanda feared that any international trial of Ntaganda could uncover incriminating details of its military involvement in eastern DRC.

The immediate events leading to Ntaganda's surrender were especially fraught for Rwanda. In April 2012, integrated rebels from the former Congrès National pour la Défense du Peuple (CNDP), led by Ntaganda, mutinied against the Congolese army and formed a new

---

[3] See, for example, D. Smith, 'Hunting The Terminator: Congo Continues Search for Bosco Ntaganda', *Guardian*, 28 November 2012, www.theguardian.com/world/2012/nov/28/terminator-search-bosco-ntaganda-congo; K. Manson, 'Tea with The Terminator: The Day I Met Bosco Ntaganda', *Financial Times*, 23 March 2013, http://blogs.ft.com/the-world/2013/03/tea-with-the-terminator-the-day-i-met-bosco-ntaganda/.

[4] See, for example, BBC, 'Bosco Ntaganda: Wanted Congolese in US Mission in Rwanda', 18 March 2013, www.bbc.co.uk/news/world-africa-21835345.

[5] United States Department of State, 'War Crimes Reward Program', www.state.gov/j/gcj/wcrp/. This rumour was still doing the rounds when I arrived in Kigali on 3 April 2013.

rebel group, the March 23 Movement (M23).[6] In November 2012, the M23 seized control of Goma, the provincial capital of North Kivu, sparking a conflict with the Congolese army and the United Nations (UN) peacekeeping mission, MONUSCO[7], which forcibly displaced nearly 200,000 civilians. After the M23 capture of Goma, several international donors, including the US, suspended part or all of their foreign aid to Rwanda, which they accused of backing the M23 rebellion.[8]

As this diplomatic controversy unfolded in early 2013, in-fighting among the M23 leadership caused a violent split between factions led by Ntaganda and Sultani Makenga, respectively. The Makenga faction quickly gained ascendancy and routed Ntaganda's forces. On 16 March 2013, Ntaganda and 200 of his men fled into the forests of the Virunga National Park.[9] Caught between his former M23 allies and an unknown fate if he found himself in Rwandan government hands, Ntaganda entered Rwanda on foot two days later and made his way to Kigali, believing the refuge of the US embassy and a ticket to face international justice in The Hague were his only means of survival.[10]

The path to the ICC, however, was not nearly as smooth as Ntaganda might have hoped. It took US and Rwandan authorities – with their own tensions over the M23 situation – four days to negotiate his fate. On 22 March 2013, they transported him under heavy security to Kigali's Grégoire Kayibanda airport. Accompanied by diplomats from the US, the United Kingdom (UK), the Netherlands, Belgium and the European Union (EU), Ntaganda was held in the airport VIP lounge waiting to board a plane sent by the Dutch government to transfer him

---

[6] The name M23 refers to the 23 March 2009 peace deal signed by the CNDP and the Congolese government. The rebels alleged that the government had reneged on the deal by not paying their salaries and threatening to disperse their ranks across the DRC, thus disrupting a parallel chain of command that the rebels maintained within the national army.

[7] MONUSCO is the abbreviation for the Mission de l'Organisation des Nations Unies pour la Stabilisation en République Démocratique du Congo (United Nations Organisation Stabilisation Mission in the Democratic Republic of Congo).

[8] See, for example, Al Jazeera, 'Germany Latest to Suspend Rwanda Aid', 29 July 2012, www.aljazeera.com/news/africa/2012/07/20127281579389961.html.

[9] See, for example, Gulf Times, 'Defeated Congo Rebels Surrender', 16 March 2013, www.gulf-times.com/story/345710/Defeated-Congo-rebels-surrender.

[10] Author's interviews, US and other foreign diplomats, Kigali, 4–10 April 2013.

to The Hague. While Ntaganda waited, the diplomats argued over which government was responsible for purchasing the fuel for his flight. The Dutch representative protested that the Netherlands had paid for the incoming flight and it was therefore the other states' responsibility to cover the return journey. The American diplomat argued that, as a non-signatory to the Rome Statute, the US could not be seen to support the ICC financially in any way. After hours of wrangling and frantic phone calls to various European capitals, the remaining officials handed over their credit cards, the plane was refuelled and Ntaganda, flanked by Dutch security guards, was led onboard.

Delivered into ICC custody in The Hague on the night of 22 March 2013, Ntaganda made his first appearance before the ICC judges four days later. He denied all of the charges against him. The charges were confirmed on 9 June 2014 – meaning that he had a *prima facie* case to answer – and his trial began on 2 September 2015, almost two and a half years after he nervously paced the embassy forecourt in Kigali.

Intervention and Intersections: Analysing the ICC's Political Impact in Africa

The broad purpose of this book is to assess critically the politics of the ICC in Uganda and the DRC – and Africa more broadly – focusing on the Court's impact on national politics and the lives of everyday citizens. The book uses the central concept of 'distance' to examine the effects in central Africa of delivering justice from afar. 'Distance' in this context denotes the physical location of the ICC in The Hague, removed from the sites where it investigates crimes and extracts suspects and witnesses; the philosophical underpinnings of the ICC's model of 'neutral and impartial' justice; and the Court's predominantly non-African staff, many of whom have limited previous experience of the people and places on which they now work. These themes are highly salient, given the recent threat by various members of the African Union (AU) to withdraw their ratifications of the Rome Statute on the grounds of the Court's neo-colonialist meddling on the continent.[11] Concerns over the ICC's political impact in Africa have

---

[11] See, for example, Guardian, 'African Leaders Plan Mass Withdrawal from the International Criminal Court', 31 January 2017, www.theguardian.com/law/ 2017/jan/31/african-leaders-plan-mass-withdrawal-from-international-criminal-court.

also gained prominence because of the Court's arrest warrants against Sudanese President Omar al-Bashir, Kenyan President Uhuru Kenyatta, Kenyan Deputy President William Ruto William Ruto, former Ivorian President Laurent Gbagbo and former Congolese Vice President Jean-Pierre Bemba.[12]

As the Ntaganda transfer highlights, enacting the high-minded ideals of international justice involves messy political and security machinations 'on the ground'. It shows the entanglement of the ICC with volatile conflict dynamics and unpredictable events such as the rupture within the M23 that led to Ntaganda's surrender; delicate political negotiations, as witnessed between the US and Rwanda over whether to send Ntaganda to The Hague; and the cooperation of states such as those that agreed to refuel Ntaganda's plane. As we will see, the ICC's reliance on state cooperation – including with states that are not signatories to the Rome Statute – and on serendipity rather than strategy have been recurring features of the Court's work in Africa to date. Later chapters will also analyse the difficulties for the ICC posed by Ntaganda's involvement in peace talks in eastern DRC and his potential eligibility for a national amnesty.

This book has three specific aims: to explore the domestic political impact of the ICC through two detailed case studies, Uganda and the DRC; to examine the resonance of these two cases in the ICC's wider work across Africa; and to highlight the theoretical relevance of these issues for broader debates about appropriate legal and non-legal responses to mass atrocity in Africa and beyond. Regarding the first aim, the book focuses heavily on Uganda and the DRC because these situations led to the ICC's first ever full investigations and thus highlight the Court's early steps and precedents established for its cases elsewhere.[13] They are also therefore the most developed of the ICC's situations, providing the Court with four out of its five completed trials to date in the cases of Thomas Lubanga, Germain Katanga, Mathieu

---

[12] On broad antagonisms between the ICC and the AU, see M. Mutua, 'Africans and the ICC', in K. Clarke, A. Knotterus and E. de Volder (eds.), *Africa and the ICC: Perceptions of Justice*, Cambridge University Press, 2016, pp. 39–46; and J-B. J. Vilmer, 'The African Union and the International Criminal Court: Counteracting the Crisis', *International Affairs*, 92, 6, 2016, pp. 1319–42.

[13] In the parlance of the ICC, a 'situation' refers to the broad conflict within which crimes are investigated (for example, the 'situation in the DRC') while a 'case' refers to the prosecution of a particular suspect or group of suspects (for example, the case of *The Prosecutor v. Bosco Ntaganda*).

Ngudjolo and Bemba, the last a Congolese national convicted of crimes committed in the Central African Republic (CAR).[14] Uganda and the DRC have also generated three out of the five trials currently ongoing at the ICC in the cases of Ntaganda, Dominic Ongwen and a new trial against Bemba and four associates for witness tampering, while another Ugandan suspect – Joseph Kony – remains at large.[15]

An in-depth analysis of two cases allows for a comprehensive exploration of the ICC's impact on specific African societies.[16] Comparing these cases then highlights structural features of the ICC's work as well as important differences that stem from the varied local contexts in which the Court operates. Furthermore, as neighbouring states, Uganda and the DRC permit an exploration of a widespread feature of the ICC's investigations across Africa, namely the complications caused by working on contiguous cases, with overlapping conflict and political dynamics and investigators shared across borders. In Chapters 3–7 – which focus on various features of the ICC's operations in Uganda and the DRC – the two country situations are analysed in sequence, highlighting key similarities and distinctions between them. Chapter 8 then provides a broad brushstroke analysis of the six other ICC situations in Africa, exploring the extent to which dynamics identified in the principal case studies manifest across the continent.

In methodological terms, this book analyses the ICC as an external *intervention* into African societies that experiences a range of *intersections* with domestic actors, institutions, networks and processes. While various authors have analysed the interventionist nature of the ICC,[17] highlighting the powerful entry of the Court into complex local environments, the focus on intersections locates the Court within a richer

---

[14] See International Criminal Court, 'Situations under Investigation', www.icc-cpi.int/pages/situations.aspx.

[15] Ibid.

[16] For a broader discussion of the need for empirically grounded, comparative analysis of the impact of transitional justice processes to substantiate the normative claims made by scholars in the field, see O. Thoms, J. Ron and R. Paris, 'State-Level Effects of Transitional Justice: What Do We Know?', *International Journal of Transitional Justice*, 4, 3, 2010, pp. 329–54.

[17] See, for example, A. Branch, *Displacing Human Rights: War and Intervention in Northern Uganda*, Oxford University Press, 2011; M. Kersten, *Justice in Conflict: The Effects of the International Criminal Court's Interventions on Ending Wars and Building Peace*, Oxford University Press, 2016.

political, social and cultural sphere and a more variegated realm of power relations, where the Court is not always the predominant actor. Mark Kersten argues that the ICC is typically expected to be among the 'first-responders' to mass conflict around the world.[18] As this book highlights, the ICC is usually a late responder, arriving long after a range of other international, national and community-level actors and processes have already begun addressing violence.

The emphasis on intersections facilitates an analysis of new dynamics created when the ICC interacts with domestic players and processes. While this book differentiates among international, national and community levels, it focuses on their dynamic interactions.[19] Crucially, the ICC's intersections at multiple levels influence one another. For example, the extent of the Court's cooperation with national governments affects its interactions with everyday citizens, many of whom hope the Court will hold state officials accountable for serious crimes.

As this book argues, the ICC generally has paid insufficient attention to these intersections, preferring to imagine Africa as a largely inert space in which it will easily wield its influence, rather than an arena of vibrant agency and contestation, much of which is fundamentally opposed to external intervention. A handful of actors within the ICC have discussed the Court's intersections with other institutional responses to conflict. For example, Matthew Brubacher, the Office of the Prosecutor's (OTP) international cooperation advisor on Uganda, argues that the Court operates 'among a multitude of other diplomatic, humanitarian and military-related initiatives, each pursuing their respective' aims.[20] Tellingly, however, Brubacher overlooks other legal or transitional justice processes – including those that may directly challenge the ICC's own jurisdiction over particular situations or cases – preferring to discuss the role of these other actors either in fostering the degree of peace and stability necessary for the ICC to

---

[18] Kersten, *Justice in Conflict*, p. 5.

[19] In this regard, the book is framed contrary to a current trend in the literature to blur these levels beyond distinction, for example the literature on the 'glocal' or melding of the global and local levels. See, for example, B. Mazlish, 'The Global and the Local', *Current Sociology*, 35, 1, 2005, pp. 93–111; and J. Brewer, *Peace Processes: A Sociological Approach*, Polity, 2010.

[20] M. Brubacher, 'The ICC Investigation of the Lord's Resistance Army: An Insider's View', in T. Allen and K. Vlassenroot (eds.), *The Lord's Resistance Army: Myth and Reality*, Zed Books, 2010, p. 263.

conduct its operations or pursuing aims such as 'social equilibrium' that he believes are beyond the purview of the Court.[21]

Reflecting this focus on intervention and intersections, this book adopts a multi-sited, multi-level methodology. It is based on eleven years of research between 2006 and 2017, encompassing 653 interviews with ICC personnel (including the first Prosecutor, Luis Moreno Ocampo), senior Ugandan and Congolese political and judicial officials (including the Ministers of Justice and other cabinet ministers in both countries), international and local civil society actors, journalists, customary and religious leaders, former rebel combatants and affected communities, with 426 of those interviews conducted with everyday people. Wherever possible, quotes are attributed to named public officials; however, some statements are anonymised either to protect respondents' security or because, especially with some ICC or political officials, they would only speak on this basis. The names of all everyday interviewees have been changed to protect their security.

The empirical research for this book comprised nineteen field trips to rural and urban areas in Uganda and the DRC (each lasting between two weeks and five months) and seven visits to the ICC headquarters in The Hague (including the observation of trials and other Court behaviour), supplemented by interviews conducted in Rwanda, South Sudan, Kenya, Tanzania, South Africa, the US, the UK, France and Belgium and an analysis of ICC judgments, court transcripts and public statements by ICC officials. Much of the literature on the ICC focuses either on international and national elites or on the Court's grassroots impact.[22] A comprehensive understanding of the ICC and its impact, however, requires examining its work in The Hague as well as in Ugandan and Congolese capitals and villages. This book attempts to

---

[21] Ibid., p. 264. For further discussion on this theme, see M. Newton, 'A Synthesis of Community-Based Justice and Complementarity', in C. De Vos, S. Kendall and C. Stahn (eds.), *Contested Justice: The Politics and Practice of International Criminal Court Interventions*, Cambridge University Press, 2015, pp. 131–8.

[22] See, for example, T. Allen, *Trial Justice: The International Criminal Court and the Lord's Resistance Army*, Zed Books, 2006; Branch, *Displacing Human Rights*; P. Kastner, *International Criminal Justice* in Bello? *The ICC between Law and Politics in Darfur and Northern Uganda*, Martinus Nijhoff, 2012; S. Nouwen, *Complementarity in the Line of Fire: The Catalysing Effect of the International Criminal Court in Uganda and Sudan*, Cambridge University Press, 2013; and Kersten, *Justice in Conflict*.

link these levels, understanding – on its own terms – the Court's objectives and modalities, as well as the ways in which the ICC is viewed and experienced by national and community elites and everyday citizens.

Underpinning this analysis is the recognition that none of these levels – international, national or local – is homogeneous. National elites, civil society and local communities in Uganda and the DRC express wide-ranging views on their intersections with the ICC. The analysis in this book therefore highlights critical disagreements within these categories of actors. Within the ICC itself – comprising the Presidency, the Judicial Division, the OTP and the Registry – there is also significant divergence over the Court's aims, approaches and perceived effects. Inevitably, this book stresses the importance of the OTP, as the organ of the Court that wields the greatest influence over the direction and impact of the institution. The OTP shapes the function of the other branches and the fundamental nature of the ICC's interventions by selecting which situations, cases and suspects the Court should pursue. This book also examines the role of the other three organs while maintaining a primary focus on the OTP's operations in Uganda and the DRC.

The period of research covers the start of the ICC's investigations in central Africa, the full duration of the ICC's first completed trials of Lubanga, Katanga, Ngudjolo and Bemba and the ongoing trials of Ntaganda, Ongwen and Bemba and his associates. This eleven-year timeframe allows an extensive analysis of the ICC's impact, which has fluctuated depending on legal developments in The Hague and broader political, economic, social and cultural dynamics in Uganda and the DRC. It also provides insights into the extent to which the ICC has 'learnt' during its first fifteen years of operation, improving its approaches based on recognised successes and missteps, and the extent to which national and community-level actors have 'learnt' how to engage with the ICC for their own purposes.

A longer timeframe facilitates a wide range of methodological approaches and different angles of analysis, extending from field-based research to participant observation in ICC cases. This comprises follow-up interviews with actors at all levels, sometimes a decade apart, to gauge changes in ICC practice and impact over time. My first field trip to Uganda and the DRC in January 2006 took place ten weeks after the issuance of the ICC's first ever arrest warrants for five commanders of the Lord's Resistance Army (LRA), including Joseph Kony.[23] I conducted interviews in the OTP in The Hague on the day of the transfer of the ICC's first ever suspect in custody, the Congolese rebel leader Thomas Lubanga, on 16 March 2006. I gained access to background meetings of the OTP discussing the Lubanga case and preparing the Prosecutor for his press conference to announce Lubanga's transfer. Later, I travelled several times to Juba in southern Sudan between 2006 and 2008 to conduct interviews around the peace talks between the Ugandan government and the LRA. In Juba, Gulu, Kampala and London, I interviewed many of the key players in the peace talks from the Ugandan government, LRA and the UN mediation team. In northern Uganda, I led a research project for the UN Office of the High Commissioner for Human Rights (OHCHR), which conducted focus group and individual interviews on peace, conflict and transitional justice with more than 1,700 internally displaced persons (IDPs) and victims of the twenty-year conflict across Acholi, Lango and Teso sub-regions. Some of the analysis in this book, especially Chapters 4 and 7, draws substantially on the OHCHR report that emerged from that research and on which I was the lead author.[24] In 2011, I was an expert witness for the ICC Defence in the case against alleged Congolese rebel leader, Callixte Mbarushimana.[25] The charges against Mbarushimana were not confirmed and the case did not reach the trial phase because the judges determined that the Prosecution had provided insufficient evidence to prosecute. In 2012, I co-produced a radio programme in northern Uganda and south-western Rwanda on local perceptions of justice, forgiveness and reconciliation, which was broadcast on Mega FM in Gulu.[26] In 2013, I travelled to Rwanda two

---

[23] International Criminal Court, 'Situation in Uganda', ICC-02/04, www.icc-cpi.int/uganda.

[24] United Nations Office of the High Commissioner for Human Rights, 'Making Peace Our Own: Victims' Perceptions of Accountability, Reconciliation and Transitional Justice in Northern Uganda', Geneva: OHCHR, 2007, www.uganda.ohchr.org/Content/publications/Making%20Peace%20Our%20Own.pdf.

[25] International Criminal Court, Pre-Trial Chamber I, 'Public Document: Decision on the Schedule of the Confirmation Hearing', Situation in the Democratic Republic of Congo, *The Prosecutor v. Callixte Mbarushimana*, 12 August 2011, www.icc-cpi.int/CourtRecords/CR2011_12170.PDF.

[26] P. Clark, N. Palmer, D. Matthee and D. Matthee et al., 'Finding it within Ourselves: Forgiveness, Reconciliation and Rescue in Post-Atrocity Rwanda and Uganda (Luo version)', 2014, www.youtube.com/watch?v=xu7nmqJLurk.

weeks after Ntaganda arrived at the US embassy and conducted interviews with embassy and diplomatic officials regarding his case. The analysis in this book builds on all of these field experiences as well as systematic qualitative research designed to elicit findings from 'on high' in The Hague as well as from 'below' at the level of Ugandan and Congolese communities.

Contributions of the Book

There is already a rich literature on the ICC, much of which has analysed it in terms of transitional justice[27], international criminal law[28] or international relations, with the last focusing on the Court's relations with the UN Security Council and major powers such as the US and the EU.[29] This book analyses the ICC in terms of African politics, exploring the various ways in which the continent has shaped the Court, and vice versa. In doing so, it views the ICC as the latest in a long line of international actors that have intervened in Africa, including European colonial powers, the World Bank and International Monetary Fund, foreign donors, humanitarian non-governmental organisations (NGOs) and multilateral peacekeeping missions. As we will see, the ICC has often failed to learn lessons from these actors' difficult entanglements in Africa, especially when engaging with post-liberation African states or rebel-movements-turned-governments such as those in Uganda and the DRC.

---

[27] See, for example, R. Lipscomb, 'Structuring the ICC Framework to Advance Transitional Justice: A Search for a Permanent Solution in Sudan', *Columbia Law Review*, 106, 1, 2006, pp. 182–212; R. Nagy, 'Transitional Justice as Global Project: Critical Reflections', *Third World Quarterly*, 29, 2, 2008, pp. 275–89; O. Okafor and U. Ngwaba, 'The International Criminal Court as a "Transitional Justice" Mechanism in Africa: Some Critical Reflections', *International Journal of Transitional Justice*, 9, 1, 2015, pp. 90–108.

[28] See, for example, T. Meron and F. Bensouda, 'Twenty Years of International Criminal Law: From the ICTY to the ICC and Beyond', *Proceedings of the Annual Meeting (American Society of International Law)*, 107, 2013, pp. 407–20; Nouwen, *Complementarity in the Line of Fire*.

[29] See, for example, C. Stahn (ed.), *The Law and Practice of the International Criminal Court*, Oxford University Press, 2014; D. Bosco, *Rough Justice: The International Criminal Court in a World of Power Politics*, Oxford University Press, 2014.

The literature on the politics of the ICC is also growing rapidly.[30] Much of it focuses on the development rather than the operation of the ICC, while some works examine general political issues such as the link between the ICC's aims and social construction[31] or popular perceptions of the Court.[32] Several prominent monographs address political dimensions of the ICC in Uganda.[33] This book differs from these in several key respects. First, this is the first book-length analysis of the ICC in the DRC, the situation that has provided the majority of the Court's completed and ongoing trials and thus gives crucial insights into the function and impact of the Court. Second, this book offers a comprehensive analysis of the ICC's mutually reinforcing operations in central Africa, including the politics of state referrals to the Court, the ICC's cooperation with states during investigations, relations with local populations, intersections with national and community-based approaches to transitional justice and impact on peace talks. The current literature tends to focus on one or two of these themes and, in particular, on either the ICC's interactions at the national[34] or community levels but not both.[35] Third, this book – through the

---

[30] See, for example, S. Roach, *Politicizing the International Criminal Court: The Convergence of Politics, Ethics, and Law*, Rowman and Littlefield, 2006; B. Schiff, *Building the International Criminal Court*, Cambridge University Press, 2008; and N. Chazal, *The International Criminal Court and Global Social Control: International Criminal Justice in Late Modernity*, Routledge, 2016.

[31] M. Struett, *The Politics of Constructing the International Criminal Court: NGOs, Discourse, and Agency*, Palgrave Macmillan, 2008.

[32] See, for example, K. Clarke, A. Knottnerus and E. de Volder (eds.), *Africa and the ICC: Perceptions of Justice*, Cambridge University Press, 2016.

[33] Allen, *Trial Justice*; Branch, *Displacing Human Rights*; Kastner, *International Criminal Justice* in Bello?; Nouwen, *Complementarity in the Line of Fire*; Kersten, *Justice in Conflict*.

[34] See, for example, William Burke-White's excellent analysis of 'multi-level global governance', examining the relationship between the ICC and the DRC government, which theorises the 'dynamic interactions' between the ICC and states (W. Burke-White, 'Complementarity in Practice: The International Criminal Court as Part of a System of Multi-level Global Governance', *Leiden Journal of International Law*, 18, 3, 2005, pp. 557–90). This book expands on such an approach by drawing in a wider range of actors and processes, including at the community level.

[35] A rare example of an analysis of the ICC's intersections with community-level transitional justice – specifically the *mato oput* ritual in Acholiland, northern Uganda – is K. Mills, *International Responses to Mass Atrocities in Africa: Responsibility to Protect, Prosecute and Palliate*, University of Pennsylvania Press, 2015, ch. 4.

exploration of the central concept of 'distance' – provides a theoretically grounded analysis of the Court's interactions in Africa and thus contributes to more general debates about external interventions on the continent and elsewhere. As elaborated further below, a key argument of this book is that the ICC represents a unique form of foreign intervention in African affairs insofar as it views distance and detachment from the domestic realm as a virtue because, it believes, this maintains the Court's neutrality and impartiality.

Broad History of the Conflicts in Northern Uganda and Eastern DRC

Before outlining the arguments of this book, it is necessary to provide some brief historical background to the main conflicts in northern Uganda and eastern DRC that have been the focus of the ICC's investigations and prosecutions to date. The two conflict cases overlap, with violence and the mass displacement of the population spilling across the Uganda–Congo border and the Ugandan army having invaded the DRC and supported DRC-based rebel movements at various stages over the last twenty years. These cases also share some common features and causes (with compounding factors at the regional, national, provincial and community levels), including crimes against civilians committed by rebel groups, government actors and large numbers of everyday citizens; tensions over land, ethnicity and access to natural resources; the political and economic marginalisation of particular regional and minority groups; the widespread use of child soldiers; and the backing of regional powers and use of proxy forces. This section sketches some primary aspects of these conflicts, while other relevant features are discussed in greater depth in later chapters as they pertain to more specific issues regarding the ICC.

Between 1986 and 2007, the civil war in northern Uganda between the Ugandan government and the LRA, a rebel force infamous for its abduction and enlistment of children, killed tens of thousands of civilians. A government policy of forced displacement meanwhile drove an estimated 1.8 million people, nearly 90 per cent of the total northern Ugandan population, into 250 squalid IDP camps.[36] The

---

[36] United Nations Office for the Coordination of Humanitarian Affairs, 'Consolidated Appeal for Uganda 2006', 30 November 2005.

civilian population suffered widespread murder, rape, torture, abduction, looting and displacement, resulting in immense social and cultural fragmentation, principally in Acholi, Lango and Teso sub-regions. The 2007 OHCHR study of perceptions among northern Ugandans mentioned above shows that the majority of the affected population considers both the government and the LRA responsible for the harm it suffered during the conflict.[37]

Crucial to the motivations and tactics of the LRA has been the personality of its leader Joseph Kony, whom Douglas Johnson and David Anderson describe as 'mantic',[38] belonging to *manti*, diviners or healers who often openly oppose mainstream social and political structures. Kony, proclaiming himself both a messenger from God and a mediator between the population and the spirit world, has often claimed that the Acholi require purification because of their failure to counter directly President Yoweri Museveni's forces in northern Uganda. There is much debate over Kony's and the LRA's precise political and military objectives.[39] Some authors dismiss the LRA as a collection of spiritual cranks with no coherent political agenda.[40] At the heart of Kony's and other LRA leaders' public pronouncements, however, has often been a clear political message about the need to address long-standing Acholi grievances, greater integration of Acholi into Ugandan national life, the dismantling of the IDP camps, as well as more spiritual claims concerning the need for cleansing and purification of the Acholi.[41] Complicating interpretations of the LRA's

[37] OHCHR, 'Making Peace Our Own', p. 3.

[38] D. Johnson and D. Anderson, 'Revealing Prophets', in D. Johnson and D. Anderson (eds.), *Revealing Prophets: Prophecy in Eastern African Studies*, James Currey, 1995, p. 14.

[39] For a thorough overview of various commentators' interpretations of the LRA's political agenda, see A. Branch, 'Neither Peace nor Justice: Political Violence and the Peasantry in Northern Uganda, 1986–1998', *African Studies Quarterly*, 8, 2, 2005, p. 4. For an excellent discussion of the community-level and national political crises that spawned the LRA, see A. Branch, 'Exploring the Roots of LRA Violence: Political Crisis and Ethnic Politics in Acholiland', in T. Allen and K. Vlassenroot (eds.), *The Lord's Resistance Army: Myth and Reality*, Zed Books, 2010, pp. 25–44.

[40] See, for example, BBC, 'Girls Escape Ugandan Rebels', 25 June 2003, http://news.bbc.co.uk/1/hi/world/africa/3018810.stm.

[41] S. Finnström, 'In and Out of Culture: Fieldwork in War-Torn Uganda', *Critique of Anthropology*, 21, 3, 2001, pp. 247–8. For a detailed critique of the role of international human rights organisations, principally Human Rights Watch, in propagating of a view of the LRA as fundamentally apolitical, see S. Finnström,

objectives is that, in seeking the greater integration of Acholi into national life, the LRA has used violence against the northern Ugandan population as a military tactic and abducted thousands of children from Acholi and other northern communities, thus weakening its ability to win popular support.[42]

Peace talks between the government and rebels in Juba, southern Sudan, between 2006 and 2008 led to the signing of a cessation of hostilities agreement. The negotiations ultimately collapsed without the signing of the final protocol that would have established a comprehensive peace accord. The LRA has now halted its operations in northern Uganda, bringing greater stability to northern communities and allowing IDPs to return to their homes.[43] The LRA, though, has not been neutralised and continues its pattern of abductions and mass violence across the region, reportedly as far away as Chad, Darfur and CAR, with several of its bases located in Garamba National Park in north-eastern DRC, highlighting the critical overlaps of the Ugandan and Congolese cases.[44]

Since the early 1990s, armed conflict has engulfed the DRC (or Zaire as it was called during the thirty-six-year reign of dictator Mobutu Sese Seko), particularly its eastern provinces, killing more than 5 million people and displacing more than 2 million.[45] The conflict has involved the deliberate targeting of the civilian population, which has suffered mass murder, rape, torture and mutilation at the hands of an array of government and rebel forces. In August and September 1996, an

---

'An African Hell of Colonial Imagination? The Lord's Resistance Army in Uganda, Another Story', in T. Allen and K. Vlassenroot (eds.), *The Lord's Resistance Army: Myth and Reality*, Zed Books, 2010, pp. 80–1. See also K. Titeca, 'The Spiritual Order of the LRA', in T. Allen and K. Vlassenroot (eds.), *The Lord's Resistance Army: Myth and Reality*, Zed Books, 2010, pp. 59–73, including on the link between spirituality and the LRA's structures of control which partly 'compensat[e] for a lack of elaborate military infrastructure' (p. 71).

[42] Branch, 'Exploring the Roots of LRA Violence', p. 41.

[43] See, for example, S. Joireman, A. Sawyer and J. Wilhoit, 'A Different Way Home: Resettlement Patterns in Northern Uganda', *Political Geography*, 31, 4, May 2012, pp. 197–204.

[44] See, for example, the extensive monitoring of LRA attacks by the LRA Crisis Tracker, www.lracrisistracker.com/.

[45] See, for example, United Nations High Commissioner for Refugees, '2014 Democratic Republic of the Congo Operations Profile', copy on file with author. B. Coghlan, R. Brennan, P. Ngoy et al., 'Mortality in the Democratic Republic of Congo: a Nationwide Survey', *The Lancet*, 367, 9504, 2006, pp. 44–51.

uprising of Tutsi from the province of South Kivu known as Banya-mulenge, backed principally by Rwanda and supported by Burundi and Uganda – which all had grievances against Mobutu and were deeply concerned by growing insecurity in eastern Zaire – led to the formation of the Alliance des Forces Démocratiques pour la Libération du Congo/Zaire (AFDL). The AFDL, whose spokesman was Laurent-Désiré Kabila, portrayed itself as the liberator of the Zairean people. It soon overran Mobutu's forces, scattering them and their *intera-hamwe*[46] allies throughout eastern Zaire. The AFDL marched across the country, capturing Kinshasa in May 1997. Kabila installed himself as President, renamed the country 'the Democratic Republic of Congo' and set about establishing a new political regime.

The DRC was soon plunged into a second continental war, from 1998 to 1999. Kabila's rebel alliance quickly disintegrated, as his association with Rwanda began to hurt him politically. Rwanda, Burundi and Uganda, having failed to receive the remuneration they expected for helping topple Mobutu and seeing various political and economic benefits to maintaining a presence in the DRC, battled Kabila's forces until the signing of a ceasefire in Lusaka in July 1999. The ceasefire had little long-term effect and conflict has since continued throughout much of eastern DRC.

Some of the most extreme violence has occurred in Ituri district[47], where in 2003 Hema and Lendu militias and their respective rebel and government backers attacked each other's communities, killing thousands of civilians over several months and displacing more than 500,000 people into Uganda and across eastern DRC. Combatants committed rape, mutilation and cannibalism, instilling fear throughout the civilian population.[48] At present, although violence in Ituri has decreased, sporadic attacks by various Mai Mai and other militias continue. Meanwhile, the situation in North and South Kivu remains

---

[46] The *interahamwe* were Hutu militias responsible for massacres during the 1994 genocide in Rwanda. Many *interahamwe* fighters fled into Zaire in mid-1994 as the Rwandan Patriotic Front (RPF) routed the Hutu-dominated government and halted the genocide.

[47] Until 2010, Ituri was a district of Orientale province. Thereafter, it was reorganised as a province in its own right under provisions in the 2005 DRC Constitution (The Constitution of the Democratic Republic of Congo, 2005, Article 2).

[48] International Crisis Group, 'Congo Crisis: Military Intervention in Ituri', 2003, p. 6.

extremely volatile, with a host of rebel groups – including the Allied Defence Forces (ADF), the Forces Démocratiques de Libération du Rwanda (FDLR) and Mai Mai militias – committing regular and widespread atrocities against civilians. As we will see in later chapters, the ICC has intervened in this dynamic terrain in Uganda and the DRC, often unprepared and ill-equipped to tackle the complexities of African conflict zones, with their various overlaps and interlinkages.

Structure and Argument of the Book

This book argues overall that the ICC's 'distance' from the African societies in which it intervenes has been damaging, both to the Court and to local polities. Failing to wrestle sufficiently with national politics and the expressed needs of local communities, while showing insufficient deference to national and community-level responses to mass conflict, the ICC has produced a range of negative effects for African societies. Not only has the Court failed to achieve distance from the domestic arena and instead become heavily enmeshed in national political and social dynamics, its failure to recognise this – because it considers itself above the political fray – has created severe problems for the Court and for the countries where it intervenes.

The book is structured as follows: Chapter 2 outlines the conceptual framework for the empirical analysis in the rest of the book. In normative and practical terms, the ICC embodies two concepts explored in this chapter: *complementarity*, with its embedded notions of deference to national institutions and cooperation with domestic actors; and *distance*, which holds that, to achieve objectivity and impartiality, the Court must insulate itself from damaging political and social influences. The purpose of this chapter is to interpret these key concepts and values at the core of the ICC, which reflect ideas central to the international criminal justice enterprise as a whole.

The rest of this book examines the practical ways in which the ICC has enacted conceptions of complementarity and distance. It shows that, while the ICC prefers to describe itself in terms of complementarity – as a partner to domestic actors and institutions – in practice, it adopts a fundamentally distanced approach to justice, seeing itself as superior to the domestic realm and often actively undermining it. The book refers to this as the *complacency of complementarity*, showing that this core principle of the ICC is not robust enough to withstand the distancing tendencies that are so heavily embedded within the Court. Throughout the book, the concepts of complementarity and distance are used to interpret the empirical issues concerning the ICC's impact on African politics, and vice versa, while the concluding chapter discusses the relevance of these empirical findings for broader theoretical debates over responses to mass atrocity.

Chapters 3–7 analyse tensions between complementarity and distance through the ICC's five main intersections in Uganda and the DRC, the first two involving relations with key actors (the Ugandan and Congolese governments and local populations) and the last three with domestic institutions and processes (national courts; domestic amnesties and peace processes; and community-based responses to mass atrocity). Chapter 3 – on dynamics between the ICC and states – situates the ICC within the study of African politics. One key purpose of this chapter is to highlight the centrality of Africa for the ICC, exploring the various ways in which the continent has shaped the Court, and vice versa. It does this through an analysis of three issues: the ICC's initiation of apparently voluntary state referrals by Uganda and the DRC; the close relationship between the ICC and these two governments throughout its investigations; and the impact of these issues on these states' behaviour during armed conflict and national elections and on the legitimacy of the ICC.

This chapter argues that the ICC has failed to thwart African states' ability to use the Court for their own purposes, especially safeguarding themselves against prosecution for international crimes and burnishing their reputation as law-abiding while continuing to commit serious violations against their citizens. The ICC has entrenched these tendencies of the Ugandan and Congolese governments by actively pursuing state referrals and other forms of cooperation, thus leaving the Court open to substantial state influence. This highlights critical pitfalls of the ICC's attempts to distance itself from the political realm, failing to contend sufficiently with domestic political dynamics and thus making it susceptible to politicisation and instrumentalisation by domestic governments. In the ICC's relations with states, the complacency of complementarity manifests in the Court's readiness to accept states' expressed unwillingness or inability to prosecute serious cases domestically and guarantees of cooperation.

Chapter 4 examines the ICC's relations with conflict-affected populations. Drawing on hundreds of community-level interviews in northern Uganda and eastern DRC, it focuses on three themes: the particular conceptions of conflict and the required responses to violence that emerge from local contexts; local actors' perceptions of the ICC generally; and, community-level perceptions of, and interactions with, specific branches and programmes of the ICC, such as the Victims and Witnesses Unit, the Outreach Unit and the Trust Fund for Victims (TFV). This chapter argues that the ICC has generally failed to secure legitimacy among local populations in Uganda and the DRC. This stems mainly from the Court's emphasis on distance in all of its operations, which reinforces popular critiques of distanced justice directed at national judicial institutions from the colonial period onwards. In these contexts, the Court's work is interpreted in light of historical and ongoing experiences of distanced legal authority.

The ICC is not alone in addressing violence and criminality. It is therefore critical to explore the ICC's impact on domestic responses to conflict. The concept of complementarity, as discussed in Chapter 2, guides the ICC's attempts to structure relations coherently with domestic prosecutions, framing the Court fundamentally as a back-stop to national institutions. Chapter 5 explores the ICC's relations with domestic courts in Uganda and the DRC, focusing on national judicial reforms and challenges to ICC jurisdiction. This chapter advances three main arguments. First, while the principle of complementarity broadly emphasises the ICC's cooperation, deference and partnership with domestic judiciaries, in Uganda and the DRC these relations have generally been competitive. This highlights the complacency of the complementarity principle and the tendency of distance – with its emphasis on the superiority of the ICC over national institutions – to predominate. Second, in both countries where the ICC has chased state referrals, the Court has assumed jurisdiction over cases that should have been handled domestically and, in doing so, has undermined vital national judicial reforms. Third, the ICC has empowered the Ugandan and Congolese governments – principally their executive branches – which have themselves attempted to weaken the domestic courts to protect state actors from judicial scrutiny. A telling feature of the Ugandan and Congolese situations is states' preference for ICC rather than domestic prosecutions as a means to weaken the latter and to pursue their wider political agenda.

Chapter 6 examines the intersections among the ICC and two major debates in transitional justice: the appropriateness of amnesties for suspected perpetrators of international crimes; and what has commonly been termed the 'peace versus justice' debate, which concerns the potential for the threat of prosecutions to scupper peace negotiations involving high-level suspects. These debates converged, for example, in the Juba peace talks between the Ugandan government and the LRA, following the ICC's issuance of arrest warrants for the five top LRA commanders. While the previous chapter explored the ICC's relations with trial processes that mirror many of its own methods, this chapter on amnesties and peace negotiations and the next on community-based responses to conflict examine its intersections with fundamentally different types of processes. This is key because, as a relatively new actor, the ICC joins the fray of addressing mass atrocity alongside much more established institutions and mechanisms, of which amnesties and peace negotiations are among the most widely used. This chapter argues that the ICC has undermined the national use of amnesties to facilitate peace negotiations and other key conflict-mitigation processes such as truth commissions, security sector reform (SSR) and disarmament, demobilisation and reintegration (DDR). In doing so, it has made achieving sustainable peace less, rather than more, likely. In this regard, the complacency of complementarity asserts in the inability of the principle to grapple with processes fundamentally different from the ICC's model of international prosecutions – again reflecting the assumption of the Court's superiority that is central to the concept of distance.

This same issue arises in Chapter 7, which explores the ICC's intersections with community-based approaches to transitional justice in Uganda and the DRC. It is becoming increasingly common, especially in central Africa, to employ forms of local, customary or traditional justice and dispute resolution following major atrocities.[49] This chapter argues that the ICC has often undermined community-based practices such as cleansing and reconciliation rituals in northern Uganda and local mediation efforts in eastern DRC. In particular, the ICC has actively opposed these practices' reliance on national amnesties and very different conceptions of justice based on forms of face-to-

---

[49] See, for example, L. Huyse and M. Salter (eds.), *Traditional Justice and Reconciliation after Violent Conflict: Learning from African Experiences*, International Institute for Democracy and Electoral Assistance (IDEA), 2008.

face engagement and presence – rather than the ICC's focus on distance – and the ultimate need for reconciliation.

Chapter 8 explores a select range of the ICC's intersections with the same categories of actors and processes in its six other African situations, CAR, Darfur, Kenya, Libya, Côte d'Ivoire and Mali. The chapter argues that the Court has confronted many of the same challenges in these countries as in Uganda and the DRC. This shows deep structural flaws in the ideology and practice of the ICC – most of which stem from its weddedness to distance over complementarity – and its general unpreparedness to address mass atrocities in Africa.

In Chapter 9, the book concludes with some theoretical insights derived from the ICC's operations in Uganda and the DRC and concrete proposals for reform of the Court. The chapter focuses on ways to return complementarity (with its embedded principles of legal humility, caution and partnership, rather than competition, with domestic processes) to the heart of the ICC. The chapter argues that a substantial reorientation of the Court is necessary for it to succeed on its own legal terms – that is, to conduct more effective criminal investigations and prosecutions – as well as to interact more productively with domestic actors and institutions across Africa; the continent that is likely to dominate the ICC's work for many years to come.

2 | Court between Two Poles
Conceptualising 'Complementarity' and 'Distance'

Introduction

In his inaugural speech as Prosecutor of the ICC in 2003, Luis Moreno Ocampo identified a critical tension at the heart of the Court. With echoes of the biblical injunction to be 'in the world but not of the world', Ocampo said:

> An international criminal court totally independent and impartial brings hope, but at the same time raises reasonable fears and misunderstandings...There seems to be a paradox: the ICC is independent and interdependent at the same time. It cannot act alone. It will achieve efficiency only if it works closely with other members of the international community.[1]

This tension – between a Court that seeks impartiality, rising above the political fray to investigate and prosecute suspects without fear or favour, and a Court dependent on domestic political and judicial actors for its daily running – frames the analysis throughout this book. The ICC's normative and operational framework oscillates between two key concepts explored in this chapter: first, *complementarity*, with its attendant notions of deference to national institutions and cooperation – even embeddedness – with domestic actors; and, second, impartiality and neutrality, which embody a discourse of *distance*, needing to separate the Court from messy political dynamics in the pursuit of a higher ideal, namely justice for serious crimes.

While Ocampo initially expressed admirable circumspection, even prescience, when describing the challenges inherent in an 'independent and interdependent' Court, such caution has dissipated and notions of distance have superseded those of complementarity. In seeking to avoid interference and politicisation by domestic actors, the ICC has

---

[1] International Criminal Court, Office of the Prosecutor, 'Ceremony for the Solemn Undertaking of the Chief Prosecutor of the International Criminal Court', 16 June 2003, p. 2.

increasingly distanced itself from the domestic sphere in various problematic ways (and, in doing so, paradoxically failed to insulate itself from interference and politicisation because of its weak grasp of the domestic terrain).

To understand this trajectory, we must first examine the development of these two concepts within the ICC and the central role they play in its practice. As this chapter will argue, these concepts derive not only from the peculiar birth of a permanent, global Court mandated to prosecute serious crimes around the world – including the unbridled optimism at the Rome conference in 1998 that led to the adoption of the ICC Statute, as David Bosco and others have described[2] – but also from the experiences of international courts and tribunals since Nuremberg and Tokyo and core principles within liberalism and liberal cosmopolitanism.[3] The purpose of this chapter therefore is to interpret these key concepts and values at the core of the ICC, which reflect ideas central to the international criminal justice enterprise as a whole. The rest of this book will examine the numerous practical ways in which the ICC has embodied and enacted conceptions of complementarity and distance and the problems created by the simultaneous pursuit of these two ideals.

A key reason for establishing this conceptual framework is to analyse the ICC on its own terms, even if those are sometimes contradictory. In a fascinating and widely cited article entitled, 'Inescapable Dyads: Why the International Criminal Court Cannot Win', Darryl

---

[2] Bosco, *Rough Justice*. See also I. Tallgren, 'We Did It? The Vertigo of Law and Everyday Life at the Diplomatic Conference on the Establishment of an International Criminal Court', *Leiden Journal of International Law*, 12, 13, 1999, pp. 683–707; M. Glasius, *The International Criminal Court: A Global Civil Society Achievement*, Routledge, 2006; and T. Krever, 'Dispensing Global Justice', *New Left Review*, 85, January–February 2014, pp. 67–97.

[3] For an excellent and detailed analysis of the Kantian cosmopolitan underpinnings of the ICC, see S. Fouladvand, 'Complementarity and Cultural Sensitivity: Decision-Making by the ICC Prosecutor in Relation to the Situations in the Darfur Region of the Sudan and the Democratic Republic of the Congo (DRC)', D.Phil thesis, University of Sussex, 2012. On the links between the ICC and liberalism – especially liberal peacebuilding – see C. Sriram, 'Justice as Peace? Liberal Peacebuilding and Strategies of Transitional Justice', *Global Security*, 21, 4, 2007, pp. 579–91. Elsewhere, Mohamed El Zeidy argues that the roots of the ICC's principle of 'complementarity' can even be found in post-First World War peace treaties (M. El Zeidy, 'The Genesis of Complementarity', in C. Stahn and M. El Zeidy (eds.), *The International Criminal Court and Complementarity*, vol. I, Cambridge University Press, 2011, pp. 71–141).

Robinson observes that in critiquing the ICC's work to date, '[m]ultiple yardsticks are plausibly employed for assessing decisions, based on recognized yet contradictory values'.[4] Analysing the structure of dominant criticisms of the ICC, he argues that the Court is frequently subjected to incommensurate critiques, for example, that it is too politicised or too apolitical in its situation and case selection.[5] Robinson ascribes these 'inescapable dyads' to opposing 'values that can be credibly regarded as values underlying international criminal justice'.[6]

While Robinson identifies important structural features of some recurring critiques of the ICC, several aspects of his argument are unconvincing. Elucidating these shortcomings is important for justifying the conceptual framework in the remainder of this chapter. Most importantly, in Robinson's discussion of the values underpinning frequent critiques of the ICC, he ignores the fact that the Court itself articulates its core principles and, by extension, the frameworks according to which it should be evaluated. Actors within the Court often express clear conceptions of the objectives the ICC should fulfil and the means by which it is equipped to do so. As this chapter will argue, the principle of complementarity – of which Robinson was a chief architect during the Rome negotiations[7] – is central in this regard. His argument belies the role of the ICC as a generator of its own norms, values and expectations, against which it is reasonable to evaluate it. The Court's self-described objectives also inspire specific practices with identifiable consequences. A further objective of this book therefore is to analyse the impact of the ways in which the ICC's driving principles are enacted in African political contexts.

While Robinson goes to great lengths to show that the argument about 'inescapable dyads' is not intended to stymie all criticism of the

---

[4] D. Robinson, 'Inescapable Dyads: Why the International Criminal Court Cannot Win', *Leiden Journal of International Law*, 28, 2015, p. 324.
[5] Robinson identifies five key dyads: selection of too high/too low suspects; pursuing situations and cases that are too hard/too easy; intervening too soon/too late; operating too close/too far from states and other powerful actors; and being too imperious/too deferential when determining whether to intervene in a particular situation (ibid., pp. 333–43).
[6] Ibid., p. 330.
[7] D. Robinson, 'The Mysterious Mysteriousness of Complementarity', *Criminal Law Forum*, 21, 2010, p. 68.

ICC,[8] he underestimates the extent to which this type of argument – echoing the 'why the ICC can't win' refrain of the article's title – is frequently deployed by ICC principals for precisely this purpose.[9] This framing is used especially to argue that the Court's critics have overly ambitious or contradictory expectations of the ICC, ignoring the fact that the Court itself has often expressed overly ambitious or contradictory objectives. In this context, the unintended consequence of Robinson's argument is the bolstering of a discourse in which the ICC 'can't lose'.

Complementarity: Admissibility and Partnership

This book's approach is to evaluate the ICC according to two virtues expressed by key actors within the Court, complementarity and distance, including the tensions created by their concurrent pursuit. Of the two framing concepts, complementarity is the more explicitly outlined in the Rome Statute and more widely discussed in the literature on the ICC.[10] As elaborated below, distance, while deeply embedded in the principles and practices of the Court, emerges most strikingly in the public statements and actions of Court officials rather than finding expression in the Statute. Distance is encoded in the DNA of the ICC and needs to be drawn out for systematic examination.

The most commonly quoted section of Ocampo's inaugural speech highlights the importance of complementarity within the Statute and suggests that, in an ideal world, this would render the ICC irrelevant:

Interdependence is also requested by the complementary nature of the Court. The Court is complementary to national systems. This means that whenever there is genuine State action, the Court cannot and will not intervene. As a consequence of complementarity, the number of cases that reach the Court

---

[8] Robinson, 'Inescapable Dyads', pp. 332–3.

[9] A good example of this type of argument is C. Chung, 'The Punishment and Prevention of Genocide: The International Criminal Court as a Benchmark of Progress and Need', *Case Western Reserve Journal of International Law*, 40, 1, 2007–8, pp. 227–42 – particularly her discussion of an 'expectations gap' between 'what observers aspire for the ICC to do and what the ICC has accomplished or attempted' (p. 235).

[10] See, for example, numerous chapters in C. Stahn and M. El Zeidy (eds.), *The International Criminal Court and Complementarity*, Cambridge University Press, 2011.

should not be a measure of its efficiency. On the contrary, the absence of trials before this Court, as a consequence of the regular functioning of national institutions, would be a major success.[11]

Despite its ubiquity in the literature, the concept of complementarity – in the way it is expressed in the Statute and by key actors within the Court – requires greater clarity and disaggregation. The OTP has stated that complementarity should be viewed as both a legal and political principle, structuring judicial procedures as well as the Court's relations with states and a wide range of other actors.[12] Four discrete, though overlapping, notions are discernible in the ICC's use of complementarity: a *legal* framework for determining the admissibility of situations and cases before the Court; a *political* conception expressing broad deference toward domestic institutions and reinforcing respect for national sovereignty; a *relational* principle that invokes partnership, interdependence and cooperation between the ICC and domestic institutions; and a *developmental* conception in which the ICC catalyses, and provides ongoing support to, domestic processes. In her analysis of complementarity in Uganda and Sudan, Sarah Nouwen argues that the term has been leading 'a double life', contrasting the 'rhetorical' deployment of complementarity in non-legal terms by ICC officials and others with the 'technical legal meaning' based on Article 17 of the Rome Statute.[13] As later chapters will show, rather than being merely 'rhetorical', non-legal interpret-ations of complementarity have always coexisted in practice with the technical legal view and have structured many of the ICC's most important political and judicial relations.

As discussed below, there are important differences among these four interpretations of complementarity. Some actors within the ICC elevate particular conceptions over others, with marked practical con-sequences. As we will see later in this book, the different conceptions are not always compatible. Within the OTP, the Jurisdiction, Comple-mentarity and Cooperation Division (JCCD) – one of three sections

---

[11] ICC, OTP, 'Ceremony for the Solemn Undertaking', p. 2.

[12] M. Brubacher, 'The ICC, National Governments and Judiciaries', presentation at Royal African Society workshop, London, 8 March 2007. For a full meeting report, see N. Waddell and P. Clark (eds.), *Peace, Justice and the ICC in Africa*, 2007, www.lse.ac.uk/international-development/Assets/Documents/PDFs/csrc-background-papers/Peace-Justice-and-the-ICC-series-report.pdf.

[13] Nouwen, *Complementarity in the Line of Fire*, p. 11.

along with the Investigation and Prosecution Divisions – is the principal actor in shaping policy on complementarity. Described by Bosco as a 'political organ at the heart of the Court'[14], the JCCD analyses referrals and communications from potential country situations and monitors national proceedings to advise the Prosecutor on when ICC intervention is warranted. The JCCD also facilitates cooperation with states during ICC investigations and prosecutions. As Carsten Stahn argues, however, '[w]ithin the ICC, each organ has sought to put its own "stamp" on complementarity. The Office of the Prosecutor has developed guidelines and policy principles on complementarity. Other aspects have been addressed by the jurisprudence of the Court or approaches of the Registry.'[15]

In the strictest *legal* sense, according to the Rome Statute, complementarity governs the ICC's decisions about which cases are admissible before the Court. Before the question of cases, situations can be referred to the ICC in one of three ways: first, when a state party to the Rome Statute refers a situation directly to the Prosecutor; second, when the UN Security Council, acting under Chapter VII of the UN Charter, refers a situation; third, when the Prosecutor initiates *proprio motu* investigations into crimes within the ICC's jurisdiction without prior referral from a state party or the Security Council.[16] Once the Court's jurisdiction over particular situations has been established, the Statute then prescribes which specific cases the ICC *should not* prosecute. These comprise cases where states with jurisdiction are already investigating or prosecuting, while displaying a genuine willingness and ability to do so; where the crimes in question are considered of insufficient gravity to concern the ICC; or where an investigation would not serve 'the interests of justice'.[17] As Robinson argues, the crux of the legal definition of complementarity is that states must have already initiated proceedings against specific suspects – and these proceedings must display a genuine willingness and ability to

---

[14] Bosco, *Rough Justice*, p. 94.
[15] C. Stahn, 'Introduction: Bridge over Troubled Waters?', in C. Stahn and M. El Zeidy (eds.), *The International Criminal Court and Complementarity*, vol. I, Cambridge University Press, 2011, p. 1.
[16] International Criminal Court, Rome Statute of the International Criminal Court, Articles 13–15.
[17] Ibid., Articles 17 and 53.

investigate and prosecute crimes – for the ICC Chambers to deem these cases inadmissible before the Court.[18]

The *political* conception of complementarity meanwhile emphasises deference to domestic institutions and the need to respect national sovereignty. In broad policy terms, complementarity holds that states have the primary responsibility to prosecute genocide, war crimes and crimes against humanity[19] but where they fail to address these adequately, the ICC can intervene to hold perpetrators accountable. The Rome Statute emphasises which cases the ICC should not pursue because the drafters of the Statute in 1998 wanted to prevent a cavalier prosecutor from riding roughshod over national sovereignty and thereby undermining domestic stability and ultimately the integrity of the Court. The drafters assumed that states would be reluctant to surrender domestic jurisdiction to the ICC, preferring to show their constituents that they could investigate and prosecute serious cases.[20] The Rome Statute consequently provides only broad principles for handling instances when states refer situations to the Court, as Uganda and the DRC have done.

The Rome negotiators also insisted that the ICC be embedded in a complementarity regime to avoid the recurrence of sovereignty-related problems encountered in the concurrent system of the International Criminal Tribunal for the former Yugoslavia (ICTY) and the International Criminal Tribunal for Rwanda (ICTR). In the Rwandan case, the concurrent operation of the ICTR, the Rwandan national courts and the *gacaca* community courts led to several jurisdictional clashes.[21] Concurrent structures emphasise a vertical relationship among different institutions in which the international level dominates.

---

[18] Robinson, 'The Mysterious Mysteriousness of Complementarity', p. 68.

[19] The ICC is also tasked with prosecuting 'the crime of aggression', the definition and conditions of which were agreed at the review conference of the Assembly of States Parties in Kampala in 2010. The ICC cannot exercise jurisdiction over the crime of aggression until the crime, and jurisdiction over it, have been ratified by thirty states, followed by the 'activation' of the Court's jurisdiction by two-thirds of States Parties after 1 January 2017 (Rome Statute, Article 121.5).

[20] M. Arsanjani and M. Reisman, 'Developments at the International Criminal Court: The Law-in-Action of the International Criminal Court', *American Journal of International Law*, 99, 2005 pp. 387–8.

[21] See P. Gourevitch, 'Justice in Exile', *New York Times*, 24 June 1996, A15; and F. Mutagwera, 'Détentions et Poursuites Judiciaires au Rwanda', in J.-F. Dupaquier (ed.), *La justice Internationale Face au Drame Rwandais*, Karthala, 1996, pp. 17–36.

The ICTR therefore claimed primacy over the national courts and *gacaca*, although there were no strict principles to resolve situations where, for example, both the ICTR and national courts claimed jurisdiction over cases involving high-ranking genocide suspects. A complementarity regime, on the other hand, in principle implies a more horizontal relationship that favours the state. Under complementarity, the state has the first call on prosecuting cases of alleged crimes committed by its nationals or within its borders. States, however, do not have free rein or absolute primacy in this regard. The ICC retains the right to intervene judicially if domestic institutions fail to show they have already initiated proceedings that display a genuine willingness and ability to investigate and prosecute crimes.[22]

Next, the *relational* understanding of complementarity comprises notions of partnership and interdependence between the ICC and domestic institutions. At the Rome conference, some states and NGOs argued that complementarity would cripple the ICC in the face of overwhelming state power.[23] The ICC, particularly the OTP, however, has maintained that complementarity not only upholds the sovereignty of states but also benefits the Court. Because the ICC has limited resources and staff to cover a global jurisdiction, the OTP argues, it relies on dividing the labour of prosecuting major crimes with domestic bodies. In a 2005 speech, Ocampo said, 'The issue for me is. . .how do we integrate the activity of the Court to prosecute the leaders with other initiatives, such as local mechanisms, because we cannot prosecute every single perpetrator.'[24]

A central feature of the relational conception of complementarity, this 'division of labour' or 'burden-sharing' stipulates that the ICC should prosecute those suspects considered the most responsible for serious crimes, while leaving 'lower level' suspects for domestic

---

[22] Rome Statute, Article 17. For a systematic discussion of deference in international criminal law, see M. Drumbl, *Atrocity, Punishment, and International Law*, Cambridge University Press, 2007, ch. 7.

[23] See, for example, J. Holmes, 'The Principle of Complementarity', in R. Lee (ed.), *The International Criminal Court: The Making of the Rome Statute*, Kluwer Law International, 1999, pp. 41–78.

[24] L. M. Ocampo, 'Keynote Address: Integrating the Work of the ICC into Local Justice Initiatives', *American University International Law Review*, 21, 4, 2005, p. 501.

prosecution or handling through some non-judicial mechanism.[25] Robinson, for example, advocates a high degree of deference toward the domestic treatment of 'lower-level' suspects but a stricter approach to evaluating the ability and willingness of domestic institutions to prosecute high-level suspects.[26] Rod Rastan argues that the legal interpretation of complementarity as an admissibility principle, outlined above, is in tension, but must coexist, with the relational interpretation of complementarity as a burden-sharing principle. He argues that the former is competitive, 'leading one forum to exercise jurisdiction to the exclusion of the other', while the latter aims at the 'consensual distribution of caseloads'.[27] Christine Chung echoes this second point by advocating a 'global system of justice' in which 'each component...is already reinforcing the others'.[28] This reinforcement takes place, she argues, through the leadership of the ICC: 'The scope, quality, and effectiveness of domestic enforcement work are enhanced by the growth and acceptance of international criminal law standards. Proceedings conducted by the ICC and other internationalized tribunals provide starting points and blueprints for proceedings involving perpetrators in the same conflicts who are tried domestically.'[29] As we will see in later chapters, this aspect of the relational conception of complementarity – which sees the ICC as the superior institution that can determine the precise division of labour between itself and domestic bodies – has been viewed as highly problematic in the Ugandan and Congolese contexts and has not led to the 'consensual distribution of caseloads' that Rastan and others have predicted.

---

[25] For an excellent analysis of the ICC's gradual shift from a court of last resort to the notion of burden-sharing with domestic institutions and, more recently, the 'voluntary relinquishment' of jurisdiction by states through self referrals, see P. McAuliffe, 'From Watchdog to Workhouse: Explaining the Emergence of the ICC's Burden-Sharing Policy as an Example of Creeping Cosmopolitanism', *Chinese Journal of International Law*, 13, 2014, paras. 1–43.

[26] D. Robinson, 'Serving the Interests of Justice: Amnesties, Truth Commissions and the International Criminal Court', *European Journal of International Law*, 14, 3, 2003, pp. 494–5.

[27] R. Rastan, 'Complementarity: Contest or Collaboration?', in M. Bergsmo (ed.), *Complementarity and the Exercise of Universal Jurisdiction for Core International Crimes*, Forum for International and Humanitarian Law, 2010, p. 83, www.toaep.org/ps-pdf/7-bergsmo.

[28] Chung, 'Punishment and Prevention of Genocide', p. 237.

[29] Ibid., pp. 237–8.

Finally, the strongest interpretation of partnership with domestic institutions takes the form of 'positive complementarity' or what some ICC actors and commentators have called 'proactive complementarity',[30] a *developmental* concept according to which the ICC should aim to catalyse and support domestic investigations and prosecutions. The OTP's 2009–12 Prosecutorial Strategy stated that positive complementarity entails 'a proactive policy of cooperation aimed at promoting national proceedings'.[31] As Robinson, who was external relations and complementarity advisor in the OTP between 2004 and 2006, argues, 'It is expected that the ICC will contribute to a climate of accountability not only through the demonstrative effect of its own prosecutions but, more importantly, through the "multiplier effect" of its complementary jurisdiction, as it encourages states to more diligently apprehend and prosecute international criminals.'[32]

The Prosecutorial Strategy states that this catalytic or multiplier effect of the Court could take various forms, including sharing information with national judiciaries, inviting domestic officials and lawyers to participate in OTP investigations and prosecutions, sharing expertise through trainings and workshops and encouraging development organisations and donors to support domestic accountability efforts.[33] In this view, the ICC is not merely a partner with domestic institutions but an active enabler of national investigations and prosecutions, although the OTP was careful to add that this would not '[involve] the Office directly in capacity building or financial or technical assistance'.[34]

Such views ascribe a 'trickle down' effect to the ICC and reflect the 'justice cascade' notion propounded by Kathryn Sikkink, represented by 'the dramatic shift in the legitimacy of the norms of individual criminal accountability for human rights violations and an increase

---

[30] See, for example, S. Arbia and G. Bassy, 'Proactive Complementarity: A Registrar's Perpsective and Plans', in C. Stahn and M. El Zeidy (eds.), *The International Criminal Court and Complementarity*, vol. I, Cambridge University Press, 2011, pp. 52–68; and W. Burke-White, 'Reframing Positive Complementarity', in C. Stahn and M. El Zeidy (eds.), *The International Criminal Court and Complementarity*, vol. I, Cambridge University Press, 2011, pp. 341–60.

[31] International Criminal Court, Office of the Prosecutor, 'Prosecutorial Strategy, 2009–2012', 1 February 2010, p. 5.

[32] Robinson, 'Serving the Interests of Justice', p. 482.

[33] ICC, OTP, 'Prosecutorial Strategy, 2009–2012', p. 5.   [34] Ibid., p. 5.

in actions (prosecutions) on behalf of those norms'.[35] Sikkink emphasises the importance of international and domestic norm entrepreneurs,
including international courts and tribunals, human rights organisations, activists and scholars, in fostering the 'international diffusion' of
norms of individual criminal accountability that culminated in the
adoption of the Rome Statute in 1998.

In recent years, though, it appears that positive complementarity has
begun to fade as a concept within the OTP's operations. The 2010–15
Prosecutorial Strategy refers to it only once (listing it as a previous
principle of the Office which now requires review) and suggests a less
strenuous relationship with domestic actors: 'Close monitoring and
frequent interaction with countries where situations are under preliminary examination result in an increased ability and willingness of
those countries to conduct genuine investigations and prosecutions.
However the Office is presently not able to sustain such high intensity
efforts due to a lack of resources.'[36] The new Strategy also states
that the OTP's primary role in 'complementarity and cooperation' is
'strengthening the Rome System in support of the ICC and of national
efforts in situations under preliminary examination or investigation'.[37]
The reference to the 'Rome System' implies that the primary support
to national institutions should come from the broader community
of the ICC's Assembly of States Parties (ASP), rather than from the
Court itself.

Highlighting this shift away from positive complementarity – and
more broadly, the evolution of interpretations of complementarity
within the Court – three months after becoming Prosecutor in June
2012, Fatou Bensouda said in a speech to the Council for Foreign
Relations:

I think that even though we talk about positive complementarity, we have to
also remember that in terms of capacity and resources, there is [only] so
much the Office of the Prosecutor can do. I think I just mentioned about even
doing our core business becoming a bit difficult for us to do, much more if we

---

[35] K. Sikkink, 'The Age of Accountability: The Rise of Individual Criminal
Accountability', in F. Lessa and L. Payne (eds.), *Amnesty in the Age of Human
Rights Accountability: Comparative and International Perspectives*, Cambridge
University Press, 2012, p. 19.
[36] International Criminal Court, Office of the Prosecutor, 'Strategic Plan, June
2012–2015', 11 October 2013, p. 12.
[37] Ibid., p. 3.

were to expand ourselves...Whether we should have gone to Uganda and investigated with them and prosecuted with them, I do not think that this is what is envisaged by the statute on complementarity.[38]

The OTP broadly interprets these four conceptions of complementarity – legal, political, relational and developmental – as mutually reinforcing (although, as mentioned above, some OTP staff such as Rastan identify tensions among them). Running through the four conceptions is a strong liberal normative thread regarding respect for national sovereignty, autonomy, equality and pluralism. The legal and political interpretations of complementarity stress that states will have the first opportunity to investigate and prosecute crimes within the ICC's jurisdiction when they are committed on their soil or by their nationals, while the ICC, acting as a back-stop, will intervene only when states fail demonstrably to do so. The relational and developmental interpretations envisage cooperation between the ICC and states, with the latter carrying the bulk of the investigative and prosecutorial burden, leaving the ICC to deal with a handful of the toughest cases that states, for whatever reason, cannot handle. Meanwhile, the Court will actively encourage and assist states in handling their own cases, which is perceived as bolstering state capacity and assisting the Court by sharing the load of delivering justice among a range of actors.

As we will see in later chapters, however, the legal conception of complementarity (which ascribes a fundamental role to the ICC in deciding when it should or should not intervene in states' affairs) has routinely dominated the ICC's practice over the other three conceptions (which stress the primacy of states and the ICC's essentially supportive role). While ICC officials and supporters of the Court often invoke complementarity broadly to express deference to domestic institutions and respect for national sovereignty, in practice they emphasise the legal conception of complementarity which, as currently conceived by the Court, establishes an extremely high threshold for states to claim jurisdiction over cases within their territory and to thwart intervention by the ICC. While the political, relational and developmental conceptions of complementarity – if they were habitually enacted – would shift

---

[38] F. Bensouda, 'The International Criminal Court: A New Approach to International Relations', transcript of speech to Council for Foreign Relations, Washington DC, 21 September 2012, www.cfr.org/event/international-criminal-court-new-approach-international-relations-0.

the balance of power toward states, these perspectives have been consistently subordinated to the legal conception, which gives enormous latitude to the ICC to determine when states should or should not be permitted to act.

In these regards, the legal conception of complementarity is imbued with many of the assumed virtues of distance, with its assertion of the superiority and insulation of international justice from the domestic sphere and its capacity to assess 'objectively' the function of national institutions when determining the admissibility of cases, as discussed in the next section. Later chapters will argue that the ICC needs to return to the view of complementarity originally expressed by Ocampo in his inaugural speech – with states playing the dominant role, the ICC intervening only in the most exceptional circumstances and, when doing so, maintaining a long-term focus on the development of domestic judicial capacity – all of which is embodied in the political, relational and developmental conceptions of complementarity. The legal conception, which currently predominates in the ICC's operations in Uganda, the DRC and (as we will see in Chapter 8) across the other ICC situations in Africa, dilutes the fundamental spirit of complementarity while also undermining the Court's efficacy and legitimacy.

Distance: Political and Philosophical Separateness

Paul Gready describes two models of transitional justice, 'distanced' and 'embedded', which require a 'correct balance' to meet the full range of needs of societies recovering from mass conflict. Gready critiques 'distanced justice', embodied principally in international courts and tribunals located beyond the atrocity sites they investigate, on four grounds:

[T]hey lack local participation in decision-making processes and management; they impoverish and undermine local legal systems through skewed resource allocation, inadequate capacity building, and by marking them with the stigma of inadequacy; they are too invisible and alien to domestic legal communities and society more generally due, for example, to their geographical remoteness and inadequate outreach; and, as a result of all of the above, they make little contribution to democratic development and peace in the country concerned.[39]

---

[39] P. Gready, 'Reconceptualising Transitional Justice: Embedded and Distanced Justice', *Conflict, Security and Development*, 5, 1, 2005, pp. 8–9.

In contrast, Gready argues, 'embedded justice', in the form of in-country institutions such as the *gacaca* courts in Rwanda or the Special Court for Sierra Leone, 'at its best involves local participation, develops local legal systems and adjudicatory mechanisms, achieves high local visibility, and, as a result, contributes to societal education, democratic development, and peace'.[40] Ultimately, Gready argues, a 'correct balance' between distanced and embedded justice requires building on their 'complementary capacities and legitimacies', namely 'due process and a position outside the intimacies of conflict [in distanced justice] alongside [embedded justice's] familiarity and...capacity to resonate with local values and culture'.[41]

This section draws on Gready's theorisation of distanced and embedded justice to interpret key norms and principles within the ICC (which reflect core ideas within international criminal law and liberal cosmopolitanism more generally). It argues that various conceptualisations of 'distance' are central to the ICC's self-identity, objectives, structures and processes. This section goes beyond Gready's view in two key respects, though: first, it provides a fuller examination of the reasoning behind the ICC's conscious embodiment of distanced justice; and, second, it casts doubt on the capacity for the kind of 'correct balance' that Gready advocates, given the sustained critique of embedded justice that is inherent in distanced justice. It does this by exploring two forms of distance – political and philosophical – that characterise the structure and function of the ICC.

A key conceptual point to emphasise initially is that 'distance' throughout this book denotes more than physical or geographical remoteness. The concept illuminates various ways in which the ICC attempts to separate and insulate itself politically, culturally and philosophically from the domestic arena, even when it engages with it physically through on-the-ground investigations, outreach and other processes. This reflects Fiona Adamson's call for a 'spatial turn' in global security studies which 'opens up "the global" and its constituent parts to interrogation and analysis, and by doing so urges us to raise questions about where security practices and discourses are located,

---

[40] Ibid., p. 9.   [41] Ibid., p. 19.

thus allowing us to juxtapose actors and connect processes that operate in very different physical (or virtual) locales.'[42]

The analysis here also echoes the rich literature critiquing the 'bunkerisation' tendencies of foreign interventions in the global South, focusing on the ways in which international development organisations and peacekeeping missions, in particular, confine their actors from the societies in which they operate, to maintain their security and impartiality.[43] Sarah Collinson, Mark Duffield et al. argue,

This 'bunkerisation' has contributed to the growing physical and social detachment of many international aid personnel from the societies in which they work, and a substantial shift towards 'remote management' techniques as aid managers attempt to administer or evaluate programmes from a safe distance, through national and local field workers, subcontracted intermediaries and new technologies. UN agencies and larger NGOs have also sought to circumvent their own security restrictions by outsourcing activities to other NGOs and for-profit subcontractors.[44]

Unlike aid and peacekeeping practices, however, which are justified predominantly in terms of assisting local populations, many practitioners and scholars argue that international justice is an inherent good or benefits a more generalised 'international community' through tackling crimes that shock the conscience of humanity and 'the moral transformation of how ordinary men and women regard political violence

---

[42] F. Adamson, 'Spaces of Global Security: Beyond Methodological Nationalism', *Journal of Global Security Studies*, 1, 1, 2016, p. 20.

[43] See, for example, M. Duffield, 'Risk-Management and the Fortified Aid Compound: Everyday Life in Post-Interventionary Society', *Journal of Intervention and Statebuilding*, 4, 4, 2010, pp. 453–74; M. Duffield, 'From Immersion to Simulation: Remote Methodologies and the Decline of Area Studies', *Review of African Political Economy*, 41, 1, 2014, pp. S75–S94; S. Autesserre, *Peaceland: Conflict Resolution and the Everyday Politics of International Intervention*, Cambridge University Press, 2014; L. Smirl, *Spaces of Aid: How Cars, Compounds and Hotels Shape Humanitarianism*, University of Chicago Press, 2015; and J. Fisher, 'Reproducing Remoteness? States, Internationals and the Co-Constitution of Aid: 'Bunkerization', in the East African Periphery', *Journal of Intervention and Statebuilding*, 11, 1, 2017, pp. 98–119.

[44] S. Collinson, M. Duffield et al., 'Paradoxes of Presence: Risk Management and Aid Culture in Challenging Environments', Humanitarian Policy Group, Overseas Development Institute, March 2013, p. iii.

against civilians'.[45] This book will show that the 'distancing' tendencies of law are particularly acute, mimicking but exceeding the 'distancing' practices of other external interventions in the global South. Unlike these other institutions, international criminal law holds that distance is an inherent virtue rather than a necessary evil.

The methodological framework of 'intervention' and 'intersections', outlined in Chapter 1, allows for an in-depth exploration of various elements of the ICC's 'distance'. As later chapters will show, the most important elements of the ICC's purposeful distancing do not flow from the idea of an external institution intervening in a foreign space – although such dynamics are important – but rather from the ways in which the ICC has structured its various intersections with national and community-level actors and institutions to preference its own modalities and objectives, underpinned by the assumption that distance enhances the Court's adjudicative capacity. Critical to the ICC's practice of distance within these intersections is its view of its own innate legal, technical and political superiority to the domestic terrain.

Political Distance

The notion of political distance at the heart of the ICC concerns the need for international justice to separate itself from powerful agendas such as states' attempts to safeguard their leaders from investigation and prosecution. Neutrality and impartiality, achieved through distancing the Court from the domestic political arena, are viewed as key to the fair and robust delivery of justice. The ICC's expression of political distance contains several mutually reinforcing components.

First, the ICC voices a consistent scepticism of state power and the likelihood that domestic political actors will seek to manipulate the Court to their own ends, including stymieing its attempts to hold them accountable. As discussed in the previous section on complementarity, political distance emphasises the ICC's independence from domestic agents and institutions, which are viewed as either responsible for atrocities or likely to interfere in the Court's efforts to prosecute

---

[45] D. Luban, 'After the Honeymoon: Reflections on the Current State of International Criminal Justice', *Journal of International Criminal Justice*, 11, 2013, p. 509. See also R. Teitel, *Humanity's Law*, Oxford University Press, 2013; and R. Teitel, *Globalizing Transitional Justice: Contemporary Essays*, Oxford University Press, 2014.

suspects. As Bensouda said in a 2012 interview, 'We are a new tool, a judicial tool, not a tool in the hands of politicians who think they can decide when to plug or unplug us.'[46] This includes an insistence on legal principles rather than political considerations as the basis for the ICC's decision-making at all stages from situation and case selection through to judgement and sentencing.

Ocampo expressed these views at a landmark international conference, 'Building a Future on Peace and Justice', in Nuremberg in June 2007. Funded by the governments of Germany, Finland and Jordan and several international NGOs[47], the event was held at the height of the Ugandan peace talks in Juba amid calls for the deferral or withdrawal of ICC charges against the LRA leadership for the sake of peace:

As the Prosecutor of the ICC, I was given a clear judicial mandate. My duty is to apply the law without political considerations...And yet, for each situation in which the ICC is exercising jurisdiction, we can hear voices challenging judicial decisions, their timing, their timeliness, asking the Prosecution to use its discretionary powers to adjust to the situations on the ground, to indict or withdraw indictments according to short term political goals. We also hear officials of States Parties calling for amnesties, the granting of immunities and other ways to avoid prosecutions, supposedly in the name of peace; we can hear voices portraying the ICC as an impediment to progressing further with peace processes. These proposals are not consistent with the Rome Statute...It is essential on the contrary to ensure that any conflict resolution initiative be compatible with the Rome Statute, so that peace and justice work effectively together...[T]here can be no political compromise on legality and accountability.[48]

In May 2012, Bensouda echoed Ocampo's views when also addressing the perennial 'peace versus justice' debate (discussed in greater detail in Chapter 6):

---

[46] Quoted in D. Smith, 'New Chief Prosecutor Defends International Criminal Court', *Guardian*, 23 May 2012, www.theguardian.com/law/2012/may/23/chief-prosecutor-international-criminal-court?newsfeed=true.

[47] 'Building a Future on Peace and Justice', Nuremberg conference, June 2007, www.jordanembassy.de/nuremberg_conference_on_peace_an.htm.

[48] L.M. Ocampo, 'Building a Future on Peace and Justice', speech at Nuremberg conference, 24 June 2007, www.icc-cpi.int/NR/rdonlyres/4E466EDB-2B38-4BAF-AF5F-005461711149/143825/LMO_nuremberg_20070625_English.pdf.

Some leaders sought by the Court threatened to commit more crimes to retain power, blackmailing the international community with a false option: peace or justice. The OTP has to follow its independent justice mandate. To guarantee its impartiality, OTP cannot take into account the prospect of peace initiatives. If politicians isolate the role of the Court and the justice component of conflict management by not cooperating, the Court's effectiveness would be seriously hampered.[49]

In these statements, Ocampo and Bensouda characterise political leaders who argue that the ICC may jeopardise peace processes as 'blackmailing the international community' in order 'to retain power'. In such a context, they argue, the Court cannot consider political arguments against ICC involvement – for example, for the sake of 'peace initiatives' – but must rather maintain impartiality by invoking legal principles contained in the Rome Statute. In short, the law is a means of operating above politics.

Second, political distance involves the notion that, given the inherent manipulativeness of domestic political actors, the ICC represents a way to *improve* politics – a 'paradigm shift', as Bensouda argued in 2011, from the Westphalian model of state sovereignty to one of international oversight and the rule of law.[50] In this view, the role of the ICC is not only to deliver impartial justice, free from political considerations, but also to improve the ways in which states treat their citizens and relate to one another. In a 2012 speech, Bensouda characterised the ICC as 'creating global governance without a global government. . .; a new paradigm in international relations, utilizing law as a global tool to promote peace and international security'.[51]

This view of the ICC as fundamentally altering the nature of international relations has been internalised by various States Parties to the Rome Statute. For example, UK Foreign Secretary, William Hague, delivered a speech in The Hague in July 2012 entitled 'International Law and Justice in a Networked World'. He described the UK's 'reliance on a rules-based international system' and international justice

---

[49] Coalition for the International Criminal Court, 'Interview with International Criminal Court Deputy Prosecutor and Prosecutor-Elect H.E. Ms. Fatou Bensouda', June 2012, www.iccnow.org/documents/Fatou_Bensouda_Full_Interview_eng.pdf, p. 1.

[50] Quoted in M. deGuzman, 'Bensouda on ICC Prosecutions', 31 March 2011, www.intlawgrrls.com/2011/03/bensouda-on-icc-prosecutions.html.

[51] Bensouda, 'A New Approach to International Relations'.

and the rule of law as 'the common thread binding many of the pressing issues we face, from building peace, widening democracy, and expanding free trade, to confronting terrorism while upholding the law and respecting human rights'.[52] Hague identified the UN Security Council's unanimous decision to refer the situation of Libya to the ICC in 2011 as a watershed for the international community's ability to address large-scale conflict collectively. In contrast, a UK Foreign and Commonwealth Office strategy paper described the lack of Security Council consensus over addressing the conflict in Syria – including on the issue of a UN referral of the Syria situation to the ICC – as a grave failure of international policymaking.[53] The UK thus views the ICC as an indispensable tool in addressing criminal behaviour during periods of mass violence, deterring future atrocities, ending wars and achieving lasting peace and security. It also views encouraging bilateral partners to sign the Rome Statute and to incorporate it into their domestic legislative frameworks – as the UK did with the International Criminal Court Act in 2001 – as signs of 'shared commitments to human rights' and the bedrock of effective international diplomacy.[54]

Third, the ICC expresses a conception of political distance by insisting on the universality of its view of justice in contrast to the self-interested nature of domestic politics and of domestic interpretations of justice. When challenged over the Court's effects on political processes such as peace negotiations, ICC principals and supporters often return to the importance of the Rome conference in 1998 as a democratic moment in which a 'global consensus' was built around the legal precepts eventually enshrined in the Rome Statute.[55] They argue

---

52 Speech by UK Foreign Secretary, W. Hague, 'International Law and Justice in a Networked World', The Hague, 9 July 2012, www.gov.uk/government/speeches/international-law-and-justice-in-a-networked-world.

53 Government of the United Kingdom, Foreign and Commonwealth Office, 'International Criminal Court Strategy Paper', London, 17 July 2013, p. 2, www.gov.uk/government/publications/international-criminal-court-strategy-paper.

54 Ibid., p. 5.

55 See, for example, Coalition for the International Criminal Court, *The Monitor: Journal of the Coalition for the International Criminal Court*, 36, May–October 2008, p. 13, www.gov.uk/government/publications/international-criminal-court-strategy-paper; and International Criminal Court, Assembly of States Parties, 'Retreat on the Future of the ICC', 18 October 2011, https://asp.icc-cpi.int/en_menus/asp/press%20releases/press%20releases%202011/Pages/pr732.aspx.

that the universality of the ICC, with the global standards it embodies, is superior to the domestic sphere, with its contested specificities and unprincipled power politics. Where the domestic is viewed as partisan and polluted – more so when it has been weakened by violent conflict – the global is framed as neutral and even-handed. Such perspectives map onto a broader liberal paradigm that views the 'local', whether domestic politics generally or domestic responses to conflict specifically, as inherently compromised and requiring international intervention.[56] The statements by Ocampo and Bensouda above also equate the ICC with modern, liberal ways of conducting domestic and international affairs, in contrast to outdated, conflictual modes of politics. In this view, the ICC's distanced justice is necessary to 'become international' rather than be hampered by states' historically self-interested conduct.[57]

Philosophical Distance

A second conception of the ICC's separateness – philosophical distance – concerns the more specific need for critical detachment, especially in the selection and judgement of individual criminal cases. In a 2014 speech, Bensouda said,

[W]e are, of course, operating in a political environment. So everything that we do is conceived to be because of politics...Which, as we know, is not the case...We proceed based solely on the evidence and the law. And I think this

---

[56] See, for example, R. Paris, 'Saving Liberal Peacebuilding', *Review of International Studies*, 36, 2, 2010, pp. 337–65.

[57] F. Mégret, 'Beyond "Fairness": Understanding the Determinants of International Criminal Procedure', *UCLA Journal of International Law and Foreign Affairs*, 14, 2010, Section IV. See also F. Mégret, 'Cour Pénale Internationale et Néocolonialisme: Audelà des Evidences', *Revue Études Internationales*, 45, 1, March 2014, p. 39; and I. Mgbeoji, 'The Civilised Self and the Barbaric Other: Imperial Delusions of Order and the Challenges of Human Security', in R. Falk, B. Rajagopal and J. Stevens (eds.), *International Law and the Third World: Reshaping Justice*, Routledge-Cavendish, 2008, p. 152, on a perceived civilisation/savagery dichotomy between the global North and South on their capacity to address mass crimes. See also Tom Young on the centrality of colonialism for the development of liberal political thought, especially its insistence on the need for societies to 'transition to modern political forms' (T. Young, 'A Project to Be Realised: Global Liberalism and Contemporary Africa', *Millennium: Journal of International Studies*, 24, 3, 1995, p. 533).

is critically important that we continue on that trajectory and not deviate. To be able to investigate and prosecute without fear or favor, wherever our jurisdiction is met. This is critically important.[58]

Following a long philosophical tradition of deontological conceptions of justice from Kant, Rawls and others – that is, the morality of an action based on its adherence to rules rather than its consequences – ICC principals regularly describe the need to separate the Court's decision-making from messy political calculations about utility and impact. Aiming to deliver what Gerry Simpson describes as 'impartial, majestic justice'[59] or the 'Godly distance, devilish understanding'[60] of the fictional Lord Chief Justice in Ian McEwan's novel *The Children Act*, the ICC seeks to extract and insulate itself from consequentialist considerations, achieving Rawls' position as the 'ideal observer' on the fraught terrain of criminality and conflict.[61] In this view, the Court should remain disinterested and thus disinfected from the domestic political sphere. As Kieran McEvoy argues, 'Claims that the "rule of

---

[58] F. Bensouda, 'Prosecuting Sexual and Gender-Based Violence: New Directions in International Criminal Justice', speech to Council for Foreign Relations, Washington DC, 11 December 2014, www.cfr.org/event/fatou-bensouda-international-criminal-court-and-gender-based-crimes-0.

[59] G. Simpson, *Law, War and Crime: War Crimes Trials and the Reinvention of International Law*, Polity, 2007, p. 30.

[60] I. McEwan, *The Children Act*, Jonathan Cape, 2014, p. 13.

[61] In Rawls' well-known theory of justice as fairness, 'mutual disinterest' is among the principal traits of the actors in the 'original position' behind the 'veil of ignorance' who are tasked with determining the fairest possible societal distribution of primary goods (J. Rawls, *A Theory of Justice*, revised edition, Harvard University Press, 1999, p. 12). See also S. Moyn, 'Judith Shklar versus the International Criminal Court', *Humanity: An International Journal of Human Rights, Humanitarianism and Development*, 4, 3, 2013, pp. 473–500, for an excellent dissection of the ICC's embodiment of liberalism and legalism. For Mahmood Mamdani, the danger with the ICC's legalist foundations is that they lead to 'human rights fundamentalism', which holds that a particular version of Western criminal justice must apply to all high-level suspects anywhere in the world, regardless of the consequences for peaceful transitions or political stability (M. Mamdani, 'Beware Human Rights Fundamentalism!', *Mail & Guardian*, 20 March 2009, https://mg.co.za/article/2009-03-20-beware-human-rights-fundamentalism). In a similarly theological vein, Thoms, Ron and Paris argue that human rights ideology – a firm belief, for example, in the need for international judicial responses to human rights violations – has often trumped finer-grained theoretical and empirical analysis, leading to 'faith-based' rather than 'fact-based' prescriptions (Thoms, Ron and Paris, 'State-Level Effects of Transitional Justice', p. 5).

law" speaks to values and working practices such as justice, objectivity, certainty, uniformity, universality, rationality and so on are particularly prized in times of profound social and political transition.'[62] This embodies what Judith Shklar in her seminal 1964 book terms 'legalism' or 'the urge to draw a clear line between law and non-law' and a 'procedure...to isolate law completely from the social context within which it exists'.[63]

Highlighting the deep entrenchment of this view of philosophical distance in the wider realm of international criminal law, previous research on the ICTR elicits similar views on the need for fundamental disengagement from local affairs. When asked whether he had travelled from the ICTR in Arusha, Tanzania, to Rwanda to gauge the impact the Tribunal was having on the Rwandan population (particularly in light of the ICTR Statute's claim that it should contribute to national reconciliation in Rwanda[64]), one senior Tribunal judge replied, 'I have never been to Rwanda and I have no desire to visit. Going there and seeing the effect we are having would only make my work more difficult. How can I do my job – judging these cases fairly – with pictures in my mind of what is happening over there? This task is already complicated enough.'[65]

At an expert roundtable in London in March 2007, Ocampo expressed similar views: 'As the Court, we can't take our impact into consideration. The law must guide us, not our effects on the ground. International justice can't bring change in a country...We have to fulfil our judicial mandate only.'[66] Such a view separates the act of punishing perpetrators from its likely political, legal, social and cultural consequences. It holds not only that considering the impact of justice is beyond the ICTR's or ICC's remit but that substantive consideration

---

[62] K. McEvoy, 'Beyond Legalism: Towards a Thicker Understanding of Transitional Justice', *Journal of Law and Society*, 34, 4, December 2007, p. 417.

[63] J. Shklar, *Legalism: Law, Morals, and Political Trials*, Harvard University Press, 1964, p. 2.

[64] United Nations, 'Statute of the International Criminal Tribunal for Rwanda', 1995, Preamble.

[65] Author's interview, ICTR Judge, Arusha, 7 February 2003.

[66] L. M. Ocampo, 'The International Criminal Court and Prospects for Peace in Africa', expert roundtable on Peace, Justice and the Dilemmas of the ICC in Africa, London School of Economics, 2 March 2007, notes on file with author.

of this will hamper these institutions' work by jeopardising their perceived impartiality.[67]

As with the four conceptions of complementarity discussed above, key actors within the ICC view the two components of distance here – political and philosophical – as mutually reinforcing. One reason that critical detachment at all stages of the Court's decision-making is paramount is that the political realm, especially the exercise of state power, is likely to wield substantial and negative influence over the Court. The ICC must therefore insulate itself from political considerations in order to deliver impartial justice. As we will see in later chapters, some actors within the ICC have, consciously or otherwise, challenged this emphasis on distance. In particular, some actors – including within the OTP – have oscillated between the deontological underpinnings of distance and framing the Court's work in more consequentialist terms. The latter view tends to emphasise the deterrence of perpetrators and the likely benefits of the ICC for atrocity victims and violence-affected societies, all of which seeks to link the ICC directly to the domestic sphere.[68] As with other international criminal justice institutions, the ICC faces a substantial tension

---

[67] For a detailed analysis of the ICTR's insistence that contributing to international jurisprudence, rather than social or political outcomes in Rwanda, is its principal objective – as well as an examination of the ICTR's impact on various dimensions of the ICC's work – see N. Palmer, *Courts in Conflict: Interpreting the Layers of Justice in Post-Genocide Rwanda*, Oxford University Press, 2015. For a sustained argument for why the ICC should be evaluated according to its manifold effects, see Kersten, *Justice in Conflict*.

[68] Eric Blumenson argues that this consequentialist camp often comprises the strongest proponents of the 'prosecute regardless' perspective (E. Blumenson, 'The Challenge of a Global Standard of Justice: Peace, Pluralism and Punishment at the International Criminal Court', *Columbia Journal of Transnational Law*, 44, 2006, p. 820). For critiques of the argument that international criminal law can deter mass crimes, see J. Snyder and L. Vinjamuri, 'Trials and Errors: Principle and Pragmatism in Strategies of International Justice', *International Security*, 28, 3, Winter 2003/4, pp. 5–44; and K. Cronin-Furman, 'Managing Expectations: International Criminal Trials and the Prospects of Deterrence of Mass Atrocity', *International Journal of Transitional Justice*, 7, 2013, pp. 434–54. Elsewhere, Vinjamuri describes the 'triumph of consequences', in which international advocacy now prefers 'results-based' justifications for international criminal law rather than 'principle or duty-based' arguments (L. Vinjamuri, 'Deterrence, Democracy and the Pursuit of International Justice', Ethics & International Affairs, 24, 2, 2010, pp. 191–211). As later chapters will argue, while this may pertain to many of the ICC's government and civil society backers, within the Court deontological justifications are still deeply entrenched.

between doing justice for its own sake (or to uphold international law) and for the benefit of individuals and communities directly affected by conflict. Analysing the practice of the ICC in Uganda and the DRC in later chapters, we will see that the Court itself is sometimes confused about how wedded it should be to notions of distance. We will also see that an institutional over-emphasis on distance causes immense difficulties for the Court and for the societies in which it operates.

Notions of political and philosophical distance in transitional justice have also been heavily contested by a vast array of authors and actors, including in the same African states where the ICC is currently operating. As suggested earlier by Gready, 'embedded' notions of transitional justice emphasise a very different set of norms and values, including engagement, access, participation and intimacy. Oliver Richmond, for example, advocates the importance of the 'everyday' and a deeper 'liberal-local' conversation in interpreting appropriate responses to mass conflict. For Richmond, the 'everyday' constitutes 'a culturally appropriate form of individual or community life and care' that challenges the liberal peace by engaging with 'the local, its cultural dynamics, welfare needs, and environment'.[69] This necessitates a 'liberal-local' conversation in which scholars and practitioners of the liberal peace (within which the ICC is assumed to be a paradigmatic actor) engage 'in a non-hegemonic manner' with everyday responses to conflict and their 'local context, culture, history, needs as well as rights and institutions'.[70]

In a similar vein, Norman Porter emphasises the importance of 'engagement', rather than distance, as a response to harm, particularly as a prerequisite for reconciliation. Porter underlines the necessity of creating fora for public discourse and debate, in which a vital element is open and fair engagement between previously antagonistic parties. Porter argues that meaningful engagement entails 'practices involving honest, committed encounters with others, not least those with whom we disagree most'.[71] In these settings, individuals make themselves

---

[69] O. Richmond, 'A Post-Liberal Peace: Eirenism and the Everyday', *Review of International Studies*, 35, 2009, p. 558.
[70] O. Richmond, 'Becoming Liberal, Unbecoming Liberalism: Liberal-Local Hybridity via the Everyday as a Response to the Paradoxes of Liberal Peacebuilding', *Journal of Intervention and Statebuilding*, 3, 3, 2009, p. 335.
[71] N. Porter, *The Elusive Quest: Reconciliation in Northern Ireland*, The Blackstaff Press, 2003, p. 108.

vulnerable to others and the most important result is that 'through [these practices] others are opened up to us and we to them, others are permitted to be heard in their terms and we in ours'.[72]

These streams of current scholarship on 'everyday' practices and 'engagement' in transitional justice critique many of the core assumptions of the 'distance' perspective espoused by the ICC. As we will see in later chapters, this scholarship also resonates with norms and values embedded in some community-based approaches to transitional justice in Uganda and the DRC, which stress the need for justice and judgement based on deep knowledge of local circumstances, calculations regarding consequences and the direct involvement of parties affected by violence. One key challenge for the ICC is how to deliver its version of distanced justice in environments where very different conceptions of justice predominate.

Liberal Underpinnings of Complementarity and Distance

The rest of this book will analyse the ICC's work in Uganda and the DRC through the lens of the two core concepts examined here, complementarity and distance. As later chapters highlight, there are inconsistencies in the way that the ICC itself, as a diverse and heterogeneous institution, interprets and acts upon these concepts. Nevertheless, the regularity with which complementarity and the claims to objectivity and impartiality that implicitly comprise distance are invoked, especially in justifying the ICC at times of vociferous critique, highlights their centrality for the Court.

As will become more apparent in analysing the ICC's operations in central Africa, complementarity and distance are often in profound tension. The 'complacency of complementarity' theme running through this book highlights that this principle invariably gives way to distance when the ICC's work is contested by different conceptions of justice or challenges to its jurisdiction. Of the two principles, distance is the stronger and more likely to predominate when the domestic

---

[72] Ibid., p. 108. See also D. Tait, 'Remote and Intimate Justice: Challenges and Paradoxes for Courts of the Future', paper presented at the 2004 Australasian Law Reform Agencies Conference, Wellington, 16 April 2004; J. Silk, 'Caring at a Distance', *Philosophy and Geography*, 1, 2, 1998, pp. 165–82; and K. Aas, '(In)security-at-a-Distance: Rescaling Justice, Risk and Warfare in a Transnational Age', *Global Crime*, 13, 4, 2012, pp. 235–53.

realm threatens ICC intervention. While some aspects of complementarity imply partnership with domestic transitional justice institutions, distance expresses a fundamental distrust of the domestic realm (a key reason that Gready's 'correct balance' between distanced and embedded justice is highly improbable). Where complementarity articulates a degree of deference to local approaches, distance implies superiority, a view of international criminal law as hovering above the political fray in order to critique it fully and to inspire it to reform according to universal principles. As we will see later, the element of complementarity that is most consistent with the above articulation of distance – namely, the *legal* definition of complementarity that governs the admissibility of situations and cases before the Court – is also the most commonly enacted by the ICC. The other three versions of complementarity (political, relational and developmental) play a negligible role in the ICC's day-to-day operation and therefore represent a much weaker impediment to the Court's fundamental and problematic emphasis on distance.

That the ICC oscillates uncomfortably between complementarity and distance reflects a core tension between pluralism and universality within liberal cosmopolitan thought, the broad philosophical realm in which the Court is strongly embedded.[73] The four conceptions of complementarity draw heavily on liberalism's adherence to the principles of autonomy, self determination, toleration regarding beliefs and practices that one finds objectionable and the fostering of pluralism in people's cultures, values, norms, traditions and identities. For this reason, complementarity begins by emphasising national sovereignty but does not automatically forbid external interference. Rather, sovereignty in this case entails states' duty to investigate and prosecute international crimes, which if they fail to fulfil may trigger intervention by the ICC.[74]

---

[73] For a discussion of international criminal law, including the ICC, as an 'overwhelmingly liberal-minded profession', see D. Robinson, 'The Identity Crisis of International Criminal Law', *Leiden Journal of International Law*, 21, 2008, pp. 925–63; and Roach, *Politicizing the International Criminal Court*.

[74] As Rastan argues, 'Objections to the exercise of ICC jurisdiction cannot be based on appeals to state sovereignty that do not in fact apply under international law.' He argues this point on two grounds: 'First, there is no general principle under international law whereby a state may seek to nullify investigations and prosecutions undertaken in another jurisdiction simply because it relates to crimes occurring on its own territory or by its nationals... Secondly, it has long

The same logic applies to another key liberal response to mass conflict, the doctrine of the 'responsibility to protect' (R2P), which begins with the obligation of states to protect their citizens from genocide, war crimes and crimes against humanity (the same crimes covered by the Rome Statute) and leaves open the possibility of foreign intervention if states fail to fulfil this duty. Bensouda has drawn a direct link between the work of the ICC and the principle of R2P. In 2012, she argued, 'The Court should be seen as a tool in the R2P toolbox. Strengthening the correlation and the interaction between both is what I think we should be concerned more with in order to maximise effectively the protection which we will give to civilians.'[75] With this perspective seemingly in mind, Ocampo argued several months after leaving the Prosecutor's post that, to ensure the maximum protection of civilians, it was imperative to 'integrate the [UN Security Council], the ICC, NATO forces'.[76] As later chapters will argue, a key point of consistency between the ICC's principle of complementarity and R2P is that the same international actors that promote these two principles also hold the power to determine when states have fulfilled their obligations and whether international intervention is therefore justified. This affords international actors enormous authority and latitude and greatly increases the likelihood of external intervention, often with highly troubling results.

While liberalism provides many of the core values behind complementarity, it simultaneously carries another set of values and norms that underpin the discourse and practice of distance, namely universality, legalism and a belief in justice delivered according to standard rules

been held in treaty law and custom that certain crimes attract universal opprobrium, rendering the culprit liable for prosecution in any state on behalf of the international community as a whole.' (R. Rastan, 'What is "Substantially the Same Conduct?": Unpacking the ICC's "First Limb" Complementarity Jurisprudence', *Journal of International Criminal Justice*, 15, 1, 2017, pp. 22–3.)

[75] F. Bensouda, 'R2P in 2022', speech to the Stanley Foundation, Iowa, 18 January 2012, http://library.fora.tv/2012/01/18/R2P_in_2022. For further discussion of the links between the ICC and R2P, see K. Ainley, 'The Responsibility to Protect and the International Criminal Court: Counteracting the Crisis', *International Affairs*, 91, 1, 2015, pp. 37–54; and Urmas Paet, Estonian Minister of Foreign Affairs, 'The Complex Relationship between R2P and the ICC: Can it Succeed?', speech at human rights conference in Reyjavik, Iceland, 10 April 2013, www.vm.ee/en/news/complex-relationship-between-r2p-and-icc-can-it-succeed.

[76] Quoted in Krever, 'Dispensing Global Justice', p. 97.

and procedures as opposed to expected consequences or other contextual factors. The ICC's conception of universality finds expression in Ruti Teitel's support for 'global citizens' delivering 'global justice' on behalf of all of humanity and in the process achieving 'the transcendence of traditional political sovereignty'.[77] Crucial to the ICC's claims of universality is the idea that the 'difficult birthing process'[78] of the Rome conference created a global consensus about the ICC as an ideal response to mass atrocity. As Chung, the ICC senior trial attorney who led the Prosecution investigations in Uganda, the DRC and Sudan between 2004 and 2007, argued,

[T]hrough ratification of the Rome Statute, States bind themselves to enforce the international rule of law within their own borders and agree that, if they fail, the ICC may intervene. This simple commitment represents a huge innovation. Like Odysseus, who bound himself to the mast in anticipation of hearing the Sirens, States that join the ICC have foreseen the possibility of their own frailty and have committed themselves to the fail-safe remedy. Member States pledge to support the permanent international criminal court in its work by means of an international cooperation network. The States also express, through the 128 articles of the Rome Statute, consensus upon the specific procedures, standards, and cooperation mechanisms by which perpetrators of genocide, crimes against humanity, and war crimes should be brought to justice under universal standards of fairness. The Rome Statute, in short, creates both a court and an international criminal justice system.[79]

As numerous commentators have argued, the tension within liberalism between universality on the one hand and toleration and pluralism on the other has often proven problematic, as witnessed in current debates over the limits of toleration when confronted with the perceived threat to liberal democracy from radical Islam and other perspectives that explicitly reject liberal precepts.[80] As we will see in later chapters, the ICC has struggled to maintain a consistent expression of complementarity – which may, in some instances, require

---

[77] R. Teitel, 'Global Transitional Justice', Project on Human Rights, Global Justice & Democracy, Working Paper No. 8, Spring 2010, p. 11.

[78] Chung, 'Punishment and Prevention', p. 227.   [79] Ibid., p. 229.

[80] See, for example, G. Crowder, 'Pluralism and Liberalism', *Political Studies*, 42, 1994, pp. 293–305; A. Phillips, 'Equality, Pluralism, Universality: Current Concerns in Normative Theory', *British Journal of Politics and International Relations*, 2, 2, 2000, pp. 237–55; and C. Joppke, 'The Retreat Is Real – But What Is the Alternative? Multiculturalism, Muscular Liberalism and Islam', *Constellations*, 21, 2, June 2014, pp. 286–95.

ceding control to domestic actors and processes – when confronted with practices that it finds objectionable. This includes claims to eschew international criminal justice for the sake of other ends such as peace or reconciliation, very different conceptions of justice in particular African contexts or domestic actors' claims of jurisdiction over the same cases being pursued by the ICC. In such instances, the ICC has tended to invoke its superiority and the need for universal application of the particular brand of legalist, procedural justice embodied in the Rome Statute, regardless of the political, social or cultural consequences or the preferences of local parties. As the conclusion to this book will argue, that the ICC speaks the language of complementarity while practising distance reflects a deep tension within liberalism, to which the ICC is yet to discover a coherent response. The ICC's insistence on distance meanwhile causes immense problems for itself and the African societies in which it operates, as the following empirical chapters will show.

3 | *Who Pulls the Strings?*
The ICC's Relations with States

Introduction

The following five chapters focus on the ICC's intersections with the Ugandan and Congolese governments, local populations and a series of domestic processes designed to address the legacies of mass conflict. This present chapter – on dynamics between the ICC and states – situates the Court in the realm of African politics and highlights theoretical tensions concerning the Court's distrust of, and reliance on, domestic governments.

When the literature has dealt with the ICC in the context of African politics, it has tended to do so through the lens of neo-colonialism, the ICC's perceived bias in targeting exclusively African conflict situations and suspects (until the 2016 opening of investigations into crimes committed during the Russia–Georgia conflict in 2008), and the ICC's often combative relationship with the AU.[1] These themes first proliferated after the ICC issued an arrest warrant for Sudanese President Omar al-Bashir in July 2008, following the referral of the Darfur situation by the UN Security Council. Critics of the ICC, including the AU, viewed this as a violation of the principles of national sovereignty and sovereign immunity. By this reckoning, as an attempt at regime change via international law, the charging of Bashir was rendered even more egregious by the fact that Sudan was not a signatory to the Rome Statute and therefore had not formally recognised the legitimacy of the Court. Some commentators have argued that the ICC

---

[1] See, for example, M. Mamdani, 'Darfur, ICC and the New Humanitarian Order: How the ICC's "Responsibility to Protect" Is Being Turned into an Assertion of Neocolonial Domination', *Pambazuka News*, 396, 17 September 2008, www.pambazuka.org/governance/darfur-icc-and-new-humanitarian-order; and P. Labuda, 'The International Criminal Court and Perceptions of Sovereignty, Colonialism and Pan-African Solidarity', *African Yearbook of International Law Online/Annuaire Africain de Droit International Online*, 20, 1, 2014, pp. 289–321.

has become a weapon for powerful states to wield against weaker ones, having twice acted on referrals by the UN Security Council, three of whose permanent members (the US, China and Russia) are not signatories to the Rome Statute.[2] Some donor states have raised similar concerns directly with the ICC Prosecutor[3], who in various speeches and articles has provided lengthy rebuttals.[4]

This chapter argues that the critiques of the ICC on the grounds of neo-colonialism, which characterise African states as weak in the face of the overwhelming power of the Court, are simplistic. Such views overstate the power of the ICC while underestimating that of African states and their ability to manipulate the Court to their own ends. This chapter argues instead that African governments have used the ICC in highly destructive ways, manifesting Bayart's concept of 'extraversion' or states' ability to 'mobiliz[e] resources derived from their (possibly unequal) relationship with the external environment'[5], actively participating in the processes that continue to render them subordinate and dependent in the global system. As a result, Bayart argues, 'occasionally the puppets pull the strings'.[6]

This chapter argues that the ICC has failed to mitigate states' ability to pull the strings of international justice, especially in protecting themselves from prosecution for serious crimes and portraying themselves globally as law-abiding while continuing to commit violations against their own citizens.[7] The ICC has further empowered the Ugandan and Congolese governments in this regard by actively pursuing state referrals and thus affording states substantial influence over the Court's investigations and prosecutions. This highlights the Court's political naiveté, complacency and lack of expertise on Africa – products of its attempts to distance itself from the domestic terrain – and its desire to

---

[2] See, for example, Mamdani, 'Darfur, ICC and New Humanitarian Order'.

[3] This issue is discussed at length in Foreign and Commonwealth Office, 'Strategy Paper on the International Criminal Court', July 2013, pp. 2–3.

[4] F. Bensouda, 'International Justice and Diplomacy', *New York Times*, 19 March 2013, www.nytimes.com/2013/03/20/opinion/global/the-role-of-the-icc-in-international-justice-and-diplomacy.html?_r=0.

[5] J. F. Bayart, *The State in Africa: The Politics of the Belly* (2nd edition), Polity, 2009, pp. 21–2.

[6] Ibid., p. 26.

[7] For an excellent analysis of the ability of domestic governments in the former Yugoslavia and Rwanda to manipulate international justice for their own gain, see V. Peskin, *International Justice in Rwanda and the Balkans: Virtual Trials and the Struggle for State Cooperation*, Cambridge University Press, 2008.

achieve rapid judicial results, which have led to it being wilfully used by states in exchange for their (often fluctuating) cooperation. While Kersten argues that 'the ICC may view being used by states as beneficial to its mandate and institutional interests'[8] – with little evidence to show that the ICC in fact holds this perspective – he ignores the extent to which states' manipulation of the ICC has been highly detrimental, both to the Court and to the societies concerned.

This chapter comprises four sections. The first outlines the process of state referrals in Uganda and the DRC and the extent to which the OTP 'chased' the cases in these countries. The second section also focuses on process, namely the nature of cooperation between the OTP and the Ugandan and Congolese governments during investigations. The third section examines the impact of these processes on the Court, in terms of its politicisation and instrumentalisation by the Ugandan and Congolese states. Finally, the fourth section analyses the effects on those governments' behaviour toward their citizens and military and political opponents during armed conflict and national elections.

Chasing Cases: The Politics of State Referrals in Uganda and the DRC

When confronted with the critique regarding neo-colonialism, senior ICC officials typically respond in one of three ways. First, they point to the 'global consensus' achieved through the ratification of the Rome Statute and the number of African states that have joined the Court.[9]

---

[8] Kersten, *Justice in Conflict*, p. 167.
[9] International Criminal Court, 'States Parties to the Rome Statute', https://asp.icc-cpi.int/en_menus/asp/states%20parties/pages/the%20states%20parties%20to%20the%20rome%20statute.aspx. For discussion of the wide range of motivations behind ratification of the Rome Statute – critiquing the argument that ratification inherently shows a credible commitment to the norms and principles of the ICC – see Terrence L. Chapman and S. Chaudoin, 'Ratification Patterns and the International Criminal Court', *International Studies Quarterly*, 57, 2, 2012, pp. 400–9. For an interesting analysis of the unexpected flood of ratifications by African states, which at the Rome conference viewed the Court as 'genuinely egalitarian' (in many cases, changing their view once the Court became operational), see W. Schabas, 'The Banality of International Justice', *Journal of International Criminal Justice*, 11, 2013, pp. 545–51; and K. Coffey, 'Why Sub-Saharan African States Supported the ICC: Equality and Exceptionalism in International Law', August 2014, draft paper used with the author's permission.

As Sanji Mmasenono Monageng, an ICC judge from Botswana (who was both a Pre-Trial and Appeals Chamber judge in cases involving suspects from the DRC), wrote in 2014,

[H]istory demonstrates the active and strong participation of African States in the drafting and adoption of the Rome Statute...African States were also among the earliest to ratify the Statute, allowing it to enter into force on 1 July 2002. Currently, of the 122 States Parties, 34 are African countries. That makes Africa the biggest regional group in the Assembly of States Parties...[10]

Second, senior ICC officials contrast African elites' criticisms of neo-colonial interference with the ICC's work on behalf of African victims, including victims of those same elites. As Bensouda told the *New York Times* in 2013, 'What offends me the most when I hear criticisms about this so-called Africa bias is how quick we are to focus on the words and propaganda of a few powerful, influential individuals, and to forget about the millions of anonymous people who suffer from their crimes.'[11]

Third, ICC officials cite the situation referrals by four out of the eight African states where cases have been opened – Uganda, the DRC, CAR and Mali[12] – as evidence of African support for the Court and the fact that the ICC has typically intervened only by invitation.[13] Until the

---

[10] S. M. Monageng, 'Africa and the International Criminal Court: Then and Now', in G. Werle et al. (eds.), *Africa and the International Criminal Court*, T. M. C. Asser Press, 2014, pp. 14–15.

[11] Quoted in R. Gladstone, 'A Life Long Passion Is Now Put into Practice in The Hague', *New York Times*, 19 January 2013, www.nytimes.com/2013/01/19/world/africa/challenging-start-for-bensouda-as-chief-prosecutor-in-the-hague.html?pagewanted=1&_r=1&ref=todays paper&.

[12] While the case of Côte d'Ivoire was not strictly a self-referral, as only States Parties to the ICC can self-refer and at the time Côte d'Ivoire was not a signatory to the Rome Statute, it echoed many of the self-referral dynamics examined in this book insofar as President Alassane Ouattara asked the Prosecutor in December 2010 to initiate a *proprio motu* investigation (A. Ouattara, 'Confirmation de la Déclaration de Reconnaissance', 14 December 2010, www.icc-cpi.int/NR/rdonlyres/498E8FEB-7A72-4005-A209-C14BA374804F/0/ReconCPI.pdf).

[13] See, for example, P. Smith, 'Interview: Luis Moreno Ocampo, ICC Prosecutor', *The Africa Report*, 21 September 2009, www.theafricareport.com/News-Analysis/interview-luis-moreno-ocampo-icc-prosecutor.html.

independent request to open investigations in Kenya in 2009[14], the Prosecutor was reluctant to initiate proceedings *proprio motu* for fear of igniting similar debates about the dangers of an untrammelled prosecutor and threats to national sovereignty that dominated the early negotiations over the Rome Statute.[15]

This section focuses on the first and third responses by exploring the nature of state cooperation with the ICC and the process and politics of state referrals in Uganda and the DRC.[16] It argues that, rather than these states referring their situations voluntarily to the ICC, as Court officials consistently claim, the OTP initiated negotiations with the Ugandan and Congolese governments before the referrals took place. Having chased these state referrals, the ICC was forced to negotiate the terms of its investigations with those governments. This is a key reason that to date the ICC has not charged any Ugandan or Congolese government officials, despite the well-documented complicity of state actors in atrocities.[17]

---

[14] International Criminal Court, Pre-Trial Chamber II, 'Situation in the Republic of Kenya: Request for Authorisation of an Investigation Pursuant to Article 15', 26 November 2009.

[15] Author's interview, Luis Moreno Ocampo, ICC Prosecutor, The Hague, 22 March 2006. A much more dismissive response to the charge of neo-colonialism was expressed by the British ICC judge, Howard Morrison, at a 2016 conference in Amsterdam attended by the author: 'People are always accusing the ICC of being a neocolonial institution, as though Africa was the only part of the world that was colonised. What people forget is that Britain is also a post-colonial society. We had the Norse and Viking invasion in the medieval period, so this issue of colonisation isn't unique to Africa.' (Author's notes, 'Pluralist Approaches to International Criminal Justice' conference, Center for International Criminal Justice, VU University Amsterdam, 7 January 2016.)

[16] The first critique is also addressed in Chapter 5, which focuses on the ICC's intersections with national prosecutions and issues concerning the national ratification and domestication of the Rome Statute. The second critique regarding the ICC's relations with victims and other community-level actors is examined in Chapters 4 and 7.

[17] See, for example, Amnesty International, 'Uganda: Fear for Safety/Fear of Torture or Ill-Treatment/Possible Extrajudicial Execution, Twenty Prisoners in Northern Uganda', 19 September 2002, Index number: AFR 59/004/2002; Amnesty International, 'Uganda: Violence against Women in Northern Uganda', 16 July 2005, Index number: AFR 59/001/2005; Human Rights Watch, 'Soldiers Who Rape, Commanders Who Condone: Sexual Violence and Military Reform in the Democratic Republic of Congo', July 2009; Human Rights Watch, '"You Will Be Punished": Attacks on Civilians in Eastern Congo', December 2009.

Uganda State Referral

For nearly a year before President Museveni referred the situation in northern Uganda to the ICC, there were substantial negotiations between The Hague and Kampala over the nature and ramifications of a state referral. The author's research was the first to uncover the extent to which the ICC 'chased' the Uganda referral[18]; a point now widely acknowledged in the literature[19] and privately by some Court officials.[20] Interviews with Ugandan government actors conducted between 2006 and 2011 indicate that Ocampo approached Museveni in 2003 and, despite the President's initial reluctance, persuaded him to refer the northern Uganda situation to the ICC. The referral suited both parties, providing the ICC with its first ever state referral and the Ugandan government with another political and legal tool to wield against the LRA.[21] Lucian Tibaruha, the Solicitor-General of Uganda, said in March 2006,

The ICC made the first move. Here the government was still discussing all the implications of the ICC becoming a legal force in the world. Then the [ICC] Prosecutor contacted the President's Office. The issue was then passed jointly to us [Ministry of Justice] and the MoD [Ministry of Defence] but it was MoD that took it forward. They started talking to the Court and they kept us informed. MoD is in charge of day-to-day ICC affairs...In our referral we told the ICC the LRA is out of reach by the Ugandan government. We asked the Court to go get them. It's clear we're unable to prosecute the LRA because they're currently outside the jurisdiction of Uganda.[22]

---

[18] P. Clark, 'Law, Politics and Pragmatism: The ICC and Case Selection in the Democratic Republic of Congo and Uganda', in N. Waddell and P. Clark (eds.), *Courting Conflict: Justice, Peace and the ICC in Africa*, Royal African Society, 2008, pp. 37–45.

[19] See, for example, Bosco, *Rough Justice*, pp. 96–8; Kastner, *International Criminal Justice*, p. 51; K. Clarke, A. Knottnerus and E. de Volder, 'Africa and the ICC: An Introduction', in K. Clarke, A. Knottnerus and E. de Volder (eds.), *Africa and the ICC: Perceptions of Justice*, Cambridge University Press, 2016, p. 14.

[20] Author's interviews and informal discussions, ICC officials, The Hague and Amsterdam, 5–7 May 2011 and 7–8 January 2016.

[21] Author's interviews, Ugandan government officials, Kampala, 2–4 March 2006.

[22] Author's interview, Lucian Tibaruha, Ugandan Solicitor-General, Kampala, 2 March 2006.

An official in the MoD who spoke on the guarantee of anonymity echoed these views:

The President's Office contacted us about communications received from the [ICC] Prosecutor. The Court wanted to discuss what a referral from our side would...mean for both parties...We didn't go looking for that – it came from them. In all truth, it was a blessing because we'd tried everything against the LRA – [peace] talks, military operations, amnesties. We needed a new approach and here was something new, something unexpected.[23]

According to the regional newspaper, *The East African*, Ambassador Adonia Ayembare, Uganda's Deputy Permanent Representative to the UN in New York and a friend of Ocampo's, met him in London in May 2003 during Uganda–Rwanda negotiations over the fallout from violence in Kisangani in 2000. In private, Ayembare introduced Ocampo to Museveni, and Ocampo raised the possibility of an ICC investigation into the LRA.[24] The same MoD official quoted above confirmed this account:

After the President came back from London, he said he'd met Ocampo. Ocampo proposed to him that we refer northern Uganda to the ICC. The President thought this would be a good way to get rid of Kony and the [other LRA leaders] but he wanted to know what we [in MoD] thought. We said it was the right approach but some in the government, like the Ministry of Justice, weren't so sure. They thought the ICC could be turned around and used against the UPDF [Uganda People's Defence Force, the national army]...Ultimately, the President agreed with us.[25]

Once the Ugandan government decided that a state referral to the ICC was in its interests, it hired a legal consultant, Payam Akhavan, who had advised on Uganda's International Court of Justice (ICJ) case against the DRC and was previously legal advisor to the OTP at the ICTY and ICTR, to guide its interactions with the ICC. Similar to Ayembare, Akhavan played an important go-between role, drawing on

---

[23] Author's interview, Ugandan MoD official, Kampala, 9 August 2011.

[24] A. Bisiika, 'Museveni's Bashir Arrest Dilemma', *The East African*, 27 July 2009, http://mobile.theeastafrican.co.ke/News/-/433842/629636/-/format/xhtml/item/ 2/-/3dorasz/-/index.html.

[25] Author's interview, Ugandan MoD official, Kampala, 9 August 2011.

his close relations with both Ocampo and senior staff in Museveni's office.[26]

The Ugandan government referred the situation in northern Uganda to the ICC in December 2003.[27] In its communication, the government underscored crimes committed by the LRA but Ocampo notified Museveni that the ICC would interpret the referral as concerning all crimes under the Rome Statute committed in northern Uganda, leaving open the possibility of investigating state crimes. In response, Tibarahu said, 'The UPDF has not involved itself in any crimes and any officer accused of such crimes would immediately be charged before the relevant court martial.'[28] Shortly after, however, the Ugandan parliament confirmed its understanding that the referral would cover all international crimes in the northern Ugandan conflict.[29] The *Daily Monitor* in Uganda reported that, one month after the referral, Ocampo wrote to Museveni via Ayembare:

In my view meaningful peace in Africa requires strong African leadership...I am confident that the successful investigation and prosecution of those bearing the greatest responsibility for the crimes committed in the North will be a critical contribution to achieving lasting peace...It will, of course, be for Uganda to decide on how to deal with any remaining issues connected to the crimes committed...However, the decision of when and where to publicise the referral is for you (President Museveni).[30]

These interactions challenge the ICC's depiction of an entirely voluntary referral by the Ugandan government, which it believes addresses the charge of neo-colonial meddling in African affairs. As we will see below, the close relationship between the ICC and the Ugandan

---

[26] Author's interviews, Ugandan Government officials, Kampala, 2–4 March 2006. See also, P. Akhavan, 'The Lord's Resistance Army Case: Uganda's Submission of the First State Referral to the International Criminal Court', *American Journal of International Law*, 99, 2, April 2005, p. 403.

[27] International Criminal Court, Office of the Prosecutor, 'Press Release: President of Uganda Refers Situation concerning the Lord's Resistance Army (LRA) to the ICC', 29 January 2004.

[28] L. Tibarahu, quoted in Uganda Human Rights Commission, 'Workshop Report: Implications of the International Criminal Court Investigations on Human Rights and the Peace Process in Uganda', 5 October 2004, p. 11.

[29] International Criminal Court, Office of the Prosecutor, 'Statement by the Chief Prosecutor, Luis Moreno-Ocampo', The Hague, 14 October 2005, p. 2.

[30] A. Izama, 'Secret Dealings that Got LRA before World Court', *Daily Monitor*, 18 May 2008, http://allafrica.com/stories/200805190624.html.

government from the Court's pursuit of the referral onwards has shaped all aspects of the ICC's intervention in Uganda.

DRC State Referral

Whereas the Uganda referral stemmed from an incidental meeting in London, the OTP was actively on the lookout for the Ituri situation in north-eastern DRC. On 16 July 2003, one month after being sworn in as Prosecutor, Ocampo announced that he had 'selected the situation in Ituri...as the most urgent situation to be followed' after his office received information showing that around 5,000 civilians had been killed in Ituri since the Rome Statute came into force in 2002.[31] When a state referral from the DRC was not forthcoming, Ocampo said that the OTP 'will use all the powers at its disposal to contribute to the prevention of future crimes and the investigation and punishment of the alleged crimes committed in Ituri'.[32] Shortly after, Ocampo issued a direct invitation to the Congolese authorities in a speech to the ASP, which increased international pressure on the Congolese government. Listing practical difficulties with initiating ICC investigations *proprio motu*, Ocampo said, 'Our role could be facilitated by a referral or active support from the DRC.'[33] That Ocampo did not initiate *proprio motu* proceedings in the DRC underscored his reluctance to use this power so early in the ICC's existence for fear of being accused of contravening national sovereignty.[34]

In February 2004, Ocampo gave a diplomatic briefing, in which he detailed the extensive discussions that had already taken place between

---

[31] International Criminal Court, 'President of the European Parliament Visits ICC', 12 November 2003.

[32] International Criminal Court, Office of the Prosecutor, 'Press Release: Communications Received by the Office of the Prosecutor of the ICC', 16 July 2003, p. 3.

[33] International Criminal Court, Office of the Prosecutor, 'Second Assembly of States Parties to the Rome Statute of the International Criminal Court, Report of the Prosecutor of the ICC', 8 September 2003, p. 4.

[34] Steven Roach argues that the fear that the Prosecutor would launch a *proprio motu* investigation, which the state would not be able to control fully, was a key catalyst for the Congolese government's self referral (S. Roach, 'Justice of the Peace? Future Challenges and Prospects for a Cosmopolitan Court', in S. Roach (ed.), *Governance, Order and the International Criminal Court: Between Realpolitik and a Cosmopolitan Court*, Oxford University Press, 2009, p. 227).

the OTP and the Congolese government and emphasised the relational conception of complementarity outlined in the previous chapter:

We have proposed a consensual division of labour with the DRC. We would contribute by prosecuting the leaders who bear the greatest responsibility for crimes committed on or after 1 July 2002. National authorities, with the assistance of the international community, could implement appropriate mechanisms to address other responsible individuals. The DRC has recently responded with a letter affirming that such a division of labour would be welcomed. I recently met in Capetown [sic] with the Minister for Human Rights of the DRC, as well as local and international NGOs. I expect to meet soon with national authorities to discuss the practical modalities of cooperation. So, good progress is being made in developing a sound and cooperative approach.[35]

Two months later on 19 April 2004, Congolese President Joseph Kabila referred the situation in the DRC to the ICC. Interviews with senior Congolese officials highlight similar divisions within the government over the possible virtues and pitfalls of an ICC referral as those witnessed in Uganda. In contrast to Uganda, however, Emmanuel Luzolo, Minister for Justice and Human Rights, said that jurists within the government were initially much more enthusiastic to engage the ICC than political leaders:

We hadn't considered engaging the ICC until the [ICC] Prosecutor raised the issue. Soon after the [September 2003] speech, some of his staff contacted my colleagues…The key now…is the politicians don't want the ICC. It doesn't matter what the jurists think. The politicians don't want it. They think the Congolese people want to see the rebel leaders flown home [to Ituri], condemned, tried and jailed.[36]

Explaining why senior political leaders such as Kabila eventually agreed to the ICC referral after discussions with OTP officials, Luzolo gave three principal reasons. First, he said, the government believed it could use the Court to bring a case of aggression against the DRC's

---

[35] International Criminal Court, Office of the Prosecutor, 'Statement by the Prosecutor, Luis Moreno Ocampo, to Diplomatic Corps, The Hague, Netherlands', 12 February 2004, p. 4.

[36] Author's interview, Emmanuel Luzolo, Congolese Minister for Justice and Human Rights, Kinshasa, 24 January 2006.

neighbours.[37] At the time of the DRC's referral, the aforementioned case involving Akhavan was underway at the ICJ, in which the DRC alleged that Uganda maintained troops on its territory illegally between 1998 and 2003. A month before the interview with Luzolo, the ICJ had ruled in the DRC's favour and ordered Uganda to pay reparations.[38] Luzolo said,

Before the [ICC] referral, we were looking for all legal avenues to deal with our neighbours. We already had the ICJ case against Uganda and the ICC offered similar opportunities. We thought, 'There's a chance of us taking Uganda to the ICC because of their aggression against us.' But Rwanda is worse. At least Uganda pays some attention to the ICJ's rulings. That's the problem with the ICC – it can investigate Uganda but not Rwanda.[39]

Such a view highlights Congolese government officials' interest in engaging with external judicial interventions to target their political opponents, including in the wider region.

Second, according to Luzolo, the announcement of Uganda's state referral in January 2004 spurred the DRC to do likewise. 'We watched the Uganda case carefully', he said. 'We could see [the Ugandan government] thought the referral suited their purposes, especially in dealing with their military opponents. We also worried that Uganda might try to use the Court against us so, if we also involved the Court, we could protect ourselves.'[40] Luzolo said that, in meetings with the OTP before the DRC referral, ICC officials cited the Ugandan example to encourage the DRC to act: '[The OTP] staff said, "You see how Uganda is inviting international law in to deal with its conflicts? Congo should do the same."'[41]

Third, Luzolo explained the DRC's self-referral in terms of crucial dynamics within the Congolese transitional government. When pushed to elaborate on his comment above that 'the politicians don't want the ICC', he said, 'It's the Vice Presidents in particular who don't want the ICC. The Vice Presidents have been pushing for us to use the [national]

---

[37] The Congolese government was mistaken in this regard. Article 5 of the Rome Statute includes the crime of aggression as one of the core crimes within the Court's remit. However, as outlined in the previous chapter, the ICC cannot currently exercise jurisdiction over this crime.

[38] International Court of Justice, 'Case concerning Armed Activities on the Territory of the Congo: *Democratic Republic of Congo v. Uganda*', Judgment of 19 December 2005.

[39] Author's interview, Luzolo, 24 January 2006.　　[40] Ibid.　　[41] Ibid.

courts in the east to tackle these [rebel] leaders.'[42] The Sun City peace agreement signed in April 2002 stipulated that, until national elections could be held, Kabila would remain President but share power with four Vice Presidents: one from the government (Abdoulaye Ndombasi from Kabila's Parti du Peuple pour la Reconstruction et la Démocratie [PPRD]); one from the unarmed political opposition (Arthur Z'ahidi Ngoma who had previously led the Rassemblement Congolais pour la Démocratie [RCD] but was an independent by the time of Sun City); and two from the main Congolese rebel groups (Azarias Ruberwa from the RCD-Goma and Jean-Pierre Bemba from the Mouvement pour la Libération du Congo [MLC]). Both the RCD-Goma and MLC continued their armed campaigns throughout the time that Ruberwa and Bemba were Vice Presidents.[43]

Reflecting these general divisions within the Congolese government, Luzolo's comments highlight splits within the executive over whether to refer the national situation to the ICC. They also suggest that Kabila (who insisted regularly and publicly on the importance of cooperating with the ICC, as discussed below) saw the referral as a way to pressure – and ultimately to sideline – Ruberwa and Bemba because of their alleged links to rebel atrocities. The OTP was aware of these dynamics within the Congolese government. Pascal Turlan, the OTP legal advisor in charge of cooperation issues in the DRC, said, 'It's true that the ICC has little knowledge about the judicial and political situation in Congo, especially the Kivus. We're still learning about the nature of reforms there, the motivations behind judicial reforms across the country and the suspicion within the government of characters like Bemba and Ruberwa.'[44]

Later interviews with other ICC officials – including within the OTP – highlight a growing realisation that the Court's lack of detailed

---

[42] Ibid.

[43] Valerie Arnould argues that the DRC's self-referral to the ICC also built on a proposed UN-run *ad hoc* tribunal – similar to the one for Rwanda – which was debated during the Sun City talks in 2002 and which the Congolese government lobbied the UN Security Council to establish in 2002 and 2003. Arnould argues, though, that dynamics within the power-sharing government that followed Sun City stifled momentum for a Congolese tribunal (V. Arnould, 'Transitional Justice in Peacebuilding: Dynamics of Contestation in the DRC', *Journal of Intervention and Statebuilding*, 10, 3, 2016, p. 327).

[44] Author's interview, Pascal Turlan, ICC, OTP Judicial Cooperation Advisor, Kinshasa, 18 January 2006.

understanding of political dynamics in both Uganda and the DRC left it open to manipulation by domestic governments. 'We always thought it suited both parties [the ICC and states] to have these referrals', said one member of the OTP.

We needed to get cases underway. States wanted to deal with crimes [committed] on their territory but it's proving more difficult than that. The governments we work with are unpredictable. They help us one day then hinder us the next. We probably didn't know enough about these countries when we went in – how politics worked, how to get governments to work with us, what their concerns were, what they were trying to achieve. How many of us had ever been to Ituri or northern Uganda before our investigations started?...There's no question it would have helped to know more before we went in. But we have to work in all these different places at once – and different places again in five, ten years time – and you can't know everything about everywhere.[45]

Analysing the Uganda and DRC State Referrals

Several elements of the state referrals by Uganda and the DRC are key to the analysis here. First, the extent to which the OTP actively pursued the referrals undermines the Court's claim that, especially in the early years of its operation, it intervened only because of the voluntary invitation by African governments. Rather than spontaneous acts, the Uganda and DRC referrals were responses to sustained lobbying by the OTP. While Ocampo's reluctance to use *proprio motu* powers to pursue the DRC situation highlights a strong institutional preference for state referrals in the ICC's early years – not wanting to appear overly interventionist and seeing such referrals as an indication of states' willingness to cooperate with the Court[46] – the Uganda and DRC situations show extensive ICC interventions behind the scenes.

Second, the Uganda and DRC experiences also challenge Ocampo's statement in his inaugural speech as Prosecutor that success for the Court would be defined as the 'absence of cases'; a view consistent with the political conception of complementarity discussed in the previous

---

[45] Author's interview, ICC, OTP official, The Hague, 7 May 2011.
[46] See, for example, International Criminal Court, Office of the Prosecutor, 'Paper on Some Policy Issues before the Office of the Prosecutor', September 2003. For further discussion of this point, see Burke-White, 'Complementarity in Practice', p. 567.

chapter, which emphasises deference to states and the ICC's self-described role as a back-stop to national processes. Within months of Ocampo's speech, the OTP was actively pursuing cases in Uganda and the DRC. This underlines a view within the Court – and particularly within the OTP – that, as a new global institution with substantial financial and diplomatic backing from States Parties, it needed to open investigations and prosecutions quickly to be seen as a legitimate actor on the world stage. As one OTP staff member said in 2006, 'What use is a court with no cases? We wanted to hit the ground running and show the world that we're a force to be reckoned with.'[47] While nothing in the Rome Statute prohibits ICC officials from actively lobbying states to refer situations to the Court, there are enormous legal and political risks in doing so, as explored below.

Third, the divisions within the Ugandan and Congolese governments over the issue of state referrals underscore a theme developed in later chapters, namely the fragmentation of many African states. The Ugandan and Congolese governments both comprise former rebel leaders as well as institutions that often lack coherence and coordination. A critical challenge for the ICC has been determining with which government officials it can legitimately engage when these states do not always function as unitary actors. The OTP's main interlocutors during discussions over state referrals were the President's Office and the MoD in Uganda and the President's Office in the DRC. That domestic Ministries of Justice and the relevant judicial branches played a largely subordinate role afforded the executive substantial influence over vital legal questions.

While the OTP showed some awareness of these issues, reflected in Turlan's comments above, its reliance on generalist, rather than country-expert, staff (a symptom of the ICC's emphasis on distance from the domestic arena), greatly undermined its ability to grapple with political complexities specific to post-liberation governments or rebel-movements-turned-governments in central Africa. While this issue has, historically, bedevilled many external interventions in Africa, the ICC lacked a coherent strategy to deal with such challenges.[48] This will prove critical as later chapters highlight divisions within the

[47] Author's interview, ICC, OTP official, The Hague, 22 March 2006.
[48] See, for example, J. F. Bayart, 'Africa in the World: A History of Extraversion', *African Affairs*, 99, 2000, pp. 217–67.

Ugandan and Congolese states over whether domestic processes, including national prosecutions, should be preferred to the ICC.

Hand in Glove? The Challenges of Cooperation

This section shifts to the ICC's investigative stage and its cooperation principally, although not exclusively, with states. This theme returns us to the core tension of an 'independent and interdependent' Court discussed in the previous chapter and the Court's desire to act autonomously of domestic actors while inevitably relying on them. As acknowledged in a 2012 speech by the late Judge Hans-Peter Kaul – a senior member of the German delegation to the Rome negotiations in 1998 and the first judge appointed to the ICC – the Court is in key respects a weak international institution.[49] A central preoccupation of many of the Rome negotiators was to avoid creating a court that would threaten national sovereignty. Kaul argued, therefore,

[a]ll States present in Rome agreed that the ICC should have no executive power on the territory of States, in particular not the power to undertake arrest actions on States' territory...The result is that the ICC...is absolutely...dependent on effective cooperation with States Parties in criminal cases, in particular when it comes to the key issue of arrest and surrender of a suspect.[50]

These structural weaknesses of the ICC, coupled with limited personnel and financial resources, mean that it depends heavily on cooperation with states where crimes are under investigation as well as international actors such as peacekeeping missions, donor agencies and NGOs to assist with security for ICC investigators, evidence gathering, the transport and protection of witnesses and the arrest and transfer of suspects. This situation, which echoes many of the constraints faced by the *ad hoc* tribunals for the former Yugoslavia and for Rwanda,[51] is likely to persist, given that the ICC's role is heavily prescribed within the Rome Statute and States Parties seem

---

[49] H.-P. Kaul, 'Ten Years of the International Criminal Court', speech at the experts' discussion, '10 Years: International Criminal Court and the Role of the United States in International Justice', Berlin, 2 October 2012, p. 5, www.icc-cpi.int/NR/rdonlyres/FB16B529-3A60-441D-8DBE-5D6A768CA6FF/284995/02102012_Berlin_DGAP_THEICCatTen_Final.pdf.
[50] Ibid., p. 7.   [51] Peskin, *International Justice in Rwanda*.

unlikely to increase substantially their financial support for the Court.[52] Furthermore, as argued below, the OTP in particular has magnified the challenges stemming from cooperation by conducting investigations and the transfer of suspects so closely with the Ugandan and Congolese governments, which has left the Court open to being wilfully used by states.

General Investigative Approaches

Before exploring cooperation issues during ICC investigations, it is important to highlight some general features of the Court's – especially the OTP's – investigative approaches that structure cooperation. Overall, there has been a significant shift in the stated Prosecutorial Strategy between the Ocampo and Bensouda eras, namely a move from 'focused' to 'open-ended, in-depth investigations'.[53] Under Ocampo, the strategy was to gather limited evidence, selecting criminal incidents and suspects early on and building a case around them, with a focus on getting through the confirmation of charges hearing and continuing to gather evidence necessary for the trial phase. Béatrice Le Fraper du Hellen, former head of the JCCD, explained Ocampo's strategy as, 'The ICC prosecutor's policy is to carry out investigations in a few months, involving as few witnesses and incidents as possible.'[54]

In contrast, Bensouda has insisted on gathering a broader range of evidence and selecting crimes and suspects only when the evidence is considered strong enough for trial.[55] One effect of Bensouda's strategy, highlighted in the case against LRA commander, Dominic Ongwen, is

---

[52] See, for example, P. Akhavan, 'The Rise, and Fall, and Rise, of International Criminal Justice', *Journal of International Criminal Justice*, 11, 3, 2013, pp. 527–36.

[53] ICC, OTP, 'Strategic Plan, June 2012–2015', 11 October 2013.

[54] Quoted in K. Glassborow, 'ICC Investigative Strategy under Fire', Institute for War and Peace Reporting, 27 October 2008, https://iwpr.net/global-voices/icc-investigative-strategy-under-fire.

[55] See comments by Michel de Smedt, ICC, OTP head of investigations, quoted in B. Evans-Pritchard and S. Jennings, 'ICC to Unveil New Investigation Strategy', Institute for War and Peace Reporting, 21 October 2013, https://iwpr.net/global-voices/icc-unveil-new-investigation-strategy. See also A. Papenfuss, '"We Should at All Costs Prevent the ICC from Being Politicized": Interview with Fatou Bensouda', *Vereinte Nationen* (German Review on the United Nations), 62, 1, 2014, pp. 16–21, www.dgvn.de/fileadmin/user_upload/DOKUMENTE/English_Documents/Interview_Fatou_Bensouda.pdf.

substantially increased charges. Whereas the initial arrest warrant against Ongwen in 2005 when Ocampo was Prosecutor listed seven charges, in September 2015 Bensouda announced a revised total of sixty-seven charges, nineteen of which relate to sexual and gender-based crimes.[56] This reflects an OTP policy document in 2014, which states that the Prosecutor will 'ensure that charges for sexual and gender-based crimes are brought wherever there is sufficient evidence to support such charges'.[57]

Three more specific features of the OTP's investigative strategy are important for the analysis below. Together, they embody the philosophical and political conceptions of distance explored in the previous chapter. First, the OTP deploys small teams of investigators who rotate between different situation countries. During the Lubanga trial, Bernard Lavigne, who oversaw the early prosecution investigations in the DRC, said that his teams never comprised more than twelve people, which he considered 'insufficient' for the task at hand.[58]

Second, the OTP has so far used only investigators who are not nationals of the situation countries in question. Despite eight of the ICC's nine situations being in Africa, only a handful of OTP investigators are even African, with most coming from western Europe, North America and Australia.[59] A 2003 OTP policy paper states that '[i]nvestigation teams will include staff members who are nationals of the countries targeted by the investigations...[which would] help the OTP have a better understanding of the society on which its work has the most direct impact, and will allow the team to interpret social behavior and cultural norms as the investigation unfolds'.[60] To date, however, the OTP has not implemented this policy in any of its cases.

Third, all OTP investigators are based in The Hague and when 'on mission' in Uganda and the DRC have spent on average only ten days in the field.[61] As Christian de Vos argues, 'The most notable aspect of

---

[56] See ICC, 'Situation in Uganda', ICC-02/04, www.icc-cpi.int/uganda.
[57] International Criminal Court, Office of the Prosecutor, 'Strategy Paper on Sexual and Gender-Based Crimes', June 2014.
[58] International Criminal Court, Trial Chamber I, 'Deposition of Witness DRC-OTP-WWWW-0582 in *The Prosecutor v. Thomas Lubanga Dyilo*', 16 November 2010, p. 16.
[59] Author's interviews, ICC, OTP officials, The Hague and Amsterdam, 7 January 2016.
[60] ICC, OTP, 'Paper on Some Policy Issues', p. 9.
[61] Author's interviews, ICC, OTP officials, The Hague, 22 March 2006.

the Prosecution's approach to evidence gathering has been its failure to locate any investigators in country on a permanent (or semi-permanent) basis. In this respect the ICC departs from the practice of predecessor tribunals like the International Criminal Tribunal for Rwanda, which had several investigators based in-country.'[62] Thijs Bouwknegt discusses this problem in the DRC context:

Only two out of the twelve investigators had a police background, including Bernard Lavigne. The team's leader testified that the others mainly included former NGO researchers, who were not up to the job. All foreigners, the [investigators] were instructed to refrain from local contact with chiefs, priests or schoolteachers. It was to protect the identities of witnesses and informants, but it barred them from gaining useful 'field knowledge'. More importantly, the team's immobility obstructed their core business: collecting information and impartially verifying prospective evidence to be used in an international court of law. Instead, the Ituri investigation was outsourced. Intelligence was borrowed from the notes of MONUC police officers and NGO researchers who had previously documented human rights violations. The very first witness was heard in The Hague 'through an NGO', a modus operandi that was soon exported to Bunia.[63]

The Trial Chamber judges in the case of alleged Ituri warlord Mathieu Ngudjolo criticised the OTP's lack of field presence in the DRC, which it argued led to various shortcomings in the Prosecution evidence. The judges noted that it would have been 'beneficial for the Prosecution to visit the localities where the Accused lived and where the preparations of the attack in Bogoro allegedly took place, prior to the substantive hearings'.[64] The judges in the Ngudjolo case had travelled to the relevant crime sites in Ituri in January 2012, the only time an ICC Chamber has done so. The judges stated that the visit afforded them 'a better understanding of the context of the events', as well as the chance to 'conduct the requisite verifications in situ of certain specific points and to evaluate the environment and geography

---

[62] C. De Vos, 'Investigating from Afar: The ICC's Evidence Problem', *Leiden Journal of International Law*, 26, 4, December 2013, p. 1016.

[63] T. Bouwknegt, 'How Did the DRC Become the ICC's Pandora's Box?', African Arguments blog, Royal African Society, 5 March 2014, http://africanarguments .org/2014/03/05/how-did-the-drc-become-the-iccs-pandoras-box-by-thijs-b-bouwknegt/.

[64] International Criminal Court, Trial Chamber II, 'Judgment Pursant to Article 74 of the Rome Statute – *The Prosecutor v. Mathieu Ngudjolo* ', 18 December 2012, para. 118.

of locations'.[65] As we will see below, the distanced form of OTP investigations described here – small teams of foreign (mostly non-African) staff, based in The Hague and spending limited time in the field – has produced severe problems, both for the Court itself and for local communities, throughout the ICC's operations in Uganda and the DRC.

State Cooperation during Investigations in Uganda

Partly because of this remote approach, the OTP has relied heavily on cooperation with states during the investigative phase. The degree of cooperation between the ICC and the Ugandan government was evident soon after the Ugandan state referral. On 29 January 2004, Ocampo and Museveni held a joint press conference at the Hotel Intercontinental in Hyde Park, London, to announce that there was a sufficient basis to begin investigations in northern Uganda. An ICC press release issued that day stated:

President Museveni met with the Prosecutor in London to establish the basis for future co-operation between Uganda and the International Criminal Court. A key issue will be locating and arresting the LRA leadership. This will require the active co-operation of states and international institutions in supporting the efforts of the Ugandan authorities.

Many of the members of the LRA are themselves victims, having been abducted and brutalised by the LRA leadership. The reintegration of these individuals into Ugandan society is key to the future stability of Northern Uganda. This will require the concerted support of the international community – Uganda and the Court cannot do this alone.

In a bid to encourage members of the LRA to return to normal life, the Ugandan authorities have enacted an amnesty law. President Museveni has indicated to the Prosecutor his intention to amend this amnesty so as to exclude the leadership of the LRA, ensuring that those bearing the greatest responsibility for the crimes against humanity committed in Northern Uganda are brought to justice.[66]

Several elements of this statement are striking, despite Matthew Brubacher from the OTP's description of the press conference as 'deliberately anodyne'.[67] First, it highlights the ICC's consciousness

---

[65] Ibid., para. 70.
[66] ICC, OTP, 'Press Release: President of Uganda Refers Situation'.
[67] Brubacher, 'The ICC Investigation of the Lord's Resistance Army', p. 268.

from the outset of the degree of cooperation required with the Ugandan government and with other 'states and international institutions'. There is also a call for international support for the reintegration of LRA combatants because 'Uganda and the Court' – framed as a single entity – 'cannot do this alone'. Finally, as a sign of Museveni's willingness to cooperate with the ICC, he stated his intention to amend the Ugandan Amnesty Act to exclude the LRA leadership; an action that could not be carried out without the ascent of the Ugandan parliament, which at that stage had not debated this matter (and would not until the Juba peace talks were well underway in 2006).

The volatile environment in which the ICC would operate in Uganda was evident soon after the London press conference. One week later, the LRA attacked an IDP camp at Abia in Lira district, killing 50 civilians, followed soon after by the murder of around 300 civilians in the Barlonyo IDP camp near Lira town. This prompted Ocampo to announce that the ICC would investigate the Barlonyo massacre.[68] On 29 July 2004, the first ICC investigators arrived in northern Uganda. Ocampo said that he expected the trial of Ugandan suspects to begin within six months, which would bring a swift end to the northern Ugandan conflict, while the 'Congo [cases] could take a little longer'.[69] This highlights the extent to which Ocampo and his staff believed that the Uganda and DRC cases would be relatively straightforward.

At the unsealing of the arrest warrants for five LRA leaders (Joseph Kony, Vincent Otti, Raska Lukwiya, Okot Odhimabo and Dominic Ongwen) in October 2005, Ocampo said that small groups of two or three ICC investigators had conducted more than fifty missions over the preceding nine months.[70] Brubacher later stated that, on the basis of these early missions, the OTP selected six criminal incidents out of 850 documented LRA attacks as the basis of the charges against the LRA commanders.[71] Two features of these investigations are important for the analysis of the ICC's cooperation with external actors. First,

---

[68] International Criminal Court, Office of the Prosecutor, 'Statement by the Prosecutor Related to Crimes Committed in Barlonyo Camp in Uganda', 23 February 2004.

[69] Quoted in P. Apps, 'ICC Hopes for Uganda Trial in 6 Months, Then Congo', Reuters, 26 January 2005, www.globalpolicy.org/component/content/article/164/28492.html.

[70] International Criminal Court, Office of the Prosecutor, 'Statement by the Chief Prosecutor on the Uganda Arrest Warrants', 14 October 2005, p. 3.

[71] Brubacher, 'The ICC Investigation of the Lord's Resistance Army', p. 270.

a key influence over the choice of atrocity sites and the specific crimes to be investigated were reports by international human organisations, principally Amnesty International (AI) and Human Rights Watch (HRW). 'NGO reports were a key source for us when we were starting investigations in both Uganda and Congo', explained a member of the OTP Investigations Division. 'Reputable international organisations had been documenting crimes for decades, so this was a critical starting point for us. We used these reports to decide which crimes and which suspects to focus on. Obviously we then had to conduct our own investigations – we couldn't just rely on those reports – but they helped frame our work.'[72]

Second, nearly all investigations were accompanied in some form by the UPDF. The same member of the investigations team explained:

We were very careful to keep the [Ugandan] army at arm's length. It would have made our work impossible if local people had linked us too closely with the army. But we often had to travel with army personnel to crime sites because of security concerns. They kept their distance but we did rely on them...The UPDF also provided useful information and intelligence. We ran our own analysis of that but much of it was extremely useful.[73]

From the outset, a major challenge for the ICC was the arrest and transfer of the LRA suspects who, by the time the ICC arrest warrants were issued, were based in the thick jungle of north-eastern DRC and highly mobile across the region. A year into the northern Ugandan investigations, Ocampo admitted that arresting Kony and the other

---

[72] Author's interview, ICC, OTP official, The Hague, 23 March 2006. Katy Glassborow critiques this investigative approach as follows: 'After this preliminary information is gathered and reviewed, investigators are told which alleged perpetrators and particular incidents – such as specific attacks on villages, mass killings or forced transfer of civilians – to focus on. However, because there is great pressure on the ICC to intervene in countries embroiled in, or emerging from, conflict, investigators say they are being sent in to investigate before an adequate analysis of this information is complete. Because they arrive in the country already focused on gathering evidence of a particular set of crimes, committed in specific locations and on specific dates, they say this means other atrocities are often overlooked. Even when investigators stumble across evidence of other crimes not on their initial list, they say they lack the time to investigate these properly, meaning that the alleged perpetrators are less likely to be charged' (Glassborow, 'ICC Investigative Strategy under Fire').
[73] Ibid.

LRA leaders represented 'the biggest challenge for the Rome Statute'.[74] In June 2006, Interpol issued wanted persons notices against the rebel leaders 'based on arrest warrants issued by the ICC'[75] in an attempt to encourage international actors to capture them. Ocampo lobbied the Ugandan government and the UN peacekeeping mission, MONUC,[76] to arrest the LRA commanders but those pleas netted little result.[77] Museveni later criticised the UN for failing to capture and arrest the commanders.[78]

The inability to arrest any of the charged LRA leaders forced the OTP to divert all of its resources away from northern Uganda to the Court's other situations in Africa. In effect, between Bensouda's inauguration as Prosecutor in June 2012 and early 2015, the OTP completely ignored the northern Ugandan cases. Given the controversies over the ICC's operations in Uganda during the Juba peace talks between 2006 and 2008 and the enormous impact these had on the entire fields of transitional justice and international criminal law (issues discussed in greater detail in Chapter 6), this represented an extraordinary shift. The OTP was forced to change direction abruptly, however, when Ongwen surrendered to US forces in CAR on 6 January 2015[79] and two weeks later was transferred to The Hague. Bensouda told the Sudanese station Radio Dabanga of the impact of this surprising development: 'We were not expecting this at all. We did not have any team ready to take [Ongwen]. I had to take resources away, including those from Darfur, and put it there to build a team, able to do the case of Ongwen.'[80]

---

[74] Quoted in J. Anderson, 'World Court Faces Biggest Challenge', Institute for War and Peace Reporting, 16 June 2006, https://iwpr.net/global-voices/world-court-faces-biggest-challenge.

[75] BBC, 'Interpol Push for Uganda Arrests', 2 June 2006, http://news.bbc.co.uk/1/hi/world/africa/5039620.stm.

[76] MONUC is the abbreviation of the Mission de l'Organisation des Nations Unies en République Démocratique du Congo, the precursor UN peacekeeping mission to MONUSCO.

[77] L. Clifford, 'Uganda: ICC Policy under Scrutiny', Institute of War and Peace Reporting, 13 April 2007, https://iwpr.net/global-voices/uganda-icc-policy-under-scrutiny.

[78] Ibid.

[79] BBC, 'LRA Rebel Dominic Ongwen Surrenders to US Forces in CAR', 7 January 2015, www.bbc.co.uk/news/world-africa-30705649.

[80] Radio Dabanga, '"Prospects of Arrests in Darfur Case Bleak": ICC Prosecutor', 31 March 2015, www.dabangasudan.org/en/all-news/article/prospect-of-arrests-in-darfur-case-bleak-icc-prosecutor.

Some details of Ongwen's capture and transfer to the ICC are still unclear but those that are known underscore the extent of the Court's reliance on cooperation with a wide array of actors, including states. Séléka rebels in CAR claimed to have captured Ongwen on the battle-field and, like the rumoured Kigali taxi driver in the Ntaganda case, demanded $5 million through the US government's War Crimes Rewards Program.[81] In US custody in Bangui, Ongwen underwent two weeks of questioning by American and Ugandan officials before the US transferred him to The Hague on 21 January 2015. As with the Ntaganda case discussed in Chapter 1, the role of the US in this instance is highly salient, given that the US is not a signatory to the ICC,[82] as is the involvement of Séléka, which 100 US special forces, supporting AU troops, had been fighting since 2011 and which in 2014 became the subject of a second wave of ICC investigations into rebel atrocities in CAR.[83] This shows the extent to which the ICC relies on cooperation with actors whose objectives diverge entirely from the Court's and may themselves be responsible for committing international crimes.

State Cooperation during Investigations in the DRC

Many of these same challenges regarding ICC cooperation in Uganda recurred in the DRC. The DRC's state referral, following the ICC's active pursuit of the situation, laid the foundation for close cooperation between the ICC and the Congolese executive. In the Bemba case, which concerns crimes committed in CAR, Congolese state cooperation was vital in the 2013 arrest and transfer of four individuals accused of witness intimidation and other attempts to undermine the Bemba trial, including Bemba's lawyer, Aimé Kilolo Musamba, and

---

[81] BBC, 'LRA's Dominic Ongwen "Capture": Séléka Rebels Want $5m Reward', 9 January 2015, www.bbc.co.uk/news/world-africa-30743647.

[82] Such are the sensitivities regarding the ICC in US politics, the State Department webpage for the War Crimes Rewards Program states that it relates only to suspects indicted by the Special Court for Sierra Leone, the ICTY and the ICTR, with no mention of the fact that it now also concerns ICC suspects (US Department of State, 'War Crimes Reward Program').

[83] International Criminal Court, 'Situation in Central African Republic II', ICC-01/14, www.icc-cpi.int/carII.

the MLC Deputy Secretary-General, Fidèle Babala Wandu.[84] Congolese government cooperation with the ICC has been even more apparent in the cases of four Ituri rebel leaders, Thomas Lubanga, Germain Katanga, Mathieu Ngudjolo and Bosco Ntaganda. At a press conference on 15 March 2012, following the ICC's first ever conviction in the Lubanga case, Ocampo announced that he would soon visit Kinshasa to meet Kabila and 'thank him for his support' during the Lubanga investigations.[85] The ICC's investigations in Ituri were greatly boosted by the government's arrest and imprisonment, with MONUC's assistance, between February and April 2005 of four Ituri rebel leaders: Lubanga, leader of the Union des Patriotes Congolais (UPC); Floribert Ndjabu, leader of the Front des Nationalistes et Intégrationnistes (FNI); Mandro Panga Kahwa, leader of the Parti pour l'Unité et la Sauvegarde de l'Intégrité du Congo (PUSIC); and Katanga, military leader of the Forces de Résistance Patriotiques en Ituri (FRPI). All four suspects were charged with involvement in the murder in February 2005 of nine Bangladeshi peacekeepers, ambushed during a MONUC patrol near the town of Kafe on Lake Albert.

Alongside the incarceration of these militia leaders, a key reason for the ICC's investigative focus on Ituri, echoing the northern Uganda situation, was the influence of international human rights groups, which had documented widespread atrocities in Ituri.[86] In the one ICC case in the DRC that concerns North and South Kivu, that of Callixte Mbarushimana, alleged rebel leader of the FDLR, however, the judges heavily criticised the OTP for its over-reliance on uncorroborated evidence, including the wholesale adoption of reports by HRW and various UN agencies.[87] Rather than gathering its own evidence and scrutinising the evidentiary basis of claims by international observers, the OTP tended to rely on single statements by alleged victims in those reports. As a result, the Pre-Trial Chamber (PTC) declined to

---

[84] International Criminal Court, 'The Prosecutor v. Jean-Pierre Bemba Gombo, Aimé Kilolo Musamba, Jean-Jacques Mangenda Kabongo, Fidèle Babala Wandu and Narcisse Arido', 29 September 2015.

[85] Quoted in M. Gouby, 'On Home Ground, Lubanga Verdict Falls Flat', Institute for War and Peace Reporting, 15 March 2012, https://iwpr.net/global-voices/home-ground-lubanga-verdict-falls-flat.

[86] Author's interviews, ICC, OTP officials, The Hague, 23 March 2006.

[87] International Criminal Court, Pre-Trial Chamber I, 'Decision on the Confirmation of Charges – The Prosecutor v. Callixte Mbarushimana ', 16 December 2011, paras. 78, 113–239.

confirm any of the thirteen charges against Mbarushimana, including eight for gender-based crimes, on the grounds that the OTP had failed to present sufficient evidence to show either that the alleged crimes had been committed or that Mbarushimana bore responsibility for them.[88]

An important difference between the Uganda and DRC situations is that, while in the former the ICC relied mainly on government troops for its security during investigations, in the latter it depended foremost on MONUC (and later MONUSCO). ICC investigators generally preferred to work with the UN rather than domestic governments, viewing the former as more impartial.[89] The absence of a UN peace-keeping mission in northern Uganda, however, rendered this approach impossible. The ICC also cooperated less with the Congolese army, the Forces Armées de la République Démocratique du Congo (FARDC), than the UPDF because the former was less in control of the relevant territory in Ituri than the latter in northern Uganda, highlighting critical differences in the nature of state authority in the two countries. The ICC did, though, often travel with the FARDC to crime sites and secured much of its evidence and information from the Congolese military.[90]

Despite seeing the UN as a more impartial partner than the Congo-lese army, the ICC's relationship with the UN in eastern Congo has often been fraught. The ICC's early investigations in Ituri were hampered by MONUC's initial reluctance to hand over evidence gathered by its own forces in cooperation with the Congolese army and police. Some MONUC officials argued that the ICC's requests distracted from their primary responsibilities, could jeopardise the security of their forces in the field and undermine attempts by the national Congolese judiciary – with which MONUC human rights and rule of law personnel worked closely – to prosecute cases of war crimes and crimes against humanity.[91] Several senior MONUC offi-cials described the unilateralism of the ICC, often assuming the role of 'top dog'[92] in this partnership. One high-level MONUC official in Bunia said,

---

[88] Ibid.
[89] Author's interviews, ICC, OTP officials, The Hague, 22–3 March 2006.
[90] Ibid.
[91] Author's interviews, MONUC officials, Bunia, 15–16 February 2006.
[92] Author's interview, MONUC official, Bunia, 15 February 2006.

[The ICC's] investigators arrived out of the blue and expected us to help them. They wanted access to sites where massacres happened. They wanted help with identifying communities that would speak to them. These are places with many vulnerable people, where we've been working for many years and where we have close working relationships...We have to keep working there long after the Court leaves, so we have to be very careful about involving ourselves too much with [ICC personnel].[93]

Difficult relations between the ICC and the UN were a key reason the Lubanga trial – the ICC's first ever trial – almost collapsed before it started. In 2008, MONUC refused to allow the OTP to make public UN-gathered evidence concerning Lubanga. The Defence argued that this compromised Lubanga's fair trial rights because potentially exculpatory evidence was not being disclosed on the basis that the UN wished to maintain the anonymity of local sources.[94] The Trial Chamber stayed the proceedings in Lubanga for almost one year until Ocampo could convince the UN to permit the public release of the relevant evidence.[95]

In 2010, the Trial Chamber imposed a second stay in the Lubanga trial after the Prosecution refused to disclose the identity of an intermediary whom the Defence accused of bribing Prosecution witnesses in the field. This led the Chamber to question the OTP's overall reliance on local intermediaries in evidence gathering and 'the system employed by the prosecution for identifying potential witnesses'.[96] In the DRC situation, the Prosecution's intermediaries have typically been

---

[93] Ibid.

[94] International Criminal Court, Trial Chamber I, '*The Prosecutor v. Thomas Lubanga Dyilo* – Decision on the Consequences of Non-Disclosure of Exculpatory Materials Covered by Article 54(3)(e) Agreements and the Application to Stay the Prosecution of the Accused, together with Certain Other Issues Raised at the Status Conference on 10 June 2008', 13 June 2008, para. 11. Tor Krever argues, 'MONUC officials had assumed that [their evidence] would merely provide the "signposts" for the Prosecutor's further investigation, and they were handed over on the expectation of confidentiality. Detailed investigation was not Ocampo's speciality, however, and his case leaned heavily on the MONUC reports' (Krever, 'Dispensing Global Justice', p. 87).

[95] ICC, Trial Chamber I, '*The Prosecutor v. Lubanga* '.

[96] International Criminal Court, Trial Chamber I, '*The Prosecutor v. Thomas Lubanga Dyilo* – Redacted Decision on the Prosecution's Urgent Request for Variation of the Time Limit to Disclose the Identity of Intermediary 143 or Alternatively to Stay Proceedings Pending Further Consultations with the VWU', 8 July 2010.

international and local human rights organisations with strong community links. Common complaints among intermediaries echoed MONUC's concerns about the Court's behaviour, particularly the tendency to demand cooperation then to leave on-the-ground actors adrift once their assistance had been extracted. As Aloycia D'Onofrio, DRC Director of the International Rescue Committee (IRC), explained,

In the middle of 2005 the ICC had a meeting with the aid agencies here. They wanted to discuss witness protection and DDR issues in particular. The meeting was hosted by UNICEF and it was basically an idiot's guide to the ICC. The Court wanted to know whether there could be information-gathering by the NGOs and they wanted our help setting up meetings with witnesses...IRC was broadly supportive but others were worried about the safety of witnesses. Since then there's been little ICC follow-up in Bunia and Goma.[97]

Joel Bisubu, Deputy Director of the Bunia-based human rights organisation, Justice Plus, described specific challenges facing local groups that acted as intermediaries for the ICC:

We've been working in communities for many years and we have close networks there...We agreed to assist the ICC Prosecutor's office because of our work with victims...But then when things went wrong with Lubanga and the other [Ituri] cases, we were blamed. In the courtroom, people kept saying, 'It was the fault of the intermediaries. Their evidence-gathering was weak. They couldn't find good witnesses. They told witnesses what to say.' Then the Prosecutor's office dropped us. We'd call them and no one returned our calls...We also had to face the victims. They heard there were problems in The Hague and they were worried Lubanga was going to be acquitted and come back for revenge. They were looking to us for answers but they should've been asking the lawyers in The Hague.[98]

According to D'Onofrio and Bisubu – and supporting Bouwknegt's analysis cited earlier – the ICC's over-reliance on intermediaries led to the out-sourcing of core investigative responsibilities such as evidence gathering and identifying, interviewing and protecting witnesses. Not only did these shortcuts cause problems for the Prosecution in the

---

[97] Author's interview, Aloycia D'Onofrio, DRC Director, IRC, Kinshasa, 30 January 2006.
[98] Author's interview, Joel Bisubu, Deputy Director, Justice Plus, Bunia, 26 August 2011.

courtroom, as highlighted in the near collapse of the Lubanga and Katanga trials and the acquittal of Ngudjolo (another trial where intermediaries played a critical role),[99] but it also jeopardised Congo-based organisations whose work will continue long after the ICC has left the DRC.[100] In the most high-profile incident, on the second day of the Lubanga trial – the first in the ICC's history – the Prosecution's star witness, a former child soldier known as 'Witness 15', stated that he had lied on the stand about his knowledge of Lubanga and had been coached on what to say by an intermediary NGO in Ituri.[101]

Finally, echoing the Ugandan case of Ongwen, the peculiar circumstances surrounding the surrender and transfer of Congolese suspect, Ntaganda, detailed in Chapter 1, highlight the ICC's constant challenges around cooperation. Most importantly, the DRC refused to hand over Ntaganda after the ICC unsealed the arrest warrant against him in April 2008. In early 2009, the DRC government integrated Ntaganda's CNDP into the national army and made him a colonel. Kabila refused to deliver Ntaganda to the ICC, arguing that his integration into the FARDC made him an agent of peace and that, as a

---

[99] International Criminal Court, Trial Chamber II, 'Judgment Pursant to Article 74 of the Statute', Situation in the Democratic Republic of Congo, *The Prosecutor v. Mathieu Ngudjolo*, 18 December 2012.

[100] See also International Refugee Rights Initative and Open Society Initiative, 'Commentary on the ICC Draft Guidlelines for Intermediaries', 18 August 2011, for a discussion of the need for greater reciprocity between the ICC and its intermediaries. In a fascinating article, Leila Ullrich argues that the ICC embodies a form of 'interactional justice' in which the 'global or local are not self-evident spaces or levels' and 'power does not only "sit" at the "top"', best exemplified by the Court's extensive use of local intermediaries in all aspects of its field engagement (L. Ullrich, 'Beyond the "Global/Local Divide": Local Intermediaries, Victims and the Justice Contestations of the International Criminal Court', *Journal of International Criminal Justice*, 14, 3, 2016, pp. 550–51). While offering an important dissection of the central role of intermediaries in the work of the ICC, this argument overstates both the importance and the justifiable use of intermediaries. The scope for intermediaries to shape fundamentally the type and modalities of justice delivered by the ICC is heavily circumscribed, given the overwhelming institutional power of the OTP and Chambers in particular. Meanwhile, as this and later chapters argue, the Court's reliance on intermediaries in Uganda, the DRC and elsewhere has often resulted in the problematic cutting of corners and out-sourcing of roles that should have been fulfilled by permanent ICC staff.

[101] See, for example, Australian Red Cross, 'The OTP vs. Thomas Lubanga Dyilo: The Challenges of Using "Intermediaries" in the International Criminal Court', Humanitarian Law Perspectives Project, July 2011.

member of the armed forces, if there were legitimate charges against him, he should be prosecuted through the Congolese military courts.[102] Ntaganda's arrival in The Hague did not result from cooperation with the DRC government but rather from his individual decision to surrender. Whereas the Ongwen transfer involved a non-signatory to the Rome Statute, the US, and a rebel group, Séléka, the Ntaganda transfer involved two non-signatories, the US again and Rwanda. As discussed in Chapter 1, four days of behind-the-scenes negotiations were required for US and Rwandan officials to question Ntaganda and for the US to decide to transfer him to the ICC (as the US embassy is sovereign territory, this was a decision solely for the US). As discussed in Chapter 1, the physical transfer of Ntaganda to The Hague was also a matter of complex cooperation, with the diplomatic wrangles over who was responsible for fuelling his plane to the Nether-lands. All of these issues regarding cooperation in the DRC highlight the complex political and conflict dynamics in which the ICC has become embroiled. Rather than hovering neutrally and objectively above the fray – as the Court's distance discourse emphasises – the ICC has become deeply embedded in the domestic arena.

Analysis of State Cooperation in Uganda and the DRC

Two key issues emerge from the ICC's cooperation with states and other actors in the situations just described. First, the Uganda and DRC examples highlight the very different types of relationships the Court has developed with a wide array of organisations. The OTP forged close working relations with the Ugandan and Congolese governments, building on dynamics surrounding the state referrals. This included travelling with the Ugandan and Congolese armed forces to investigation sites and sharing evidence. In contrast, the ICC's – especially the OTP's – other key collaborators, including the UN and international and local NGOs, viewed the Court as adopting a superior stance and advancing its objectives over theirs, even if this risked jeopardising the longer-term work of these organisations. Meanwhile, the ICC has also developed incidental – and highly ambivalent – relations with bodies such as Séléka and the Rwandan government

---

[102] J. Gettleman, 'An Interview with Joseph Kabila', *New York Times*, 3 April 2009, www.nytimes.com/2009/04/04/world/africa/04kabilatranscript.html.

and, as discussed further below, a complex and ever-evolving relationship with the US government. All of these dimensions challenge the view, which is central to the ICC's distance discourse, that the Court can and should insulate itself from domestic politics, to safeguard its objectivity and neutrality. The ICC's close relations with a wide range of political actors have rather embedded the Court deeply in national and regional dynamics.

Second, the Ugandan and Congolese examples underscore the highly conditional nature of state cooperation. The ICC enjoyed substantial cooperation when its endeavours cohered with these governments' objectives – particularly when targeting their political and military opponents – but much less when it threatened state interests. The Congolese government, for example, assisted the Court comprehensively in the cases of Lubanga, Katanga, Ngudjolo and especially Bemba, who posed the greatest threat to Kabila's government (explored further below), but refused to arrest and transfer Ntaganda who was vital to the national military integration programme. Similarly in Uganda, the government has cooperated consistently with the ICC, seeing it as a vital tool against the LRA. Museveni openly criticised the Court, however, when it prosecuted the Kenyan President Uhuru Kenyatta and Deputy President William Ruto, with whom the Ugandan government has forged close alliances, not least over attempts to thwart al-Shabaab terrorism in the two countries.[103] While the ICC relies heavily on states, their cooperation is often fickle, and in key instances the Ugandan and Congolese governments have used their substantial leverage to block the Court's operations.

This highlights a critical shortcoming of the distance perspective, namely the Court's inability to tackle the complexities of domestic politics because of its apolitical stance. The ICC's heavy reliance on state cooperation inevitably enmeshes it in fluctuating political machinations. Eschewing contextual political expertise and insisting on its status above the political arena – key components of the distance perspective – however, has left the Court unable to address the domestic political dynamics that are central to its operation and, as we will see, open to manipulation by domestic actors.

[103] Daily Nation, 'Uganda's President Museveni Calls for Africa to Review its Ties with ICC', 9 October 2014, www.nation.co.ke/news/Africa-should-review-ties-with-ICC–Museveni/-/1056/2480492/-/138otwdz/-/index.html.

Wilfully Used? Politicisation and Instrumentalisation of the ICC

Having examined two key processes of the ICC in Uganda and the DRC – situation referrals and cooperation with states during investigations – the remainder of this chapter focuses on the impact of these initiatives. This section explores their effects on the ICC in terms of its politicisation and instrumentalisation by states, while the following section analyses their impact on those states' policies and behaviour. Together, these sections argue that the overly close relationship between the ICC and states from the point of referral onwards has had negative consequences both for the Court and for the societies where it operates.

In conceptual terms, politicisation should be interpreted as the substitution of political for legal criteria in the Court's key decision-making, while instrumentalisation entails the extent to which political actors have used the Court for ends that contradict elements of the Rome Statute and the ICC's stated aims. This section argues that the politicisation of the ICC can be seen in the selection of solely non-state suspects in Uganda and the DRC, where government crimes have been widespread and widely documented. Instrumentalisation manifests in the extent to which states have insulated themselves from ICC investigation and prosecution, while using the Court as a weapon against their military and political opponents and a means to legitimise themselves internationally. Throughout the Uganda and DRC investigations, senior ICC officials expressed some awareness of the risks in their relations with domestic political actors and consciously engaged in a trade-off of some of their independence for the sake of state cooperation. Greater knowledge of the domestic terrain – which the ICC's emphasis on distance, in the name of objectivity and impartiality, does not permit – however, may have allowed the Court to secure cooperation without forfeiting such a high degree of its independence.

Politicisation and Instrumentalisation in Uganda

In the Ugandan situation, the ICC's investigations into LRA and not UPDF crimes have created a perception of the Court as one-sided and heavily politicised. A common view among community leaders and members of the political opposition in Kampala and northern Uganda is that, as one politician argued, 'the ICC has become Museveni's political tool'.[104] The OTP has so far failed to dispel this perception. Local and international human rights groups have reported regular atrocities by the UPDF in northern Uganda, including the forced displacement of around 1.8 million people into IDP camps. As mentioned earlier, the 2007 OHCHR qualitative study highlighted the widespread view among northern Ugandan victims that both the LRA and the government are responsible for the immense harm they suffered during the conflict.[105]

Meanwhile, Museveni highlighted the government's intentions by describing only LRA crimes in Uganda's referral to the ICC. As Stephen Oola from the Refugee Law Project said, 'Museveni let the cat out of the bag with that initial referral. From the government's perspective, involving the ICC was only ever about targeting the LRA.'[106] While the OTP informed the Ugandan government that it could not limit the referral to LRA atrocities in northern Uganda, the OTP has in practice investigated only those crimes. The ICC argues that the focus on LRA crimes is justified because these constitute the gravest violations perpetrated in northern Uganda. Both Ocampo and Bensouda have stated repeatedly that the ICC may yet investigate UPDF crimes.[107] It appears highly unlikely, however, that the ICC will prosecute UPDF suspects, given its reliance on the government for its continued presence in Uganda and its generally good relations with senior Ugandan officials, especially in the MoD. The extent of the negotiations between the ICC and the Ugandan government before Uganda's referral raises questions about promises the Court may have made to Museveni to ensure his cooperation, particularly guarantees against investigations into UPDF crimes. Even if there were no such explicit deal, the extent of the ICC's reliance on state cooperation has severely limited the Court's ability to investigate and prosecute government crimes. It has also embroiled the ICC in domestic political dimensions contrary to the claims of neutrality and impartiality that underpin the Court's distance discourse.

---

[104] Author's interview, Ugandan member of parliament, Kampala, 2 March 2006.
[105] OHCHR, 'Making Peace Our Own', p. 3.
[106] Author's interview, Stephen Oola, Programme Manager, Conflict, Transitional Justice and Governance, Refugee Law Project, Kampala, 6 April 2015.
[107] Author's interview, Ocampo, 22 March 2006.

Politicisation and Instrumentalisation in the DRC

In the DRC situation, the OTP's singular focus on Ituri highlights important degrees of politicisation and instrumentalisation. First, of the various conflicts in the DRC, that in Ituri is the most isolated from the political arena in Kinshasa. In particular, there is less clear evidence to connect Kabila to atrocities committed in Ituri, although it is suspected that he has previously supported rebel groups in the province, including Germain Katanga's FRPI.[108] This differs from violence in other provinces, particularly North and South Kivu and Katanga, where government forces and Mai Mai militias backed by Kabila are directly implicated in serious crimes.[109] Investigations and prosecutions in Ituri therefore display the least capacity to destabilise Kabila and his supporters. In contrast, when the OTP began its investigations in Ituri, there was a significant chance of uncovering evidence concerning Bemba's MLC, which suited Kabila's political interests within the transitional government.

The ICC also wanted to avoid implicating government officials in the lead-up to Congo's first post-independence elections in July 2006. Foreign donor pressure on the ICC to avoid causing political instability was severe, as the international community (principally the UN and the EU) poured US$500 million towards the elections, the most expensive UN-run poll ever.[110] David Bosco cites a Wikileaks cable after ICC Deputy Prosecutor Serge Brammertz's visit to the US embassy in Kinshasa in August 2004: '[Brammertz] left American officials convinced that the ICC would be targeting militia leaders who had not joined the unity government and remained outside the peace process.'[111] The cable in question states, '[Brammertz] hopes that [the] ICC's initial

---

[108] See, for example, Human Rights Watch, 'ICC/DRC: Second War Crimes Suspect to Face Justice in The Hague', 18 October 2007; and P. Kambale, 'The ICC and Lubanga: Missed Opportunities', Social Science Research Council, 16 March 2012, http://forums.ssrc.org/african-futures/2012/03/16/african-futures-icc-missed-opportunities/.

[109] See, for example, International Crisis Group, 'Katanga: The Congo's Forgotten Crisis', 9 January 2006.

[110] United Nations News Centre, 'Security Council Urges DR of Congo to Meet Next June's Election Deadline', 7 November 2005, https://reliefweb.int/report/democratic-republic-congo/security-council-urges-dr-congo-meet-next-junes-election-deadline.

[111] Bosco, *Rough Justice*, p. 101.

investigations, which will focus on abuses committed by actors outside the transition, such as the Ituri armed groups, will help bring the transitional government closer together.'[112] In January 2006, Turlan from the OTP echoed these views: 'Electoral processes are central to our thinking because elections affect everything the Court does. I'm in Kinshasa this week meeting with government officials and NGOs to discuss exactly this.'[113] Reflecting these concerns, the ICC did not issue an arrest warrant for Bemba until 2008 after he had lost the 2006 presidential election to Kabila. This shows some political awareness on the Court's part – and willingness to tailor its activities according to political realities – but without a sufficiently clear strategy to avoid the instrumentalisation discussed below.

Second, the ICC's focus on Ituri also raises crucial questions about politicisation in the OTP's regional calculations. The OTP has resisted investigating the wider dimensions of Lubanga's crimes, notably the alleged training and financing of Lubanga's UPC by the Ugandan and Rwandan governments. At the time of writing, the OTP has also avoided submitting evidence of Uganda's and Rwanda's support for Ntaganda, a former Rwandan army officer who between 2000 and 2012 was a leading figure in various Congolese armed groups, including the UPC (alongside Lubanga), the CNDP and the M23, as well as a colonel in the Congolese army. Such investigations could implicate key figures in Kampala and Kigali, including Salim Saleh, Museveni's half-brother and a former UPDF commander.

Turlan highlighted the importance of regional dimensions in the Ituri cases:

We have plenty of information about Uganda and Rwanda's role in the Lubanga case. As things move along, we'll see what we are able to do with this...We've had lots of bad reports here about the Prosecutor's press conference [with Museveni] in London. The DRC government is very worried, lots of paranoia. Everyone thinks we're favouring Uganda, which will disadvantage the DRC. They see it as talking with the enemy.[114]

---

[112] Quoted in ibid., p. 101. For an excellent analysis of the broader tensions between power-sharing and transitional justice in the DRC, see L. Davis, 'Power Shared and Justice Shelved: the Democratic Republic of Congo', *International Journal of Human Rights*, 17, 2, 2013, pp. 289–306.
[113] Author's interview, Turlan, '18 January 2006'.   [114] Ibid.

Despite the regional issues highlighted by the Lubanga case, the Prosecutor indicated that he did not wish to widen its scope.[115] Voices within the ICC criticised this. Following Lubanga's confirmation of charges hearing, the PTC's 29 January 2007 ruling stated that the Prosecutor's charges against Lubanga were insufficient as they failed to recognise the 'international' nature of the Ituri conflict, implying the role of Uganda and Rwanda. The Prosecutor appealed to the PTC, requesting that references to crimes in the 'international' conflict be removed from the charges against Lubanga, as the OTP's evidence related only to crimes committed in the 'internal' conflict.[116]

In the context of violence in Ituri, Lubanga is in key respects a middle-ranking perpetrator, with more senior regional actors responsible for the crimes committed through their direct involvement and use of proxy rebel forces. One symptom of the OTP's strategy to date – pursuing cases in inter-locking countries in the same region, with conflicts flowing across the borders of the DRC, CAR, Sudan and northern Uganda – is that it must maintain effective relations with political leaders who may be implicated in crimes elsewhere in the region. This requires a more coherent cross-border approach than the OTP has displayed to date.

Third, Kabila has effectively instrumentalised the ICC to paint his government as law-abiding despite continuing state atrocities across the DRC. In a letter to the Registry regarding the admissibility of the Katanga and Ngudjolo cases in June 2009, Kabila's office stated, 'His Excellency Mr Joseph Kabila Kabange, President of the DRC, has demonstrated to the world his determination to fight resolutely against impunity by making the DRC to date an unequalled model of cooperation with the ICC.'[117] Two months earlier, Kabila told Jeffrey Gettleman from the *New York Times*, 'There is no other country in Africa that has cooperated with the ICC like Congo. Out of the four people at the ICC, four are Congolese. That shows you how cooperative we've

---

[115] International Criminal Court, Pre-Trial Chamber I, '*The Prosecutor vs. Thomas Lubanga Dyilo* – Prosecutor's Information on Further Investigation', 28 June 2006.

[116] International Criminal Court, Pre-Trial Chamber I, '*The Prosecutor v. Thomas Lubanga Dyilo* – Decision on the Confirmation of Charges', 5 February 2007.

[117] International Criminal Court, Registry, 'Transmission par le Greffier des observations écrites des autorités congolaises telles que présentées à l'audience du 1er juin 2009', 4 June 2009.

been.'[118] While Kabila was making such claims, the Congolese armed forces were accused of committing atrocities against civilians in Bas-Congo and supporting the FDLR and various militias in attacks against civilians in North and South Kivu.[119] This underscores the capacity of states to use cooperation with the ICC as a legitimation tool – portraying themselves as dedicated to the rule of law and international accountability – while simultaneously cracking down violently against dissident voices at home.

Taken together, the Uganda and DRC cases embody Bayart's theory of extraversion and the ability of African states to use international institutions for their own political ends. Seeking state referrals and state cooperation throughout its investigations, the ICC allowed itself to be politicised and instrumentalised by the Ugandan and Congolese governments, while expressing some – though insufficient – awareness of the risks involved. This points to the distancing of the ICC from the domestic arena: failing to engage country-specific expertise on political dynamics in Uganda and the DRC and to spend sufficient time *in situ* to understand fully the local context, the Court left itself open to this government manipulation. Believing itself to be above politics – and therefore paying insufficient attention to political machinations in the two countries – the ICC has become vulnerable to the vicissitudes of state behaviour.

'Changing the Game on the Ground': The ICC's Domestic Political Impact

In a 2006 interview, Ocampo stated that the ICC was 'changing the game on the ground'[120] in Uganda and the DRC, deterring future crimes, making states more respectful of the rule of law and contributing to general peace and stability. This section analyses this statement in terms of two key political domains in Uganda and the DRC since the ICC's intervention: these states' military responses to armed opponents; and their behaviour during national elections. These issues reinforce the acute difficulty of the ICC's task, investigating and prosecuting crimes amid ongoing conflict and fraught electoral dynamics.

[118] Quoted in Gettleman, 'An Interview with Joseph Kabila'.
[119] See, for example, Human Rights Watch, 'Democratic Republic of Congo (DRC): Events of 2008', *HRW World Report*, 2009, pp. 61–6.
[120] Author's interview, Ocampo, 22 March 2006.

This section argues that the involvement of the ICC has bolstered the Ugandan and Congolese states, which have committed widespread and sustained violations against their own citizens, rigged elections, used violent force against their political opponents (including civilian pro- testers) and avoided justice for their own crimes. In short, because of the politicisation and instrumentalisation described above, the ICC has helped entrench incumbent leaders and their corrupt, undemocratic and militarised practices.

ICC Impact on State Responses to Armed Opponents in Uganda and the DRC

The ICC has contributed to the militarisation of the Ugandan and Congolese governments' responses to armed actors in the region. By making peace talks less feasible (an issue discussed in greater detail in Chapter 6) and encouraging the militarised capture and arrest of suspects, the Court has in effect legalised violent conflict and made armed behaviour by states more, rather than less, likely. Critical in this regard has been the confluence of the ICC, US military operations and campaigns by foreign NGOs, all of which have cooperated with regional governments and championed military responses.

The ICC has actively courted the US government, which it believes is vital to the provision of security to investigators and assistance with evidence gathering and the transfer of suspects. 'The US is an import- ant player for us', Ocampo said in 2006. 'Their reach and their resources can certainly help us, especially in arresting suspects at large...We are regularly in contact with US officials.'[121] In May 2009, Judge Sang-Hyun Song made his first visit to the US as ICC President. A leaked cable reported his meeting with Ambassador Rosemary DiCarlo, US Deputy Permanent Representative to the UN, and other US officials:

President Song said that he welcomes the apparently improving relationship between the ICC and the United States, noting that previously the ICC President was 'not allowed to visit' the U.S. Mission to the United Nations...President Song [said] that he has already noticed a change of attitude on the part of the United States, including a very good recent meeting with War Crimes Ambassador Clint Williamson. President Song

[121] Ibid.

concluded by saying that he hoped that the working relationship between the ICC and the United States will continue to improve.[122]

The US is unlikely to ratify the Rome Statute any time soon, more so since the election of President Donald Trump. The US, however, will probably continue various forms of unofficial cooperation with the Court when these suit its interests. During Obama's presidency, the US increasingly warmed to the ICC. Along with the US's assistance in the transfers of Ntaganda and Ongwen and the provision of rewards for information leading to the arrest of international – including ICC – suspects, the US has also attended all ASP summits as an observer since 2008 and the ICC review conference in Kampala in 2010, as well as supporting the UN Security Council referral of the Libya situation to the ICC (as it had done regarding Darfur during the Bush administration[123]). In 2010, Stephen Rapp, the US Ambassador-at-Large for War Crimes Issues, said, 'At the present...we will be considering ways in which we may be able to assist the ICC, consistent with our law, in investigations involving atrocities.'[124]

The ICC has also courted a wide range of international NGOs and civil society groups, including the US-based Invisible Children, the Enough Project and the Resolve LRA Crisis Initiative, all of which have close ties to the US State Department and have advocated a robust US military role in tackling the LRA and other armed groups in central Africa.[125] Ocampo's relationship with Invisible Children – best known for its Kony2012 internet advocacy campaign, which after its launch on 2 March 2012 was viewed more than 100 million

---

[122] Wikileaks, 'Ambassador DiCarlo Meets with International Criminal Court President Song', 19 May 2009, https://wikileaks.org/plusd/cables/09USUNNEWYORK519_a.html.

[123] While the US abstained on the vote regarding Darfur, it voted in favour of the Libya referral.

[124] Mission of the United States to Switzerland, 'Press Briefing with Stephen J. Rapp, Ambassador-at-Large for War Crimes Issues', 22 January 2010, https://webcache.googleusercontent.com/search?q=cache:3RlA8TYqWm4J:https://geneva.usmission.gov/2010/01/22/stephen-rapp/+&cd=1&hl=en&ct=clnk&gl=tr.

[125] For a systematic critique of the role of these three organisations in the context of the LRA conflict, including their close relationship with the US State Department, see K. Titeca and T. Costeur, 'An LRA for Everyone: How Different Actors Frame the Lord's Resistance Army', *African Affairs*, 114, 454, 2015, pp. 92–114.

times[126] – is illustrative in this regard. In April 2012, Ocampo was the guest of honour at an Invisible Children fundraising event in Los Angeles, designed to introduce the organisation to Hollywood directors, actors and producers. At the event, he said, 'I love Invisible Children. I love them. Their video is making a huge change in stopping Kony...Invisible Children will, I think, produce the arrest of Joseph Kony this year.'[127]

One week after the release of the Kony2012 video, the US House of Representatives supported a resolution condemning Kony and advocating an increased military response 'to assist governments in the region to bring Joseph Kony to justice and end LRA atrocities'.[128] This resolution led to a ramping up of the US's military efforts against the LRA, following the dispatch of 100 American military advisors in October 2011 to support regional governments, including those of Uganda and the DRC, in their fight against the LRA. This move was precipitated by the Lord's Resistance Army Disarmament and Northern Uganda Recovery Act signed by President Barack Obama in May 2010, legislation strongly supported by Invisible Children, as the group highlighted in the Kony2012 video.[129] In 2012, the US also funded and trained the African Union Regional Task Force against the LRA, which

---

[126] The Kony2012 campaign was widely criticised on numerous grounds, including its portrayal of miserable Africans and white saviours, its depiction of the northern Ugandan conflict solely in terms of the demonic behaviour of Kony, the suggestion that violence continued to rage in northern Uganda (when it had almost entirely abated since 2007 and spread elsewhere in the region) and its silence on atrocities committed by the Ugandan government. See, for example, various contributions to the Critical Investigations into Humanitarianism in Africa blog, www.cihablog.com/category/home/.

[127] M. Slosson, 'ICC Prosecutor Courts Hollywood with Invisible Children', Reuters, 1 April 2012, www.reuters.com/article/2012/04/01/us-kony-campaign-hollywood-idUSBRE8300JZ20120401.

[128] United States House of Representatives, 'Resolution Expressing Support for Robust Efforts by the United States to See Joseph Kony, the Leader of the Lord's Resistance Army, and his Top Commanders Brought to Justice and the Group's Atrocities Permanently Ended', 3 March 2012, pp. 5–6, http://royce.house.gov/uploadedfiles/mcgovern_royce_res_spotlights_kony_and_lra_3.13.12.pdf.

[129] Invisible Children, 'Kony2012', www.youtube.com/watch?v=Y4MnpzG5Sqc. For a wide-ranging critique of military operations against the LRA, including the historical pattern of such attempts leading to LRA revenge attacks against civilians and generally exacerbating conflict, see R. Atkinson et al., 'Do No Harm: Assessing a Military Approach to the Lord's Resistance Army', *Journal of Eastern African Studies*, 6, 2, 2012, pp. 371–82.

included Ugandan and Congolese troops. An Enough Project report in October 2013 stated, 'The efforts by US military advisors to train troops from the region show how a small US investment in a challenging environment can still pay dividends in promoting sustainable regional solutions and improving security.'[130] In August 2015, Resolve published a report entitled, 'The Kony Crossroads: President Obama's Chance to Define his Legacy on the LRA Crisis', calling for 'renewed diplomatic and military initiatives' to finally eradicate the LRA.[131]

The dispatch of the military advisors in 2011 was the latest move in long-standing military relationships between the US and the Ugandan and Congolese governments. Since the 1990s, Washington has viewed Museveni's government as a key regional ally against the Sudanese government during Khartoum's wars in southern Sudan and Darfur, the 'terrorist' threat of the LRA, and most recently al-Shabaab in Somalia.[132] In December 2008, the US military supported the failed Operation Lightning Thunder by the UPDF against the LRA in Dungu, north-eastern DRC, which led to LRA revenge massacres against the local population at Christmas in both 2008 and 2009.[133] Throughout, Washington's political, military and economic aid to Uganda has propped up Museveni's regime and strengthened the role of the armed forces in everyday politics.[134]

Since 2006, the US has also actively supported the Congolese army through the Democratic Republic of the Congo Relief, Security, and Democracy Promotion Act, which included substantial funding for

---

[130] Enough Project, 'Completing the Mission: US Special Forces Are Essential for Ending the LRA', October 2013, p. 6, www.enoughproject.org/files/
Completing-The-Mission-US-Special-Forces-Essential-to-Ending-LRA.pdf.

[131] Resolve LRA Crisis Initative, 'The Kony Crossroads: President Obama's Chance to Define his Legacy on the LRA Crisis', August 2015, p. 4, www.theresolve.org/wp-content/uploads/2015/08/The-Kony-Crossroads-August-2015.pdf.

[132] For two excellent analyses of the various effects of the joint UPDF and US policy of militarisation, see M. Schomerus, '"They Forget What They Came For": Uganda's Army in Sudan', *Journal of Eastern African Studies*, 6, 1, 2012, pp. 124–53; and Branch, *Displacing Human Rights*, pp. 80–9.

[133] Human Rights Watch, 'Trail of Death: LRA Atrocities in Northeastern Congo', March 2010, www.hrw.org/sites/default/files/reports/drc0310webwcover_0.pdf.

[134] For a systematic account of this issue, see, Branch, *Displacing Human Rights*, ch. 7.

military training and equipment as part of a wider attempt at SSR.[135] This legislation was first tabled by Obama, then a senator, in 2005 and signed into law by President George W. Bush in December 2006. In 2012, members of the 391st Commando Battalion of the FARDC, which two years earlier had undergone eight months' training by US special forces, committed mass rapes and other serious crimes in the South Kivu town of Minova.[136] FARDC contingents sent to Garamba National Park as part of the regional fight against the LRA were also accused of looting, smuggling and a range of other crimes against the civilian population.[137]

The ICC has openly supported the armed campaigns of the US, Ugandan and Congolese militaries[138] and built strong relations with US-based civil society actors that have lobbied for increased military action against rebel groups in the region, particularly the LRA. Given that the ICC relies so heavily on national armies to capture, arrest and transfer suspects to The Hague, it has cooperated closely with these governments, even when their military activities have led to substantial civilian death tolls across the region. As we will see in Chapter 6, the ICC has expressed immense scepticism toward peace negotiations involving Ugandan and Congolese suspects whom it has charged – especially when those talks involve the offer of amnesty – but has strongly supported militarised responses to these suspects and their respective rebel movements. In short, the ICC has viewed ongoing armed conflict rather than peace talks as more useful for its own purposes. In doing so, the ICC has highlighted the implausibility of its distance philosophy. While the Court's conception of political

---

[135] United States Congress, 'Democratic Republic of the Congo Relief, Security, and Democracy Promotion Act', 16 December 2005, www.govtrack.us/congress/bills/109/s2125.

[136] C. Whitlock, 'US-Trained Congolese Troops Committed Rapes and Other Atrocities, UN Says', *Washington Post*, 13 May 2013, www.washingtonpost.com/world/national-security/us-trained-congolese-troops-committed-rapes-and-other-atrocities-un-says/2013/05/13/9781dd88-bbfe-11e2-a31d-a41b2414d001_story.html.

[137] Conciliation Resources, 'A People Dispossessed: The Plight of Civilians in Areas of the Democratic Republic of Congo Affected by the Lord's Resistance Army', July 2014, www.c-r.org/downloads/People_dispossessed_report_2014.pdf.

[138] See, for example, quotes by Ocampo in M. Odokonyero, 'Ugandans Edgy over US Move against LRA', Institute for War and Peace Reporting, 22 July 2010, https://iwpr.net/global-voices/ugandans-edgy-over-us-move-against-lra.

distance expresses a deep distrust of state power and the need to insulate itself from domestic politics, the Court's quest for close cooperation with states and support for their military campaigns shows the weakness of the distance concept. The notion of distance also falters in its belief that the ICC can both supersede and improve the practice of domestic politics, given that the Court has helped entrench state actors who continue to commit widespread crimes against civilians.

ICC Impact on National Elections in Uganda and the DRC

Since the involvement of the ICC, state violations have continued in the context of national elections in Uganda and the DRC. Both countries held presidential and parliamentary elections in 2006 and 2011 while ICC investigations and prosecutions were underway. Uganda held presidential and parliamentary elections in February 2016, with delayed national elections in the DRC now slated for 2018 at the earliest.[139] An overview of the Ugandan and Congolese governments' electoral behaviour highlights three important political problems concerning the ICC.

First, while these states have launched military campaigns against their armed opponents, they have adopted increasingly violent tactics against their political adversaries and opposition supporters before and during elections.[140] While the ICC is not a direct cause of these violations, it has failed – contrary to the predictions of various actors within the Court and among its supporters[141] – to deter criminal behaviour by states. Because of the ICC's close relations with these governments, they have little to reason to fear investigation and prosecution for crimes committed during elections. This underlines the deep problems

---

[139] J. Burke, 'DRC Minister Says Country "Can't Afford" to Hold Election This Year', *Guardian*, 16 February 2017, www.theguardian.com/world/2017/feb/16/delayed-drc-elections-could-be-put-back-further-by-cash-shortage.

[140] For an excellent analysis of the increasing ethnicisation of the Ugandan military and national politics under Museveni, see S. Lindemann, 'The Ethnic Politics of Coup Avoidance: Evidence from Zambia and Uganda', *Africa Spectrum*, 2, 2011, pp. 3–41.

[141] See, for example, G. Dancy, K. Sikkink et al., 'The ICC's Deterrent Impact – What the Evidence Shows', openDemocracy, 3 February 2015, www.opendemocracy.net/openglobalrights/geoff-dancy-bridget-marchesi-florencia-montal-kathryn-sikkink/icc%E2%80%99s-deterrent-impac.

stemming from the ICC's close cooperation with states that are responsible for regular and systematic crimes against their citizens.

In Uganda, the build-up to, and results of, the presidential and parliamentary elections in February 2006 – the first multi-party vote in Uganda for twenty-six years – highlighted the deep divisions in Ugandan national life, particularly between the north and south. These elections came nearly eighteen months after the start of ICC investigations and four months after the unsealing of the arrest warrants against the LRA leaders. Human rights groups documented serious government violations against opposition candidates and supporters during the campaign and systematic electoral fraud, including the stuffing of ballot boxes and multiple registration of voters.[142] The most serious example of the government's heavy-handed tactics during the campaign involved charges brought in the civilian and military courts against Kizza Besigye, the Forum for Democratic Change (FDC) presidential candidate. Besigye went into exile in South Africa after losing the 2001 elections. Soon after his return to Uganda on 26 October 2005 – eleven days after the ICC issued arrest warrants for the LRA leaders – he was arrested and charged with rape and treason for allegedly attempting to establish a rebel force, the People's Democratic Army (PDA), in the DRC.[143]

Similarly, the lead-up to the 2011 and 2016 presidential and parliamentary elections in Uganda was marred by rampant corruption and violence, including the murder, torture and arbitrary arrest of opposition leaders and supporters and independent journalists. During an FDC rally in June 2010, a *kiboko* (stick) squad mobilised by the government attacked Besigye and other FDC leaders.[144] Three months after losing the presidential election to Museveni, Besigye was arrested in May 2011 for organising 'walk to walk' protests, which brought thousands of protesters onto the streets across the country.[145] Besigye

---

[142] See, for example, Human Rights Watch, 'Uganda: Electoral Irregularities Require Judicial Probe', 2 March 2006.

[143] Besigye's arrest followed similar government tactics in April 2005, when two FDC members of parliament, Ronald Reagan Okumu (co-chair of the FDC) and Michael Ocula, were arrested on murder charges. Okumu and Ocula were later acquitted but only after Besigye's arrest (ibid.).

[144] Human Rights Watch, 'World Report 2011: Uganda – Events of 2010', *HRW World Report*, 2011, pp. 185–94.

[145] Al Jazeera, 'Uganda Opposition Leader "Under House Arrest"', 16 May 2011, www.aljazeera.com/news/africa/2011/05/20115169413805969.html.

was again arrested in October 2015 and three times during the week of the February 2016 vote, while government-backed 'crime preventers' and local militias murdered and harassed opposition supporters at rallies throughout the election campaign.[146]

In the DRC, following the Sun City agreement in 2002, national elections were delayed five times until they were finally held in July 2006. Veteran politician Etienne Tshisekedi and his Union pour la Démocratie et le Progrès Social boycotted the elections because of delays in candidate and voter registration, which they argued were another attempt by Kabila's PPRD to cling to power. While Kabila won the presidential vote after a run-off against Bemba, the PPRD failed to win an absolute majority in the National Assembly, forcing it to form an alliance with minor parties, including the Union des Démocrates Mobutistes, led by one of Mobutu's sons, François. While the election campaign itself was relatively peaceful, due largely to MONUC's security presence across the country, violence surrounded the lengthy waits for results between the first round of voting and the run-off. On the eve of the announcement of the run-off result, Kinshasa was paralysed for three days by fighting between Kabila's and Bemba's forces, including an attack on the MLC by Kabila's republican guard outside Bemba's residence as he met with foreign ambassadors and the leadership of MONUC.[147]

The post-election period produced further violence and instability. In January 2007, the Congolese army and police mounted a violent crackdown against a religious sect, Bundu dia Kongo, which protested the appointment of a pro-Kabila governor in Bas-Congo, leading to more than 100 civilian deaths.[148] In March 2007, government troops and Bemba's armed guards, who defied a government order to disband after the elections, fought each other in the streets of Kinshasa, killing

---

[146] See, for example, M. Taylor, 'Game ON BETWeen Uganda's Former Liberation Allies', International Crisis Group, 7 October 2015, http://blog.crisisgroup.org/africa/uganda/2015/10/07/game-on-between-ugandas-former-liberation-war-allies/. Meanwhile, Valerie Freeland argues that the Ugandan government has used the ICC primarily as a means to preserve NRM patronage networks, including in the context of national elections (V. Freeland, 'Rebranding the State: Uganda's Strategic Use of the International Criminal Court', *Development and Change*, 46, 2, 2015, pp. 293–319).

[147] T. Caryannis, 'Elections in the DRC: The Bemba Surprise', United States Institute of Peace, February 2008, p. 14.

[148] Ibid., p. 13.

around 600 civilians.[149] This fighting weakened the opposition forces and led to the UN negotiating for Bemba to go into exile in Portugal three weeks later. A week after Bemba's departure, the Congolese Attorney-General, Tshimanga Mukeba, announced that Bemba's senatorial immunity had been removed. Less than a year later, on 24 May 2008 Bemba was arrested on a family visit to Brussels and transferred to the ICC on 3 July 2008 on charges relating to crimes committed in CAR.

While international donors funded the 2006 elections, the DRC alone financed the 2011 vote as well as the elections originally scheduled for 2016, with less security support by MONUSCO in the latter cases. Both the 2011 and 2016 campaigns were characterised by violent crackdowns against opposition supporters which, in 2011, continued after the announcement of Kabila's victory over Tshisekedi in the presidential vote, leading to the deaths of at least thirty opposition protesters in Kinshasa at the hands of the security forces.[150] Similar levels of state violence followed widespread protests in late 2016 against the delay to the December election and the possibility that Kabila would change the constitution to run for a third presidential term.[151] That election-related violence occurred in Uganda and the DRC throughout the period of ICC investigations shows the inability of the Court to regulate state behaviour. The Ugandan and Congolese governments had little fear of ICC prosecutions, given assurances by the ICC from the pre-referral negotiations onwards and their close cooperation with the Court.

Second, the ICC's refusal to prosecute government cases has left the incumbent Presidents, Museveni and Kabila, free to continue contesting elections despite their various human rights violations. In the case of the DRC, Kabila's political position has been bolstered further by

---

[149] Reuters, 'UN Council Deplores Congo Violence, Urges Talks', 4 April 2007, www.alertnet.org/thenews/newsdesk/N03244140.htm.

[150] See, for example, United Nations Joint Human Rights Office, 'Report of the United Nations Joint Human Rights Office on Serious Human Rights Violations Committed by Members of the Congolese Defense and Security Forces in Kinshasa in the Democratic Republic of Congo between 26 November and 25 December 2011', March 2012.

[151] J. Burke, 'Clashes in Kinshasa Leave 50 Dead, Say DRC Opposition Groups', *Guardian*, 20 September 2016, www.theguardian.com/world/2016/sep/19/democratic-republic-congo-demonstrations-banned-police-killed-joseph-kabila-etienne-tshisekedi.

the ICC's prosecution of Bemba, who was convicted of all charges in March 2016. The ICC's targeting of Bemba and not Kabila has completely altered the national political landscape. Bemba was one of the few opposition figures capable of mobilising substantial support across the DRC. While most of his support centred on his home province of Equateur, he was the leading candidate throughout western DRC, including Kinshasa, during the 2006 elections. Among many Bemba supporters, the ICC's custody of Bemba was simply an extension of his exile, which they perceived as an attempt by Kabila, with the support of the UN and other international actors, to sideline his main political rival. An MLC supporter in Kisangani said in 2008,

The ICC is part of the foreigners' game. Everyone knows the Europeans and the Americans prefer Kabila. They say they can do business with him, just as they did business with his father…Bemba threatened to spoil that so they had to eliminate him. The foreigners tried at the ballot box. They let Kabila get away with buying the vote. Then they tried to disarm [Bemba] and when that failed, they used the ICC.[152]

Third, the factors just explored have deepened national political divisions in both Uganda and the DRC. In the former, showing how isolated the north had become from the rest of the country and the depth of northern animosity toward the Ugandan government, in 2006 Museveni won less than 20 per cent of the vote in most northern constituencies, followed by a slight increase in the northern vote in 2011 and a return to almost 2006 levels by 2016.[153] In 2006, National Resistance Movement (NRM) candidates were defeated across northern Uganda, signalling a major political shift. 'The north sees itself as completely alienated', said Norbert Mao of the Democratic Party, who won 77 per cent of the 2006 vote against the NRM's incumbent Walter Ochora for the LC5 (Local Council) chairmanship of Gulu district, a post Ochora had held for a decade. Mao said,

One senior politician has even talked about a northern cessation. The vote in the north was a vote of no confidence in Museveni's policies, especially in relation to the [IDP] camps. Also, Museveni is bent on a military solution to the conflict and the people reject that…Look at the anti-Museveni vote in conflict areas. The map of the elections is a conflict map. The country is now

---

[152] Author's interview, MLC supporter, Kisangani, 14 September 2008.
[153] Electoral Commission of Uganda, www.ec.or.ug/.

deeply divided. Will Museveni interpret it correctly or dismiss it as he has in the past?[154]

A sub-chief in the Pabbo IDP camp said, 'Museveni's win in the elections was devastating. It was yet another trauma for my people. For them, it means another five years in the camps.'[155]

By focusing only on northern Uganda (and not conflicts in other parts of the country such as West Nile and Karamoja) and only on LRA crimes (and not those by the government), the ICC has reinforced a colonial era narrative, further entrenched by the government in recent decades, that northern Uganda is uncivilised and incapable of governing itself, in contrast to the civilised south.[156] As Andrew Mawson, a long-time UN observer in Uganda, stated,

The ICC thinks the LRA is the problem but the other issue is the government, which has been responsible for the [IDP] camps and the lack of protection there, as well as direct crimes by the government in the camps. The ICC seems to have no view on the government's counter-insurgency...The Acholi also say the ICC is aligned with the southerners. They say, 'We're the number one victims of this conflict. We've been made the scapegoats and the government simply doesn't care.'[157]

Similarly, in the DRC, the ICC approach to investigations and prosecutions has deepened long-standing divisions between the east and west of the country. Many Congolese from western provinces interpret the prosecution of Bemba as an attempt to block the shift of power from Kabila's support base in Katanga and the eastern provinces more broadly. A widespread view in western DRC is that, while the transitional government after the Sun City accords provided a relatively even distribution of power across the country, Kabila (and his perceived foreign backers) would always seek to grab control, especially once the Sun City power-sharing arrangement ended with the 2006 elections. As a Bemba supporter in Kinshasa said four months before the elections, 'The international community will never let a

---

[154] Author's interview, Norbert Mao, LC5 chairman of Gulu District, Gulu, 9 March 2006.
[155] Author's interview, sub-chief, Pabbo, 11 March 2006.
[156] See, for example, R. Atkinson, *The Roots of Ethnicity: The Origins of the Acholi of Uganda*, Fountain Publishers, 1999, especially ch. 1.
[157] Author's interview, Andrew Mawson, UNICEF, Kampala, 3 March 2006.

westerner dominate here. Our politics are always about the east. That's where the wealth is. That's where the conflict is.'[158]

Another common view expressed in interviews was that Bemba represented the legacy of Mobutu, as both hailed from Equateur and one of Bemba's earliest battles with President Laurent Kabila, following the toppling of Mobutu, was the systematic exclusion of political actors from Equateur. One of Bemba's three sisters is married to Nzanga Mobutu, the former dictator's son. Bemba also elevated several senior Mobutu officials to prominent positions within the MLC, including the Secretary-General of the movement, François Muamba, who had been Minister of Economy and Industry under Mobutu.[159] The ICC's targeting of Bemba therefore taps into these divisive undercurrents in Congolese politics.[160]

Through the politicisation and instrumentalisation discussed above, the ICC has solidified the position of both Museveni and Kabila and entrenched long-standing national divisions in Uganda and the DRC. Despite violent tactics against their political opponents – often conducted by the same armed forces supported by the US and the ICC as the likeliest actors to capture and arrest suspects – Museveni and Kabila have avoided prosecution and continued contesting elections. In the most extreme case, the DRC, the ICC removed Bemba, Kabila's main political rival, thus completely transforming the national political arena.

Conclusion

Museveni and Kabila have proven masterful at making themselves indispensable to international actors. Generally unquestioning international cooperation with the Ugandan and Congolese governments has allowed them to appear as agents of peace, security and justice while continuing, emboldened, to commit abuses against their citizens. Thus, they have used the ICC's version of distanced justice to distance

---

[158] Author's interview, MLC supporter, Kinshasa, 26 January 2006.
[159] Caryannis, 'Elections in the DRC', p. 4.
[160] For an interesting analysis of the ways in which the ICC's prosecution of Bemba has also collectively criminalised the Banyamulenge minority in South Kivu, see F. Ndahinda, 'The Bemba–Banyamulenge Case before the ICC: From Individual to Collective Criminal Responsibility', *International Journal of Transitional Justice*, 7, 2013, pp. 476–96.

themselves from accountability for mass crimes. The claim by the ICC and its supporters that the Court deters criminal behaviour and therefore contributes to lasting peace rings hollow when state crimes are committed under its watchful eye.

International military and judicial interventions in central Africa to date risk not only ignoring government atrocities but reinforcing them. As we will see in the following chapters, the extraversionary capacities of the Ugandan and Congolese governments to 'pull the strings' of the ICC have also undermined the Court's relations with conflict-affected populations and domestic institutions designed to address atrocities. While various African elites have accused the ICC of neo-colonialist interference in African affairs (including Museveni who sought solidarity with other AU leaders in the wake of the Kenyatta and Ruto prosecutions in Kenya),[161] the ICC's shortcoming has rather been its failure to insulate itself from political manipulation by African states. This stems from the OTP's state-cooperation-at-all-costs approach as well as the general distancing of the ICC from the domestic political sphere in Uganda and the DRC, eschewing country-specific experts and contextual knowledge in favour of generalist staff with technical, template approaches to investigations and prosecutions. As the Court has become ever more embroiled in domestic politics, it required a deeper understanding of national political dynamics. Rather than claim separateness from the political realm, it needed to become politically savvier. The ICC's inability to grapple fully with domestic political complexities has had deeply damaging effects both for the Court and for the conduct of national politics in Uganda and the DRC.

---

[161] The East African, 'Museveni to Move Motion for Africa to Withdraw from the ICC', 13 December 2014, www.theeastafrican.co.ke/news/Museveni-to-move-motion-for-Africa-to-withdraw-from-the-ICC/-/2558/2555174/-/ilne4k/-/index.html.

4 | *In Whose Name?*
The ICC's Relations with Affected Communities

Introduction

Commentators have long debated on whose behalf international justice should be enacted, including whether justice should be victim-centred, geared fundamentally toward the fair prosecution of suspects or some other audience, including 'affected populations' or the more nebulous 'international community'.[1] This chapter is not intended to resolve this broad issue but rather to explore the various intersections between the ICC and local communities. It explores local actors' perceptions of, and engagements with, the ICC, focusing on customary and civil society leaders but especially everyday citizens.

Limited research has been conducted into these issues, and the research that has occurred has tended to involve large-N quantitative studies based on perception surveys of affected populations.[2] While

---

[1] For recent debates over these issues, see A. Macdonald, 'Local Understandings and Experiences of Transitional Justice: A Review of the Evidence', Justice and Security Research Programme, London School of Economics, July 2013; and F. Megret, 'In Whose Name? The ICC and the Search for Constituency', in C. De Vos, S. Kendall and C. Stahn (eds.), *Contested Justice: The Politics and Practice of International Criminal Court Interventions*, Cambridge, 2015, pp. 23–45.

[2] See, for example, International Center for Transitional Justice and the Human Rights Center, University of California, Berkeley, 'Forgotten Voices: A Population-Based Survey of Attitudes about Peace and Justice in Northern Uganda', July 2005; International Center for Transitional Justice and the Human Rights Center, University of California, Berkeley, 'When the War Ends: A Population-Based Survey on Attitudes about Peace, Justice and Social Reconstruction in Northern Uganda', December 2007; International Center for Transitional Justice and Human Rights Center, University of California, Berkeley, 'Living with Fear: A Population-Based Survey on Attitudes about Peace, Justice, and Social Reconstruction in Eastern Democratic Republic of Congo', August 2008; P. Vinck and P. Pham, 'Searching for Lasting Peace: Population-Based Survey on Perceptions and Attitudes about Peace, Security and Justice in Eastern Democratic Republic of the Congo', Harvard Humanitarian Initiative and UNDP, 2014; C. Hemedi, 'Thomas Lubanga Dyilo's Arrest: Survey on the Ground Indicates an Overall Positive Reaction', *Insight on the International*

these analyses provide a useful overview of popular perspectives, they give limited insight into the contextual factors that underpin these perceptions, including local values, norms, beliefs, narratives and experiences, and the meanings that local actors ascribe to key survey terms such as 'justice', 'peace' and 'reconciliation'.[3] For example, these studies tend to argue that large segments of affected communities support the idea of prosecutions for high-level atrocity suspects, including through the ICC, but without interpreting the reasons and conditions underlying these views and whether they may change based on respondents' individual and collective circumstances.

The ICC itself, especially the OTP, regularly invokes the findings of these surveys to justify its operations.[4] This raises key questions about the effects of more disembodied research methodologies and statistical representations of large aggregated population samples on attempts to legitimise the modes of justice delivered by the ICC and other international judicial institutions. In effect, more 'distanced' methodologies that fail to probe the specificities and nuances of respondents' perceptions and experiences are often deployed to legitimise distanced approaches to justice.

The analysis in this chapter focuses on qualitative material drawn from the author's community-level interviews in Uganda and the DRC from 2006 to 2016. This includes 426 interviews with everyday citizens (229 in the Acholi, Lango and Teso sub-regions of northern Uganda and in Kampala and 197 in Ituri, North and South Kivu and Equateur provinces of the DRC and in Kinshasa) and 97 interviews with customary leaders and civil society actors (53 in Uganda and 44 in the DRC). These community-level interviews over a decade give critical insights into the changing views and attitudes of local actors. The chapter also draws on the OHCHR report on popular perceptions of

---

Criminal Court: Newsletter of the NGO Coalition for the ICC, 8, July 2006, p. 3. For an excellent in-depth qualitative study of popular interpretations of, and direct interactions with, international justice, see T. Kelsall, *Culture under Cross-Examination: International Justice and the Special Court for Sierra Leone*, Cambridge University Press, 2009.

[3] For a penetrating analysis of the need to understand these subjective and inter-subjective dimensions of people's experiences of conflict, see E. Porter, *Connecting Peace, Justice and Reconciliation*, Lynne Rienner, 2015, especially ch. 1 and 2.

[4] Author's interview, Ocampo, 22 March 2006. See also, International Criminal Court, The Registry, 'Outreach Report 2007', Outreach Unit, 2007, pp. 15–16.

transitional justice mechanisms in northern Uganda, discussed in Chapter 1, and other civil society reports. This chapter highlights dominant trends in this heterogeneous empirical material, with interview quotes selected to illustrate widespread perspectives. A key aspect of this analysis is attempting to understand why and on the basis of which local values and experiences community-based actors hold particular views.

This chapter is organised according to three themes: first, the particular conceptions of conflict and the necessary responses to violence that emerge from local contexts in Uganda and the DRC; second, local actors' perceptions of the ICC generally; and, finally, local perceptions of, and interactions with, specific branches and programmes of the ICC, such as the Victims and Witnesses Unit, the Outreach Unit and the TFV, all located within the Registry. The chapter argues that, both in Uganda and the DRC, the ICC has generally failed to deliver justice and associated goods in ways that resonate with local populations' experiences of conflict, conceptions of justice and expressed needs after violence. In particular, common perceptions of the causes and principal actors of conflict – in complex situations that combine elite orchestration of violence with a high degree of perpetration by everyday citizens – do not cohere with the more distant, generalised interpretations of conflict that undergird the ICC's work. This calls into question the appropriateness of fundamental aspects of the ICC's response to the types of violence witnessed in Uganda and the DRC (and elsewhere in Africa, as we will see in Chapter 8).

Local Conceptions of Conflict and Necessary Responses to Violence

Various commentators have highlighted the tendency of 'law's lens on the African continent'[5] to impose conceptions of conflict that do not comport either with local communities' expressed understandings of violence or with sociological accounts of the principal causes of conflict. Richard Wilson argues that this stems from the fact that 'the international criminal law courtroom operates within a hermetically-sealed

---

[5] R. Wilson, 'Through the Lens of International Criminal Law: Comprehending the African Context of Crimes at the International Criminal Court', *Studies in Ethnicity and Nationalism*, 11, 1, 2011, p. 107.

textual universe of tightly-controlled documentary evidence'.[6] In particular, international criminal legal interpretations of violence – drawing heavily on the understanding of Nazi crimes that informed the Nuremberg trials – tend to reflect strictly hierarchical conceptions, with linear chains of command and an emphasis on the role of a handful of powerful leaders as opposed to a more diffuse array of individuals or structural societal causes.[7]

A good example of the legal imposition of foreign understandings of conflict on complex African contexts arose in the ICC case against the Kenyan suspects, Francis Muthaura, Uhuru Kenyatta and Mohammed Ali. Judge Hans-Peter Kaul delivered a dissenting opinion against the PTC's decision to issue summonses for the three suspects. Kaul argued that it was unimaginable that a criminal gang such as Mungiki – which the Prosecution alleged the suspects had deployed to commit coordinated attacks against opposition supporters – possessed the necessary degree of 'state-like' organisation with the capacity, including the means, to target the civilian population on a large scale.[8] This was despite the substantial academic and other literature describing Mungiki's high degree of organisational sophistication and long history of collaborating with powerful government and non-government figures in committing widespread atrocities against civilians.[9]

---

[6] Ibid., p. 114.

[7] See also S. Dersso, 'The ICC's Africa Problem: A Spotlight on the Politics and Limits of International Criminal Justice', in K. Clarke, A. Knottnerus and E. de Volder (eds.), *Africa and the ICC: Perceptions of Justice*, Cambridge University Press, 2016, p. 69. Arguing similarly regarding the tendency of international humanitarian aid and peacekeeping to rely on distorted accounts of violence in the DRC, see S. Autesserre, 'Dangerous Tales: Dominant Narratives on the Congo and their Unintended Consequences', *African Affairs*, 111, 443, 2012, pp. 202–22.

[8] International Criminal Court, Pre-Trial Chamber II, 'Dissenting Opinion by Judge Hans-Peter Kaul to Pre-Trial Chamber II's "Decision on the Prosecutor's Application for Summonses to Appear for Francis Kirimi Muthaura, Uhuru Muigai Kenyatta and Mohammed Hussein Ali"', 15 March 2011, Situation in the Republic of Kenya, *The Prosecutor v. Francis Kirimi Muthaura and Uhuru Muigai Kenyatta and Mohammed Hussein Ali*, 15 March 2011.

[9] See, for example, D. Anderson, 'Vigilantes, Violence and the Politics of Public Order in Kenya', *African Affairs*, 101, 405, 2002, pp. 531–55; P. Kagwanja, 'Facing Mount Kenya or Facing Mecca? The Mungiki, Ethnic Violence and the Politics of the Moi Succession in Kenya, 1987–2002', *African Affairs*, 102, 406, 2003, pp. 25–49; J.-C. Servant, 'Briefing: Kikuyus Muscle in on Security and Politics: Kenya's Righteous Youth Militia', *Review of African Political Economy*, 34, 113, September 2007, pp. 521–6; and A. Atieno, 'Mungiki, "Neo-Mau Mau"

Similarly, in the Darfur situation, Kenneth Rodman critiques the ICC's 'fiction'[10] of President Bashir as 'the mastermind...[with]... absolute control...at the apex of...the state's hierarchical structure of authority'[11] when so much of the scholarship on structures of political authority in Sudanese politics details the collective leadership and decision-making of the ruling National Congress Party.[12] These examples underscore the immense difficulties confronting ICC personnel who must evaluate conflict-related evidence from social and political contexts that often differ substantially from their own.

This section focuses on three categories of local understandings that impinge on the ICC's interventions in Uganda and the DRC: popular conceptions of the gravity of crimes; the actors considered most responsible for atrocities; and local views on the required responses to conflict. These themes are crucial for the ICC because criminal cases

and the Prospects for Democracy in Kenya', *Review of African Political Economy*, 34, 113, September 2007, pp. 526–31.

[10] K. Rodman, 'Justice as a Dialogue between Law and Politics: Embedding the International Criminal Court within Conflict Management and Peacebuilding', *Journal of International Criminal Justice*, 12, 3, 2014, p. 448. Megret provides a similar example from the Special Court for Sierra Leone, where the dissenting opinion of one judge, George Gelaga King – himself Sierra Leonean – expressed disbelief at the majority Appeals Chamber's finding that a former traditional doctor, Allieu Kondewa, could be considered a commander of the Civil Defence Forces and guilty of commanding war crimes: 'It boggles the imagination to think that on the basis of purporting to have occult powers...Kondewa could be said to qualify as a "commander" in a superior/subordinate relationship. Without remarking on the novelty of its finding, the Appeals Chamber Majority Opinion, for the first time in the history of international criminal law has concluded that a civilian Sierra Leonean juju man or witch doctor...can be held to be a commander of subordinates in the bush and guerrilla conflict in Sierra Leone, "by virtue" of his reputed superstitious, mystical, supernatural and suchlike fictional and fantasy powers!' (Special Court for Sierra Leone, Appeals Chamber, *The Prosecutor v. Moinina Fofana and Allieu Kondewa*, Case No. SCSL-04-14-A, Judgement, Partially Dissenting Opinion of Honourable Justice George Gelaga King, 28 May 2008, para. 69, quoted in Mégret, 'Cour Pénale Internationale et Néocolonialisme', p. 8.)

[11] International Criminal Court, 'Prosecutor's Application for Warrant of Arrest under Article 58 of Omar Hassan Ahmad al Bashir', Situation in Darfur, the Sudan, 17 April 2008, p. 1.

[12] See, for example, D. Johnson, *The Root Causes of Sudan's Civil Wars*, James Currey, 2003; and J. Burr and R. Collins, *Revolutionary Sudan: Hasan al-Turabi and the Islamist State, 1989–2000*, Brill, 2003.

are only admissible to the Court if they concern sufficiently grave crimes and the suspects considered the most responsible for their commission.

In the Ugandan and Congolese contexts, many respondents link the issues of gravity and greatest responsibility, emphasising that the identity of the perpetrators – rather than the scale or psychological impact of crimes – is the primary determinant of gravity. Two identity-related aspects expressed by local actors clash with the ICC's approach in Uganda and the DRC. First, local respondents emphasise the gravity of crimes committed by government actors because these violate core expectations of how states should engage with their citizens. That the ICC has eschewed investigating and prosecuting state actors in both countries, for the reasons explored in the previous chapter, delegitimises the Court in the eyes of affected communities. In the DRC, this includes sustained criticism of the ICC's refusal to investigate regional governments such as Uganda and Rwanda as well as the Congolese state.

Second, particularly in the Uganda case, local accounts regarding gravity emphasise the proximity of perpetrators, including neighbours who have committed egregious crimes and today live side by side with victims. The key identity at work in these depictions is not necessarily that perpetrators are considered 'high-ranking' in political or military terms, which has been a key feature of ICC admissibility determinations to date, but rather that more harmonious behaviour was expected of intimate actors who knew their victims personally and whose crimes undermine the prospects for peaceful cohabitation.

As discussed in the next chapter, the ICC's four gravity criteria – the scale, nature, manner of commission and impact of crimes[13] – focus on the number of victims of particular atrocities. This quantitative emphasis overlooks crucial qualitative dimensions of these same criteria, including the identity of perpetrators and the subjective effects of crimes on victims. This jarring with local interpretations greatly undermines the ICC's legitimacy among affected populations and, by extension, its efficacy in investigating and prosecuting cases.

---

[13] International Criminal Court, Office of the Prosecutor, 'Regulations of the Office of the Prosecutor', ICC-BD/05-01-09, 23 April 2009, p. 17.

Local Conceptions of Conflict and Necessary Responses in Northern Uganda

Empirical evidence from northern Uganda highlights significant diversity of opinion regarding the nature and causes of conflict and the required remedies, including differences across the three most affected sub-regions of Acholiland, Lango and Teso. Nevertheless, some consistent issues recur, specifically the spiritual dimension of harm, the idea of many perpetrators being 'children of the community' and the profound impact of forced displacement.

Interviewees highlighted two categories of perpetrators considered to have committed particularly grave crimes, intimately known perpetrators and government actors. Regarding the former, numerous respondents across the sub-regions, but especially among Acholi, argued that crimes by intimate offenders were acutely grave because they were known to their victims, who were often their clan members and neighbours. Furthermore, the future looked bleak because victims would inevitably have to live alongside these perpetrators once they were reintegrated into the community. Many respondents also emphasised the spiritual harm wrought by individuals who had previously lived in the same compounds where they returned with the rebels to commit crimes. Margaret, a forty-six-year-old victim of LRA violence in Amuru district of Acholiland, said,

The worst crimes here were by people we knew, even some of our loved ones. How is it possible for someone to kill their own family members? That is unimaginable. Now these people are back in the community and we have to find ways to live with them after what they have done...These people bring back bad spirits, which must be cleansed. The places where they killed are also full of bad spirits.[14]

During interviews for the aforementioned radio programme the author co-produced in 2012, Concy, a young former LRA abductee from a village an hour and a half east of Gulu, described the community's hostile reception when she returned from the bush: 'When I had just returned home, things were very hard for me as every time I went walking in the community people would be pointing fingers saying, "There goes the girl who killed her own father." It got so bad that my

---

[14] Author's interview, Margaret, Amuru, 11 August 2011.

mother said I should move to town and let her stay at home in the village.'[15] Robert, the middle-ranking LRA commander who was in charge of Concy in captivity, described the rebels' deliberate tactic of forcing young abductees to perpetrate intimate violence: 'There are two reasons why the [LRA] generals take people back to their homes to kill someone close to you. One is to make you strong, make you into a fighter, and the second is to make you never think of going back home again.'[16]

Even more consistently across the three northern sub-regions, interviewees emphasised the immense gravity of atrocities committed by the Ugandan government. This includes the direct crimes of forced displacement, murder, rape and torture and indirect crimes such as the failure to protect the population from LRA attacks. Many respondents argued that such actions violated the social contract between the state and its citizens. 'We expect the government to protect us', said Michael, a forty-two-year-old man in Pabbo IDP camp in Acholiland who had lost his wife and two children to LRA violence.

Not only have they failed to protect us, they have murdered us. . .People start screaming when they know the LRA is coming but the UPDF does nothing. It does nothing to stop the rebels and it violates us. Soldiers always come into the camp at night. They rape our women and girls and abduct the men they say collaborate with the rebels.[17]

The crime of forced displacement weighs heavily on the local population because it drove entire communities from their ancestral lands, which are vital for livelihoods, collective identity and spiritual meaning.[18] Displacement also reinforces an entrenched narrative among northern Ugandans that Museveni's government has deliberately marginalised and subjugated the north, which it considers a hotbed of opposition to the NRM regime.[19]

Northern Ugandan communities also express complex views on the question of who should be considered most responsible for the crimes they have suffered. These discussions focus equally on two categories

---

[15] Quoted in Clark et al., 'Finding it within Ourselves'. Interview conducted by Nicola Palmer, Debbie Matthee and Jacob Candano, Gulu, 21 August 2012.

[16] Quoted in Clark et al., 'Finding it within Ourselves'. Interview conducted by Phil Clark, Daniel Matthee and Jacob Candano, Gulu, 21 August 2012.

[17] Author's interview, Michael, Pabbo, 11 March 2006.

[18] See OHCHR, 'Making Peace Our Own', section I.   [19] Ibid.

of actors, high-ranking LRA and government perpetrators, but also with some discussion of rank and file rebel combatants. When discussing the rebels, there is a degree of nuance that is absent when describing the role of the government. A widespread perception in Acholiland is that all of the LRA, including leaders such as Kony and Otti, are 'our children' who have been failed by the entire community.[20] Underpinning such a view is the oft-cited account that Kony took the LRA to the bush and returned to attack Acholi civilians because Acholi customary leaders refused to support him in the fight against Museveni's regime.[21] Many Acholi respondents therefore ascribe some collective Acholi responsibility for the crimes of the LRA. This view is most pronounced when discussing the role of young combatants, most of whom are abductees and therefore possess a complex victim-perpetrator identity. Among a large proportion of respondents, this view also extends to the LRA commanders, highlighting that many northern Ugandans – particularly in Acholiland – do not distinguish categorically between high- and low-level LRA combatants. 'All of the LRA are our children', said Kato, a fifty-six-year-old man in an IDP camp near Kitgum. 'If they behave badly, if they kill people, this is because of us. We didn't raise them well. They must come back so that we can educate them to behave right.' When pushed on whether this extended to the senior LRA commanders, Kato said, 'Even Kony, even Otti. Where did they come from originally? They came from here. They are our responsibility.'[22]

Meanwhile, some northern Ugandan respondents question the extent to which former abductees should be absolved of all responsibility simply because they were young or forcibly recruited into the LRA. Unsurprisingly, these views are strongest in Lango and Teso, where many victims attribute collective blame to the Acholi for spawning and failing to constrain the LRA.[23] Such views, however, also have substantial currency among Acholi respondents. 'They were young when they were taken but they still did these terrible things', said Thomas, a farmer in Amuru district. 'We should not punish them

---

[20] See OHCHR, 'Making Peace Our Own', section II.
[21] Author's interviews, local population, Acholi sub-region, 2006–15.
[22] Author's interview, Kato, Kitgum, 13 March 2006.
[23] Author's interviews, local population, Lango and Teso, 2006–15. See also OHCHR, 'Making Peace Our Own', section II.

harshly but it would be wrong not to punish them at all.'[24] Numerous Acholi interviewees argued that rank and file rebels should be held accountable because they were directly responsible for perpetrating grave crimes by wielding the machete or *panga* or throwing the grenade, rather than the faceless rebel leader who may have given the orders. That perpetrators were already known to their victims and could be individually identified as responsible for violent attacks were key factors in ascribing accountability.[25] As Judith, a forty-two-year-old woman in Pader, described an LRA attack on her village:

The man who most needs punishment is Rubangakene. He used to live over there [points to a neighbouring compound]. He came here with the rebels and hacked my aunt to death. We saw him enter the compound with the machete. We watched him pull her from her hut and kill her right in front of us...Maybe someone ordered him but he was the one who did it. No one forced him. Only he did it.[26]

Other commentators have uncovered similar perspectives in their field research, emphasising the agency and rational calculation of many abductees who committed crimes during their time in rebel ranks and the salience of this for discussions of accountability.[27]

These nuanced accounts about the relationship between the LRA leaders and the wider northern Ugandan society and their degree of responsibility are central to the case of Dominic Ongwen, whose ICC trial at the time of writing had just opened in The Hague. Ongwen was reportedly abducted as a child[28] and initiated violently into the LRA before rising to the rank of commander. Ongwen's defence team has

---

[24] Author's interview, Thomas, Amuru, 7 May 2008.

[25] For a discussion of these complex distinctions between responsibility and accountability among northern Ugandan respondents, see OHCHR, 'Making Peace Our Own', section II.

[26] Author's interview, Judith, Pader, 14 March 2006. [The name of the alleged assailant has also been changed.]

[27] See, for example, C. Blattman and J. Annan, 'On the Nature and Causes of LRA Abduction: What the Abductees Say', in T. Allen and K. Vlassenroot (eds.), *The Lord's Resistance Army: Myth and Reality*, Zed Books, 2010, p. 133; Branch, *Displacing Human Rights*, pp. 134–5; and M. Drumbl, *Reimagining Child Soldiers in International Law and Policy*, Oxford University Press, 2012.

[28] Some sources, such as JRP, claim that Ongwen was as young as ten years old when he was abducted (Justice and Reconciliation Project, 'Complicating Victims and Perpetrators in Uganda: On Dominic Ongwen', JRP Field Note 7, July 2008, p. 1, http://justiceandreconciliation.com/wp-content/uploads/2008/07/JRP_FN7_Dominic-Ongwen.pdf.

already indicated that his identity as a victim of LRA crimes will form a central plank of their case.[29] In July 2008, seven years before Ongwen's arrest and transfer to the ICC, the Gulu-based Justice and Reconciliation Project (JRP) published a report entitled, 'Complicating Victims and Perpetrators in Uganda: On Dominic Ongwen'. The report states,

> Our point is not to prove [Ongwen's] innocence or guilt, but to place his life into historical context and to complicate his status, urging current justice pursuits in Uganda to do likewise. We argue a legal approach is limited in this regard, and that the ICC may have been incorrect in identifying Ongwen as one of the 'most responsible' given his ambiguous political status. To be clear, this does not deny that Ongwen committed heinous crimes, but to complicate his status as a perpetrator, as well as a victim.[30]

Throughout popular accounts, vehement condemnation is reserved for government crimes, for the reasons discussed above as well as for the government's support for other actors who were armed and trained to counter the LRA such as the Arrow Boys militia in Teso.[31] Local and international human rights groups have reported regular atrocities committed by the UPDF in northern Uganda, while many commentators identify the government's desire for control over the population as the primary reason that so many northern Ugandans were forced to live in inhumane conditions in the IDP camps.[32] 'We have been attacked by both sides', said Vincent, a forty-six-year-old man in the Bobi IDP camp. 'The LRA and the UPDF have killed people here. The government said it would protect us but instead it herded us like cattle into these camps and left us to be slaughtered or starve.'[33] Brubacher, the OTP analyst in charge of cooperation matters in the Uganda

---

[29] See, for example, S. van den Berg, 'Defence Tactics Exposed in Ongwen Case at ICC', *International Justice Tribune*, 6 December 2016, www.justicetribune.com/blog/defence-tactics-exposed-ongwen-case-icc.

[30] JRP, 'Complicating Victims and Perpetrators', p. 2.

[31] Author's interviews, local population, Acholi, Lango and Teso sub-regions, 2006–15. See also, OHCHR, 'Making Peace Our Own', sections I and II.

[32] See, for example, Refugee Law Project, 'War as Normal: The Impact of Violence on the Lives of Displaced Communities in Pader District, Northern Uganda', Working Paper No. 5, June 2002; Human Rights Watch, 'Army and Rebels Commit Atrocities in the North: International Criminal Court Must Investigate Abuses on Both Sides', 20 September 2005; C. Dolan, *Social Torture: The Case of Northern Uganda, 1986–2006*, Berghahn Books, 2009.

[33] Author's interview, Vincent, Bobi, 13 March 2006.

situation, acknowledged that many northern Ugandans view the government – particularly the UPDF – as a principal perpetrator of violence against the civilian population. He argued, however, 'the prosecutor's office cannot open itself to being influenced by popular sentiment, as to do so would subject the ICC to subjectivity, incoherence and external pressure'.[34]

Finally, northern Ugandan communities provide complex accounts of the necessary responses to conflict, including on issues of justice. Central to these perspectives is the view that intimate violence has wrought immense and lasting harm on individuals and communities. The intimate post-conflict environment, in which victims and perpetrators are likely to live side by side, also requires particular attention. Several themes emerge consistently from field research on the necessary responses to conflict: the need for face-to-face resolution among parties to the conflict; national political reform; compensation; and truth-telling.

The intimacy of conflict and its aftermath underpins a widespread emphasis on the need for victims and perpetrators to confront one another directly, to deliver and receive apologies and to engage in a dialogue about the crimes of the past and their causes. These views are also closely linked to victims' concern that, with large numbers of former rebels returning to the community (including to live in the same communities where they committed crimes), the potential for renewed conflict is immense.[35] This necessitates direct engagement and mediation to avert new forms of violence and to achieve long-term peace and reconciliation. In recent years, since the dismantling of the IDP camps and the return home of much of the northern Ugandan population, many respondents express fears of new forms of conflict – especially

[34] Brubacher, 'The ICC Investigation of the Lord's Resistance Army', p. 269.

[35] Such views are also widespread among former combatants who express concerns about the 'home' to which they have returned, which is rarely as peaceful, stable or welcoming as many conceptions of 'reintegration' assume. See, for example, B. Mergelsberg, 'Between Two Worlds: Former LRA Soldiers in Northern Uganda', in T. Allen and K. Vlassenroot (eds.), *The Lord's Resistance Army: Myth and Reality*, Zed Books, 2010, pp. 156–75; S. Atri and S. Cusimano, 'Perceptions of Children Involved in War and Transitional Justice in Uganda', Trudeau Centre for Peace and Conflict Studies, University of Toronto, 2012; P. Clark, 'Bringing Them All Home: The Challenges of DDR and Transitional Justice in Contexts of Displacement in Rwanda and Uganda', *Journal of Refugee Studies*, 27, 2, 2014, pp. 234–59.

land disputes[36] – and the possibility of renewed LRA crimes. As long as the LRA exists, even further afield in the region, many northern Ugandans fear they could return in small numbers to commit atrocities, as they did in the past. 'We need to bring the fighters together with the victims', said Patience, a forty-eight-year-old victim of LRA attacks in Amuru district. 'They should apologise to the victims and ask their forgiveness. Only when that happens will we know that they won't go back to the bush and continue the killing.'[37]

The desire for direct engagement between victims and perpetrators, in many interviews, also extends to the senior leaders of the government or the LRA. 'Kony and Museveni should come here to Gulu. They should stand in front of all of us, apologise and ask for forgiveness', said Henry, an Acholi shop owner in Gulu.[38] Margaret, a trader in Kitgum, said, 'The LRA did so many bad things to my family. Let Kony come here and face us. Let us ask him why he did these things and let him apologise to us, so we can see if he is sincere.'[39] The widespread emphasis on responses to conflict that include face-to-face interactions with perpetrators is usually linked to notions of apology, forgiveness, the need to gauge the sincerity of perpetrators and to cleanse the locations where crimes were committed from *cen*, the malevolent spirits that haunt the perpetrators and the people and locations affected by their crimes.[40] Other commentators, based on extensive research in northern Ugandan communities, echo these findings. Lucy Hovil, for example, argues that people's experiences in IDP camps elicit a strong desire for greater trust, political accountability and sustainable peace and these objectives may be best reached through Kony and the other LRA leaders returning 'home' rather than landing in the dock.[41]

---

[36] See, for example, J. Hopwood, 'Women's Land Claims in the Acholi Region of Northern Uganda: What Can be Learnt from What Is Contested', *International Journal on Minority and Group Rights*, 22, 2015, pp. 387–409.

[37] Author's interview, Patience, Amuru, 11 August 2011.

[38] Author's interview, Henry, Gulu, 13 August 2011.

[39] Author's interview, Margaret, Kitgum, 12 August 2011.

[40] Author's interviews, local population, Acholi, Teso and Lango sub-regions, 2006–15.

[41] L. Hovil, 'A Poisoned Chalice? Local Civil Society and the International Criminal Court's Engagement in Uganda', International Refugee Rights Initative, Discussion Paper No. 1, October 2011.

A further reason that many respondents emphasise themes of engagement and proximity is that state institutions mandated to address crimes – particularly the national courts and the LCs – are considered distanced from the population, either in geographical terms or from the needs of local populations. This is critical because it highlights that a strong local critique of distance and the inaccessibility of justice predates the ICC's intervention in northern Uganda.[42] The Ugandan judiciary, especially in the north, lacks the infrastructure and personnel to meet the population's legal needs. Civilian courts in particular have always been under-resourced, and recent decades of conflict have further undermined their capacity, particularly in rural communities. In northern Uganda, for example, only three courts are capable of dealing with serious crimes – the High Court in Gulu (the only court able to handle capital offences) and the Magistrates Courts in Gulu and Kitgum. In Kitgum and Pader districts, there is almost no judicial presence; Kitgum has only two magistrates for a population of around 300,000.[43] In early 2005, after no High Court judge had sat in Gulu for nearly six months, Justice Peter Onega, head of the Amnesty Commission and a support judge for the High Court in Gulu, left his Commission duties in Kampala to preside in Gulu for one month.[44]

All court proceedings are in English, which many rural claimants in particular do not speak, and costs for interpreters are prohibitive. With limited access to the courts, the population takes the majority of their cases – even those involving serious offences – to the LCs. As Stephen, a thirty-four-year-old man in Pabbo IDP camp, said, 'There are always cases here that should go to the courts but we can't go to [the courts in] Gulu. It's expensive to travel there. And we have to wait a long time – a year sometimes, two years even – for our cases to be heard.'[45] Where

---

[42] This echoes broader analyses of the distance of domestic courts from local populations throughout the global South and problems of access to justice for the poor. For an excellent appraisal of these issues, see R. Gargarella, '"Too Far Removed from the People" Access to Justice for the Poor: The Case of Latin America', UNDP Issue Paper, Christian Michelsen Institute, 2002. Gargarella argues that in this context judicial distance represents 'insensitivity' to disadvantage and structural inequality and displays a fundamental distrust of the population, from which the courts also aim to achieve 'social distance', insulating themselves from the social and economic concerns of those they are mandated to serve.

[43] Author's interview, Justice Peter Onega, chairman, Ugandan Amnesty Commission, Kampala, 3 March 2006.

[44] Ibid.   [45] Author's interview, Stephen, Pabbo, 11 March 2006.

courts do function around the country, they often lack the necessary materials to carry out their work, while many judges and lawyers are underpaid and widely considered corrupt.

Reflecting concerns over patronage, corruption and neglect by the state, another commonly identified response to conflict was the necessity for national political change. Many respondents across the northern sub-regions argued that, while Museveni's government remains in power and northern Uganda is still regarded as inferior to the rest of the country, the scope for future conflict is substantial. Odongo, a thirty-seven-year-old man in Pabbo IDP camp, said, 'Until Museveni is gone, nothing will get better here. The government takes the money for themselves and leaves us with nothing. They have forgotten the whole of the north.'[46]

Across the author's interviews and the OHCHR study, respondents discuss two further needs after conflict: compensation and truth-telling. The OHCHR report also found that these constituted the essential elements of any transitional justice process designed to deal with crimes committed by the Ugandan government and the LRA. Many victims argue that they are willing to accept former combatants back into the community, provided they receive restitution from the perpetrators' clans. Vincent, a thirty-four-year-old man in Gulu town, whose younger brother was abducted by the LRA and whose sister was killed by the UPDF during an attack on the LRA near the Sudanese border, said,

These people who have murdered many others come back now and the government gives them money and other things to help them live. Some of them have big houses now. They live well. I went to the big [Ker Kwaro Acholi cleansing] ceremony, where [former LRA commanders] Banya and Kolo apologised, and it made me angry. They said they were sorry and people cheered. I tell you, I wasn't cheering...Who gives money to those who have suffered? If somebody gave us money to help us live, maybe then I would cheer.[47]

The Acholi paramount chief, Rwot David Acana, said,

Some people think there is no punishment in the Acholi rituals. But in our practices, punishment means compensation...Normally, compensation is

---

[46] Author's interview, Odongo, Pabbo, 11 March 2006.
[47] Author's interview, Vincent, Gulu, 10 March 2006.

paid by the offender's clan to the victim's clan. We stress collective redress because individuals do not have the means to pay reparation. It is not just individuals who feel the damage done and it is the clan's responsibility to ensure its members do not harm others...The people believe that you can't let perpetrators get away with their crimes. Once someone has committed a crime in the community, the person has to tell why they did it and they have to be ready to go through the necessary rituals and face the consequences.[48]

As we will see in Chapter 7, a key reason that local rituals have become such a prevalent mechanism for northern Ugandan communities to address the legacies of conflict is that they combine central features identified in this section, namely the key role of intimate perpetrators, the desire for face-to-face redress for crimes, apology, truth-telling and clan-based compensation. Crucially, as discussed below, many local respondents argue that the ICC fails to address all of these issues, imparting a foreign mode of justice that clashes with community perceptions.

Local Conceptions of Conflict and Necessary Responses in Eastern DRC

Important similarities and differences manifest between northern Ugandan and eastern Congolese communities' views on the three issues examined here: the perceived gravity of crimes; the actors considered most responsible for those crimes; and the necessary responses to mass violence. Among the various harms that Congolese respondents have suffered, two categories recur in their discussions of those considered most grave: large-scale massacres, especially when committed along ethnic lines; and crimes committed by the Congolese and regional governments and their proxies. Importantly for the ICC, crimes committed by child soldiers, which have featured in several ICC prosecutions in Ituri, or rebel groups perceived to originate from

---

[48] Author's interview, Rwot David Acana II, Acholi Paramount Chief, Gulu, 27 February 2007. For a further discussion of the centrality of punishment in many northern Ugandan community-based practices, see Beyond Juba Project, 'Tradition in Transition: Drawing on the Old to Develop a New Jurisprudence for Dealing with Uganda's Legacy of Violence', Working Paper No. 1, July 2009, pp. 19–23.

outside the target community rarely appear in local accounts of the gravest crimes.[49]

Congolese respondents discuss massacres as the gravest atrocities more readily than their Ugandan counterparts, perhaps because the scale and frequency of murder in eastern DRC surpass even the horrific situation in northern Uganda. While the northern Ugandan conflict is replete with cases of large-scale killings in tightknit communities, a greater proportion of the population in eastern DRC has directly experienced these crimes. Francis, a thirty-five-year-old Hema man in Bogoro in Ituri, said, 'We have suffered so many crimes here but the worst are the big killings. The FNI killed so many people here, whole families, women, children. This leaves the whole community scared. Many people have fled and will never come back.'[50] Marie, a twenty-nine-year-old victim of a rebel attack near Rutshuru in North Kivu, said, 'When the rebels come and kill 50, 60 people in one day, that's what people fear most. It happens so quickly. People run but how can they get away? The rebels surround the village so no one can escape.'[51]

Many Congolese respondents, particularly in Ituri, describe massacres committed by other ethnic groups with which they cohabit as the gravest crimes they have suffered. This concurrence of intimacy and ethnicity differs from the Ugandan case where intimacy is linked to gravity because of its rupture of long-term relations and grave consequences for future cohabitation. In the DRC, where many communities are multi-ethnic – as opposed to the largely mono-ethnic communities in Acholiland, Lango and Teso – massacres carried out by ethnic groups that have historically lived in the same communities are considered especially grave because they rupture previously harmonious relations and reflect the likely recurrence of such crimes. Francis, quoted above, continued, 'After the Lendu attacked, all of the Hema were scared. We looked at our Lendu neighbours and wondered if they

---

[49] For vehement criticisms by members of Congolese civil society of the OTP's decision to focus so heavily on child soldier crimes in all of the Ituri cases, see the DRC National Coalition for the ICC's letter to the Prosecutor cited in P. Kambale, 'A Story of Missed Opportunities: The Role of the International Criminal Court in the Democratic Republic of Congo', in C. de Vos, S. Kendall and C. Stahn (eds.), *Contested Justice: The Politics and Practice of International Criminal Court Interventions*, Cambridge University Press, 2015, pp. 181–2.

[50] Author's interview, Francis, Bogoro, 14 September 2008.

[51] Author's interview, Marie, Rutshuru, 8 February 2006.

were part of this. Did they know the attacks were coming? Why didn't they tell us?'[52]

Echoing the northern Ugandan case, eastern Congolese respondents interpret crimes committed by government actors and their perceived proxies as especially grave. The Congolese military has routinely committed atrocities against civilians, either through direct FARDC attacks or by supporting various rebel groups and militias.[53] Government crimes are considered extremely grave because they violate citizens' expectation of protection by the state. Furthermore, such crimes – as in northern Uganda – tap into a deep-seated antagonism toward a government that is widely perceived as neglecting the eastern Congolese population in its provision of services and security. 'It has always been like this', said Faustin, a sixty-eight-year-old man near Uvira in South Kivu. 'First it was the Belgians, then it was Mobutu, then Kabila *père*, then Kabila *fils*. The government is always attacking our people. No one can feel safe when their own government kills them.'[54]

Congolese respondents' views on the actors considered most responsible for atrocities also echo some of the perspectives recorded in Uganda but with important differences. Similar to the Ugandan case, many eastern Congolese emphasise the role of the government in committing atrocities. 'The government gives us nothing but problems', said Niyonkuru, a victim of Mai Mai violence in Uvira. 'We get no services here. No water, no schools. But the army attacks our people and the government supports all these militias.'[55] Reflecting such views, in her dissenting judgement in the Germain Katanga case, Judge Christine Van den Wyngaert criticised the OTP's and the other judges' framing of the Ituri conflict foremost in ethnic terms, belying the role of the Congolese government in fomenting much of the violence:

Whereas ethnicity sometimes does play an important role in the type of conflict that took place in Ituri, it is essential not to fall into the trap of oversimplification. There is a real danger in treating entire populations, or vast categories within a population, as abstract entities with a mind of their own... [I]f we are to believe the Majority, we have to accept that the Ngiti

---

[52] Author's interview, Francis, 14 September 2008.
[53] See, for example, International Crisis Group, 'Congo: Five Priorities for a Peacebuilding Strategy', Africa Report No. 150, 11 May 2009.
[54] Author's interview, Faustin, Uvira, 22 February 2006.
[55] Author's interview, Niyonkuru, Uvira, 22 February 2006.

fighters of Walendu-Bindi were so afraid of the impending rise of the 'Hema-Tutsi empire' that they developed an 'anti-Hema ideology' which was so strong that they wanted to eliminate all Hema from Bogoro...Apart from the fact that there is simply no good evidence for this proposition, it is a lot more plausible that the initiative to drive out the UPC from Ituri by military force originated from the authorities in Kinshasa and Beni, who enlisted several Ngiti commanders, including Germain Katanga and some former APC officers, for that purpose.[56]

Beyond the strong emphasis on state actors, Congolese respondents also highlighted the central role of rebel and militia leaders who orchestrated and incited widespread violence. Unlike the Ugandan case, Congolese interviewees broadly did not interpret these leaders as members of their own communities or 'our children' for whom the community should take responsibility. They were instead typically described as outsiders who arrived to foment strife or to occupy territory so that they could tax the local population and steal their property.[57]

Such views were pervasive in the lead-up to the 2006 elections, the first since Congolese independence in 1960. In particular, the expectation that the Tutsi-dominated rebel group, the RCD, would lose much of its influence over the Kivus because of the minority Banyarwanda's lack of electoral clout and the RCD's inability to forge genuine political alliances drove it to pursue violence as a means of control.[58] In early 2005, previously integrated RCD troops, under the command of Gen. Laurent Nkunda and supported by the Governor of North Kivu, Eugene Serufuli, redeployed to North Kivu, where they regularly attacked non-Banyarwanda civilians. Nkunda's troops attacked Rutshuru on 9 February 2006, several hours after the author left the town. An eyewitness told the author later that day:

Nkunda's men came out of their camps in the hills and attacked the town. I didn't see Nkunda himself with them. It was about 4 o'clock [in the afternoon], when it was still light. They started shooting at a hotel in the

---

[56] International Criminal Court, Trial Chamber II, 'Dissenting Opinion of Christine Van den Wyngaert', Situation in the Democratic Republic of Congo, *The Prosecutor v. Germain Katanga*, 20 May 2013, paras. 258–60.

[57] Author's interviews, North and South Kivu and Ituri, 2006–15.

[58] The term 'Banyarwanda' denotes people assumed to have cultural and linguistic roots in Rwanda, including belonging to the main Rwandan ethnic groups, Hutu, Tutsi and Twa.

main street, because there was a rumour that a meeting of [non-Banyarwanda] community leaders was going on there...Everyone was running. Some people were hurt. A few were killed. Women and children ran into the bush...It will be a long time before they come back now...Everyone is scared of Nkunda. These rebels can come down so quickly from the hills then disappear.[59]

At the same time, there was often disagreement, even within the same communities, over which specific rebel leaders should be considered principally responsible for mass crimes. This reflects the often shadowy nature of many rebel movements in the DRC, whose backers, leaders and alliances change constantly. Relevant for the ICC cases in Ituri, many local respondents criticised the focus on Lubanga and Ngudjolo because they were perceived as middle-ranking, with more prominent figures such as Ntaganda, Katanga and others viewed as having fundamental control over the commission of crimes.[60] Similarly, in North and South Kivu, local actors who had suffered FDLR atrocities rarely discussed the ICC suspects, Mbarushimana and Mudacamara, who are accused of directing the FDLR from afar, but rather prominent FDLR commanders in the field who were often seen directly orchestrating attacks against civilians.[61]

Another common view expressed by eastern Congolese interviewees was that regional actors – especially Uganda and Rwanda – were responsible for coordinating attacks through their Congolese proxies and should therefore be held accountable. A recurring feature of local narratives of violence is the view that conflict is generated by powerful regional figures who can mobilise local forces while remaining invisible. The impact on the local population of the Ugandan and Rwandan armed invasions of eastern DRC since the mid-1990s cannot be overstated. Whereas among northern Ugandan communities a crucial dimension of intimacy defines views on those most responsible, in eastern DRC notions of faceless, distanced perpetrators dominate discussions. 'Our biggest problem is Rwanda', said Gaspard, a victim

---

[59] Author's telephone interview, general population, Rutshuru, 9 February 2006 [author's translation].

[60] Author's interviews, local population, Bunia, Bogoro, Djugu, Nioka, Mahagi, 2006–15. See also Kambale, 'A Story of Missed Opportunities' , pp. 178–9.

[61] Author's interviews, local population, Goma, Rutshuru, Walikale, Masisi, Beni, Bukavu, Uvira, Fizi, 2006–15.

of RCD violence now living in Goma. 'The rebels attack us here but it's Kagame who gives the orders.'[62]

These perspectives on the gravity of crimes and the actors considered most responsible for atrocities determine the most commonly expressed views on the necessary responses to conflict in eastern DRC. Echoing the Ugandan case, local respondents most often cite the need for peace and mediation, coupled with political reform, reflecting the lived reality of ongoing conflict and deep suspicion of the state. 'The most important thing for us is peace', said Mireille, a fifty-two-year-old woman in Beni. 'But how can we have peace when we can't trust the government? No one will have peace until Kabila goes.'[63] For many local respondents, it is difficult to countenance the types of transitional justice measures discussed in other contexts – such as war crimes trials, truth commissions or reparations programmes – before peace and stability have been achieved and government institutions such as the army and police have been fundamentally reformed.[64]

A common theme in eastern Congolese discussions of peace is the need for face-to-face mediation between conflictual parties, including different ethnic groups and between rebel leaders and community authorities. 'To stop the fighting, people must talk', said Françine, a victim of FDLR violence in Walikale in North Kivu. 'You must gather the leaders controlling the fighters and ask them why they are fighting so we can make them stop. You can't have peace through more fighting, only talking together.'[65] As we will see in Chapter 7, such perspectives underpin the widespread support for community-level mediation processes such as the *Barza Inter-Communautaire* in North Kivu and the *Réseau Haki na Amani* (RHA) in Ituri, including their role in negotiating with senior armed actors.

Similar to the northern Ugandan experience above, many Congolese respondents emphasise the need for face-to-face practices and proximity because of the long-standing distance of the domestic courts, which

---

[62] Author's interview, Gaspard, Goma, 10 February 2006. See also P. Dixon, 'Reparations and the Politics of Recognition', in C. De Vos, S. Kendall and C. Stahn (eds.), *Contested Justice: The Politics and Practice of International Criminal Court Interventions*, Cambridge University Press, 2015, p. 335.

[63] Author's interview, Mireille, Beni, 12 February 2006.

[64] Author's interviews, North and South Kivu and Ituri, 2006–15.

[65] Author's interview, Françine, Walikale, 11 February 2006.

are broadly viewed as inaccessible, corrupt and symbolic of the population's broader neglect by the state from the colonial period to the present.[66] The civilian and military courts have historically faced immense challenges in delivering justice in the DRC. Only around 2,500 judges currently oversee the judicial system, three-quarters of them in the civilian courts, providing approximately one judge per 29,000 inhabitants.[67] Most of the population cannot access the court system, which is located primarily in urban centres despite a 1979 law providing for the establishment of courts or *tribunaux de paix* in most rural areas. A 2005 report by Global Rights concluded:

There is no legal presence in most of the interior, where many human rights violations have been noted. Judges are rarely compensated and some, who were appointed by the rebels, have an ambiguous status because they are not recognized by the government...All judicial personnel are forced to live off the backs of victims. Despite the lack of means made available to them by the government, the courts nevertheless try to operate, but their performance is very limited and their independence is often sacrificed for survival necessities.[68]

These views were echoed by Marie, a fifty-three-year-old farmer near Rutshuru in North Kivu:

None of my friends or family has ever used the courts. The system in Rutshuru doesn't work and it is too far for us to go to the courts in Goma. Even if we could travel there, we don't have the money to pay the judges, who ask for very large payments. We deal with our problems ourselves, family to family.[69]

[66] B. Rubbers and E. Gallez, 'Why Do Congolese People Go to Court? A Qualitative Study of Litigants' Experience of Two Justice of the Peace Courts in Lubumbashi', *Journal of Legal Pluralism and Unofficial Law*, 44, 66, 2012, pp. 79–108, citing the principal impediments to justice as distrust of lawyers, physical distance, multiple adjournments and the financial costs associated. See also, Vinck and Pham, 'Searching for Lasting Peace'. The key findings of the latter survey for the themes explored in this chapter are that 54 per cent of Congolese respondents viewed the national justice system as corrupt; there was increasing awareness of the ICC over time (from 28 per cent of respondents claiming some knowledge of the Court in 2008 to 53 per cent in 2013); and, that 48 per cent believed the national justice system was a more appropriate forum for the prosecution of high-ranking suspects of international crimes than the ICC.
[67] Global Rights, 'S.O.S. Justice: Assessment of the Justice Sector in North and South Kivu, Maniema and North Katanga', August 2005, p. 6.
[68] Ibid., p. 8. [69] Author's interview, Marie, Rutshuru, 8 February 2006.

Distrust of the civilian and military courts is rife because of the population's inability to access the legal system and because the courts are still identified with the repressive dictatorship of Mobutu, who used them to ensure impunity for himself and his supporters and as part of his divide and conquer strategy in fractious communities, for example to enforce citizenship legislation. Many Congolese view the military courts in particular, with their lack of an appeals process, as repressive and a means to increase the army's influence over civilian life. The head of a local human rights group in Goma said:

Corruption within the military and especially in the military tribunals is widespread...The problem is that many of the perpetrators have been integrated into the FARDC in the last few months and no one wants to prosecute them...There are huge problems with corruption and the military courts are often the worst offenders. Money and protecting their own people are their biggest concerns. The justice sector is simply a huge marketplace of influence.[70]

Much of the population also suspects widespread collusion between the national judiciary and various armed groups, which wield major political influence in the eastern provinces.[71] As discussed further in the next chapter, overcoming popular perceptions of the legal system as distant and corrupt is one of the biggest challenges facing the Congolese judiciary.

When Congolese respondents move beyond peace and political reform to discuss other responses to violence, two themes recur. In contrast to Uganda, there is a strong emphasis on the need to punish the perpetrators of mass atrocity. In Uganda, a consistent discourse regarding amnesty (discussed in greater detail in Chapters 6 and 7) reflects the reality that most amnesty recipients are young former abductees, often considered the 'children' of affected communities, and the national Amnesty Act is widely perceived to have successfully reintegrated thousands of former combatants and substantially depleted the ranks of various rebel groups. In eastern DRC, amnesty is broadly equated with high- and middle-ranking rebel actors who receive plum positions in the FARDC and, once embedded in the army, continue to commit crimes against civilians. 'We have never had justice here', said Samuel, a Lendu victim who was badly injured by the UPC

[70] Author's interview, local human rights worker, Goma, 2 February 2006.
[71] Ibid.

in Bunia in 2002. 'We need to punish those responsible to send a message that the violence must stop. If we don't punish the murderers, they will do the same thing over and over.'[72] The eastern Congolese experience is marked by less of the assumed solidarity between victims and perpetrators witnessed in northern Uganda – especially in Acholiland – which influences local perceptions regarding amnesty and punishment.

Finally, a wide range of local Congolese actors emphasise the need for systematic truth-telling about crimes. A common feature of the conflict landscape in both northern Uganda and eastern DRC – but discussed more regularly in the latter – is the impact of rumour and intrigue in people's understandings of the causes of conflict. 'The FDLR often attack at night', said Belvie, a victim of violence in Masisi in North Kivu. 'You can't see their faces. The attacks happen quickly so you can't be sure who is attacking you.'[73] Linked to the point above that many local actors discern shadowy and sinister forces such as regional governments behind local conflict, there is a widespread desire for greater clarity about the main orchestrators, motivations and means of violence.

These findings from Uganda and the DRC critically shape community-based perceptions of the ICC, explored in the next section. Local conceptions in both countries clash with key aspects of the ICC's approach, which centre around its imposition of particular notions of 'gravity' and the suspects considered 'most responsible' for crimes. In particular, local interpretations contest the ICC's eschewing of crimes committed by domestic and regional governments, which local respondents routinely cite as among the gravest of crimes (along with those committed by intimate actors, a category the ICC considers 'low-level' suspects and therefore the exclusive purview of domestic transitional justice institutions; a theme discussed in greater detail in Chapters 5 and 7).

Connected to this issue, respondents in both countries emphasise the need for substantial political reform as a response to violence and general circumstances of deprivation and marginalisation. A major problem for the ICC is not only that it has avoided investigating and prosecuting government atrocities but, as argued in the previous

[72] Author's interview, Samuel, Bunia, 24 August 2011.
[73] Author's interview, Belvie, Masisi, 11 February 2006.

chapter, it has bolstered the same states whose citizens call for their fundamental reform. While there appears to be greater popular appetite in the DRC than Uganda for the punishment of atrocity perpetrators, the ICC's singular focus on non-state actors in the DRC undermines its legitimacy among local actors. Furthermore, in both Uganda and the DRC, the sustained emphasis on the need for transitional justice processes to be delivered face-to-face, with a high degree of public engagement, calls into question the ICC's fundamental approach to distanced justice, delivered far from the populations most affected by violence.

Popular Perceptions of the ICC as a Whole

This section focuses on local perceptions of the ICC generally, while the final section of this chapter examines communities' direct interactions with specific branches of the Court. As this section highlights, the overall conceptions of conflict and the necessary responses to violence examined earlier underpin local actors' views of the ICC. Broadly, most everyday Ugandan and Congolese interviewees express either ignorance or criticism of the ICC as an institution. Local actors' views have inevitably changed across the ten years during which fieldwork was conducted. However, the most marked change – communities' gaining more information about the Court – has led to increased scepticism of the ICC. As we will see in the final section of this chapter, such perceptions profoundly shape local actors' expectations of the Court and their willingness to participate directly in its operations, including as witnesses in trials.

Popular Perceptions of the ICC in Northern Uganda

Fieldwork in northern Uganda identified four general perspectives on the ICC over four distinct periods between 2006 and 2016. In early 2006, less than a year after the ICC issued arrest warrants for the five LRA commanders, the two dominant and mutually reinforcing views of the ICC among northern Ugandan interviewees were distrust of the close relationship between the Court and Museveni's government and insufficient information about the workings of the ICC, which interviewees perceived as lacking visibility. This echoes the popular views above regarding the gravity of government crimes, the desire for national political reform and doubts over institutions that do not deliver face-to-face accountability for mass crimes (including criticisms of the distanced national courts from the colonial period onwards).[74] The majority of northern Ugandan respondents had heard of Museveni's joint press conference with Ocampo in London in 2004, as it had been widely reported by Mega FM and other local radio stations. 'If the ICC and Museveni are working together, there can't be justice', said Ketty, a victim of LRA violence in the Bobi IDP camp. 'Who will deal with the government's crimes? What is Museveni telling the ICC about what happened here?'[75]

The majority of interviewees also said they knew little about the ICC and had received minimal information about the Court's aims and plans. Many respondents consequently held misconceptions of the Court, principally that it possessed its own police force capable of arresting the LRA suspects. 'We have heard of the ICC but only that they want to catch Kony and put him on trial', said Candano, a thirty-eight-year-old man in Lira. 'We haven't heard anything else.'[76] As Stephen Okello, the coordinator of the Uganda Conflict Action Network, said in March 2006,

The ICC has been very fuzzy about its objectives. It hasn't explained why it is present in the north. You hear many rumours – the ICC has an army and police, it can arrest and kill the LRA fighters. These rumours have persisted and have had a big impact on the LRA. There were many [combatants] coming from the bush because of the [national] amnesty but after the ICC most of them have stopped coming.[77]

In his 2006 book, *Trial Justice*, Tim Allen argues that a widespread desire among northern Ugandans for the punishment of atrocity perpetrators indicates substantial support for the ICC. '[T]he idea that some kind of external agency might intervene to allocate accountability and punish those found guilty seemed more appealing [among the general population] than activists in Gulu suggested', Allen claims.[78] He quotes the finding of an International Center for Transitional

---

[74] On these themes, see also H. Porter, *After Rape: Violence, Justice and Social Harmony in Uganda*, Cambridge University Press, 2017.
[75] Author's interview, Ketty, Bobi, 13 March 2006.
[76] Author's interview, Candano, Lira, 11 November 2006.
[77] Stephen Okello, Coordinator or Uganda Conflict Action Network, Kampala, 1 March 2006.
[78] Allen, *Trial Justice*, p. 147.

Justice (ICTJ)/Berkeley survey of nearly 2,600 people in northern Uganda in early 2005 that of the respondents who had heard of the ICC, 91 per cent believed it could contribute to peace and 89 per cent believed it could contribute to justice.[79] The same survey, however, found that only 27 per cent of respondents had heard of the ICC, which casts serious doubt on claims about extensive support for the Court during this period.[80]

Father Carlos Rodriguez, who conducted qualitative research on accountability mechanisms on behalf of the Acholi Religious Leaders Peace Initiative (ARLPI) in 2005, also found that a surprising percentage of respondents supported the ICC's operations in northern Uganda. He discovered, though, that this perception stemmed principally from the common view that the ICC had a military and police force capable of arresting the LRA commanders. When respondents were informed that this was not the case, the vast majority questioned the virtues of the ICC's operations.[81] A follow-up ICTJ/Berkeley survey in 2007 showed that 60 per cent of the northern Ugandan population knew about the ICC (a substantial increase from two years earlier) but that 54 per cent of those respondents still believed that the ICC could enforce its own arrest warrants.[82] My own interviews as well as the ICTJ/Berkley survey and Rodriguez's qualitative research suggest that in the early years of the ICC's operations in northern Uganda, the overriding popular sentiment toward the ICC was neither support nor antipathy but lack of information, tinged with suspicion over the seemingly cosy relationship between the ICC and Museveni's government.

Throughout the Juba peace talks from 2006 to 2008, northern Ugandan respondents questioned – often vociferously – the timeliness of the ICC's intervention, underpinned by the persistent view that the ICC lacked presence among affected communities. Numerous sources argued, consistent with the perceptions of the most pressing responses to conflict discussed above, that the ICC displayed insensitivity to local attempts to achieve peace (particularly through the Juba process) and the smooth reintegration of LRA combatants, including those considered 'children of the community' (through the Amnesty Act and

[79] Ibid., pp. 147–8.   [80] ICTJ, 'Forgotten Voices', p. 32.
[81] Author's interview, Father Carlos Rodriguez, Gulu Catholic Diocese and ARLPI, Gulu, 10 March 2006.
[82] ICTJ, 'When the War Ends', p. 36.

local rituals). The sub-chief in Pabbo camp quoted in the previous chapter said,

The ICC isn't really talked about here because they can't arrest anyone. Until the LRA leaders are captured, the ICC means nothing to us. People also worry that the ICC means the LRA won't come back from the bush to receive amnesty. It won't change the fact that people walk outside the five kilometre perimeter [of the camp] and get shot, killed or abducted. Look at our children. They know only life in the camp, this life of disease and poverty.[83]

Norbert Mao, the LC5 chairman of Gulu district, expressed similar sentiments:

The Acholi people are very practical. We're waiting to see if the ICC can produce arrests then we'll see. Some people say, 'Let's just give Kony a mansion in Gulu if he gives us peace. This won't end impunity but you can't raise the dead.' Ultimately our focus here is on peace, not how long Kony will spend in jail...Ocampo needs to come here to tell people how the arrest warrants will help them if they've been living in the camps waiting for the end of the war. The ICC needs to prove it isn't a callous organisation. Originally, they thought the LRA would be an easy target. They haven't been persuasive in terms of their choice of cases. The ICC's actions haven't been wrong but untimely. There was a lack of groundwork before they jumped in, including having no champions on the ground.[84]

For several years following the collapse of the Juba peace talks in late 2008, the dominant view expressed by local respondents – particularly victims of violence – was one of abandonment by the ICC. One victim of an LRA attack in Amuru district who had given evidence to Prosecution investigators in 2006 said,

Where is the ICC now? When they came here, they told us our evidence was important and we could help punish Kony and the [other LRA leaders]...It was very difficult for us to speak to them. We took risks because we didn't know who was listening. All this time has passed and we've heard nothing from them. Now we don't know what will happen.[85]

A regular observation in interviews during this time was that the ICC had disrupted the Juba negotiations but had soon lost interest in

[83] Author's interview, James, sub-chief, Pabbo, 11 March 2006.
[84] Author's interview, Mao, 9 March 2006.
[85] Author's interview, ICC witness, Amuru, 12 March 2006.

northern Uganda because of the failure to arrest the LRA commanders. As Martin, a trader in Lira town, said in 2009, 'For years all we heard was "ICC, ICC". When the talks were happening in Juba, it was still, "ICC, ICC". Then the ICC lost interest. They decided everything here was too hard, so they went elsewhere. Now I hear they're in Kenya, even Central African Republic.'[86] Some respondents noted that the perceived abandonment by the ICC coincided with the immense international aid industry moving from LRA-affected areas in Acholiland, Lango and Teso to other parts of Uganda such as Karamoja and to South Sudan. 'The foreigners always do this', said Priscilla, an amputee in Barlonyo who had been a victim of an LRA attack.

They come here and say they want to help then they leave. They never tell us when they're going, they just leave. The UN was here when we were in the camps. Now where are they? It's the same with the ICC. They were here asking us all these questions when we were in the camps. Once we left the camps, they left too.[87]

Such views underline the extent to which local communities experience the ICC as one external intervention among many and the Court absorbs and reinforces many of the criticisms of these other practices.

More recent perceptions among northern Ugandan respondents reflect the arrest and transfer to The Hague of Dominic Ongwen in January 2015. For some respondents, Ongwen's capture represented a reminder that the ICC was even involved in northern Uganda. 'We had forgotten about the ICC here', said Godfrey, a mechanic in Gulu. 'People were busy leaving the camps and starting their lives again...But now with Ongwen, we remember that this ICC is still around.'[88] Field interviews indicate that the Ongwen case has generated further uncertainty rather than increased legitimacy for the Court among the affected population. In particular, as discussed earlier, the fact that Ongwen was abducted by the LRA before he rose to the rank of commander provoked some sympathy among everyday Ugandans as well as questions about the applicability of the Amnesty Act in his case. 'Why doesn't Ongwen get an amnesty like Banya or Kolo?' asked Boniface, a teacher in Amuru.[89]

---

[86] Author's interview, Martin, Lira, 3 September 2009.
[87] Author's interview, Priscilla, Barlonyo, 6 September 2009.
[88] Author's interview, Godfrey, Gulu, 10 April 2015.
[89] Author's interview, Boniface, Amuru, 12 April 2015.

Various civil society actors in Acholiland meanwhile argued that Bensouda's visit to northern Uganda in late February 2015 was welcome but failed to address their concerns over the Ongwen case and the wider work of the ICC. 'It was good that [Bensouda] came here', said one NGO representative. 'Ocampo never came here when he was Prosecutor so we were happy that Bensouda visited. But she didn't provide many answers to our questions, which frustrated many of us.'[90] Henry Komakech, a Gulu-based lawyer who had undergone legal training through an ICC programme in The Hague and is currently representing victims in the Kwoyelo case before the Ugandan International Crimes Division, expressed similar views:

I went to the meeting with Bensouda. I met her. She stayed here only two days, at the Bomah Hotel. One meeting was deliberately moved to Golden Peace Hotel to confuse people and distract the critics. Many people didn't make it. She said she needed three more months to finalise the charges against Ongwen. People criticised her. They said, 'Why are you waiting so long and why are you prosecuting Ongwen? We can forgive him and cleanse him here.' Bensouda disagreed and said, 'We have to honour the indictment and follow this through to The Hague.'[91]

These different phases of opinion show that northern Ugandan communities do not hold static views of the ICC and the Court is interpreted according to its changing practices and the variable circumstances of the local population. Nevertheless, some criticisms of the ICC persist, namely its close relationship with the Ugandan government, disruption to peace talks and lack of responsiveness to local needs and concerns. Local respondents therefore, implicitly, express scepticism of the ICC's claimed neutrality and distance from domestic politics, viewing it as inextricably tied to – and interfering directly in – the national political arena.

Popular Perceptions of the ICC in Eastern DRC

As in Uganda, the Congolese population's general perceptions of the ICC have varied over time, depending on the changing work of the Court or people's living conditions. Drawing on the author's interviews in Ituri, the Kivus, Equateur and Kinshasa as well as other

---

[90] Author's interview, NGO representative, Gulu, 8 April 2015.
[91] Author's interview, Henry Komakech, lawyer, Gulu, 7 April 2015.

sources, this section identifies three main periods with distinct perceptions of the Court. The early years of the ICC's operations in the DRC
in 2006 and 2007 were dominated by cautious optimism about what
an international court could achieve in a country where the national
judiciary had historically failed the local population. Throughout my
interviews in early 2006 – eighteen months after the start of the ICC's
investigations in the DRC but before any suspects had been transferred
to The Hague – respondents expressed muted hope that the ICC would
improve this situation. 'It is good that the ICC is in Congo now', said
Aude, a seamstress in Goma. 'Our courts here do nothing. Finally there
might be justice for the rebels and the government.'[92] A July
2006 survey of around 2,600 people in fifteen cities across the DRC,
conducted by the Kinshasa-based National Coalition for the ICC,
suggested that many Congolese responded favourably to Lubanga's
arrest and transfer to The Hague.[93] Turlan, from the OTP, confirmed
this was the Prosecution's general interpretation of popular sentiment
toward the Court: 'There's much greater popular support for the ICC
in Congo than in Uganda. There's little infrastructure here, so the
people are grateful for any judicial presence.'[94]

Echoing the Ugandan case, however, a common view among everyday Congolese respondents in early 2006 was that the ICC lacked
visibility and therefore reflected a problematic distance than the population had already witnessed with the domestic courts.[95] There were
signs at this time that the population's initial optimism about the Court
was waning, particularly outside of Kinshasa or Ituri where the ICC
had almost no presence. One strong thread of popular sentiment
during this period was that the ICC mimicked justice as it had been
delivered in the colonial period and under Mobutu. 'When the Belgians
were here then when Mobutu was President, the courts were always in
Kinshasa', said Gautier, a trader in Bukavu. 'People couldn't use them
because they were too far away, too expensive. The ICC looks like
that. It's even further away than Kinshasa.'[96] Etienne, a doctor in
Goma, expressed a similar view: 'When justice happens out of sight,

---

[92] Author's interview, Aude, Goma, 2 February 2006.
[93] Hemedi, 'Thomas Lubanga Dyilo's Arrest', p. 3.
[94] Author's interview, Turlan, 18 January 2006.
[95] Author's interviews, local population, Kinshasa, Goma, Bunia, Bukavu, 19
    January–21 February 2006.
[96] Author's interview, Gautier, Bukavu, 23 February 2006.

all Congolese worry. The colonials did that, so did Mobutu. Don't let the people see what's happening. Hide the courts away, close the doors. Here we worry that the ICC won't let us see what's happening.'[97]

Lack of information about, and confusion regarding, the ICC were rife during this period. Many inhabitants of Ituri and the Kivus, especially in rural areas, claimed to have never heard of the ICC or conflated it with the ICJ, about which there was much discussion in these provinces because of high-profile ICJ cases several months earlier, the first of which saw Uganda found guilty of crimes of aggression on Congolese soil and ordered to pay damages to the DRC government;[98] the second resulting in Rwanda being found not guilty of similar crimes in the DRC.[99] When asked what he knew of the ICC's work in the DRC, a teacher in Rutshuru, who was a prominent figure in the community, said, 'I've never heard of the International Criminal Court. Do you mean the court for Rwanda?'[100] That a well-educated man in a town in North Kivu was at that time better-informed of the work of the ICTR in Tanzania than of the ICC's work in the DRC says much about the ICC's lack of outreach among the Congolese population, especially in the eastern provinces.[101]

Repeating concerns over treatment of intermediaries discussed in Chapter 3, many Congolese NGOs in particular claimed during this period that the ICC had made little attempt to foster relationships with local actors, thus forfeiting much of its legitimacy in their eyes and those of the wider Congolese population. A human rights lawyer in Kinshasa expressed a common perspective:

---

[97] Author's interview, Etienne, Goma, 2 February 2006.
[98] International Court of Justice, 'Armed Activities on the Territory of Congo', Judgment in *Democratic Republic of Congo vs. Uganda*, 19 December 2005.
[99] International Court of Justice, 'Armed Activities on the Territory of Congo', Judgment in *Democratic Republic of Congo vs. Rwanda*, 3 February 2006.
[100] Author's interview, local population, Rutshuru, 8 February 2006.
[101] Like issues of staffing discussed earlier, problems with the ICC's outreach programme appear to be a combination of lack of ICC will to improve performance and lack of funding from States Parties. Some States Parties, however, have argued that much more funding should be directed to ICC outreach in the field, to increase knowledge of the ICC among the general population in the countries where the Court operates (Budget and Finance Team of the Coalition for the International Criminal Court, 'Submission to the 3rd Meeting of the Assembly of States Parties: The Report of the Committee on Budget and Finance', 26 August 2004, pp. 17–18, 29–30).

The destiny of the ICC rests in the DRC. It faces an immense test here. Because we are so disaffected with our own justice system, we are looking for alternatives and we believe the ICC offers this. We are used to disenfranchisement. We understand realpolitik and now we wonder if the ICC will be the same as all these other [justice] institutions. Will it put realpolitik above the needs of the population and the interests of justice? There is a danger that the ICC will suffer a death in the heart...The ICC says it has limited means for its work in the DRC, so they come to Kinshasa for two days, talk to the government, then leave. The ICC ignores us, the intellectuals of the country, and even more so the bulk of the population...We experienced colonisation in this country, so people look at the ICC, these Europeans, and they ask, 'Are they here to liberate us?...The Belgians were here until the 1960s, they learnt classic Swahili, moved among the people, promised us great things. Now they're back with the ICC...Will the ICC just be colonisation all over again? What will it bring us?'[102]

NGOs in eastern DRC expressed these views even more strongly during this period because they felt that the ICC engaged mainly with local actors in Kinshasa. One senior human rights worker in Goma said,

I told Prosecutor Ocampo in 2003 that if he neglected the Kivus this would hurt the ICC in the long run. It won't be treated as a serious court. If he neglects NGOs here this will also hurt the ICC. NGOs act as interlocutors between the ICC and the population, especially when it comes to spreading the word about the ICC and gathering witness statements...Has the ICC really privileged the DRC over other conflicts in the world? If so, where are they? I can assure you they are not here in North Kivu. They have no presence here whatsoever.[103]

Fieldwork conducted between 2008 and 2012 when proceedings against five Congolese suspects (Lubanga, Katanga, Ngudjolo, Bemba and Mbarushimana) were underway elicited even more divided opinion of the ICC. Popular perceptions tended to cleave along ethnic and political lines, with divisions most acute in 2010 in the build-up to the national elections in November 2011. One symptom of the OTP's perceived ethnic balancing in prosecuting Lubanga, leader of the Hema-dominated UPC, and Katanga and Ngudjolo, leaders of the

---

[102] Author's interviews, roundtable of local human rights workers, Kinshasa, 26 January 2006.
[103] Author's interview, local human rights worker, Goma, 1 February 2006.

Lendu-dominated FRPI and FNI, respectively, was that Hema and Lendu constituencies in Ituri viewed the ICC proceedings through an explicitly ethnic lens. Routinely, the prosecution of the other ethnic group's leader was viewed as justifiable and a credit to the ICC, while the prosecution of one's own ethnic group was viewed as exacerbating the group's victimhood.[104] Many Hema welcomed the stays of proceedings against Lubanga, while many Lendu viewed this as the incompetence of the OTP and its inability to gather effective evidence in Ituri.[105]

Many Lendu also criticised the ICC's refusal to bring charges against Ugandan government officials perceived as backing Lubanga's UPC, echoing the issue above regarding the role of regional actors in the Ituri conflict. 'Everyone knows Lubanga committed extreme crimes', said a Lendu chief near Mahagi in Ituri. 'But he was only obeying orders from Museveni. The ICC is wasting its time with Lubanga. They should be punishing Museveni.'[106] Similarly, the acquittal of Ngudjolo in December 2012 was widely celebrated by Lendu but denounced by many Hema respondents, who again interpreted this as the ICC's single-minded pursuit of the Hema, best represented by the conviction of Lubanga in March 2012. A Hema chief in Nioka in Ituri said, 'The ICC is only for the Lendu. We could see that straight away. They went after Lubanga but they were never serious about Ngudjolo. They tried to make it seem it was equal by dealing with him but it was never serious.'[107] Meanwhile, the ICC judges' refusal to confirm the charges against Mbarushimana, alleged leader of the Hutu-dominated FDLR, elicited comparable ethnic-based reactions in North and South Kivu and across the border in Rwanda. Many Tutsi viewed this as a conspiracy between Kabila – under whose command the FARDC has historically been accused of backing the FDLR[108] – and the ICC to protect the FDLR and by extension the Hutu of eastern DRC.[109]

---

[104] Author's interviews, local population, Bunia, Bogoro, Djugu, Nioka, Mahagi, 2008–12.
[105] Ibid.   [106] Author's interview, Lendu Chief, Mahagi, 15 September 2008.
[107] Author's interview, Hema Chief, Nioka, 15 April 2013.
[108] See, for example, Global Witness, '"Faced with a Gun, What Can You Do?" War and the Militarisation of Mining in Eastern Congo', July 2009, section 7.
[109] Author's interviews, local population, Goma, Rutshuru, Walikale, Masisi, Rusizi, Rubavu, 2012–15.

As discussed in the previous chapter, interviews with everyday Congolese citizens in Kinshasa and Kisangani about the ICC inevitably turned to the Court's treatment of Bemba, with stark political faultlines similar to the ethnic divisions around the ICC in Ituri and the Kivus. Kabila supporters often framed the ICC's prosecution of Bemba as long overdue, given Bemba's alleged rebel atrocities in the DRC and CAR, while Bemba supporters viewed his arrest in Belgium and transfer to The Hague as the continuation of the long-standing targeting of a perceived Mobutu/Bemba power base, often with the assistance of external actors.[110] Such views were expressed most acutely in 2010 at the start of campaigning for the 2011 elections, which were due to proceed without Bemba at the helm of the MLC. As quoted earlier, many Bemba supporters viewed this as affording Kabila a clear run at the presidency. These findings from different parts of the DRC and the wider region highlight the extent to which local actors interpret the ICC through the lens of historical and prevailing domestic political and ethnic dynamics. In such views, the ICC – while it may claim to function apolitically, a key component of its distanced approach – is not considered immune to domestic politics and instead interpreted as yet another political actor among many.

From 2013 onwards, empirical sources in eastern DRC echo views expressed in the first two phases while raising new issues concerning the transfer of Ntaganda to The Hague in March 2013. While respondents acknowledged the more pronounced activity of the ICC, which by the time of Ntaganda's transfer had convicted Lubanga, acquitted Ngudjolo and dismissed the charges against Mbarushimana, with the trial of Katanga ongoing, many continued to view the ICC as a foreign institution fundamentally detached from domestic affairs and lacking any obvious presence among affected communities.[111] The transfer of Ntaganda also exacerbated several recurring themes in interviews, namely the ICC's inability to address government crimes; its ignoring violations by regional powers; and continued perceptions of targeting some ethnic groups while overlooking crimes committed by others.

On the issue of government crimes, while Ntaganda had been a colonel in the Congolese army and based in North Kivu, the ICC charges against him concern only crimes allegedly committed while

---

[110] Author's interviews, local population, Kinshasa and Kisangani, 2008, 2010.
[111] Author's interviews, local population, Goma, Rutshuru, Bunia, 2013–15.

he acted as the UPC chief of military operations under Lubanga's command in Ituri. 'It's very good news that Bosco [Ntaganda] is now at the ICC', said Alain, a merchant in Goma.

He has been walking around here freely for years. It makes us angry to see him living so comfortably. But now we hear the ICC will only ask him about those old crimes [in Ituri in 2002 and 2003]. What about M23? What about CNDP? They killed so many people. Will he have to talk about that too?[112]

The focus of the Ntaganda case on Ituri rather than the Kivus also raised fresh criticisms of the ICC's geographical limits, neglecting the part of eastern DRC where conflict today is much more pronounced. While violence has continued sporadically in Ituri since 2003, punctuated by periods of relative peace, most parts of North and South Kivu have experienced more sustained violence, including the large-scale massacres described earlier.

Regarding regional actors, many respondents questioned the ICC's reluctance to address the role of Uganda and Rwanda in supporting Ntaganda during his time in the UPC, CNDP and M23. Alain continued, 'Bosco wasn't the main leader. He was only following orders from Kigali. Will Kagame end up at the ICC? It's impossible!'[113] Meanwhile, many of the same Tutsi respondents in the Kivus and Rwanda who criticised the dropping of charges against Mbarushimana viewed the Ntaganda transfer through the lens of ethnic victimisation. 'The FDLR are still committing crimes against Tutsi but the ICC doesn't care about the FDLR. They only want to go after Tutsi like Bosco', said Solange, a Tutsi community leader in Rutshuru. These views echoed many Tutsis' concerns over the UN Force Intervention Brigade (FIB), a bolstered unit within MONUSCO established in March 2013 to 'neutralise and disarm' rebel groups in eastern DRC. While the FIB was nominally mandated to target three main groups – the M23, the FDLR and the ADF – it focused mainly on the M23, which it successfully drove out of the Kivus in October 2013. That the FIB has targeted the Tutsi-dominated M23, only minimally engaged the ADF and appears to have completely ignored the Hutu-dominated FDLR has created a widespread perception of ethnic bias among many Tutsi.[114] In numerous interviews, Tutsi respondents viewed the ICC

---

[112] Author's interviews, Alain, Goma, 9 April 2013.   [113] Ibid.
[114] Author's interviews, local population, Goma, Rutshuru, Rusizi, Rubavu, 2013–15.

and the FIB as twin international mechanisms designed to target Tutsi while ignoring armed actors associated with other ethnic groups.

These community-level findings from northern Uganda and eastern DRC highlight the extent to which the ICC is interpreted through the lens of broader past and unfolding political and social dynamics, in particular the history of colonialism, the behaviour of successive domestic political regimes, interventions by other international actors, continuing widespread violence and local actors' perceptions of the conflicts they have experienced first hand and their proposed remedies. Crucially, the ICC has not achieved its intended status as a neutral, objective arbiter of the domestic terrain, viewed instead as deeply embedded in local political, social and cultural dynamics. Emphasising distance from the domestic arena, the Court has rarely shown sufficient awareness of these matters to enable it to intervene effectively in these two countries and to secure legitimacy among local populations. Constant across a decade of field research in the two countries is the refrain concerning a detached and invisible Court, lacking field presence, distrusted because of its close relations with the two governments in question and seen as deepening rather than alleviating key political, regional and ethnic divisions, while stymieing attempts at national political reform. These interpretations of the ICC as a whole profoundly shape Ugandan and Congolese populations' interactions with specific organs and initiatives of the Court.

Popular Interactions with Specific ICC Branches

This final section focuses on Ugandan and Congolese communities' perceptions of specific ICC branches and programmes. Whereas the previous section explored the views of broad segments of society, this section examines those of local actors who have interacted directly with the Court. Specifically, it analyses local interactions with Prosecution and Defence investigators as well as three Registry processes: witness protection, outreach and the Trust Fund for Victims TFV.

This section highlights that, while the population engages differently with these organs of the ICC and these bodies themselves often disagree about the ICC's overarching objectives and modalities, most local respondents view each as synonymous with the Court overall and judge the entire institution according to their interactions with particular branches. Furthermore, the effects of engaging with different

ICC sections are compounding, as many actors have interacted with multiple branches and carry their experiences with one into their engagements with the others. A recurring theme in interviews with ICC officials is that the Registry sees itself as often 'cleaning up the mess'[115] of the other branches of the Court, particularly the OTP, by explaining the work of the ICC overall and providing more of the 'personal touch'[116] that the others neglect. Carolyn Hoyle and Leila Ullrich even argue that the TFV operates with a fundamentally different conception of justice – which they term 'transformative justice and gender justice' – from the rest of the ICC.[117] My research, however, indicates that local respondents do not distinguish so definitively between the different branches of the ICC, ensuring that the Registry is bedevilled by the actions of the rest of the Court, principally the OTP.

Popular Interactions with Specific ICC Branches in Northern Uganda

Community-level interviews over nearly a decade in northern Uganda highlight some of the key localised effects of the ICC's interventions, only some of which Court officials acknowledge explicitly. Interviews regarding interactions with ICC investigators do not highlight substantial differences between Prosecution or Defence and concern witnesses who have given evidence to investigators in the field rather than being called as witnesses in The Hague. A dominant perspective among these respondents is that they experienced a great deal of individual agency in giving their testimony to ICC investigators. 'I have wanted to tell my story for many years', said Apio, a victim of LRA violence in Barlonyo. 'When the [OTP] investigators came

---

[115] Author's interview, ICC Registry official, The Hague, 6 May 2011.

[116] Ibid. Sara Kendall even finds that many local actors consider the TFV as a 'donor', which complicates the work of both the TFV and the ICC more broadly. S. Kendall, 'Beyond the Restorative Turn: The Limits of Legal Humanitarianism', in C. de Vos, S. Kendall and C. Stahn (eds.), *Contested Justice: The Politics and Practice of International Criminal Court Interventions*, Cambridge University Press, 2015, p. 370.

[117] C. Hoyle and L. Ullrich, 'New Court, New Justice? The Evolution of "Justice for Victims" at Domestic Courts and at the International Criminal Court', *Journal of International Criminal Justice*, 12, 14, 2014, p. 691.

here, it was the first time I told anyone what happened to me and my family. It made me feel strong.'[118]

Some respondents, however, were often unclear about how their evidence would be used, and there was very little follow-up by investigators once they left the field. This was particularly the case between 2012 and 2015 when the OTP froze the situation of northern Uganda because of the inability to capture the LRA leaders. Richard, another victim of LRA violence in Barlonyo, said, 'I spoke to the investigators in 2006, I think it was. They met me several times and I gave them lots of information. Since then I haven't heard from them and I don't know what's happening.'[119] As Sarah Kasande from the ICTJ Uganda office said, 'There's a big problem with witnesses saying the ICC has neglected them. They were previously mobilised and ready to testify in The Hague then the ICC disappeared. There's a lot of anger around this.'[120]

These experiences hampered the various programmes conducted by the Registry in northern Uganda, particularly witness protection. Andrew Mawson from UNICEF indicated that from the beginning of ICC investigations in northern Uganda there was major friction between the OTP and other ICC branches over this issue:

At a meeting in Florence in December 2005, some of the other ICC departments had misgivings about how the Prosecutor's office was doing investigations, especially in the IDP camps. Were they getting informed consent? Who was advising children approached by the ICC?...This got a very defensive response from the OTP. It also showed that there are different responses by different [ICC] departments.[121]

Numerous interviewees across the three conflict-affected sub-regions of northern Uganda said they did not trust the ICC witness protection programme because of the close working relationship between the OTP and the UPDF, which they had observed in the field. 'The investigators came here and asked if anyone had seen with their own eyes what the LRA did', said Kintu in Barlonyo in 2009.

[118] Author's interview, Apio, Barlonyo, 6 September 2009.
[119] Author's interview, Richard, Barlonyo, 6 September 2009.
[120] Author's interview, Sarah Kasande, ICT, Kampala, 10 August 2011.
[121] Author's interview, Andrew Mawson, UNICEF, Kampala, 3 March 2006.

Most of us here could tell you everything that happened when the LRA came, everything. But we were very worried. When the investigators were here, over there [pointing beyond some low scrub] were the army vehicles...It got us thinking, if we talk to the ICC, will they tell the army? And what happens if we talk about what the army did to our people? The ICC leaves then it's just us and the military here.[122]

Echoing the controversies over the ICC's use of intermediaries discussed in Chapter 3, many local and international NGOs working in northern Uganda resent the ICC's reliance on them when identifying and protecting witnesses but refusal to heed their advice about how to work more effectively in local communities. 'Recently the ICC came to see us about witness protection issues', said one local NGO worker in Gulu. 'But as we pointed out to them, we should've been brought into the process from the very beginning. Apparently we're a tap that can be turned on and off when it suits them.'[123]

Exacerbating many of these issues, the Registry's outreach programme was slow to begin throughout Uganda, including the north, and it was widely perceived as vague and unresponsive to questions from affected communities. 'We know the ICC has investigators here', said an FDC party member in Gulu in 2006, 'but the ICC doesn't tell us what it intends to do. We don't expect sensitive information about the nature of their investigations but why can't they give us more general information about why they're here?'[124] When the ICC's outreach did finally begin in Uganda, it amounted to an information pamphlet inserted in the *New Vision*, the government-owned English-language newspaper, in December 2005 and sensitisation meetings in Gulu district in 2006, more than two years after the opening of the northern Uganda situation.[125] The ICC's general outreach strategy has been to sensitise civil society intermediaries who are encouraged to inform the broader population of the ICC's operations.[126] Interviews show that this strategy has resulted in the effective sensitisation of northern

---

[122] Author's interview, Kintu, Barlonyo, 6 September 2009.
[123] Author's interview, local humanitarian worker, Gulu, 20 February 2007.
[124] Author's interview, LC official, Gulu, 10 March 2006.
[125] ICC information pamphlet inserted in the *New Vision*, 14 December 2005, on file with author.
[126] International Criminal Court, The Registry, 'Strategic Plan for Outreach of the International Criminal Court', Doc. ICC/ASP/5/12, 29 September 2006, pp. 22–3.

Ugandan civil society but much less so among the general populace, especially when people lived in the IDP camps.[127]

Stephen Lamony, formerly interim coordinator for the Uganda Coalition for the ICC and currently the global Coalition's head of advocacy and policy for UN, AU and Africa situations, admitted to these problems in March 2006:

Only last week the ICC outreach posts were advertised. The outreach officers won't be appointed for another month. In the meantime, people in the north keep asking what the ICC is all about. There is very little popular knowledge about the ICC except that the ICC and the government are working together. The only information people are getting about the ICC comes from civil society groups like the Coalition for the ICC, which has made some trips north. Much of the damage [to the Court's reputation] could be undone by ICC sensitisation.[128]

At an event at Makerere University in Kampala in 2008, at which two members of the ICC Outreach Unit delivered a presentation on the Court's investigations in Uganda, further problems with the ICC's overall communication strategy became apparent. Repeating dynamics witnessed at similar events in northern Uganda, the highly didactic presentation focused mainly on the ICC's website and the different organs and functions of the Court. During the subsequent audience discussion, the representatives refused to answer questions about political and social dynamics surrounding the ICC's work, including its impact on the Juba peace talks that were ongoing at the time. They stated that such concerns should be raised with ICC principals in The Hague.[129]

Finally, questions about the Registry's northern Uganda programme, through the TFV, elicited a wide range of perspectives from local respondents. Between 2008 and 2015, two local NGOs received nearly $2 million from the TFV to deliver material support to affected communities and physical and psychological rehabilitation to conflict victims. An external evaluation of the TFV programme in northern

---

[127] Author's interviews, general population, Kampala, Gulu, Lira, March 2006–February 2007.

[128] Author's interview, Stephen Lamony, interim coordinator of Ugandan Coalition for the ICC, Kampala, 3 March 2006.

[129] ICC Outreach Presentation, 'Peace, Justice and the International Criminal Court in Africa' seminar, Makerere University, Kampala, 2 May 2008, notes on file with author.

Uganda indicated that approximately 40,000 northern Ugandans benefited from these initiatives between 2008 and a pause in programming at the end of 2013.[130] In 2013, the TFV Board in The Hague decided to phase out the material component of the TFV's work in northern Uganda, including support for micro-credit and loan schemes in communities directly affected by LRA violence. The Board decided that the TFV should carry on the physical and psychological support work through six new NGOs, with funding that ended in mid-2016.[131] Interviews with local actors before 2013 showed that specific victims as well as broader communities had benefited substantially from the TFV's work. 'I was able to get a loan to buy seeds and equipment for my family's farm', said Doreen, a victim of LRA violence in Amuru. 'The Trust Fund made a big difference to our livelihoods. It was the first loan I've ever received.'[132]

Interviews after 2013, however, indicated a high level of disquiet over the ending of the material component of the TFV's support – which was key to supporting wider communities – in favour of focusing on the more individualised support for specific victims through the physical and psychological programmes. While the latter approach, which includes provision of prothestic limbs for amputees and counselling for traumatised victims, garnered substantial support,[133] many respondents emphasised the importance of collective assistance, given the impact of violence on entire communities, as well as the need to support victims who may have suffered less visible harm than amputees and outwardly traumatised victims.[134] Such views reflect local conceptions of justice, discussed earlier, particularly redress for collective harm. As we will see in more detail in Chapter 7, this includes a strong emphasis on collective reparations delivered between clans.

---

[130] International Center for Research on Women, 'External Evaluation of the Trust Fund for Victims Programmes in Northern Uganda and the Democratic Republic of Congo: Towards a Perspective of Upcoming Interventions', November 2013, www.icrw.org/publications/external-evaluation-of-the-trust-fund-for-victims-programmes-in-northern-uganda-and-the-democratic-republic-of-congo-towards-a-perspective-for-upcoming-interventions/.
[131] International Criminal Court, The Registry, 'Assistance and Reparations: Achievements, Lessons Learnt and Transitioning', TFV, Programme Progress Report, 2015, www.legal-tools.org/doc/370265/pdf/, pp. 38–47
[132] Author's interview, Doreen, Amuru, 11 August 2011.
[133] Author's interviews, Acholi, Teso, Lango sub-regions, 2008–13.   [134] Ibid.

Numerous northern Ugandan respondents also argued that, while the work of the TFV was highly visible and often had a tangible impact on the lives of beneficiaries, they either could not determine how this connected to the broader work of the ICC – which they framed in highly detached terms – or viewed it as contradicting other ICC operations. 'It is good that the Trust Fund helps our people with these programmes', said one community elder in Apac. 'But why aren't the ICC chasing the LRA leaders in the bush? Why don't they get Kony and get him to tell us why he did all these terrible things?...It's like those people at the ICC have forgotten about us down here.'[135]

Interviews with northern Ugandan civil society actors, including within NGOs commissioned to carry out TFV-funded programmes, uncovered key perceptions of the work of the TFV and the ICC more broadly. Not surprisingly, all interviewees in this category emphasised the importance of the TFV's activities and its positive impact among the local population. One civil society representative in Gulu said, 'The finance from the Trust Fund enables us to carry out work in the community that we otherwise couldn't do. This helps victims and helps us as an organisation because people now see what we can achieve when we have the funding.'[136] Some NGO actors conducting TFV-supported programmes, however, expressed resentment that ICC staff either in The Hague or Kampala held such sway over their local operations. The Registry has no permanent staff in northern Uganda, running all of its programmes, including the TFV, from Kampala.[137] Complaints by northern Ugandan NGOs echoed common civil society critiques of international donors, located faraway but heavily determining the objectives, priorities and strategies of local organisations. 'This is particularly the case with amputees and other disabled victims', said a civil society leader from the Association of Volunteers in International Service, which has worked with the TFV since 2008. 'There is pressure from above to help those who are most obviously victims. The message from the top is clear: we have to be seen to be doing good so find the people who are most visibly victims.'[138]

---

[135] Author's interview, community elder, Apac, 14 August 2011.
[136] Author's interview, civil society representative, Gulu, 12 August 2011.
[137] Author's interviews, civil society representatives, Gulu, Lira, 11–15 August 2011.
[138] Author's interview, representative of Association of Volunteers in International Service, Gulu, 12 August 2011.

Some civil society actors also expressed similar concerns to the intermediaries discussed in Chapter 3, namely that in the field they were increasingly viewed as extensions of the ICC. This caused difficulties for these organisations when local communities criticised the Court, as occurred repeatedly during the Juba peace talks. A representative of one organisation that has run a TFV-funded psychological rehabilitation programme said, 'Sometimes it's difficult to talk about the ICC when we visit communities. We prefer to talk about "the Trust Fund for Victims" rather than "the ICC" because some of our partners are hostile to the Court.'[139] Other organisations working with the TFV said they often had to answer communities' questions about why the ICC was engaging in development activities. 'People ask why a court is doing NGO work', said one Gulu-based civil society leader. 'People had given up on the ICC because it couldn't capture the LRA leaders. Then they heard the Court was supporting victims through the Trust Fund. It caused a lot of confusion.'[140]

Popular Interactions with Specific ICC Branches in Eastern DRC

Interviews conducted over seven years with everyday Congolese citizens and civil society actors highlight some of the major impacts of the ICC's interventions, with echoes from the Ugandan case. Regarding respondents' interactions with Prosecution and Defence investigators, they voiced concerns about their own safety, the identity of investigators who were often local NGO intermediaries rather than ICC investigators and, paralleling the Ugandan case, the lack of follow-up as trials progressed.[141] 'We met the people from Justice Plus who were going to record our stories and give them to the ICC', said Jules, a victim of FNI violence in Bogoro. 'They were very helpful, very calm. We trusted them very much. But we keep asking

---

[139] Author's interview, civil society representative, Lira, 14 August 2011.
[140] Author's interview, civil society representative, Gulu, 12 August 2011.
[141] These critical tensions between the desired voice and agency of some
community-level participants in international legal processes and the tendency
of those processes toward the anonymity of witnesses and other key
participants, usually for security reasons, are discussed further in N. Palmer and
P. Clark, 'Testifying to Genocide: Victim and Witness Protection in Rwanda',
REDRESS Trust, 2012.

them what happens now and they tell us they don't know. This is very confusing for us.'[142]

Various interviewees in Ituri said they believed the ICC was giving mixed messages about the role of victims during the investigative stage. While the Registry's early community sensitisation in Ituri, discussed further below, stressed the centrality of victims in providing evidence and helping to shape the elements of any criminal cases, developments during the Lubanga trial directly challenged this view. During the Lubanga case, a rift emerged between the PTC and the OTP over the participation of victims. The Rome Statute allows victims to be represented by their lawyer during trials at the ICC, to pose questions to suspects and to argue for reparations at the end of a trial.[143] On 17 January 2006, the PTC ruled that six Congolese victims, whose case was brought to the ICC by the Fédération Internationale des Ligues des Droits de l'Homme (FIDH), could be represented during investigations in the DRC, although their exact role was not specified. The PTC stated that its decision recognised the 'growing emphasis placed on the role of victims by the international body of human rights law and by international humanitarian law'.[144] The Prosecutor voiced his objection to victim participation during the investigation stage of cases: 'We [in the OTP] disagree with some areas [of the decision], which could be very dangerous for the victims. In the compensation part they will have participation [but in] the investigation stage it is more complicated because security is a big issue.'[145] The Prosecutor argued there was an insufficient causal link between the harm suffered by the six victims, whose participation was permitted by the PTC, and the specific crimes with which Lubanga was charged. The PTC agreed with the Prosecutor and on 29 June 2006 handed down a decision barring the participation of the six victims in the Lubanga case.[146]

---

[142] Author's interview, Jules, Bogoro, 14 September 2008.

[143] Rome Statute, Article 15.

[144] International Criminal Court, Pre-Trial Chamber I, 'Situation in the Democratic Republic of Congo: Decision on the Applications for Participation in the Proceedings of VPRS1, VPRS2, VPRS3, VPRS4, VPRS5, VPRS6', Doc. ICC-01/04-101-tEN-Corr, 17 January 2006, p. 13.

[145] L. M. Ocampo, quoted in J. Anderson, 'ICC Enters Uncharted Territory', Institute for War and Peace Reporting, 24 March 2006, https://iwpr.net/global-voices/icc-enters-uncharted-territory.

[146] International Criminal Court, Pre-Trial Chamber I, 'Situation in the Democratic Republic of Congo in the Case of the Prosecutor vs. Thomas

Some observers have interpreted these arguments regarding victim participation as a broader battle between the OTP and the PTC over control of the investigation stage of trials.[147] At the local level, respondents who had given evidence to the ICC were aware of the controversies over victim participation in the Lubanga case. Various interviewees said that this made them reluctant to continue cooperating either with the Prosecution or the Defence because they had hoped to play a more central role in the framing of cases against several suspects and to see the suspect first hand in the dock, echoing the themes of direct voice and agency expressed in northern Uganda.[148]

Concerning local actors' engagement with the three key Registry processes – witness protection, outreach and the TFV – respondents were generally more favourable than about Prosecution and Defence investigations, while expressing sustained critiques of the Registry. The difficulties expressed regarding investigations underpinned criticisms of the Registry's attempts at witness protection. The most common view among respondents who had given evidence to ICC investigators was that they did not trust the Registry to protect them. Principal reasons cited for this view were that the suspects transferred to The Hague were powerful actors with local connections who could cause harm to anyone who testified against them; the overall security situation remained tense during a period of ongoing violence; and the ICC's use of intermediaries meant that many witnesses did not know who precisely was responsible for their protection.[149] 'Lubanga's men are still living here', said Wembe, a Prosecution witness in Bogoro.

It's frightening for those of us who spoke to the people from the ICC. They don't live here, so they don't know what happens to us. Some other people I know have been harassed for giving evidence. Some of them were harassed and they hadn't even given any evidence. It was just that Lubanga's supporters suspected them of talking to the ICC. It can be enough for people just to think you give evidence, even if you don't.[150]

Lubanga Dyilo: Decision on the Applications for Participation in the Proceedings Submitted by VPRS1 to VPRS6 in the Case of of the Prosecutor vs. Thomas Lubanga Dyilo', Doc. ICC-01/04-01/06-172-tEN, 29 June 2006.

[147] See, for example, Anderson, 'ICC Enters Uncharted Territory'.

[148] Author's interviews, ICC witnesses, Bunia, Bogoro, Nioka, September 2008 and August 2011.

[149] Author's interviews, local population, Bunia, Bogoro, Djugu, Nioka, Mahagi, 2006–15.

[150] Author's interview, Wembe, Bogoro, 15 September 2008.

Congolese respondents were even more critical than their Ugandan counterparts of the Registry's outreach programme. 'We never see anyone from the ICC here', said Tabu, a victim of UPC violence living in Bunia. 'Sometimes they speak on the radio but we can't tell if they're in Ituri or in Europe. If you have a question about what's happening, you can't ask them.'[151] Whereas in Uganda over time the Registry has held more community-level meetings to discuss the ICC's work, the Registry in the DRC has conducted outreach almost entirely through local media. Nicola Kuyaka from the ICC's field office in Bunia said in 2011,

This office has two main activities: working with local media, for example radio interviews and TV appearances, and preparing press releases for local newspapers. For TV, each Wednesday we show a DVD from The Hague. For radio, every two weeks we have an interactive session where we respond to questions...MLC supporters have been asking us lots of questions. Can Bemba still stand as a candidate? There have been lots of rumours that Bemba will be provisionally released before the elections.[152]

While the Registry's engagement with radio reaches a wide audience across eastern DRC, only a small elite can access print and TV journalism, greatly limiting the ICC's audience. Such practices – coupled with the OTP's and Defence's broad approach of conducting investigations through intermediaries – magnify a local perception that the ICC lacks physical presence and thus responsiveness in eastern DRC.

Finally, the TFV's work in eastern DRC has been even more extensive than in northern Uganda and has elicited a wider range of reactions from local actors who have engaged with it directly. Since November 2008, the TFV has provided nearly $9 million to nine Congolese civil society groups for projects covering the same three domains as in Uganda – material, physical and psychological support to victims – in Ituri and North and South Kivu.[153] In 2016 and 2017, respectively, the ICC Trial Chamber also ordered the TFV to award individual and collective reparations to victims of Lubanga's and Katanga's crimes because of the convicted perpetrators' indigence.[154]

---

[151] Author's interview, Tabu, Bunia, 24 August 2011.
[152] Author's interview, Nicolas Kuyaku, ICC Field Office, Bunia, 25 August 2011.
[153] ICC Registry, 'Assistance and Reparations', pp. 24–38.
[154] International Criminal Court, Trial Chamber II, 'Order Approving the Proposed Plan of the Trust Fund for Victims in Relation to Symbolic Collective

The most extensive TFV-funded programme has been the Caravan of Peace, run by the RHA – discussed in greater detail in Chapter 7 – which delivers psychosocial and economic assistance to conflict-affected communities as well as collecting the population's first hand accounts of violence.

In interviews, the Caravan of Peace was widely considered an effective programme because the RHA was well known in Ituri for its long-standing conflict mediation work and the Caravan combined individual and collective assistance.[155] Interviewees found the story-gathering component of the Caravan of Peace particularly beneficial, allowing them to narrate their direct experiences of conflict in a way that had not been previously possible. 'We know *Haki na Amani* well here because they've been coming for many years', said Marcel, a victim of violence in Djugu. 'We like the Caravan of Peace because we know the people who organise it. We trust them when we tell our stories. They keep everyone calm and encourage us to speak.'[156]

Several respondents, however, questioned whether this approach to gathering popular narratives meshed with the ICC's trial-based methods, linking it to concerns over victim participation and agency discussed earlier. 'It is good that I can share my story during the Caravan', said Vanda, a victim of violence in Bogoro. 'But I wanted to talk about my experiences at the ICC. The investigators told me they would need me in The Hague to tell what I saw when Ngudjolo's men came here. But I never heard from them again.'[157] Another interviewee, Evette, in Djugu said, 'It's good that *Haki na Amani* has recorded my story. I want my family and my community to know what I suffered. But the whole world should know what happened to us here. If *Haki na Amani* works with the ICC, why can't the world hear our experiences?'[158] These perspectives suggest that many community actors view the ICC as an important international arena for the

Reparations', Situation in the Democratic Republic of Congo, *The Prosecutor v. Thomas Lubanga Dyilo*, 21 October 2016; International Criminal Court, Trial Chamber II, 'Order of Reparations under Article 75 of the Statute', Situation in the Democratic Republic of Congo, *The Prosecutor v. Germain Katanga*, 24 March 2017.

[155] Author's interviews, local population, Bunia, Bogoro, Djugu, Nioka, Mahagi, 2008–15.
[156] Author's interview, Marcel, Djugu, 16 April 2013.
[157] Author's interview, Vanda, Bogoro, 18 April 2013.
[158] Author's interview, Evette, Djugu, 16 April 2013.

amplification of their first hand accounts of conflict. Several interviewees, however, also questioned whether providing conflict narratives to the RHA automatically qualified them as victims who could legitimately claim reparations if any of the Ituri suspects prosecuted at the ICC were found guilty.[159] This issue has become particularly fraught given the lengthy delays to the reparations decisions in the recently completed Lubanga and Katanga cases, and questions of over whether reparations should be delivered individually and collectively, who qualifies as a victim in reparative terms and whether it is the responsibility of the convicted perpetrators or the TFV to pay reparations.[160]

Across numerous Ugandan and Congolese communities between 2006 and 2016, specific ICC programmes have generated a range of fluctuating perceptions. Most consistent is uncertainty among local witnesses about how their evidence will be deployed, and the extent to which they can participate fully, during ICC trials. The ICC's use of intermediaries as investigators, limited time spent in the field as well as suspicions around its relations with the Ugandan and Congolese governments – key features of the ICC's distanced approach – are particularly damaging in this regard. While there is wider support for the work of the Registry than that of the Prosecution or Defence – given that a larger number of people engage with the Registry and the TFV oversees provision of direct material support to communities – the Registry has often struggled to overcome perceived failures by the other branches of the ICC. This includes pervasive uncertainty over how particular Registry programmes, such as development-oriented practices and the gathering of community-level narratives, connect to the broader trial-focused and more distant work of the Court.

---

[159] Author's interview, local population, Bogoro, Djugu, Nioka, Mahagi, 2008–15.

[160] See, for example, International Criminal Court, The Registry, 'Draft Implementation Plan for Collective Reparations to Victims', Situation in the Democratic Republic of Congo, *The Prosecutor v. Thomas Lubanga Dyilo*, 3 November 2015; International Criminal Court, 'Press Release: Lubanga Case: Trial Chamber II Orders Trust Fund for Victims to Add Information to the Reparations Plan', Situation in the Democratic Republic of Congo, *The Prosecutor vs. Thomas Lubanga Dyilo*, 9 February 2016; Open Society Justice Initiative, 'Factsheet: ICC Katanga Reparations', March 2017.

Conclusion

When the ICC launched its operations in Uganda and the DRC, many of its staff across the different branches of the Court expected to be welcomed warmly by local communities, especially victims of violence.[161] The analysis in this chapter shows that, while some sections of the Court enjoy a certain degree of popular legitimacy, the ICC broadly has failed to establish constructive working relations with local actors. In particular, it has failed to communicate its aims and modalities effectively; to respond convincingly to local queries and concerns; to make itself visible to local actors; and to consider the appropriateness of its particular mode of international justice when delivered in local contexts where there are entrenched interpretations of the nature of conflict and the required remedies to violence. This latter dimension includes conceptions of conflict and justice that challenge key aspects of the ICC's approach.

Taken together, these elements highlight a distanced Court that, hovering above the local terrain, has failed to wrestle sufficiently with the complex political, social, cultural and economic circumstances that characterise communities affected by mass violence. Nonetheless, local communities do not view the ICC as having attained an objective or impartial detachment from the domestic terrain. Interviewees instead typically perceive the Court as part and parcel of national and community political dynamics while remaining aloof and unresponsive to local needs.

Emerging strongly from communities in both northern Uganda and eastern DRC is a discourse of presence – the need to resolve conflicts face-to-face, with victims, perpetrators and mediators visible and responsive to communal concerns. Adhering to its central principle of distance, the ICC has therefore failed to deliver justice in ways that make sense to, and respond systematically to the expressed needs of, local actors. This causes confusion and disillusionment among many everyday Ugandans and Congolese. In the process, these shortcomings also undermine the ICC's trial-based work, which relies heavily on the legitimacy, trust and cooperation of local communities.

---

[161] Author's interviews, ICC staff, The Hague and Amsterdam, 22–4 March 2006, 5–7 May 2011 and 7–8 January 2016.

5 | *When Courts Collide*
The ICC and Domestic Prosecutions

Introduction

The following three chapters analyse the ICC's intersections with domestic processes that address the manifold legacies of mass conflict: national prosecutions; amnesties and peace negotiations; and community-based transitional justice. This current chapter focuses on the ICC's relations with the institutions that are arguably most like itself, namely domestic courts. Complementarity represents the ICC's view on the most effective means to structure relations with national judiciaries, framing the Court as a last resort when domestic institutions fail to address crimes adequately. This chapter explores these relations through two principal themes: the ICC's role in catalysing national judicial reforms, which focuses on the developmental conception of complementarity discussed in Chapter 2; and issues of admissibility or the extent to which the ICC justifiably assumed jurisdiction over particular cases in Uganda and the DRC, which focuses on the legal conception of complementarity (but also impinges on the political, relational and developmental interpretations).

This chapter advances three main arguments. First, while the ICC's political, relational and developmental conceptions of complementarity emphasise cooperation, deference and partnership, relations between the ICC and domestic prosecutions in Uganda and the DRC have typically been competitive. The distance inherent in the ICC's approach – which is more consistent with the legal conception of complementarity – imparts a notion of superiority over national processes, which are typically viewed as less technically adept than the Court and more open to political manipulation, especially by domestic elites. This challenges a widespread view among many transitional justice commentators – echoing Gready's 'correct balance' outlined in Chapter 2 – that multi-institutional or multi-tiered responses are required to deliver 'holistic' remedies to atrocity, for example through

150

some combination of international, national and community-based mechanisms.[1] Increasingly in African states, these three levels of transitional justice processes coincide and frequently clash.[2] Such systems are usually the product of accident rather than design, with different actors creating different layers of institutions at different times, with little, if any, coordination.

Second, in both Uganda and the DRC, where the ICC has chased state referrals, the Court has suppressed new legalities and local innovation by assuming jurisdiction over cases that could have been addressed by domestic institutions. This has undermined national processes that are better equipped to handle the particular types of conflict experienced in these two countries, are more visible to local populations and will carry the load of delivering justice long after the ICC has moved on.

Third, in the process, the ICC has empowered the Ugandan and Congolese governments, which have themselves sought to undermine domestic courts to protect their own officials and to advance their broader political agendas. These states have belatedly used domestication of the Rome Statute, assisted by donors and a wider 'rule of law' industry, to standardise domestic judiciaries according to international norms but in ways that hamper national judicial effectiveness and, like the ICC, give cover to state actors. A peculiar feature of the Ugandan and Congolese experiences is the tendency of the respective governments to prefer the ICC to domestic institutions as a means to weaken the latter and to insulate state actors from judicial scrutiny.

The ICC's Role in Domestic Judicial Reforms

This section examines the ICC's role within domestic judicial reforms in Uganda and the DRC, focusing on the civilian and military courts in both countries. Despite some commentators' suggestion that Africa

---

[1] See, for example, A. Boraine, 'Transitional Justice: A Holistic Interpretation', *Journal of International Affairs*, 60, 1, Fall/Winter 2006, pp. 17–27; and T. Olsen, L. Payne and A. Reiter, *Transitional Justice in Balance: Comparing Processes, Weighing Efficacy*, United States Institute of Peace, 2010.

[2] See, for example, M. Morris, 'The Trials of Concurrent Jurisdiction: The Case of Rwanda', *Duke Journal of Comparative and International Law*, 7, 1997, pp. 349–74; and Palmer, *Courts in Conflict*.

lacks judicial momentum in addressing atrocities,[3] many African states, including Uganda and the DRC, over the last decade have created new judicial institutions, passed legislation concerning international crimes and conducted trials of high-profile atrocity suspects. This section explores the extent to which the ICC has embodied the developmental conception of 'positive complementarity' by catalysing, and providing ongoing support to, these reforms of national prosecutions. Some commentators have argued that such improvements in Uganda and the DRC are primarily attributable to the ICC and would not have occurred without states' desire to avoid ICC intervention through building robust domestic courts or their wholesale adoption of the Rome Statute in domestic law.[4] This section examines whether the ICC has played a catalytic, neutral or even negative role vis-à-vis national reforms. It argues that the ICC has not been the principal catalyst in this respect, although it has offered some minor support. As argued in the next section on admissibility issues, however, this positive role for the ICC has been greatly undermined by the Court's competitiveness with domestic courts and tendency to usurp jurisdiction over cases that could have been handled domestically.

Domestic Judicial Reforms in Uganda

In Uganda, the civilian and military courts have historically displayed major deficiencies – including their distance and inaccessibility to the local population, discussed in the previous chapter – but in recent years, the civilian courts have proven more effective. This includes holding the government to account in key political moments such as the Supreme Court ruling after the 2006 presidential election that the ruling party had won the vote fraudulently.[5] The ICC's intervention in Uganda, however (because it chased the LRA cases and built such a close relationship with the Ugandan government), has bolstered the

[3] See, for example, K. Roth, 'Africa Attacks the International Criminal Court', *New York Review of Books*, 6 February 2014.
[4] See, for example, S. Horovitz, 'Uganda: Interactions between International and National Responses to Mass Atrocities', DOMAC project, Paper No. 18, January 2013, and DOMAC Project, 'Project Final Report', 30 June 2011.
[5] International Bar Association, 'Judicial Independence Undermined: A Report on Uganda', September 2007.

government's attempts to weaken the domestic judiciary's capacity to hold the state accountable.

Three major legal and judicial reforms concerning the handling of serious human rights violations all stem from the 2006–8 Juba peace talks between the Ugandan government and the LRA: the creation in 2008 of the War Crimes Division (later named the International Crimes Division [ICD]) of the High Court; the launch of the Transitional Justice Working Group (TJWG) within the Justice, Law and Order Sector (JLOS) in 2008, which was mandated to implement the accountability and reconciliation agreement signed in Juba; and the passing of the International Criminal Court Act in 2010. As discussed further in the next chapter, accountability issues were central to the Juba negotiations because the LRA saw the talks as an opportunity to remove the ICC arrest warrants against its leaders. Debates over complementarity – including the admissibility of northern Ugandan cases before the ICC and the relationship between the ICC and domestic approaches to justice – featured heavily in Juba and continued to shape the transitional justice sphere in Uganda even though the final peace agreement was never signed.

While on paper these reforms appear substantial, in practice they have delivered very little accountability for perpetrators of serious crimes. At a systemic level, the TJWG, which comprises five thematic sub-committees (war crimes prosecutions, truth and reconciliation, traditional justice, sustainable funding and integrated systems), drafted a National Transitional Justice Strategy in 2008. The National Strategy was designed to harmonise the various components of the Juba accountability and reconciliation agreement. This included balancing disparate elements such as the Amnesty Act, the ICD, traditional practices and victim reparations. Now in its sixth draft, the Strategy remains unimplemented and looks unlikely to be enacted any time soon.[6]

---

[6] For useful critiques of the National Transitional Justice Strategy, especially its focus on the LRA as opposed to other national conflicts and accountability solely for non-state actors, see M. Otim and S. Kasande, 'On the Path to Vindicate Victims' Rights in Uganda: Reflections on the Transitional Justice Process since Juba', International Center for Transitional Justice, June 2015; and A. Macdonald, 'Justice in Transition? Transitional Justice and its Discontents', Ph.D. thesis, King's College London, 2016.

More specifically, the passing of the International Criminal Court Bill in May 2010, following its initial tabling in parliament in December 2006,[7] was designed to embed the Rome Statute in Ugandan law and to strengthen further the government's resolve to pursue the LRA judicially.[8] De Vos argues that the start of the ICC review conference in Kampala on 31 May 2010 pressured the Ugandan parliament to pass the Bill.[9] That it stalled in parliament for three and a half years highlighted the government's reluctance to commit fully to the domestication of the Rome Statute, which some state actors feared could open new avenues for the prosecution of government atrocities during the LRA conflict. 'Within JLOS and all of the parliamentary committees, this was the biggest worry', said one NRM member of parliament who spoke on the guarantee of anonymity. 'The ICC was still new to us [in 2006]. We were still learning about it. We thought it would help deal with Kony but our lawyers were telling us to be careful. Once you start using international law, you can't always control it and it can be turned against you.'[10] As discussed in Chapter 3, though, the government's concerns that the ICC might pursue cases against state officials were short-lived.

Once it was passed, the ICC Act enabled the ICD to try cases of genocide, crimes against humanity and war crimes. Reflecting the agreements signed in Juba, however, this was limited to the prosecution of senior LRA leaders. 'The government got exactly what it wanted with the ICD', said Lyandro Komakech, senior researcher at

[7] J. Namutebi and J. Odyek, 'International Criminal Court Bill Out', *New Vision*, 5 December 2006, www.newvision.co.ug/new_vision/news/1135544/international-criminal-court.

[8] The ICC Bill, first drafted in 2004 and since modified, was designed to cement relations between Uganda and the ICC on complementarity and cooperation issues. Owiny-Dollo petitioned the government to withdraw the Bill on the grounds that it excluded the possibility of using alternative accountability mechanisms, such as northern Ugandan reconciliation rituals, a situation he describes as unacceptable to the LRA delegation in Juba, discussed further in the next chapter (quoted in H. Mukasa, 'Withdraw ICC Bill, Former Minister Pleads', *New Vision*, 17 December 2006, www.newvision.co.ug/new_vision/news/1134759/withdraw-icc-minister-pleads).

[9] C. De Vos, 'All Roads Lead to Rome: Implementation and Domestic Politics in Kenya and Uganda', in C. De Vos, S. Kendall and C. Stahn (eds.), *Contested Justice: The Politics and Practice of International Criminal Court Interventions*, Cambridge University Press, 2015, p. 380.

[10] Author's interview, NRM member of Ugandan parliament, Kampala, 9 August 2011.

the Refugee Law Project in Kampala. 'It was the vehicle to bring the ICC Statute into national law. That presented Uganda well to the world – "Look, we're in line with international law." But the ICD will deal only with rebel cases, not government cases. So the government can look good but also protect itself.'[11]

Even regarding LRA cases, the ICD has been heavily criticised for focusing only on relatively minor rebel leaders.[12] To date, the only case to have come before the ICD is that of Thomas Kwoyelo, a middle-ranking LRA commander charged with twelve counts of kidnapping with intent to murder. A more senior LRA commander, Maj. Gen. Caesar Acellam, was captured by Ugandan government forces in CAR in May 2012.[13] Acellam's crimes were investigated for two years and the government stated repeatedly that he would be prosecuted through the ICD.[14] In 2014, however, Acellam was integrated into the UPDF and granted an amnesty in March 2015.[15] The reasons behind Acellam's amnesty – and, more broadly, the apparent contradiction between the ICD and the national Amnesty Act – are explored in greater detail in the following chapter. As examined further in the next section, the Ugandan government also did not contest the transfer of LRA commander Dominic Ongwen to the ICC so that he could be prosecuted through the ICD, even though it had the domestic legislative and judicial means to do so.

Throughout these national judicial reforms, the ICC has played a highly variable role. It has arguably had a greater impact on the reform agenda in Uganda than the DRC but the depth of reform has been

---

[11] Author's interview, Lyandro Komakech, senior researcher, Refugee Law Project, Kampala, 6 April 2015.

[12] See various community-level and other perspectives expressed in A. Macdonald and H. Porter, 'The Trial of Thomas Kwoyelo: Opportunity or Spectre? Reflections from the Ground on the First LRA Prosecution', *Africa*, 86, 4, 2016, pp. 698–722.

[13] For a discussion of the ambiguity over whether Kwoyelo and Acellam defected or were captured and the relevance of this for amnesty determinations, see S. Ross, 'A Rebel's Escape – an LRA Commander Tells his Story', Justice in Conflict blog, 31 July 2013, https://justiceinconflict.org/2013/07/31/a-rebels-escape-an-lra-commander-tells-his-story/.

[14] See, for example, IRIN News, 'No More Amnesty Certificates for Rebels', 1 June 2012, www.irinnews.org/report/95569/uganda-no-more-amnesty-certificates-rebels.

[15] A. Otto, 'Top LRA Commanders, Returnees Undergo Ritual Cleansing', Uganda Radio Network, 9 March 2015, http://ugandaradionetwork.com/story/top-lra-commanders-returnees-undergo-ritual-cleansing.

substantially greater in the latter, as discussed below. Without the threat of ICC prosecutions of the LRA leadership, issues of account-ability are unlikely to have become so prominent during the Juba talks and to have led to the establishment of the ICD. At Juba, the LRA lobbied hard for national and community-based approaches to accountability, seeing these as a potential substitute for the ICC.[16] The Ugandan government, on the other hand, appeared to have more complex motives during these negotiations. While it could have insisted on the ICC as the only judicial mechanism necessary to handle the LRA, interviews with senior Ugandan officials and civil society participants in Juba suggest three issues shaped the government's eventual assent to national judicial reforms.

First, a critical factor was Museveni's pragmatic desire to keep on the table all possible responses to the LRA – a military solution, the Amnesty Act, the ICC and national prosecutions. One senior official in the MoD said in 2007, 'The President wants to keep his options open. The situation with the LRA changes so often. Sometimes they're weaker, other times they're stronger. They also move about the region a great deal. It would be unwise to remove one possible approach in favour of another until we know what we're dealing with.'[17]

This pragmatism includes creating a domestic judicial option that could thwart any future attempts by the ICC to pursue government cases. In this vein, Nouwen cites a statement in 2010 by Justice James Ogoola, the Principal Judge of the ICD, that it should be seen as a 'court of complementarity'[18] designed to bolster the state's capacity to address crimes within the ICC's remit. Nouwen argues that this shows that the ICC rather than the Juba agreement on accountability and reconciliation was the template for the creation of the ICD.[19] Boniface

---

[16] The following chapter dissects this issue in great detail.

[17] This degree of pragmatism extends beyond Museveni. Two key figures in the debates around Juba, Betty Bigombe and Alphonse Owiny-Dollo – both of whom had previously been Minister of State for Northern Uganda – were initially ardent opponents of the ICC and prosecutorial mechanisms generally, strongly favouring the national Amnesty Act. Later, though, both publicly advocated the ICC and the ICD – Owiny-Dollo was named a judge on the latter – as means to tackle the LRA. Bigombe's opposition to the ICC on the grounds that it jeopardised the peace talks she initiated with the LRA in 2004 and 2005 is discussed in detail in the next chapter.

[18] Nouwen, *Complementarity in the Line of Fire*, p. 181.   [19] Ibid., p. 185.

Ojok, then Director of the JRP in Gulu, echoed these views: 'The ICD is a back-up in case there are ever international investigations of the UPDF. That is one of the government's main motivations – to protect itself, just in case.'[20] Such thinking and the desire to leave all options open perhaps explains the continued legal tensions between the Amnesty Act and the ICD, which have arisen consistently in the Kwoyelo trial, and the government's lack of dedication to resolving these issues.[21]

Second, throughout the Juba negotiations there was severe external pressure on the Ugandan government to support the ICC and to block attempts to pause the ICC arrest warrants against the LRA for one year renewable, which is permissible under Article 18 of the Rome Statute. Strident advocacy by international human rights organisations and foreign donor support for the Court while opposing domestic remedies involving amnesties – coupled with pressure on domestic civil society to do likewise – heavily influenced the national agenda. During the Juba talks, HRW and AI issued numerous press releases emphasising Uganda's obligations to facilitate the ICC prosecution of the named LRA leaders and opposing the LRA's proposal that their leaders receive amnesties or pass through 'alternative accountability mechanisms' such as localised rituals.[22] The OTP issued similar statements, arguing that anything short of prosecution by the Court would violate international law.[23] Many Ugandan NGO representatives, especially in the north, criticised these international interventions in domestic debates. One NGO leader in Gulu said,

At Juba, our situation got hijacked by all these foreign groups like Amnesty [International] and ICTJ, using our case to support the ICC and say that there should always be international trials. But what about the voices of local people? We went to Juba but couldn't get our voices heard because all these

---

[20] Author's interview, Boniface Ojok, Director, JRP, Gulu, 15 August 2011.
[21] See also Macdonald and Porter, 'The Trial of Thomas Kwoyelo'.
[22] Human Rights Watch, 'Benchmarks for Assessing Possible National Alternatives to International Criminal Court Cases against LRA Leaders: A Human Rights Watch Memorandum', May 2007; Amnesty International, 'Amnesty International Letter to Security Council', AI Index: AFR 59/003/2008, 1 April 2008.
[23] International Criminal Court, Office of the Prosecutor, 'Statement by Luis Moreno Ocampo', 6 July 2006.

outsiders shouted louder than us. Then they turned to us and said, 'Don't you know about your international obligations? Do you want Kony to walk free?'[24]

Third, the Ugandan government sensed an opportunity to use the momentum after Juba to strengthen relations with international donors around law and order issues and to be seen to promote the rule of law. As Margaret Ajok, Transitional Justice Advisor to JLOS, said,

The ICD is the follow-up to Juba, guaranteeing accountability for war crimes. We never had any prosecutions here previously, only treason and other political cases, after all these rebellions. So the ICD is in line with our international obligations, showing our complementarity with the ICC. The government wants to test whether it can [deliver national justice] after the Juba outcry over the ICC and the disruption to the peace talks. The ICD has no problem with the ICC arrest warrants because complementarity is still in place. If the ICC relinquishes these cases, we would prosecute them here, then we would be fulfilling our obligations to the Rome Statute.[25]

Soon after the start of the Juba talks, international donors increased their sector-wide support for JLOS, particularly the transitional justice section that oversaw the establishment of the ICD. The JLOS Strategic Investment Plan for 2006/7 to 2010/11 underlines the increased coordination between the Ugandan government and international donors in two principal domains, criminal and commercial law, underpinned by Uganda's international legal obligations.[26]

Many local civil society actors and customary leaders view JLOS's donor-driven agenda as emphasising legalistic, prosecutorial approaches to transitional justice that are designed to assuage international concerns. In doing so, it diminishes processes that are viewed as more systematically addressing the legacies of mass conflict, including community-based reintegration rituals and victim reparations. Stephen Oola from the Refugee Law Project argues that JLOS, with heavy donor backing, rushed the ICC Bill through parliament and

[24] Author's interview, NGO representative, Gulu, 10 April 2015.
[25] Author's interview, Margaret Ajok, Transitional Justice Advisor, JLOS, Kampala, 30 August 2011.
[26] Justice, Law and Order Sector, 'JLOS Strategic Investment Plan II 2006/7 – 2010/11', p. 23, www.laspnet.org/index.php?view=document&alias=267-jlos-strategic-investment-plan-ii-20067-201011&category_slug=strategicplans& layout=default&option=com_docman& Itemid=837.

actively blocked debate over issues such as national reconciliation and reparations that were being advanced by various civil society and community-level actors.[27] Similarly, an NGO representative in Lira said, 'These days it's all about trials. If you support trials, the government is with you and the donors are with you. You can get funding and the government will listen to you. If you oppose trials, no one listens.'[28]

On this point, there is an apparent disjunct between some rural northern and other Ugandan civil society actors. A leader of a rural community-based organisation in Lango sub-region said,

Trials just stir up trouble. Those big NGOs in Gulu now just do what the government tells them. They take the money and they say, fine, we support prosecutions now. They used to criticise the ICC all the time. Now they say, 'Well, the ICC is already here, Ongwen is already there [in The Hague], so let's work with the ICC.'[29]

Numerous rural respondents argued that some civil society organisations have been swayed by the immense resources available for the national rule of law agenda, minimising any challenge to the government's and external actors' insistence on prosecutorial responses to the conflict in northern Uganda. In a general environment of civil society fatigue and state crackdown on NGOs – for example, through the 2014 Anti-Homosexuality Act and the 2015 NGO Act, both of which increased state surveillance and possible sanction of domestic civil society[30] – many respondents argue that some organisations have simply adopted the government's overall transitional justice approach.[31]

---

[27] S. Oola, 'In the Shadow of Kwoyelo's Trial: Complementarity in Practice in Uganda', in C. De Vos, S. Kendall and C. Stahn (eds.), *Contested Justice: The Politics and Practice of International Criminal Court Interventions*, Cambridge University Press, 2015, p. 166.

[28] Author's interview, civil society representative, Lira, 11 April 2015.

[29] Author's interview, civil society representative, Lira, 11 April 2015.

[30] See, for example, S. Thapa, 'LGBT Uganda Today Continue to Face Danger despite Nullification of Anti-Homosexuality Act', Human Rights Campaign, 30 September 2015, www.hrc.org/blog/lgbt-ugandans-continue-to-face-danger-despite-nullification-of-anti-homosex.

[31] Author's interviews, civil society representatives, Kampala, Gulu, Lira, 2013–15. For an astute analysis of the NRM's deliberate use of prospective legislation to divide and stifle Ugandan civil society, see T. Goodfellow, 'Legal Manoeuvres and Violence: Law Making, Protest and Semi-Authoritarianism in Uganda', *Development and Change*, 45, 4, 2014, pp. 753–6.

The confluence of ICC and donor impetus in Uganda reflects the broader pressure for domestic systems to mimic the Rome Statute if they wish to ward off the threat of international judicial intervention and to secure donor funding. De Vos argues that this reflects international criminal law's desire for uniformity[32] or what Luis Eslava calls the tendency of international law to smooth over the 'jumbledness' of local decision-making[33] in seeking the routinisation and internalisation of international norms.[34] This is magnified by donors' push for domestic systems to adopt 'international best practice' established through 'guidelines' such as the Rome Statute or the Commonwealth Model Law and stifles national and community-level decision-making regarding appropriate responses to mass violence.[35]

Assessing the ICC's role in domestic reforms, given the factors just discussed, it can be concluded that the Court's principal contribution was to structure the negotiations in Juba that led to the bolstering of JLOS and ultimately to the ICD, although other actors and interests were also crucial to these reforms. In practice, since Juba the national courts have lain largely dormant in terms of dealing with international crimes, with the ICD prosecuting only Kwoyelo for LRA atrocities. The broader legalism of JLOS's approach, though, has stifled national discussion of non-prosecutorial transitional justice options, including

---

[32] De Vos, 'All Roads Lead to Rome', pp. 380–1.
[33] L. Eslava, *Local Space, Global Life: The Everyday Operation of Law and Development*, Cambridge University Press, 2015, p. 17.
[34] Ibid., p. 19.
[35] De Vos, 'All Roads Lead to Rome', pp. 382–4. De Vos cites a statement by David Donat Cattin, Secretary-General of the influential Parliamentarians for Global Action, in 2012 that the principle of complementarity 'implies that States shall fully implement the Rome Statute in their domestic legal orders in order to comply with their primary responsibility to realize the object and purpose of the treaty (and [Rome Statute] system)', which is 'to put an end to the impunity of the [individual] perpetrators of the most serious crimes of concern to the international community as a whole and to contribute to the prevention of such crimes' (quoted in De Vos, 'All Roads Lead to Rome', p. 382). See also S. Dersso, 'The ICC's Africa Problem: A Spotlight on the Limits and Politics of International Criminal Justice', in K. Clarke, A. Knottnerus and E. de Volder (eds.), *Africa and the ICC: Perceptions of Justice*, Cambridge University Press, 2016, p. 67; S. Nouwen and W. Werner, 'Monopolizing Global Justice: International Criminal Law as Challenge to Human Diversity', *Journal of International Criminal Justice*, 13, 2015, pp. 157–76; Aas, '(In)security-at-a-Distance'; and P. Dixon and C. Tenove, 'International Criminal Justice as a Transnational Field: Rules, Authority and Victims', *International Journal of Transitional Justice*, 7, 2013, pp. 393–412.

the Amnesty Act and local rituals, as discussed in Chapters 6 and 7. The ICC's greatest legacy in this domain has been to precipitate an entrenched donor-driven rule of law industry in Uganda, with an overriding emphasis on trial-based approaches to transitional justice. This reflects the dominance of the legal conception of complementarity – and the superiority inherent in the distance perspective – in the ICC's attempts to reshape domestic judiciaries in the Court's image. As a result, a consistent feature of both the Ugandan government's judicial reforms and the work of the ICC is that they focus singularly on prosecuting LRA and not state crimes.

Domestic Judicial Reforms in the DRC

The DRC situation has followed a similar trajectory to Uganda's, with the civilian and military courts historically suffering enormous shortcomings – including a perception of distance from the local population, discussed earlier – some of which have been addressed through systematic reforms over the last decade. In contrast to the Ugandan case, the military courts in the DRC have been the focus of the most fundamental changes. Intervention by the ICC, however (because of chased cases and an overly cosy relationship with the Congolese government), risks undermining many of these reforms and the long-term prospects of a robust judiciary and the rule of law in the DRC.

The Congolese judicial system arguably started from a lower point than the Ugandan system but has witnessed more substantial reforms and greater effectiveness in dealing with serious crimes over the last decade, including those committed by state actors. A European Commission (EC)-funded reform process has bolstered the domestic courts, especially in Ituri, and enabled them to investigate and prosecute a wide range of war crimes and crimes against humanity. Within this process, the military courts have been the focus of attempts to address international crimes because, until an amendment in April 2013, Congolese law prohibited civilian courts from handling these cases.[36] Since then, the civilian courts have prosecuted very few such cases, perhaps

---

[36] Democratic Republic of Congo, 'Projet de Loi Modifiant et Complétant la Loi Organique No 13/011-B of April 11, 2013 portant Organisation, Fonctionnement, et Compétences des Juridictions de l'Ordre Judiciaire en Matière de Répression des Crimes de Génocide, des Crimes contre l'Humanité et des Crimes de Guerres', April 2014.

because the population generally prefers to seek redress through the military courts given their longer track record in this domain.

Since July 2003, the EC's Ituri-centred investment of more than US $40 million towards reforming the Congolese judiciary has seen considerable progress in local capacity. The EC launched the project to rebuild the judicial system in Bunia after a UN assessment team reported that the system in the town had completely collapsed.[37] This programme became the basis of the much broader Restoration of Justice in the East of the DRC (REJUSCO) initiative funded by the EC, Belgium, the Netherlands and Sweden, which extended to the Kivus and other provinces.[38] Implemented by the Belgian NGO Réseau des Citoyens-Citizens' Network (RCN), the project in Bunia aimed to establish the minimal operation of the local police and judiciary and to improve arrest and detention processes and facilities. The EC funded the purchase of new judicial offices and equipment and provided training and salaries for investigators and magistrates. Since 2003, MONUC (followed by MONUSCO) has provided around-the-clock protection to all judges in Bunia.[39] These developments have helped increase the efficiency of the Bunia judiciary. A year after the commencement of the EC project, 440 cases were under investigation in Bunia, mostly into low-level crimes but around 40 related to serious human rights violations, and 42 judgments had been handed down.[40] The last six months of 2004 produced 88 judgments in Bunia, rising to 258 in 2005, 312 in 2008 and 337 in 2016.[41] Chris Aberi, State Prosecutor in Bunia, said in 2006,

We have a different working spirit [in the judicial sector] in Ituri now because of the EC's involvement here. MONUC's protection has helped greatly as well. Judges now feel they can do their job without fear of intimidation. We have a different philosophy and energy for justice. The

---

[37] Author's interview, Esther Elkrieff, Consultant on Justice Sector in the DRC, EC, Kinshasa, 27 January 2006.

[38] European Commission, 'Press Release: The European Commission Contributes to the Restoration of Justice in the East of the Democratic Republic of Congo', 26 June 2006.

[39] Author's interviews, MONUC officials, Bunia, 15 February 2006.

[40] F. Borello, 'A First Few Steps: The Long Road to a Just Peace in the Democratic Republic of Congo', International Center for Transitional Justice, 2004, p. 27.

[41] Author's interviews, Chris Aberi, State Prosecutor, Bunia, 14 February 2006 and 11 September 2008. Author's telephone interviews, senior Bunia judicial official, 4 March 2016 and 13 January 2017.

appeals system works here. It is not like Kisangani, for example, where there have not been the same reforms, criminals are constantly freed and there is a loss of confidence in the justice system.[42]

These reforms enabled the Ituri courts to prosecute a string of high-level suspects for international crimes. In 2006, the military tribunal in Bunia prosecuted the case of Chef Mandro Panga Kahwa, a senior member of the UPC and later founder and president of PUSIC, who in 2005 had been imprisoned in Kinshasa along with Thomas Lubanga and Germain Katanga. Kahwa was found guilty of crimes against humanity, including the murder of villagers in Zumbe and Bedu Eze-kere in 2002, sentenced to twenty years in prison and ordered to pay compensation of up to $75,000 each to fourteen of his victims.[43] Among other serious cases before the Bunia courts, in 2006 the same military tribunal convicted a Congolese army captain, Blaise Bongi Massaba, for the murder of five students accused of looting during clashes between the FARDC and several Ituri rebel groups.[44] In 2007, the same tribunal sentenced five former FNI militiamen to life imprisonment for killing two MONUC military observers in Mongbwalu in 2003 and convicted Congolese army captain, François Mulesa Mulomba, and fourteen other FARDC soldiers for murder and rape in the village of Bavi in 2006.[45] The next year, the Bunia military tribunal convicted a Congolese army lieutenant and a sergeant for the use of rape and threats of violence against civilians in Fataki and Nioka.[46] That the Bunia courts have investigated and prosecuted such serious cases involving rebel leaders and senior Congolese military personnel highlights the substantial increase in domestic judicial capacity since the start of the EC reform programme.

---

[42] Author's interview, Chris Aberi, 14 February 2006.

[43] Trial Watch, 'Yves Mandro Kahwa Panga', last modified 14 June 2016, https://trialinternational.org/latest-post/yves-mandro-kahwa-panga/.

[44] Democratic Republic of Congo, Military Tribunal of Ituri, '*Military Prosecutor v. Massaba (Blaise Bongi)*, Criminal Trial Judgment and Accompanying Civil Action for Damages', RP No 018/2006, RMP No 242/PEN/06, ILDC 387 (CD 2006), 24 March 2006.

[45] Avocats sans Frontières, 'Analyse de Verdict: Condamnation des Militaires de la 1ere Brigade Integrée pour Crimes de Guerre, Tribunal Militaire de Garnison de Bunia, RD Congo – 19.02.2007', 23 March 2007, www.congoforum.be/fr/nieuwsdetail.asp?subitem=2&newsid=26121&Actualiteit=selected.

[46] United Nations Mission in the Democratic Republic of Congo, 'Human Rights Monthly Assessment: March 2008', 14 May 2008, section 34.

One of the most important reforms in the DRC judicial system has been the widespread use of mobile courts in eight provinces to address a wide range of cases, including those concerning international crimes. The most extensive mobile courts programme has focused on sexual and gender-based crimes in South Kivu and Maniema. A key innovation here is an international–domestic collaboration, with the mobile courts overseen exclusively by Congolese judges and lawyers but with funding and technical support from the American Bar Association/Rule of Law Initiative (ABA/ROLI), the Open Society Justice Initiative (OSJI) and the Open Society Initiative for Southern Africa (OSISA). The mobile courts are also an attempt to make justice more accessible to local populations by holding hearings close to the sites of alleged crimes. In their three years of operation between 2009 and 2012, 20 mobile courts heard 382 cases, leading to 204 rape convictions, 82 convictions for other crimes and 67 acquittals.[47] One of the highest-profile cases before the mobile courts led to the conviction of Lt. Col. Kibibi Mutuara and eight of his subordinates for crimes against humanity, specifically the rape and imprisonment of more than sixty women in the town of Fizi in South Kivu on New Year's Day in 2011. The court sentenced Mutuara to twenty years in jail.[48] Interviews with community-level actors in South Kivu elicit broad support for the mobile court process. 'I never thought I would see these army officials on trial', said Djoëlle, a victim of FARDC violence in Fizi. 'We have never seen this happen here. We thought it was completely impossible to hear them questioned about what they did.'[49] Armandine, a trader in Fizi, said,

Normally we can't get to the courts to watch the trials. They're far away in Bukavu and we can't leave our work to get there. To see the trials happening right here, in the middle of the town, is very important for the people...You can watch how the suspect acts. Is he nervous? You can hear what the judge says. And the army comes too [to observe], so we are all in one place watching – us and the army.[50]

---

[47] Open Society Foundations, 'Justice in DRC: Mobile Courts Combat Rape and Impunity in Eastern Congo', 14 January 2014, p. 7.
[48] BBC, 'DR Congo Colonel Kibibi Mutware Jailed for Mass Rape', 21 February 2011, www.bbc.co.uk/news/world-africa-12523847.
[49] Author's interview, Djoëlle, Fizi, 11 April 2013.
[50] Author's interview, Armandine, Fizi, 11 April 2013.

As in Uganda, the ICC has played a fluctuating role in the reforms of the Congolese national judiciary – such as those witnessed in the mobile courts – that have enabled them to address international crimes. The Rome Statute has helped clarify key aspects of the domestic legislative framework.[51] When the DRC ratified the Rome Statute in 2002, it also enacted a new Military Penal Code. The revised law, however, included amended definitions of genocide, crimes against humanity and war crimes that do not correspond with the Rome Statute. The military courts have found the new Penal Code difficult to implement, prompting some courts to apply the Rome Statute directly in their proceedings, for example in the Kahwa and Massaba cases.[52] Antonietta Trapani argues, 'The result on an individual case basis has been a move toward defining crimes more in line with international norms as perceived through the Rome Statute, and an increase in the use of international jurisprudence to support judicial decision making.'[53] In one early and prominent case in April 2006, seven soldiers from the 9th battalion of the FARDC (who represent mainly integrated militiamen from Jean-Pierre Bemba's MLC) were sentenced to life imprisonment by a military tribunal for their part in the gang rape of at least 119 women in the northern province of Equateur in December 2003.[54] For the first time in Congolese law, rape was characterised as a crime against humanity. 'The decision to [define rape in this way] is in line with the criteria laid down by the International Criminal Court', said Luc Henkinbrant, head of MONUC's Human Rights division in Kinshasa. 'The fact that the Congolese justice system has adopted these criteria is a very encouraging sign in

---

[51] For a comprehensive examination of this issue, see P. Labuda, 'The ICC in the Democratic Republic of Congo: A Decade of Partnership and Antagonism', in K. Clarke, A. Knottnerus and E. de Volder (eds.), *Africa and the ICC: Perceptions of Justice*, Cambridge University Press, 2016, pp. 277–99; and P. Labuda, 'Applying and "Misapplying" the Rome Statute in the Democratic Republic of Congo', in C. De Vos, S. Kendall and C. Stahn (eds.), *Contested Justice: The Politics and Practice of International Criminal Court Interventions*, Cambridge University Press, 2015, pp. 408–31.

[52] A. Trapani, 'Complementarity in the Congo: The Direct Application of the Rome Statute in the Military Courts of the DRC', DOMAC Project, DOMAC Paper 11, November 2011.

[53] Ibid., p. 5.

[54] IRIN News, 'DRC: Ex-Militiamen Get Life for Murdering UN Soldiers', 21 February 2007, www.irinnews.org/report/70288/drc-ex-militiamen-get-life-murdering-un-soldiers.

the fight against impunity in the Congo.'[55] It is not clear what motivated the military court's decision to define rape as a crime against humanity in this case nor why it chose this moment to adopt legal definitions from the Rome Statute. One senior Congolese NGO worker, however, claimed that such a move was intended to highlight crimes committed by former MLC militamen, to discredit Bemba and his party ahead of the 2006 elections.[56]

Despite these important legislative contributions, in practice the ICC has undermined national reforms, principally in the cases of the Ituri rebel leaders who were being investigated domestically before they were transferred to The Hague. As discussed in detail below, this move has demoralised key judicial actors in Ituri and sent a clear message throughout the Congolese judicial system that, despite wholesale improvements in the sector and even when tangible investigations are underway, the ICC will fight to prosecute such cases itself. Furthermore, as discussed in greater detail in the next section, the ICC has delayed on technical grounds the DRC's prosecution of Germain Katanga, following his trial and serving of his sentence in The Hague. Thus, the ICC has generally failed to live up to the three conceptions of complementarity discussed earlier, namely the political, relational and developmental perspectives, which emphasise deference, partnership and a catalytic potential, respectively.

More fundamental to these reforms in the DRC has been activism from within the Congolese judicial community, complex dynamics within the DRC transitional government (especially the activist role of the Vice Presidents, discussed in Chapter 3), with the support of external actors such as the EC, MONUSCO, ABA/ROLI, OSJI and OSISA. Crucially, these international actors have played a supportive and subordinate role to the Congolese courts, providing finance, evidence and logistical assistance but without undermining the ownership of national personnel. The ICC, in contrast, has competed directly with the military courts for jurisdiction over high-profile cases. This includes the ICC's refusal to share evidence that could be useful for domestic institutions; a point that Bernard Lavigne, the lead OTP investigator in

---

[55] Quoted in Agence France-Presse, 'DRC Soldiers, Serial Rapists, Jailed for "Crimes against Humanity"', 12 April 2006, www.reliefweb.int/rw/RWB.NSF/db900SID/ABES-6NSRRL?OpenDocument.

[56] Author's telephone interview, local human rights worker, Kinshasa, 15 April 2006.

the early phases of the Ituri cases, acknowledged in an interview with Katy Glassborow from the Institute for War and Peace Reporting (IWPR):

Lavigne said it was a 'mistake' not to hand over to the local judiciary evidence of sexual violence crimes gathered in the Lubanga investigation, after ICC prosecutors decided to focus exclusively on charges relating to child soldiers. 'It is a pity that we didn't hand over evidence [so local courts could organise sexual violence trials]', he said. 'Thanks to our resources, we collected forensic evidence that could have been useful for them, but the prosecutors were not interested in handing it over.'[57]

The irony of this situation is that the ICC has undermined national courts that have attempted a more difficult judicial task, namely pursuing the most serious charges – including murder and rape – against suspects, including government actors, which the ICC has avoided for the reasons of state cooperation discussed in Chapter 3. In both Uganda and the DRC, the ICC has thus adopted a distanced stance, viewing itself as superior to domestic judiciaries and thus undermining the political, relational and developmental conceptions of complementarity.

To Be or Not to Be Involved: Assessing Admissibility

This section examines issues of admissibility and the extent to which the ICC has legitimately claimed jurisdiction over particular cases or whether these should have been handled by the national courts in Uganda and the DRC. Building on the previous discussion of domestic judicial reforms, this section examines concrete moments of jurisdictional contestation between the ICC and domestic courts. In conceptual terms, this entails a fundamental focus on the legal conception of complementarity, which centres on admissibility determinations. As discussed in Chapter 2, the rules of admissibility in the Rome Statute include three instances in which the ICC *should not* investigate or prosecute cases: where states with jurisdiction are already investigating or prosecuting particular cases, while displaying a genuine willingness and ability to do so; where the crimes in question are considered of insufficient gravity to concern the ICC; or, where an investigation

---

[57] Glassborow, 'ICC Investigative Strategy under Fire'.

would not serve 'the interests of justice'. Rod Rastan, legal advisor to the OTP, argues that these three criteria constitute a 'contest model'[58] of admissibility in which 'the Rome Statute establishes the competence of the ICC judges to review the *bona fides* of national proceedings and, moreover, empowers the Court to recall cases previously deferred where it deems this appropriate'.[59] As Alexander Greenawalt argues, the Statute gives the Court extremely broad discretion to evaluate the adequacy of states' transitional justice policies, including criminal investigations and prosecutions; a highly controversial provision given ICC judges may not be familiar with the nuances and intricacies of domestic systems.[60]

This section analyses the ICC's case selection in Uganda and the DRC according to these three criteria within the legal conception of complementarity. The ICC's actions in moments of contestation with domestic courts, however, also impinge on the political, relational and developmental conceptions. Overall, this section argues that in both Uganda and the DRC, the ICC's chasing of state referrals undermined the legitimacy of its admissibility determinations and the efficacy of the national courts in handling international crimes. It also weakened the Court's claim to achieve distance from the domestic political terrain and underscored its role as one highly political actor among many.

Admissibility in Uganda

On 13 October 2005, the ICC issued arrest warrants for five LRA commanders: Joseph Kony, Vincent Otti, Raska Lukwiya, Okot Odhiambo and Dominic Ongwen. The warrants had originally been sealed on 8 July 2005, after the Prosecutor's application to PTC II for

---

[58] Rastan, 'Complementarity: Contest or Collaboration?', p. 104.

[59] Ibid., p. 87.

[60] A. Greenawalt, 'Complementarity in Crisis: Uganda, Alternative Justice, and the International Criminal Court', *Virginia Journal of International Law*, 50, 1, 2009, p. 110. As Nirej Sekhon argues, 'the prospect of a European-based court making political judgments about the quality of justice available in post-colonial states is symbolically fraught, to say the least' (N. Sekhon, 'Complementarity and Postcoloniality', *Emory International Law Journal*, 27, 2013, p. 816). See also C. Deprez, 'Foundations and Scope of the Human Rights Obligations of the International Criminal Court: Brief Overview of an Unsettled Question', *Revue de la Faculté de Droit de l'Université de Liège*, 3, 2014, pp. 475–93, on the extent to which the ICC functions as its own authority when determining its human rights obligations and those of states.

the warrants was brought forward following a press leak of his intended request.[61] The charges against the five commanders comprised a range of alleged war crimes and crimes against humanity during LRA attacks between July 2002 and July 2004.[62] The warrant for Kony's arrest accused him of thirty-three separate counts (twelve for crimes against humanity and twenty-one for war crimes) deriving from six separate attacks,[63] during which he was allegedly responsible for rape, murder, enslavement, sexual enslavement and forced enlisting of children.[64] The heavily redacted warrant did not indicate to which specific attacks the ICC's case referred. Announcing the unsealing of the arrest warrants, Ocampo justified the selection of LRA rather than UPDF cases on the basis of their relative gravity, invoking Article 53 of the Rome Statute, although he did not rule out investigating UPDF crimes in the future.[65] At a workshop in London in March 2007, Ocampo said, 'LRA killings were 100 times worse than those by the UPDF. There's no question we had to start by investigating LRA crimes.'[66] At the time of writing, three of the LRA commanders charged by the ICC (Lukwiya, Otti and Odhiambo) have died, leaving only Kony (who is still at large) and Ongwen (whose trial has commenced in The Hague).

The issue of admissibility in the LRA cases highlights three problems for the ICC and its legal conception of complementarity. First, the ICC's grounds for admissibility in these cases are questionable because of the Court's own limited capacity. The ICC's decision to open investigations in the Uganda situation was based on the gravity of the crimes

---

[61] International Criminal Court, Pre-Trial Chamber II, 'Situation in Uganda: Prosecutor's Application to Disclose to Internal Auditor Certain Information relating to the Amended Application for Warrants', 13 June 2005, p. 3. *Le Monde* published the leaked information on 12 June 2005 (S. Maupas, 'Le Procureur de la Cour Pénale Internationale Veut Inculper Deux Chefs Rebelles Ougandais', *Le Monde*, 12 June 2005, www.lemonde.fr/international/article/2005/06/11/le-procureur-de-la-cour-penale-internationale-veut-inculper-deux-chefs-rebelles-ougandais_660980_3210.html).

[62] International Criminal Court, Office of the Prosecutor, 'Statement by the Chief Prosecutor, Luis Moreno-Ocampo', 14 October 2005, p. 4.

[63] International Criminal Court, Pre-Trial Chamber II, 'Situation in Uganda: Warrant of Arrest for Joseph Kony Issued on 8 July 2005 as Amended on 27 September 2005', 27 September 2005.

[64] ICC, OTP, 'Statement by the Chief Prosecutor on the Uganda Arrest Warrants', p. 4.

[65] Ibid.

[66] Ocampo, 'The International Criminal Court and Prospects for Peace in Africa'.

reported and the fact that Uganda had not initiated judicial proceedings against suspected perpetrators of these crimes.[67] The latter, however, was not due to the inadequacy of the Ugandan judiciary – even in its referral, the Ugandan government claimed that '[t]he Ugandan judicial system is widely recognised as one of the most independent, impartial and competent on the African continent...There is no doubt that Ugandan courts have the capacity to give captured LRA leaders a fair and impartial trial'[68] – but rather the inability of Ugandan authorities to capture and arrest the LRA commanders who at that stage were located in southern Sudan. This differs from the DRC situation, discussed below, where the referral to the ICC was based on the perceived ineffectiveness of the entire Congolese judiciary.[69]

While the Rome Statute permits ICC investigations and prosecutions wherever domestic jurisdictions are not seeking to prosecute the same cases, the Uganda situation nonetheless poses problems in terms of the ICC's broader policy of complementarity. Even if it is considered justifiable for the ICC to open investigations on the basis that Uganda's military and police (rather than judicial) capacity was insufficient to address serious crimes, the ICC itself has neither military nor police capacity. The ICC therefore opened cases in northern Uganda on grounds for which it is not adequately equipped to respond. The ICC could not secure the transfer of any LRA suspects (and, as discussed earlier, had to hibernate the Ugandan situation) until the unexpected capture of Ongwen in 2015. Given the crucial role of Séléka in the transfer of Ongwen to The Hague, the ICC cannot reasonably claim that it inspired this move. It was rather the ICC's good fortune that a CAR-based rebel group – which was later subject to ICC investigations – cooperated with the US government, a non-signatory to the ICC, to hand over Ongwen.

This issue highlights the need to revisit the criteria of admissibility in the Rome Statute, particularly Article 17, which concerns the investigative and prosecutorial capabilities and actions of domestic

---

[67] International Criminal Court, Office of the Prosecutor, 'The Investigation in Northern Uganda: ICC OTP Press Conference', 14 October 2005.

[68] Government of Uganda, 'Referral of the Situation concerning the Lord's Resistance Army Submitted by the Republic of Uganda', 16 December 2003, section 25.

[69] Government of the Democratic Republic of Congo, 'Referral of the Situation in the Democratic Republic of Congo', 19 April 2004.

governments. None of these criteria concerns the reasonable capacities of the ICC to investigate and prosecute crimes effectively. The LRA cases highlight that, while the Ugandan state did not fulfil the admissibility criteria, neither did the ICC, which could not display a genuine ability to facilitate the arrest and transfer of any of the LRA suspects. As it stands, Article 17 places the onus on states to show that they fulfil the criteria for admissibility but assumes that the ICC will always be able and willing to deal with cases, despite its inherent reliance on cooperation with states (including principally in this instance the same state, Uganda, that was already deemed unable to arrest or transfer LRA suspects). Embedded within the 'burden-sharing' component of the ICC's relational conception of complementarity, as discussed in Chapter 2, is the belief that the ICC is always equipped to handle the cases of those considered most responsible for serious crimes and to determine the ideal 'division of labour' with domestic institutions. This sense of superiority is central to the ICC's distance discourse but problematic for all of the Court's conceptions of complementarity, including the legal interpretation.

Second, the Ongwen case highlights a further problem with the ICC's intervention in Uganda and its relations with domestic judiciaries more broadly, namely uncertainty over how to respond when states claim an inability to prosecute cases, despite possessing the clear capacity to do so. At the time of Ongwen's arrest, Uganda had established the ICD in the High Court. Not only did the ICD provide the legislative framework and operational structures to deal with a case such as Ongwen's but the Ugandan authorities possessed substantial evidence of his crimes, much of which they had shared with the ICC.[70] It is unclear therefore why the Ugandan government did not insist on Ongwen being prosecuted in the ICD. One explanation provided by several Ugandan sources is that Museveni viewed an ICC rather than domestic prosecution as less likely to involve close examination of UPDF crimes, given that the ICC's heavy reliance on state cooperation curtailed any investigations into the latter. This directly challenges the ICC's claims to delivering distanced, impartial justice. In contrast, any trial on Ugandan soil – in a febrile political atmosphere and closer to

---

[70] Author's interviews, Ugandan Ministry of Justice officials and ICC investigators, Kampala and The Hague, 2006–15.

affected communities – would inevitably generate extensive discussions of state complicity.[71]

Third, extending the argument developed in Chapter 3, Ocampo's claim that LRA crimes were clearly more grave than government crimes and therefore warranted prosecution requires closer scrutiny. At the London workshop in 2007 mentioned earlier, Ocampo and Brubacher from the OTP conceded that when they opened investigations in northern Uganda, they did not have a clear working definition of gravity beyond a quantitative assessment of the number of atrocity victims.[72] The OTP's four-criteria framework regarding gravity – the scale, nature, manner of commission and impact of crimes – emerged later.[73] This calls into question whether the OTP had developed sufficiently clear guidelines for its selection of crimes and suspects in northern Uganda.

Even taking into account the OTP's initial quantitative framework for gravity, though, it is still unclear why government crimes would not be considered sufficiently grave. Systematic analyses by numerous sources since 2002 when the Rome Statute came into force have documented serious crimes committed by the UPDF, including the mass forced displacement of the population into IDP camps as well as widespread murder, rape and torture, all of which constitute international crimes under the Rome Statute. The evidence for these crimes includes reports by international human rights groups upon which the OTP relied heavily in framing its own investigations.[74]

By the time the OTP had clarified its gravity criteria, investigations in northern Uganda were still in their early stages. This would have permitted a reappraisal of the OTP's strategy in line with these new criteria. In terms of the scale, nature and manner of the commission of Ugandan government crimes, it is unclear why these would not

---

[71] Author's interviews, Ugandan Ministry of Justice and JLOS officials, Kampala, 2–3 April 2015.

[72] Luis Moreno Ocampo and Matthew Brubacher, 'Peace, Justice and the ICC in Africa' workshop, Royal African Society, London, 8 March 2007, notes on file with author. David Bosco also argues that, before the ICC had opened any cases, its metric for determining possible situations was the number of violent deaths, leading to a three-country shortlist of the DRC, Colombia and Uganda (Bosco, *Rough Justice*, p. 90).

[73] International Criminal Court, Office of the Prosecutor, 'Policy Paper on the Interests of Justice', September 2007.

[74] Author's interviews, ICC officials, The Hague, 22 March 2006 and 7 May 2011.

warrant ICC prosecution. Furthermore, there can be no doubting the immense impact of UPDF crimes on the northern Ugandan population. As discussed in the previous chapter, the extreme gravity of government crimes is central to northern Ugandan populations' narrated experiences of the LRA conflict and their views on the actors most responsible for serious crimes.

Thus, in the Ugandan situation, the ICC's decision not to prosecute government cases is highly problematic. Given the close relationship between the ICC and the Ugandan state, it appears that, rather than a careful determination regarding gravity, the ICC has eschewed prosecuting state actors because of its heavy reliance on the government for the situation referral, on-the-ground security and evidence-sharing.[75] When challenged on this issue, Ocampo and other senior OTP officials have emphasised the Court's limited resources, which ensure that it cannot investigate and prosecute all cases at all times.[76] However, as Uganda was the first of the ICC's investigations and the Court at the time did not suffer the severe overstretch across Africa that it experiences today, the resource argument is unconvincing.

While the ICC's sole focus on LRA crimes is unjustifiable according to its own principles in the Rome Statute and its working criteria regarding gravity, the Court also – along with foreign donors – should have pressed the Ugandan government more strongly to handle the Ongwen case through the domestic ICD. That the Ugandan government ultimately did not contest Ongwen's transfer to The Hague highlighted the state's belief that its political and legal interests were better served by an international prosecution, even though it possessed the capacity to prosecute Ongwen at home. Some JLOS officials argued that Ongwen should be prosecuted in the ICD on the grounds that Uganda's new legislative framework was designed specifically for such a case and this would provide an ideal opportunity to showcase the extent of Uganda's judicial reforms. It would also increase the popular legitimacy of the ICD, which has been heavily criticised for the lengthy and fraught prosecution of Kwoyelo and confusion over why Acellam received an amnesty.[77] Echoing the earlier theme regarding state

---

[75] For further discussion on this point, see W. Schabas, 'Prosecutorial Discretion v. Judicial Activism at the International Criminal Court', *Journal of International Criminal Justice*, 6, 2008, pp. 731–61.

[76] See, for example, 'Peace, Justice and the ICC in Africa' workshop.

[77] Author's interviews, JLOS officials, Kampala, 2–3 April 2015.

referrals, crucial to these dynamics around the Ongwen case is the primacy of the executive branch – even when contested by domestic judicial actors – and the ICC's tendency to favour relations with the executive rather than the judiciary when determining the admissibility of cases. This has bolstered these executives and weakened the role of national judicial actors, with lasting and negative consequences. In turn, this has greatly undermined the political, relational and developmental conceptions of complementarity.

Admissibility in the DRC

In the DRC, the ICC has charged six suspects – Thomas Lubanga, Bosco Ntaganda, Germain Katanga, Mathieu Ngudjolo, Callixte Mbarushimana and Sylvestre Mudacumura – the first four concerning crimes in Ituri and the last two in North and South Kivu. The ICC charged Lubanga with three counts of war crimes: enlisting children under the age of fifteen years, conscripting them to the armed forces of the UPC and using them to participate actively in hostilities.[78] In 2012, he was found guilty of all charges and sentenced to fourteen years in jail. Ntaganda, whose trial is ongoing, was charged with thirteen counts of war crimes and five counts of crimes against humanity, including murder, rape and conscription of child soldiers. Katanga and Ngudjolo were both charged with six counts of war crimes and three of crimes against humanity, including murder, sexual slavery and conscription of children, all stemming from a joint FRPI–FNI attack on the village of Bogoro in Ituri on 24 February 2003.[79] In 2012, Ngudjolo was acquitted on all charges, while in 2014 Katanga was found guilty of five out of the nine charges against him and sentenced to twelve years' imprisonment. As discussed earlier, in 2011 PTC I declined to confirm any of the thirteen charges (eight for war crimes and five for crimes against humanity) against Mbarushimana.

---

[78] International Criminal Court, Pre-Trial Chamber I, 'Decision on the Confirmation of Charges', Situation in the Democratic Republic of Congo, *The Prosecutor v. Thomas Lubango Dyilo*, 29 January 2007.

[79] International Criminal Court, Pre-Trial Chamber I, 'Decision on the Confirmation of Charges', Situation in the Democratic Republic of Congo, *The Prosecutor v. Germain Katanga and Mathieu Ngudjolo Chui*, 30 September 2008.

Meanwhile, Mudacumura, who is still at large, is charged with nine counts of war crimes, including murder, mutilation, rape and torture.[80]

In the early DRC cases, the OTP had a tougher task convincing the PTC judges of the admissibility of the cases than in Uganda. In the four Congolese cases to reach trial – those of the Ituri rebel leaders, Lubanga, Ntaganda, Katanga and Ngudjolo – the OTP initially argued that there were no domestic investigations or prosecutions underway against these individuals and regardless, in its current condition, the Congolese judiciary did not display a genuine willingness or ability to handle these cases. Regarding Lubanga, Ocampo told the Pre-Trial judges that the Congolese file against him was 'literally empty'.[81] The judges found, however, that 'certain changes' in the function of the Congolese judiciary – namely the EC reforms in Ituri outlined earlier – contradicted Ocampo's depiction.[82] They ruled the four Ituri cases admissible nonetheless based on the 'same person, same conduct' test, which holds that the ICC can pursue cases against suspects who are also subject to domestic investigations, provided the criminal conduct with which they are charged differs from the domestic charges. That the OTP charged Lubanga and Ntaganda only with crimes regarding child soldiers (the charges against Ntaganda were expanded in 2012), while the Congolese judiciary charged them with genocide and war crimes, rendered these cases admissible to the ICC under the Rome Statute because, as the judges reasoned, the Congolese authorities were not acting on 'the specific case before the [ICC]'.[83] Similarly, while Katanga and Ngudjolo were charged domestically with a range of

[80] International Criminal Court, Office of the Prosecutor, 'Mudacumura Case', Situation in the Democratic Republic of Congo, *The Prosecutor v. Sylvestre Mudacumura*.

[81] International Criminal Court, Pre-Trial Chamber I, 'Redacted Version of the Transcript of the Hearing Held on 2 February 2006 and Certain Materials Presented during That Hearing', Situation in the Democratic Republic of Congo, *The Prosecutor v. Thomas Lubango Dyilo*, 22 March 2006, p. 39.

[82] International Criminal Court, Pre-Trial Chamber I, 'Decision concerning Pre-Trial Chamber I's Decision of 10 February 2006 and the Incorporation of Documents into the Case against Mr. Thomas Lubanga Dyilo, Annex I: Decision on the Prosecutor's Application for a Warrant of Arrest, Article 58', 27 February 2006, para. 36.

[83] Ibid., paras. 38–9.

genocide crimes and crimes against humanity, the OTP's charges were different and thus the PTC ruled their cases admissible.[84]

The rest of this section highlights several major admissibility problems in the ICC's Ituri cases. First, while the 'same person, same conduct' test used in these cases is legally valid, it is heavily skewed toward ICC rather than national jurisdiction. The test requires only that the OTP's charges against a suspect differ from those brought domestically. These charges do not need to be more grave or comprehensive than the domestic charges, only different. The scope for the OTP to bring charges even slightly divergent from those brought domestically appears infinite when the OTP can wait until national institutions lay their charges before announcing their own. In other words, in any tussle between the ICC and national judiciaries over admissibility issues involving the 'same conduct' test, the ICC is effectively guaranteed to prevail.

These issues came to a head when Katanga challenged the admissibility of his case in 2009. Katanga's defence counsel argued that, rather than the 'same conduct' test, the Court should apply a test of 'comparative gravity' or 'comprehensive conduct'.[85] Because the domestic charges against him were both more grave and more comprehensive than the OTP's (genocide and war crimes as opposed to the ICC's charges regarding child soldiers), the Defence argued that he should be prosecuted in the DRC. The Appeals Chamber ultimately rejected the Defence argument, not on substantive grounds regarding the relative gravity and comprehensiveness of the respective charges but on the

---

[84] International Criminal Court, Pre-Trial Chamber I, 'Decision on the Evidence and Information Provided by the Prosecution for the Issuance of a Warrant of Arrest for Mathieu Ngudjolo Chui', Situation in the Democratic Republic of Congo, *The Prosecutor v. Germain Katanga and Mathieu Ngudjolo Chui*, 6 July 2007; International Criminal Court, Appeals Chamber, 'Judgment on the Appeal of Mr. Germain Katanga against the Oral Decision of Trial Chamber II of 12 June 2009 on the Admissibility of the Case', Situation in the Democratic Republic of Congo, *The Prosecutor v. Germain Katanga and Mathieu Ngudjolo Chui*, 25 September 2009.

[85] International Criminal Court, Trial Chamber II, 'Motion Challenging the Admissibility of the Case by the Defence of Germain Katanga, Pursuant to Article 19 (2) (a) of the Statute', Situation in the Democratic Republic of Congo, *The Prosecutor v. Germain Katanga and Mathieu Ngudjolo Chui*, 11 March 2009, paras. 46–7.

legal grounds that the 'same conduct' test comports with the admissibility criteria outlined in the Rome Statute.[86]

Considering those substantive grounds, the 'same conduct' threshold does not appear to serve the purposes of complementarity or the wider pursuit of justice for serious crimes.[87] Arguably little is gained by denying the DRC the opportunity to prosecute Lubanga, Ntaganda, Katanga and Ngudjolo simply to enable the ICC to prosecute them on narrower charges. The singular focus on child soldier crimes in Lubanga and Ntaganda is particularly questionable in this regard. As Katy Glassborow from IWPR wrote in 2008, based on interviews with various current and former ICC investigators:

> Those investigating war crimes in DRC expressed frustration that one day, without explanation, prosecutors told the team probing...Lubanga, to drop a year and a half of investigative work and focus solely on the use of child soldiers. In the course of investigating incidents like mass killings in a village, they say they had also found evidence of torture, pillage, rape, and enslavement. 'It was bizarre and surprising', said a former investigator. 'We had been investigating killings, attacks on villages, the flow of illegal weapons – but one day a decision was made to focus just on child soldiers.' The same ex-employee says he thought that this might have happened because the investigation had already taken a long time, and prosecutors wanted something to present at court as soon as possible.[88]

Ocampo was well aware of these problems at the opening of the Lubanga prosecution. At the press conference on 17 March 2006 to announce Lubanga's arrival in The Hague that day – the ICC's first ever suspect in custody – Ocampo stated that, while only limited charges had been brought against Lubanga, the OTP left open the possibility of bringing further charges as more evidence emerged. Without stating it, he may have believed such pragmatism was necessary to avoid interminable trials such as that of Slobodan Milošević at the ICTY. Milošević had died in The Hague six days earlier, before his

---

[86] ICC, Appeals Chamber, 'Judgment on the Appeal of Mr. Germain Katanga'.

[87] Rastan provides a solid doctrinal defence of the 'same person, same conduct' test. However, he fails to address the problem of the ICC's capacity to amend charges to guarantee jurisdiction or the extent to which the conceptions of complementarity other than the strictly legal one are served by the 'same person, same conduct' approach (Rastan, 'What is "Substantially the Same Conduct?"').

[88] Glassborow, 'ICC Investigative Strategy under Fire'.

trial could be completed.[89] In an earlier closed door session attended by the author, OTP staff played the role of journalists to prepare Ocampo for the historic press conference. This included posing questions about the narrow charges against Lubanga. When Ocampo ventured that there would be scope for expanding the charges later, several staff advised him strongly against this response, as it made the OTP seem at best ill-prepared and at worst cherry-picking the charges considered most likely to secure a conviction rather than arguably more serious charges such as murder and rape.[90] That Ocampo ignored this advice and during the press conference repeated the line about the possibility of amending the charges against Lubanga provoked immense consternation among OTP staff and several barbed questions from journalists.[91]

The ICC's determination of admissibility in the Ituri cases is also highly problematic in light of national political dimensions. Crucial to any consideration of the ICC's operations in the DRC is the opposition to the Court's intervention by senior judicial officials in Ituri. In the Ituri cases, the ICC accepted the Congolese government's argument that it was unwilling and unable to prosecute the cases of Lubanga, Ntaganda, Katanga and Ngudjolo. As mentioned earlier, Katanga's defence counsel contested this point in 2009 on the grounds that legal proceedings were already underway against their client in the DRC before the ICC intervened.[92] They cited the Pre-Trial judges' rejection in the Lubanga case of the OTP's assertion that the Congolese judiciary was inactive in investigating Lubanga and Ntaganda, which included a detailed description of the nature of the domestic investigations.[93] The Trial judges rejected this argument, citing 'the explicit statements of the representatives of the authorities of the DRC' that they had not commenced legal proceedings against Katanga and had referred the DRC situation to the ICC in order to stem impunity in the country.[94]

---

[89] BBC, 'Milosevic Found Dead in his Cell', 11 March 2006, http://news.bbc .co.uk/1/hi/world/europe/4796470.stm.

[90] ICC, OTP meeting, The Hague, 17 March 2006, notes on file with author.

[91] ICC, OTP press conference, The Hague, 17 March 2006, notes on file with author.

[92] ICC, Trial Chamber II, 'Motion Challenging the Admissibility of the Case by the Defence of Germain Katanga'.

[93] Ibid., para. 30.

[94] International Criminal Court, Trial Chamber II, 'Reason for the Oral Decision on the Motion Challenging the Admissibility of the Case (Article 19 of the

The 'authorities of the DRC' in this instance, however, were representatives of the Congolese executive – the main category of Congolese state actors with which the OTP interacted – as well as the Director of the Immediate Office of the Chief Prosecutor of the High Military Court in Kinshasa, who sent a letter to the ICC Prosecutor stating that the Military Prosecuting Authority had not initiated proceedings against Katanga.[95] However, interviews with senior judicial officials in Ituri – who are also state-appointed (nominated by the President and elected by the Ministry of Justice) – indicated that they did not share the Kinshasa authorities' view regarding unwillingness and inability to investigate and prosecute serious cases such as those of the four Ituri suspects. In contrast to Kabila and other Kinshasa-based officials, the two most senior Ituri-based prosecutors, Chris Aberi, the State Prosecutor, and John Penza, the Military Prosecutor, argued that the Bunia courts were already investigating a range of serious cases, including those of Lubanga, Ntaganda, Katanga and Ngudjolo. 'When the ICC first came here', Aberi said, 'we showed them the dossiers we had already assembled on Lubanga and others. We were ready to try those cases here. We had the capacity to do this and it would have had a major impact for the people here, to see these [rebel] leaders standing trial in the local courthouse.'[96] Penza argued:

You only have to look at our record here to know what we are capable of. With MONUC's help, we prosecuted Kahwa here – MONUC detained him and we prosecuted him...We found the mass grave at Bavi and we prosecuted [Congolese army captain François Mulesa] Mulombo and his men in connection with that...The ICC is certainly a necessary thing but it should be handling bigger cases than those [it is currently prosecuting].[97]

Given such views of the senior judicial officials closest to the Ituri situation, the ICC Trial judges erred in claiming that the Congolese state had voluntarily relinquished jurisdiction over the Lubanga, Ntaganda, Katanga and Ngudjolo cases. The judges should also have given greater weight to the account of the domestic investigations cited in the Pre-Trial judgment, as opposed to the statements of the Kinshasa officials. This points to a lacuna in the Trial judges' reasoning, as well

---

Statute)', Situation in the Democratic Republic of Congo, *The Prosecutor v. Germain Katanga and Mathieu Ngudjolo Chui*, 16 June 2009, para. 92.
[95] Ibid., para. 93.   [96] Author's interview, Chris Aberi, 11 September 2008.
[97] Author's interview, John Penza, Military Prosecutor, Bunia, 10 September 2008.

as the arguments formulated by Katanga's defence counsel, namely treating the Congolese state or the 'Congolese authorities' as a unitary actor when in fact there may be substantial disagreement within the state on matters pertaining to serious criminal cases. In such a situation, it is insufficient for the ICC to accept the claims of one group of state actors when others – particularly provincial-level judicial officials with detailed knowledge of local capacity and the progress of local investigations – strongly contest these claims. The Trial Chamber's failure to address more systematically the nature of the domestic proceedings against the Ituri warlords (and arguably also the Defence's failure to fully reflect this reality in its case) denied the Court the opportunity to establish a clearer set of criteria for a 'genuine domestic proceeding', which would be key in adjudicating future admissibility challenges in other countries, as discussed in Chapter 8.[98]

This is critical in situations such as in the DRC (arguably more so than in Uganda), which, as discussed in Chapter 3, manifest a high degree of state fragmentation and internal contestation over government authority. Crucial in the DRC case are political divisions between Kabila on the one hand and two of the Vice Presidents, Bemba and Ruberwa, on the other, regarding the benefits of involving the ICC rather than the national courts in the prosecution of serious crimes. While Kabila and his coterie informed the ICC that the DRC was unwilling and unable to deal with serious cases, this view was directly challenged by a range of other actors, including Ituri-based judicial actors and the international donors and MONUC that were assisting judicial reform in Ituri. 'Ituri is easy for the ICC', one foreign diplomat in Kinshasa said. 'MONUC have all the information on cases there. The dossiers are ready to go. Did we really fight all those political and legal battles to create the ICC only to have it try the easiest cases?'[99]

---

[98] In 2010, Brubacher from the OTP admitted to the problems created by the lack of clear criteria in this respect. He stated that, in the absence of criteria established by any Trial Chamber ruling, the OTP was adopting a strict interpretation of the 'interests of justice' when considering whether to relinquish jurisdiction over particular cases. In this regard, 'the direction in which the OTP [was] going' reflected an HRW report advocating a strict approach that would cede jurisdiction to domestic institutions or halt ICC investigations for the sake of peace processes only in the most exceptional circumstances (Brubacher, 'The ICC Investigation of the Lord's Resistance Army', p. 267).

[99] Author's interview, foreign diplomat, Kinshasa, 25 January 2006.

The ICC judges' reasoning also did not account for the possibility that, in referring the DRC situation to the ICC, the Congolese authorities may have instrumental political interests. Similar to the Ugandan situation, for example, they may have wished to aid the Court in prosecuting rebel leaders to deflect attention from atrocities committed by state actors, or simply to gain international legitimacy by being seen to cooperate with the ICC. The Trial judges' own decision incorporates evidence suggesting the latter motivation underpinned the Congolese authorities' reasoning. The judges cite the letter from DRC government representatives, partly quoted earlier, which states that they

consider that the ICC must reject the challenge to admissibility made by the Defence for Germain Katanga so that Mr. Katanga may effectively be prosecuted before the ICC. In rejecting this challenge, the ICC will be doing justice to the DRC, a country devastated by the countless number of victims of atrocities (5 million dead and 3 million war-displaced), regarding which His Excellency Mr Joseph Kabila Kabange, President of the DRC, has demonstrated to the world his determination to fight resolutely against impunity by making the DRC to date an unequalled model of cooperation with the ICC. This is the official position of the DRC regarding the challenge to admissibility.[100]

That a state claims it is unwilling or unable to address serious crimes does not inherently mean that is the case, and further analysis of these claims must be undertaken. The negotiators of the Rome Statute assumed a high degree of state reluctance to engage with the ICC and to refer situations to the Court.[101] Key aspects of the Statute and much of the thinking of Court officials – particularly judges – appear grounded in this assumption and therefore neglect the possibility that states will seek to manipulate the referral process for their own political gain. Furthermore, the ICC's distancing from the local terrain through the almost exclusive use of generalist and non-African, rather than Africa-specialist, staff casts doubt on the capacity of all branches of the Court to analyse the function of domestic judiciaries and the motives behind domestic political decision-making. This critical

---

[100] Quoted in ICC, Trial Chamber II, 'Reason for the Oral Decision on the Motion', para. 94.
[101] For further discussion of this point, see W. Schabas, *An Introduction to the International Criminal Court* (5th edition), Cambridge University Press, 2017, ch. 2.

component of the ICC's distance – forgoing country-specific experts in favour of legal and technical specialists – weakens the Court's ability to judge these complex and nuanced issues that are central to admissibility determinations.

In the Ituri cases, the ICC's decisions on the basis of complementarity have been overly determined by Kabila and the Congolese executive. The impact of these decisions domestically has been widespread disappointment among judicial actors in Ituri that, despite the extensive legal reforms of the last fourteen years, they will not be able to prosecute some of the most important atrocity suspects in local courtrooms.[102] This has important ramifications for the long-term legitimacy and efficacy of the domestic judiciary. It also leads some domestic judicial actors to believe they are receiving mixed messages from the international community, which has invested heavily in legal reform but maintains that such reforms are insufficient to warrant domestic trials of high-profile suspects.[103] Overall, in the DRC situation, the ICC's active pursuit of a referral by the Congolese state has afforded national political authorities considerable influence over the nature and scope of the Court's operations, to the detriment of complementarity and the long-term cause of domestic justice in the DRC.[104]

Echoing the Uganda case above, further questions arise over whether the ICC itself is capable of investigating and prosecuting cases in a complex environment of ongoing conflict such as Ituri. The 'burden-sharing' aspect of complementarity does not appear to countenance this possibility, as it assumes that in principle there will always be a role for the ICC. The only question raised by the relational conception of complementarity is whether – and regarding which specific criminal cases – there is a justifiable role for the national courts. To date, the Ituri cases before the ICC suggest that the Court has struggled to conduct robust proceedings and, in some instances, even to match the judicial performance of the domestic courts in Ituri. The Lubanga, Ngudjolo and Katanga cases before the ICC were bedevilled by

[102] Author's interviews, Congolese judicial officials, Bunia, 2008–15.
[103] Author's interviews, Congolese judicial officials, Bunia, 9–13 September 2008.
[104] This reinforces Sekhon's observation that the ICC's practice of complementarity to date reinforces notions of governmentality insofar as it structures a dialogue among technocratic elites at the international and national levels, limiting 'deliberate openness' and various subaltern voices (Sekhon, 'Complementarity and Postcoloniality', p. 826).

investigative problems and the cutting of corners examined in Chapter 2, not least the over-reliance on intermediaries and evidence supplied by international human rights organisations.[105] Similar issues are likely to arise in the Ntaganda case, given this was investigated at the same time and with the same methods as the other three Ituri suspects. Numerous commentators have argued that the Lubanga case was fortunate not to collapse twice, rather than being stayed, given the Prosecution's evidentiary blunders.[106] Similar issues arose in the Katanga trial and led to the acquittal of Ngudjolo (in which, as discussed earlier, the judges who had travelled to the atrocity sites in Ituri criticised the OTP investigators for their distanced approaches). A Congolese investigator in Bunia who had worked on the Ngudjolo case in the Ituri courts said, 'That is the tragedy of this situation. The ICC stole these cases from us and has done a worse job. What was the point of sending these suspects to The Hague, to face a lower standard of justice?'[107]

The Bunia courts have faced some of the same challenges as the ICC but possess inherent advantages over distanced prosecutions in The Hague, including a greater willingness to investigate state crimes. Highlighting the immense difficulties confronting national prosecutions, during one period of fieldwork in 2006, the State Prosecutor in Bunia was investigating three high-level militia leaders – Ngudjolo of the FNI, Prince Mugabo of PUSIC and Aimable Rafiki of the UPC – for their alleged involvement in the massacre of around 100 civilians in the Ituri village of Tchomia in May 2004. At the time, all three suspects were detained in the MONUC barracks in Bunia.[108] Because it had proven impossible to gather sufficient evidence regarding the Tchomia massacre, however, the State Prosecutor was forced to indict the militia leaders on less serious counts. Mugabo, suspected of committing major atrocities, was eventually convicted for the armed robbery of a stereo

---

[105] See also Kambale, 'A Story of Missed Opportunities'.
[106] See, for example, D. Jacobs, 'The Lubanga Trial Is Stayed, the Slapstick Comedy Continues…But Isn't the Joke Wearing a Little Thin?', Spreading the Jam blog, 9 July 2010, https://dovjacobs.com/2010/07/09/the-lubanga-trial-is-stayed-the-slapstick-comedy-continues-but-isnt-the-joke-wearing-a-little-thin/; and Radio Netherlands Worldwide, 'ICC's First Trial at Risk as Prosecutor Ignores Judges' Orders', 14 July 2010, www.rnw.org/archive/iccs-first-trial-risk-prosecution-ignores-judges-orders.
[107] Author's interview, Congolese investigator, Bunia, 15 April 2013.
[108] Author's interview, Chris Aberi, 14 February 2006.

system, while Ngudjolo and Rafiki were each convicted for committing single murders. The case against Ngudjolo nearly fell apart when all Prosecution witnesses bar one withdrew their statements against him and the remaining witness withdrew his testimony after receiving death threats.[109]

These examples underscore why we should not romanticise the capacity of the national courts to address serious crimes and the low base from which they have begun reforms. Nevertheless, to date the ICC has not shown that it is capable of prosecuting cases to a higher standard than the Bunia courts. On the contrary, the substantial difficulties confronting the ICC cases, which led to the two stays in proceedings against Lubanga and the acquittal of Ngudjolo, show that it has fundamentally struggled in this regard. Despite the inevitable challenges facing both international and domestic prosecutions in this context, domestic trials have two further inherent advantages to the ICC, namely a higher degree of visibility among the local population (especially given the OTP's consistent opposition to holding *in situ* ICC hearings in Ituri)[110] and the bolstering of the domestic judicial system that will remain responsible for handling cases of international crimes long after the ICC has moved on from the Congolese situation.

Finally, in December 2015 Katanga returned to the DRC, having served his sentence in The Hague. He now faces a domestic prosecution in the DRC on the original charges levelled against him before the ICC assumed jurisdiction over his case. Having served a relatively lenient sentence courtesy of the ICC – twelve years, reduced to five because of the time he spent in custody during his trial – Katanga has returned to face trial for more serious charges in the DRC, which judicial actors in Ituri argue he should have faced in the first instance. More vexing for local actors is the fact that, according to the Rome Statute, the DRC was forced to wait for the ICC's approval to prosecute Katanga on these new charges, which was granted in April 2016.[111] In the eyes of the Ituri jurists, they were required to seek the

---

[109] Ibid.

[110] See, for example, W. Wakabi, 'Challenges of Holding Ntaganda's Trial in Congo', International Justice Monitor, 20 March 2015, www.ijmonitor.org/2015/03/challenges-of-holding-ntagandas-trial-in-congo/.

[111] International Criminal Court, The Presidency, 'Decision Pursuant to Article 108(1) of the Statute', Situation in the Democratic Republic of Congo, *The Prosecutor v. Germain Katanga*, 7 April 2016.

permission of the foreign institution that stole Katanga's case so that they can now prosecute him in the way they had intended before the ICC intervened.[112]

This section has highlighted key problems with the ICC's admissibility determinations in both Uganda and the DRC. While the selection of suspects and criminal cases has typically cohered with the legal interpretation of complementarity, it poses substantial difficulties for the other three conceptions. Regarding the political interpretation, the Court has displayed limited deference to domestic judicial institutions even when, as in the DRC case, national actors were already investigating the same suspects who were eventually transferred to The Hague. These actions also undermine the relational conception of complementarity, with the ICC preferencing its own jurisdiction over the claims of national actors, thus weakening any notion of partnership, interdependence or division of labour between international and domestic courts. This leaves limited scope for the developmental conception of complementarity, specifically the notion of positive complementarity, as the ICC has replaced rather than catalysed domestic prosecutions. In both Uganda and the DRC, domestic judicial infrastructure is being developed but circumvented by the ICC.

Conclusion

As analysed throughout this chapter, by stymieing key domestic judicial reforms and elevating ICC over domestic admissibility in Uganda and the DRC, the ICC has embodied the political and philosophical conceptions of distance outlined in Chapter 2. This includes viewing itself as superior to domestic prosecutions while eschewing the fine-grained contextual analysis of judicial processes and the motives behind them that should have made the Court more reluctant to intervene in the two countries. This highlights the complacency of complementarity. While the Court has expressed a weddedness to notions of deference, partnership and cooperation, in practice it has insisted on its own jurisdiction whenever challenged by domestic courts. The net result is that the ICC, which has failed to show itself to be technically superior to, and beholden to the same logistical and

---

[112] Author's telephone interviews, Congolese prosecutors and lawyers, January–February 2016.

political challenges as, domestic courts has weakened the capacity of national institutions to investigate and prosecute international crimes. This includes undermining domestic judicial institutions that, particularly in the DRC case, are currently engaged in a tussle with the national executive over the extent of their authority and their ability to hold state actors accountable. When coupled with the ICC's bolstering of the national executives in Uganda and the DRC, as examined in earlier chapters, this blunts the effectiveness of the judiciary in checking executive power, with deep and lasting consequences for the conduct of national politics.

6 | *Peace versus Justice* Redux

The ICC, Amnesties and Peace Negotiations

Introduction

This chapter examines the ICC's intersections with two domestic conflict resolution processes, national amnesties and peace negotiations. In
doing so, it connects to two overarching debates, namely the appropriateness and legality of amnesties as opposed to prosecutions for
suspected perpetrators of international crimes,[1] and the 'peace versus
justice' debate over whether the threat of prosecution imperils peace
negotiations that involve high-level suspects.[2] These issues coincided
during the Juba peace talks between the Ugandan government and the
LRA, starting in 2006, the year after the ICC issued arrest warrants for
the top five LRA commanders while a national amnesty for all rebel
combatants was still in place. The tensions around Juba ignited the
entire field of transitional justice, as witnessed in the 2007 Nuremberg
conference mentioned earlier. The conference was attended by the ICC
Prosecutor, Registrar and other senior Court officials, who used it as a
platform to pronounce on developments in Juba.[3] This included

---

[1] See, for example, Robinson, 'Serving the Interests of Justice'; M. Pensky,
    'Amnesty on Trial: Impunity, Accountability and the Norms of International
    Law', *Ethics and Global Politics*, 1, 1–2, 2008, pp. 1–40; L. Mallinder, *Amnesty,
    Human Rights and Political Transitions: Bridging the Peace and Justice Divide*,
    Hart Publishing, 2008; and M. Freeman, *Necessary Evils: Amnesties and the
    Search for Justice*, Cambridge University Press, 2011.
[2] See, for example, D. Orentlicher, 'Settling Accounts: The Duty to Prosecute
    Human Rights Violations of a Prior Regime', *Yale Law Journal*, 100, 8, 1991,
    pp. 2537–615; C. Nino, 'The Duty to Punish Past Abuses of Human Rights Put
    into Context: The Case of Argentina', *Yale Law Journal*, 100, 8, 1991,
    pp. 2619–40; D. Orentlicher, 'A Reply to Professor Nino', *Yale Law Journal*,
    100, 8, 1991, pp. 2641–3; N. Waddell and P. Clark (eds.), *Courting Conflict:
    Justice, Peace and the ICC in Africa*, Royal African Society, 2008; and
    R. Mnookin, 'Rethinking the Tension between Peace and Justice: The
    International Criminal Prosecutor as Diplomat', *Harvard Negotiation Law
    Review*, 18, 2013, pp. 145–72.
[3] 'Building a Future on Peace and Justice'.

Ocampo's lament, quoted in Chapter 2, that 'we...hear officials of States Parties calling for amnesties, the granting of immunities and other ways to avoid prosecutions, supposedly in the name of peace'.

Ocampo reiterated these views at the ICC review conference in Kampala in May 2010. Reflecting the controversies around the Juba talks, Uganda was chosen as the location for this 'stocktaking' exercise, which the Rome Statute stipulated must be convened seven years after the inauguration of the ICC. On the opening panel of the conference, Ocampo – in strongly consequentialist terms, belying some of his previous statements about the need for justice to rise above the political and social terrain – argued that the ICC was the main reason the LRA was no longer militarily active in northern Uganda. 'I am very glad that the situation in Northern Uganda has changed so drastically since the Court's arrest warrants forced Joseph Kony to leave his safe haven in the Sudan and move to the DRC', Ocampo said.

Let me conclude on peace and justice. The drafters of the Rome Statute took great care to exclude political considerations from the work of the Court. The Prosecutor and Judges cannot and will not take political considerations into account. This was a conscious decision, to force political actors to adjust to the new legal limits. We cannot both claim that we will 'never again' let atrocities happen and continue to appease the criminals, conducting 'business as usual'.[4]

While the previous chapter explored the ICC's relations with trial-based approaches that echo its own methods, this chapter on amnesties and peace negotiations and the next on community-based transitional justice examine its relations with fundamentally different types of processes. As a relative newcomer, the ICC joins the fray alongside much more established responses to atrocity, of which amnesties and peace negotiations are among the most widely deployed. This chapter is structured in two parts: the first explores domestic amnesties in Uganda and the DRC; and the second examines peace negotiations, in which amnesties have played a critical role.

This chapter argues that the ICC has generally ridden roughshod over national choices to employ amnesties to facilitate peace negotiations and other responses to violence. The ICC's and its supporters' vehement insistence on a narrow brand of international criminal justice

---

[4] L. M. Ocampo, 'Review Conference – General Debate Statement', 31 May 2010, p. 5.

has undermined these other important attempts to resolve conflict and often made peace less, rather than more, likely. In the process, the ICC's practice of complementarity highlights the complacency of the principle, given the Court's tendency to invoke notions of superiority and distance when confronted with conflict resolution and transitional justice modalities very different from its own. Furthermore, the confusion regarding the ICC's ultimate purpose – between having positive effects on the ground as opposed to hovering above the fray – exacerbates this problem. While these factors have played out differently in Uganda and the DRC, the ICC has displayed a consistent unwillingness to bow to domestic pragmatic decisions regarding amnesties and peace processes and has often interfered directly in their implementation.

Domestic Amnesties

International criminal law is now a central feature of most peace negotiations around the world, especially those involving UN mediation. The UN increasingly holds that international law prohibits the use of amnesties for suspects of genocide, war crimes and crimes against humanity and therefore insists on prosecutions within the framework of peace negotiations.[5] Meanwhile, the ICC has regularly briefed international mediators about the illegality of using amnesties for this category of suspects during peace talks.[6] This signifies a substantial shift since the Rome conference in 1998, where many delegates expressed sympathy for the model of amnesty central to the South African Truth and Reconciliation Commission (TRC), which was underway at the time.[7] Philippe Kirsch, the chair of the Preparatory Commission in Rome and later the first President of the ICC, stated

---

[5] A 2009 report on amnesties by the UN Office of the High Commissioner for Human Rights states, 'The United Nations policy of opposing amnesties for war crimes, crimes against humanity, genocide or gross violations of human rights, including in the context of peace negotiations, represents an important evolution, grounded in long experience' (United Nations Office of the High Commissioner for Human Rights, 'Rule-of-Law Tools for Post-Conflict States: Amnesties', 2009).

[6] See, for example, Nouwen, *Complementarity in the Line of Fire*, p. 18.

[7] Greenawalt, 'Complementarity in Crisis', p. 133.

that the Rome Statute purposely contains a 'creative ambiguity'[8] that gives substantial discretion when considering amnesties.[9]

As various commentators have pointed out, international criminal law does not clearly prohibit the use of amnesties for serious crimes.[10] The Rome Statute does not mention amnesties, although as discussed elsewhere in this book, the ICC's definition of the 'genuine proceedings' by domestic institutions that would prevent ICC intervention encompasses only national prosecutions. Other international criminal law statutes and conventions meanwhile are less prescriptive or say very little about this issue. This suggests that the international legal basis for the trend against amnesties is significantly weaker than many advocates have proposed, necessitating a different set of justifications by the UN and other international practitioners for their anti-amnesty stance. Various scholars also challenge the widespread assumptions that international trials inherently deter crimes and produce long-term stability and that amnesties foster impunity and ultimately undermine peace and social order.[11]

The advent of the ICC as a permanent global court has increased debate over the legality and efficacy of administering domestic amnesties. This section explores the impact of the ICC on the use of national amnesties in Uganda and the DRC. A key complicating factor in this regard is that both states had instituted amnesties for high-ranking suspects of international crimes years before the ICC intervened, often with the financial and diplomatic backing of the same international agencies and foreign donors that later advocated ICC prosecutions.

---

[8] Quoted in M. Scharf, 'The Amnesty Exception to the Jurisdiction of the International Criminal Court', *Cornell International Law Journal*, 32, 1999, p. 522.

[9] For a broader discussion of the extent to which the Rome Statute is a 'flexible instrument' affording the Prosecutor in particular a high degree of discretion, see K. Ambos, 'The Legal Framework of Transitional Justice: A Systematic Study with a Specific Focus on the ICC', in K. Ambos, J. Large and M. Wierda (eds.), *Building a Future on Peace and Justice: Studies on Transitional Justice, Peace and Development*, Springer, 2014, p. 20.

[10] See, for example, Pensky, 'Amnesty on Trial'; Mallinder, *Amnesty, Human Rights and Political Transitions*; Freeman, *Necessary Evils*; and M. Freeman and M. Pensky, 'The Amnesty Controversy in International Law', in F. Lessa and L. Payne (eds.), *Amnesty in the Age of Human Rights Accountability: Comparative and International Perspectives*, Cambridge University Press, 2012, pp. 42–65.

[11] See, for example, Snyder and Vinjamuri, 'Trials and Errors'; and Vinjamuri, 'Deterrence, Democracy and the Pursuit of International Justice'.

This section argues that both countries have sound reasons for deploying amnesties for a wide range of armed actors, including high-level suspects. Both states, however, have experienced substantial difficulties in implementing amnesty policies and both have used strategic ambiguity around amnesty and prosecution issues to their advantage. Insisting on the supposed illegality and damaging effects of domestic amnesties, the ICC has undermined national decision-making – including widespread popular support for amnesties in the Ugandan case – and reduced national options for addressing large-scale conflict.

Domestic Amnesties in Uganda

As discussed in Chapter 3, from the start of the ICC's pre-referral negotiations with the Ugandan government, the Court opposed the use of Uganda's Amnesty Act for high-level suspects of international crimes on the grounds that it violated the Rome Statute and entrenched impunity. This opposition reached a crescendo during the Juba peace talks, where the OTP issued regular dismissals of the LRA's attempts to secure an amnesty for its leaders, amplified by a constant stream of press releases and communiqués by international human rights organisations.[12] This section argues that the pronouncements by the ICC and its supporters belied the long-term use of amnesties in Uganda even before the emergence of the LRA; the widespread support for the Amnesty Act among everyday Ugandans, including its use for senior LRA commanders; and the tangible, positive effects of the amnesty policy.

The Amnesty Act stemmed from lobbying by the ARLPI during the 1999 peace talks between the Ugandan government, the LRA and the LRA's principal backer, the Sudanese government. Following President Museveni's statement in July 1998 that he would accept a ceasefire with the LRA, the ARLPI – along with the Acholi Parliamentary Group and Acholi in the diaspora – campaigned for an amnesty for all rebels

---

[12] International Criminal Court, Office of the Prosecutor, 'Statement by the Chief Prosecutor Luis Moreno-Ocampo', 12 July 2006. See also Ocampo's quotes in F. Osike and H. Musaka, 'ICC Insists Kony Must Face Prosecution', *New Vision*, 11 October 2007, www.newvision.co.ug/new_vision/news/1217697/icc-insists-kony-prosecution; HRW 'Benchmarks for Assessing Possible National Alternatives'; AI, 'Amnesty International Letter to Security Council'.

in northern Uganda to halt the violence permanently. The ARLPI conducted widespread consultations with northern victims' groups and concluded there was a strong desire among the population for personal and collective healing and reconciliation with the rebels.[13] The ARLPI argued that an amnesty would therefore reflect what Rt Rev. Macleord Baker Ochola II, co-founder and vice chairman of the ARLPI, called an Acholi 'cultural conflict resolution approach'.[14]

There are several precedents for employing amnesties in Uganda. In 1987, the NRM offered an amnesty to the Uganda People's Democratic Army (UPDA) and the Uganda People's Army in exchange for a cessation to their rebel insurgencies against the newly formed government.[15] Thereafter, several army commanders, working with traditional and cultural leaders, used unofficial amnesties to help end conflict. Beginning in 1996, Maj. Gen. Katumba Wamala encouraged large numbers of rebels from the West Nile Bank Front (WNBF), which had attacked western Uganda from bases in southern Sudan and eastern Zaire, to lay down their arms and return from the bush. Assuring the rebels that no returnees would face prosecution and the army would facilitate their reintegration into their home communities, Wamala succeeded in ending the WNBF's insurgency in 1998.[16]

Rare among amnesty legislation around the world, the Amnesty Act passed by the Ugandan parliament in January 2000 was explicitly conceived as an expression of the broader population's, and especially victims', concerns. The preamble to the Amnesty Act claims that the legislation reflects 'the expressed desire of the people of Uganda to end

---

[13] G. Khadiagala, 'The Role of the Acholi Religious Leaders Peace Initiative (ARLPI) in Peace Building in Northern Uganda', Appendix in USAID/ Management Systems International, 'The Effectiveness of Civil Society Initiatives in Controlling Violent Conflicts and Building Peace: A Study of Three Approaches in the Greater Horn of Africa', March 2001, pp. 4–6.

[14] M. B. Ochola II, 'Hope in the Storm: Experience of ARLPI in Conflict Resolution of the Northern Ugandan Armed Conflict', paper delivered at 'Seminar on Northern Uganda', Mission Church of Uppsala, Sweden, 15 April 2004, p. 5.

[15] B. Afako, 'Reconciliation and Justice: "Mato Oput" and the Amnesty Act', in O. Lucima (ed.), *Protracted Conflict, Elusive Peace: Initiatives to End the Violence in Northern Uganda*, Conciliation Resources/Accord, 2002, p. 65.

[16] Refugee Law Project, 'Negotiating Peace: Resolution of Conflicts in Uganda's West Nile Region', Working Paper No. 12, June 2004, pp. 18–21. See also, A. Bogner and D. Neubert, 'Negotiated Peace, Denied Justice? The Case of West Nile (Northern Uganda)', *Africa Spectrum*, 48, 3, 2013, pp. 55–84.

armed hostilities, reconcile with those who have caused suffering and rebuild their communities'.[17] The Act establishes the Amnesty Commission to oversee the amnesty process. The Commission is a temporary institution, with its mandate renewed every two years (until an amendment to the Act in 2006, the renewal period was six months) until parliament deems that it has succeeded or ceased to be useful in helping to end conflict.[18] Linking the amnesty directly to wider DDR efforts, the Act also establishes a Demobilisation and Resettlement Team to decommission the arms of combatants seeking amnesty and to demobilise, resettle and reintegrate them into their home communities.[19]

The Amnesty Act is at once both broader and more limited than that proposed by the ARLPI. Whereas the ARLPI lobbied for an amnesty only for rebels in northern Uganda, the Act covers combatants nationwide. The Amnesty Act also does not afford the sort of blanket amnesty the ARLPI proposed but rather an individualised amnesty in which each rebel wanting to benefit from the provision must voluntarily return from the bush, register with a designated government official (usually an army or police officer or a local magistrate), sign a declaration renouncing conflict and surrender any weapons in his or her possession. The reporter, as a returned combatant seeking amnesty is known, does not have to admit to any particular crime, only to 'renounce or abandon involvement in the war or rebellion'.[20] Once satisfied with a reporter's case, the Commission issues an amnesty certificate, which entitles him or her to a resettlement package containing 263,000 Ugandan shillings in cash, a mattress, blankets, saucepans, plates, cups, maize seeds and flour.[21] Most of the funding for the packages has come from a US$4.2 million World Bank Multi-Country Demobilisation and Reintegration Program grant, issued in March 2005.[22]

---

[17] Republic of Uganda, 'The Amnesty Act', 2000, Preamble (from hereon, referred to as 'Amnesty Act').
[18] Author's interview, Lucian Tibarahu, Attorney-General, Republic of Uganda, Kampala, 2 March 2006.
[19] Amnesty Act, Section 12.   [20] Ibid., Section 4.1.c.
[21] Author's interview, Onega, 3 March 2006. The cash amount provided is equivalent to three months' salary for a policeman or teacher, at the passing of the Amnesty Act, plus 20,000 Ugandan shillings for transport costs.
[22] Ibid.

The impact of the Ugandan amnesty process has been substantial. To date, approximately 30,000 rebels have come in from the bush under the DDR process facilitated by the amnesty, although fewer than half of these have received their resettlement packages.[23] While most debates around the Amnesty Act in Uganda focus on the return of LRA combatants, LRA returnees comprise around only half of the amnesty recipients, with the rest from twenty-eight other rebel groups.[24] It is also unclear how many former LRA combatants have returned to northern Uganda without passing through the amnesty process. A 2005 survey by Tim Allen and Mareike Schomerus of 248 formerly abducted persons who had transited through reception centres, for example, showed that only 25 per cent of respondents had received an amnesty card, applied for amnesty or heard of the Amnesty Commission.[25]

Most amnestied LRA combatants – including senior LRA commanders such as Brig. Kenneth Banya and Brig. Sam Kolo – have resettled in Gulu and Kitgum districts. In Gulu, Banya, whom the UPDF considered 'the main military and technical brain behind the [LRA] rebellion',[26] now oversees a government farm at Labora, where around 600 LRA returnees work as part of their repatriation. Established jointly in 2004 by the government, UPDF and Gulu District LC5, Labora Farm was designed to facilitate the former rebels' 'economic empowerment and reintegration into society'.[27]

Because of the quantifiable impact of the amnesty process, various empirical studies highlight widespread popular support for the policy.[28]

---

[23] Author's telephone interview, Amnesty Commission official, Kampala, 17 January 2017.

[24] Ibid. See also, K. Agger, 'The End of Amnesty in Uganda: Implications for LRA Defections', Enough Project, August 2012.

[25] T. Allen and M. Schomerus, 'A Hard Homecoming: Lessons Learned from the Reception Center Process in Northern Uganda – An Independent Study', report commissioned by USAID and UNICEF for Management Systems International, June 2006, p. 37.

[26] Quoted in IRIN News, 'Uganda: Senior LRA Commander Captured by the Army', 15 July 2004, www.irinnews.org/news/2004/07/15/senior-lra-commander-captured-army.

[27] Internal UNICEF document, on file with author.

[28] Blattman and Annan, 'On the Nature and Causes of LRA Abduction'; Refugee Law Project, 'Whose Justice? Perceptions of Uganda's Amnesty Act 2000', Working Paper No. 15, 28 February 2005; ICTJ, 'Forgotten Voices'; ICTJ, 'When the War Ends'.

'Amnesty is a good option since it has encouraged a number of children to come back', said a member of a community-based organisation in Oyam district of Lango, quoted in the 2007 OHCHR report.

It can encourage more to return from the bush. When the majority have returned and very few remain in the bush, these few – say if about nine in number – will find it so easy to escape from the bush and they will eventually come back as well. If there is no amnesty, those in the bush will not return because of the uncertainty of knowing what could happen to them.[29]

'The amnesty is not perfect', said Henry, a farmer in Amuru, in 2015, 'but look how many of our people it brought back from the bush. We need them here to work on the farms now that we have left the [IDP] camps.'[30]

In 2012, the Ugandan government let the Amnesty Act lapse for the first time since its promulgation. The move was consistent with the increasingly legalistic and prosecutorial focus of JLOS and the government as a whole, discussed in the previous chapter. Sustained pressure from northern Ugandan civil society, however, forced the government to reinstate the Amnesty Act in 2013.[31] This sparked a vociferous reaction from JLOS, including a letter to the Chief Justice calling for the Act to be rescinded.[32] Since then, hundreds more fighters from the LRA and other rebel groups have returned from combat and taken up the amnesty provision.[33]

Despite the clear successes of the Amnesty Act, the northern Ugandan population is not universal in its praise of the amnesty process. The OHCHR study showed that much of the population supports the Act but views it as lacking in two key respects, reflecting popular needs discussed in Chapter 4: an inability to compel returnees to tell the truth about their crimes; and a lack of compensation for victims of violence.[34] These problems stem from the fact that former combatants must simply renounce their involvement in hostilities against the state, rather than divulge their specific participation in human rights violations. Through the reintegration packages and training at Labora

---

[29] OHCHR, 'Making Peace Our Own', p. 61.
[30] Author's interview, Henry, Amuru, 12 April 2015.
[31] See, for example, Refugee Law Project, 'A Renewed Promise for Peace and Justice: The Reinstatement of Uganda's Amnesty Act 2000', 29 May 2013.
[32] Oola, 'In the Shadow of Kwoyelo's Trial', pp. 168–9.
[33] See LRA Crisis Tracker.   [34] OHCHR, 'Making Peace Our Own', section III.

Farm, returnees then receive the kind of material support that many victims believe they have been denied. 'We see what these people get', said Sabiti, an elderly woman in Gulu town, 'and it makes us angry. These people have killed others – killed women and children. And now they get food and money from the government, while the government ignores us.'[35]

The Ugandan government has also confused many everyday citizens with its changeable position on the Amnesty Act. On occasions, President Museveni has stated that LRA commanders are eligible for the amnesty – a point criticised by the ICC, which saw this as an about-face after Uganda's state referral[36] – while sometimes claiming that only the LRA rank and file may qualify.[37] In the weeks preceding the Juba peace talks in May 2006, the government amended the Amnesty Act to exclude the LRA commanders charged by the ICC (an issue explored in greater detail below).

The Amnesty Act also contradicts other aspects of national legislation, fuelling suspicion, especially among the LRA, of the government's amnesty offer. In 2002, the government passed the 'Suppression of Terrorism Act', which outlaws groups considered terrorist organisations, including the LRA, ADF and PDA, and makes it a punishable offence to be a member of, or to make contact with, such groups.[38] More recently, the Ugandan government has failed to explain the precise relationship between the Amnesty Act and either the ICD or the ICC. Several senior LRA commanders, including Kolo, Banya, Acellam, Lt. Col. Charles Otim and Lt. Col. Francis Okwanga, have received amnesties, while the lower-ranking Kwoyelo is being prosecuted through the ICD. Similar uncertainty surrounds the case of Ongwen, currently on trial at the ICC. Soon after Ongwen's capture in CAR, an audio recording surfaced of him claiming that the government had granted him an amnesty and he would soon return to his

---

[35] Author's interview, general population, Gulu, 9 March 2006.
[36] Bosco, *Rough Justice*, p. 129.
[37] See, for example, ICC, OTP, 'Press Release: President of Uganda Refers Situation'; M. Wilkerson and F. Nyakairu, 'Museveni Offers Kony Amnesty', *Daily Monitor*, 5 July 2006, www.allafrica.com/stories/200607051328.html.
[38] Sam Kolo, former LRA commander, Gulu, 10 March 2006.

home community in northern Uganda.[39] Stephen Oola from the Refugee Law Project said,

[Many Ugandan civil society actors] have heard the recording of Ongwen expecting an amnesty. He also asked forgiveness from Museveni...There was never a serious consideration of prosecuting Ongwen in Uganda. He never set foot in Uganda – Museveni ensured that. He didn't want any troubles with combining the ICC and the Amnesty Act, so he sent UPDF leaders to CAR to liaise with the US, get intel from Ongwen, then let the US handle him.[40]

Michael Otim, head of the ICTJ office in Kampala, who had also heard the recording, said, 'Ongwen thought he was getting an amnesty. Initially the government made statements about him going home. Ongwen started sending messages to one of his wives who had already returned. Only late in the process, he was transferred to Bangui and informed that he was going to The Hague.'[41]

Despite all of these challenges surrounding the Ugandan amnesty, including the government's strategic legal ambiguity, the opposition to the Act by the ICC and its supporters is highly problematic for two main reasons. First, these actors ignore the substantial support for the Act among everyday Ugandans. In the late 1980s and 1990s, there was considerable support for amnesty processes because of their success in disarming and reintegrating the WNBF, UPDA and other armed groups. This track record largely explains why the population backed the adoption of the Amnesty Act in 2000. Furthermore, it must be recognised – as the OHCHR report in 2007 found – that widespread approval for processes of amnesty, forgiveness and reconciliation (which most respondents define discretely) emerges because many northern Ugandans view the perpetrators of violence as their own children who must be treated leniently and eventually reintegrated into the community.[42] Support for amnesty therefore is based not only on the positive use of such measures in the past but also the identity of

---

[39] The author heard a recording provided by Stephen Oola and Lyandro Komakech, Refugee Law Project, Kampala, 6 April 2015.

[40] Author's interview, Oola, 6 April 2015.

[41] Author's interview, Michael Otim, Head of ICTJ-Uganda, Kampala, 6 April 2015. On this issue, see also Refugee Law Project, 'Ongwen's Justice Dilemma: Perspectives from Northern Uganda', 26 January 2015.

[42] OHCHR, 'Making Peace Our Own', section II.

many perpetrators and the intimacy of relations between victims and perpetrators.

As discussed in Chapter 4, this often extends to LRA leaders such as Kony, whom many northern Ugandans consider a 'child of the community' who should be encouraged through the amnesty process to halt the rebellion and return 'home'. These community-level interpretations challenge the ICC's and various observers' insistence on a strict dichotomy between high-level suspects of international crimes (who, they argue, should never be eligible for amnesties) and low-level suspects (who, under certain conditions, could be considered eligible) as well as the broad 'division of labour' policy inherent in the relational conception of complementarity. The Uganda case also directly challenges commentators who argue that the use of amnesty hampers a long-term transition toward democracy. Uganda represents an example of a democratic amnesty, which resulted from civil society lobbying and widespread popular consultations, rather than government diktat. International opposition to such a democratic amnesty may therefore undermine democracy in the long run.

Second, the confusion over the applicability of the Act – whether the amnesty is still in place and to whom it applies – generated both by the ICC and the Ugandan government has greatly undermined the Act's effectiveness in incentivising the disarmament, return and reintegration of LRA and other rebel combatants. The Amnesty Commission and various civil society groups have reported over the last decade the substantial reduction in combatants returning from the bush under the Amnesty Act, which they attribute directly to the perceived threat of prosecution.[43] Many LRA combatants are still unaware of, or confused by, the amnesty generally or its specific modalities. While the Gulu-based radio station Mega FM has broadcast messages into the bush explaining the amnesty to LRA fighters, returnees such as Kolo claim that knowledge of the system is still minimal and many rebels do not trust the government sufficiently to return. 'Many fighters in the bush still don't know about the amnesty', Kolo said.

---

[43] Author's interview, Onega, 3 March 2006; Refugee Law Project, 'Ongwen's Justice Dilemma'. For further views of various civil society actors on this issue, see IRIN News, 'War Crimes Trial May Affect LRA Defections – Analysts', 29 July 2011, http://reliefweb.int/report/uganda/war-crimes-trial-may-affect-lra-defections-analysts.

Sometimes they haven't heard about it and other times they're told [by their commanders] that it's a trap...If any bad news about the returnees reaches the bush, it dissuades them from coming in...I can personally encourage fighters to come in from the bush but there are limits to the advice I can give. I can't just say, 'Don't worry about it. Come in and everything will be fine.' Those in the bush want to know about conditions here. They want reassurances that life will be better than what they currently have.[44]

In a context of such distrust between the LRA and the government, the further doubts over the amnesty policy sowed by the government's and the ICC's insistence on prosecutions for high-ranking LRA combatants have proven extremely damaging. In broader terms, they also highlight the extent to which the ICC's principle of complementarity does not permit an analysis of the genuineness and effectiveness of non-prosecutorial approaches such as Uganda's amnesty policy.

Domestic Amnesties in the DRC

The DRC has instituted a much wider range of amnesty processes than Uganda for a broader set of purposes. Whereas Uganda has used a single Amnesty Act, connected to an overarching DDR process for returning rebels, the DRC has passed four amnesty laws since 2002, linked explicitly to a TRC and an SSR programme involving the *brassage* or 'mixing' of former rebels into the national Congolese army. In contrast to the Ugandan situation, these amnesties have tended to result from, rather than to precede, peace negotiations. Furthermore, an implicit amnesty underpins the DDR process that facilitates the return of Congo-based rebels to Rwanda. In the past, rebel leaders, including Bemba, Katanga and Ngudjolo, have even established military tribunals separate from the Congolese state and issued amnesties to their own fighters.[45]

---

[44] Author's interview, Kolo, 10 March 2006.
[45] International Criminal Court, Pre-Trial Chamber III, 'Public Redacted Version: Amended Document containing the Charges', Situation in the Democratic Republic of Congo, *The Prosecutor v. Jean-Pierre Bemba Gombo*, 17 October 2008, para. 76; International Criminal Court, Pre-Trial Chamber I, 'Public Redacted Version: Decision on the Confirmation of Charges', Situation in the Democratic Republic of Congo, *The Prosecutor v. Germain Katanga and Mathieu Ngudjolo Chui*, 30 September 2008, para. 542.

The ICC has thus intervened into a highly complex amnesty terrain in the DRC. Generally, the ICC has not publicly contested the DRC's amnesty processes as it has Uganda's because the former excludes genocide, war crimes and crimes against humanity and therefore the Court does not view these as a direct threat to its own operations. When the ICC asked the Congolese government why it had permitted the visit of Sudanese President and ICC suspect Omar al-Bashir in 2014, for example, the government stated that its exclusion of these crimes under the amnesty provisions highlighted its 'commitment to justice'.[46]

That the DRC's four amnesty laws cover different periods and conflict sites but all exclude international crimes reflects the DRC's monist system, in which international treaties and conventions signed by the Congolese government are automatically subsumed into national law.[47] While these amnesty laws have not covered suspected perpetrators of international crimes, however, the majority of such suspects in the DRC have not been prosecuted and many have risen to senior positions in the government or military.

The first Congolese amnesty law, signed in 2003, stemmed from the peace agreement signed in Sun City in 2002.[48] Its primary purpose was to weaken the numerous rebel movements challenging the Congolese state – still reorienting after the assassination of President Laurent Kabila in January 2001 – through incorporating rebel leaders either into the national executive or the national army. This led to the elevation of two rebel leaders later charged by the ICC, Jean-Pierre Bemba as one of four Vice Presidents in the transitional government in July 2003 and Bosco Ntaganda to the position of colonel in the national army in December 2004.

The second amnesty law, signed in 2005, was connected explicitly to the creation of a TRC, as stipulated under the Sun City agreement. The

[46] International Criminal Court, The Registry, 'Transmission to Pre-Trial Chamber II of the Observations Submitted by the Democratic Republic of Congo Pursuant to the "Decision Requesting Observations on Omar al-Bashir's Visit to the Democratic Republic of Congo" dated 3 March 2014', 17 March 2004, p. 8.

[47] D. Zongwe, F. Butedi and P. Clément, 'The Legal System of the Democratic Republic of the Congo (DRC): Overview and Research', Hauser Global Law School Program, January/February 2015.

[48] Government of the Democratic Republic of Congo, 'Amnesty Decree-Law', *Journal Officiel de la République Démocratique du Congo*, No. 03–001, 15 April 2003.

TRC was mandated to investigate political, economic and social crimes committed between Congo's independence in 1960 and the beginning of the transitional period in June 2003. A crucial feature of the TRC was its ability to grant amnesty to perpetrators of 'acts of war, political crimes and crimes of opinion' committed between the beginning of the rebellion against Mobutu on 20 August 1996 and the establishment of the transitional government on 30 June 2003, in exchange for a full confession of their crimes.[49]

The third and fourth amnesty laws, passed in May 2009 and February 2014, respectively, resulted from peace negotiations with two main rebel groups, the CNDP in 2009, which by 2014 had evolved into the M23. The 2009 amnesty covers only crimes committed in North and South Kivu between June 2003 and the promulgation of the law[50], while the 2014 amnesty covers all 'insurrectional acts, acts of war and political offences' committed within the DRC between 20 December 2005 and 20 December 2013.[51] During these peace talks, both the CNDP and M23 lobbied unsuccessfully for the inclusion of international crimes in the amnesty laws. Under the 2014 law, former rebels

---

[49] Government of the Democratic Republic of Congo, 'Loi No. 04 Portant Amnistie Pour Faits de Guerre, Infractions Politiques et d'Opinion', 30 November 2005, Articles 1 and 5. The adoption of the 2005 Amnesty Law was highly controversial, as the National Assembly voted for it in the absence of President Kabila's ruling PPRD, which boycotted the vote, claiming that the Law would free thirty men convicted of the murder of Laurent Kabila in 2001; an act that the PPRD argues constitutes a 'political crime' under the terms of the legislation (IRIN News, 'DRC: Amnesty Law Passed without MPs from Kabila's Party', IRIN, 30 November 2005, www.irinnews.org/report/57408/drc-amnesty-law-passed-without-mps-kabilas-party). Opposition groups accused the PPRD of blocking the Amnesty Law to justify its continued imprisonment of opposition figures convicted of Kabila's assassination and to avoid the possibility of members of armed groups such as the MLC and RCD, the PPRD's strongest political opponents, receiving amnesties for their crimes (H. Kabungulu Ngoy-Kangoy, 'Parties and Political Transition in the Democratic Republic of Congo', Election Institute of Southern Africa, Research Report No. 20, 2006, p. 46). Three weeks after the National Assembly adopted the Amnesty Law, Joseph Kabila was forced to promulgate it to maintain parliamentary stability.

[50] Government of the Democratic Republic of Congo, 'Loi No. 09/003 du 7 mai 2009 portant Amnistie pour Faits de Guerre et Insurrectionnels Commis dans les Provinces du Nord-Kivu et du Sud-Kivu', 7 May 2009.

[51] Government of the Democratic Republic of Congo, 'Loi No. 14/006 du 11 février 2014 portant Amnistie pour Faits Insurrectionnels, Faits de Guerre et Infractions Politiques', 11 February 2014.

were given six months to vow 'in writing, on their honour, not to commit any acts that come under the present amnesty' to qualify for the provision.[52]

Finally, concurrent to all four DRC amnesty laws, an implicit amnesty policy has supported an extensive DDR programme for Congo-based Rwandan rebels. Three phases of DDR since 1998 – the first managed by UNDP and the last two by the Rwanda Demobilisation and Reintegration Commission, building on a framework established through the Lusaka peace agreement in 1999, which ended the Second Congo War[53] – have demobilised around 35,000 mainly Hutu former combatants from eastern Congo. The majority of these fighters are members of the FDLR and the former Rwandan army which fled across the border after the 1994 genocide.[54]

Broadly speaking, the DRC's amnesty laws have not affected the ICC to the same extent as the Ugandan Amnesty Act, and vice versa, because of their explicit exclusion of international crimes. Two important problems regarding the ICC and amnesties nevertheless have manifested in the DRC. First, the Congolese government has displayed a much greater readiness to give amnesties to senior military and rebel leaders as part of the country's SSR programme than implied by its self-portrayal as an unyielding friend of international justice (echoed in many senior ICC officials' depictions of the government such as Ocampo's statement earlier on the need to travel to Kinshasa to thank Kabila for his cooperation throughout the Lubanga case). Acting outside of the 2005 amnesty law, Kabila pardoned Mathieu Ngudjolo and all 10,000 members of his Ituri rebel coalition, the Mouvement Révolutionnaire Congolais, as well as the rebel groups led by Peter Karim and Cobra Matata, in exchange for their surrender, the decommissioning of their weapons and their integration into the FARDC.[55] As a result,

---

[52] Ibid.

[53] IRIN News, 'DRC: Summary of Lusaka Accord', 21 July 1999, www.irinnews.org/news/1999/07/21/summary-lusaka-accord.

[54] Rwanda Demobilisation and Reintegration Commission, 'Demobilisation', http://demobrwanda.gov.rw/.

[55] BBC, 'DR Congo Militias Lay Down Arms', 27 July 2006, http://news.bbc .co.uk/1/hi/world/africa/5219076.stm. For further discussion of the overlaps between the ICC and these Ituri cases, see K. Rodman, 'The Peace versus Justice Debate at the ICC: The Case of the Ituri Warlords in the Democratic Republic of the Congo', workshop paper, March 2016, http://web.colby.edu/karodman/ files/2016/03/ICCWorkshop_DRC.pdf.

all three leaders were promoted to the rank of colonel in the Congolese army. Such a practice was common in the lead-up to the 2006 national elections, as the government sought to minimise the impact of militia groups capable of intimidating voters and disrupting preparations for the poll. MONUC supported the scheme as part of the UN's broader disarmament programme in eastern DRC. Kemal Saiki, a MONUC spokesperson, defended the amnesty-for-peace deals with Ngudjolo, Karim and Matata: 'The most important thing is to bring an end to the bloodshed. Since these deals have been signed, there has not been any large-scale fighting in Ituri.'[56]

The Congolese government's strategic ambiguity on questions of amnesty continued when in February 2008 it arrested Ngudjolo at a military training camp in Kinshasa following an ICC warrant issued in July 2007. This amounted to a 'bait and switch', with Ngudjolo lured into surrender from his rebel ranks and integrated into the Congolese army, only to be arrested and transferred to The Hague for prosecution eighteen months later. While the Congolese government was widely hailed for its cooperation in arresting and transferring Ngudjolo to the ICC, its duplicity toward an amnesty recipient undermined the broader use of amnesty as an incentive for members of rebel groups to disarm.[57] Interviews with former rebels from Ngudjolo's FNI and FRPI in Bunia who had been integrated into the Congolese army underscored this point. 'This is the big problem with *brassage*', said one former FNI combatant. 'The government gives us an amnesty, so we join the army and get a new uniform. But look what happened to Ngudjolo. He also got an amnesty but now he's in The Hague. We all wonder whether this will happen to us next.'[58] A former mid-ranking FRPI commander echoed these views: 'You can't trust the government or the ICC. These amnesties mean nothing. They can change their mind at any time, which makes us all vulnerable.'[59]

---

[56] Quoted in T. McConnell, 'Measures to Keep Peace in Congo Draw Fire', *Christian Science Monitor*, 5 September 2006, www.csmonitor.com/2006/0905/p04s02-woaf.html.

[57] This also challenges the view expressed by some transitional justice scholars that trials can follow amnesties, delivering the perceived benefits of both approaches. See, for example, Olsen, Payne and Reiter, *Transitional Justice in Balance*.

[58] Author's interview, integrated former FNI combatant, Bunia, 24 August 2011.

[59] Author's interview, integrated former FRPI combatant, Bunia, 25 August 2011. The case of Cobra Matata elicits similar concerns. He was arrested in Ituri in January 2015 and transferred to Kinshasa to face trial on charges of war crimes

Second, the ICC's interventions in the DRC potentially weaken the unofficial amnesty that underpins the extensive DDR programme, which has demobilised and returned tens of thousands of rebels to Rwanda. This could have jeopardised the ICC's case against Ntaganda, a Rwandan-born former Rwandan Patriotic Army (RPA) officer. As a Rwandan national, Ntaganda could have been eligible to participate in the DDR process and thus avoid prosecution by the Rwandan authorities. It appears, however, that Ntaganda feared Rwanda would deal with him harshly, as witnessed in the perpetual house arrest without trial of his former comrade, Laurent Nkunda, who was captured by the Rwandan army in January 2009. During the diplomatic negotiations around Ntaganda's transfer to The Hague, discussed in Chapter 1, Rwanda reportedly lobbied the US and the ICC to handle Ntaganda's case domestically but eventually acceded to international demands to deliver him to the ICC.[60] The complications inherent in the Ntaganda case again highlight the potential for fraught relations between the ICC and, in this case, a UN-supported DDR process. A key challenge for the UN and other international bodies in the Great Lakes is that many support amnesty-based SSR and DDR as well as the ICC, highlighting a problem for peace mediators and related actors in navigating the new peacebuilding terrain since the advent of the Court.

Similar sentiments to those of the former FNI and FRPI rebels above were expressed by former Congo-based rebels in the Mutobo demobilisation centre in Rwanda:

We heard what happened to Bosco. He was bigger than us and did the same as we did, coming across the border. Now he's at the ICC. Is that going to happen to us too?[61]

The [Rwandan] government here said that if we come back, we won't be punished. Even when there was [the possibility of prosecution through] *gacaca*, we wouldn't be punished because they wanted us to come home. We trusted them but, after Bosco, none of us are sure we made the right choice.[62]

---

and crimes against humanity. The Matata case differs somewhat from Ngudjolo's, though, in that following Matata's integration into the Congolese army in 2006 he defected in 2010 to form a new rebel group in Ituri, the Front Populaire pour la Justice au Congo, and surrendered to the Congolese authorities in November 2014.

[60] Author's interviews, foreign diplomats, Kigali, 4–10 April 2013.
[61] Author's interview, former FDLR combatant, Mutobo, 19 April 2013.
[62] Ibid.

The Bosco case sends a bad message to others in Congo. Many of them won't come back now. Some people say Bosco wanted to go to the ICC but why would he do that? He could've been reintegrated and gone back to his family in Virunga.[63]

The Uganda and DRC situations highlight the ICC's outright dismissal of national decisions to employ amnesties as a central means of conflict resolution. While the two governments in question have adopted deliberately ambiguous policies on amnesties – at times persisting with them even while cooperating with ICC investigations – amnesties have continued to be highly effective in encouraging combatants to lay down their arms and reintegrate into their home communities. Despite these observable successes, when confronted with approaches such as amnesties that are fundamentally opposed to its own prosecutorial method, the ICC holds that complementarity determinations – including the possibility of deferring to domestic mechanisms – are not required. The Court instead invokes the inherent superiority and neglect of outcomes that is central to the distance discourse, insisting on international prosecutions while viewing amnesties as a means to entrench impunity, despite their long track record as effective tools of conflict mitigation, especially in terms of DDR in Uganda and the DRC. The Ugandan and Congolese experiences also highlight that the ICC's decision to overrule domestic amnesties in the cases of high-ranking suspects can dampen the effectiveness of amnesties for lower-ranking combatants, who often believe they too will be subject to criminal prosecution.

Peace Negotiations

This section analyses the ICC's intersections with peace negotiations in Uganda and the DRC, including negotiations over the applicability of amnesties for high-ranking suspects. These concerns have affected various international criminal justice institutions in the past, for example in the Balkans and Sierra Leone,[64] but have escalated since

---

[63] Ibid.
[64] See, for example, J. Jones, 'The Implications of the Peace Agreement for the International Criminal Tribunal for the Former Yugoslavia', *European Journal of International Law*, 7, 1996, pp. 226–44; and A. Tejan-Cole, 'The Complementary and Conflicting Relationship between the Special Court for

the advent of the ICC. Because the Court's temporal mandate means it can only intervene in situations since July 2002, it invariably does so in cases of ongoing or recently halted conflict, which increases the likelihood of its involvement when peace negotiations are underway.

As explored in the Uganda and DRC situations below, the binary framing of 'peace versus justice' discussions has proven decidedly unhelpful. During the Juba peace talks between the Ugandan government and the LRA, it generated fiercely opposed camps of advisors and commentators, constraining the options debated around the table and creating a generally antagonistic atmosphere that hampered the talks. The 'peace versus justice' structure at Juba presupposed that justice must entail punishment rather than other forms of accountability such as perpetrator apologies, public acknowledgement of harm and material reparations.[65] During the talks, these alternative formulations garnered some attention – principally among northern Ugandan civil society actors who travelled to Juba – but were stymied by the polarised debates among the negotiators and their principal interlocutors.

Three brief conceptual remarks are necessary to progress the 'peace versus justice' discussion and to inform the empirical analysis below. First, a more helpful framing of the intersections of international justice and peace talks comes from Nick Grono and Adam O'Brien who argue that the objectives of justice and peace, while not necessarily incompatible, are inevitably in tension.[66] This counters the claim by numerous ICC officials and observers that peace and justice are always mutually reinforcing.[67] Grono and O'Brien acknowledge the possibility of pursuing peace and justice sequentially but stress that some trade-off will probably be required, depending on the circumstances of particular conflict-affected societies and the nature of the proposed justice and peace interventions.

Sierra Leone and the Truth and Reconciliation Commission', *Yale Human Rights and Development Journal*, 6, 1, 2014, pp. 139–59.

[65] For an excellent analysis of broader notions of accountability, see L. Mallinder and K. McEvoy, 'Rethinking Amnesties: Atrocity, Accountability and Impunity in Post-Conflict Societies', *Contemporary Social Science*, 6, 1, 2011, pp. 107–28.

[66] N. Grono and A. O'Brien, 'Justice in Conflict? The ICC and Peace Processes', in N. Waddell and P. Clark (eds.), *Courting Conflict: Justice, Peace and the ICC in Africa*, Royal African Society, 2008, pp. 13–20.

[67] See, for example, Ocampo's comments at Osike and Musaka, 'ICC Insists Kony Must Face Prosecution'.

Second, it is important to recognise that what is being debated in situations such as Uganda and the DRC is rarely whether peace or justice are the desired outcomes – few actors would contest the necessity of both – but rather whether negotiations or prosecutions are the preferred processes by which to achieve these ends. A 'negotiations versus prosecutions' formulation has the advantage of not pre-empting the result of particular mechanisms, while remaining open to the likelihood that such processes may have multiple (and even unexpected) outcomes. The 'peace versus justice' debate assumes that peace negotiations produce peace and prosecutions produce justice, neither of which inherently holds. Peace talks can fail to achieve peace, just as trials can fail to achieve justice. Peace negotiations can also, if tailored in particular ways, pursue certain conceptions of justice (including those that include conditional amnesties), while prosecutions can, if approached in contextually sensitive ways, contribute to peace.

Third, when analysing the nature and impact of negotiations and prosecutions as processes, it is necessary to move beyond a fixation on the set-pieces of formal peace talks and criminal trials. A range of processes preceding, during and following formal negotiations, as well as the prevailing environment in which they take place, are vital for understanding the impact that prosecutions have on negotiations and vice versa. Similarly, as emphasised throughout this book, understanding the nature and effects of prosecutions involves more than an analysis of core legal practices such as investigations, courtroom arguments and judgments. This also requires close examination of the political, social, cultural and economic context in which these legal processes unfold and their intersections with a wide range of other actors and mechanisms.

Peace Negotiations in Uganda

This section explores the impact of the ICC on four peace-related phases in northern Uganda: the 2004–5 peace talks led by Betty Bigombe; the general atmosphere of violence in northern Uganda in 2005; the kickstarting of the Juba talks in 2006; and the Juba negotiations themselves from 2006 to 2008. This section argues that the ICC contributed to a broader set of factors that pushed the LRA to the Juba talks but ultimately undermined all of these peace efforts. Once the

Juba negotiations got underway, the ICC was a consistent stumbling block that, along with other issues, precipitated the collapse of the talks. As either a catalyst or impediment to peace negotiations, the ICC was an enabling – though never the decisive – factor. Nevertheless, a better grasp by the Court of key political and social dynamics surrounding Juba and greater flexibility about the scope of the ICC's prosecutions – neither of which the ICC's distance discourse permits – would have greatly aided a negotiated solution to the conflict between the government and the LRA.

After the Barlonyo massacre in February 2004, Bigombe left her World Bank job in Washington DC to launch a series of negotiations with the LRA leadership – principally with Kony's deputy Vincent Otti – between March 2004 and April 2005. This mirrored Bigombe's negotiations with the LRA in 1993 and 1994 when she famously walked unguarded into the bush to meet Kony and his commanders.[68] By May 2005, however, Bigombe was holed up at the Acholi Inn in Gulu, with the LRA refusing to take her calls and the prospects for peace seemingly dashed. Unbeknown to Bigombe, the LRA had begun meeting representatives of the Sudan People's Liberation Movement/ Army (SPLM/A), which now controlled all of southern Sudan. This led to a meeting between Kony and Riek Machar, Vice President of the government of southern Sudan, in May 2006 that paved the way for the Juba talks.[69]

Bigombe and various Acholi civil society leaders argued that the threat of ICC prosecution jeopardised peace talks between her mediation team and the LRA commanders and would deter combatants from returning from the bush under the amnesty provision.[70] 'The peace process is currently on the shelf, stalled', Bigombe said in March 2006.

---

[68] B. O'Kadameri, 'Protracted Conflict, Elusive Peace: Initiatives to End the Violence in Northern Uganda', Accord Issue 11, Conciliation Resources, 2002.
[69] For fuller dissections of the Juba process, see R. Atkinson, '"The Realists in Juba"? An Analysis of the Juba Peace Talks', in T. Allen and K. Vlassenroot (eds.), *The Lord's Resistance Army: Myth and Reality*, Zed Books, 2011, pp. 205–21; M. Schomerus, 'Even Eating You Can Bite Your Tongue: Dynamics and Challenges of the Juba Peace Talks with the Lord's Resistance Army', Ph.D. thesis, London School of Economics and Political Science, 2012; Macdonald, 'Justice in Transition'; and L. K. Bosire, 'Judicial Statecraft in Kenya and Uganda: Explaining Transitional Justice Choices in the Age of the International Criminal Court', D.Phil thesis, University of Oxford, 2013.
[70] Author's interviews, Acholi Civil Society members, Gulu, 7–10 March 2006.

I'm in daily contact with Otti...Otti expects my mediation to continue...Ocampo expects mass surrender of the LRA and the war will end in
three months but this is impossible. We need to involve Kony and Otti in all
discussions...Otti called me two weeks ago, angry, saying, 'Do you still want
to talk?...If tomorrow Kony says I'll talk, what flexibility will there be from
the ICC?' The current rigidity of the ICC complicates this process so much.
Otti asked if he could talk to Ocampo through me. But he also said, 'I know
the cells are already ready', so this is a big problem.[71]

Lars Erik Skaansar, the UN envoy to the northern Uganda peace
process, whose team supported Bigombe throughout the 2004–5 negotiations, echoed her views:

The main effect of the ICC warrants is that Kony is much more reluctant to
call Bigombe. Otti is still in regular contact but not Kony. Initially Bigombe
told Otti he could still use the amnesty but that train has gone...After the
ICC, the UN peace team can't meet the LRA. The peace team approached
Ocampo about the arrest warrants. The Rome Statute says that justice can be
put on hold for the sake of peace processes. Ocampo made a taped broadcast
on [Mega FM] in the north. He changed his wording on the advice of the
peace team, a meeting I participated in. He said, 'We support the UN and its
peace efforts but we also have the support of the international community.'
Ocampo promised to cooperate with the peace team but he has never
been here.[72]

Reflecting these concerns, the ARLPI sent delegations to The Hague in
March and April 2005 to lobby against ICC investigations.[73]

The ICC countered these claims, arguing that the Bigombe peace
talks had stalled long before the issuance of the warrants and that new
initiatives were necessary to achieve peace and security. Ocampo
stated that the dramatic change in LRA tactics in mid- to late 2005,
particularly the movement of large numbers of LRA combatants,
including Kony and Otti, into north-eastern DRC, stemmed from the

[71] Author's interview, Betty Bigombe, Gulu, 10 March 2006.
[72] Author's interview, Lars Erik Skaansar, UN humanitarian affairs officer and UN
special envoy to the northern Uganda peace process, Gulu, 8 March 2006.
[73] IRIN News, 'The ICC and the Northern Uganda Conflict', 9 June 2005,
www.irinnews.org/fr/node/222384. For a detailed discussion of the interactions
between the ARLPI and the ICC, see, K. Apuuli, 'Peace over Justice: The Acholi
Religious Leaders Peace Initiative vs. the International Criminal Court in
Northern Uganda', *Studies in Ethnicity and Nationalism*, 11, 1, 2011,
pp. 116–29.

threat of ICC prosecution and showed the ICC's inherent contribution to lasting peace.[74]

The reality probably lies somewhere between Bigombe's and Ocampo's depictions. By the time the ICC unsealed arrest warrants for the LRA commanders in October 2005, Bigombe's negotiations had already faltered, due mainly to the signing of the Comprehensive Peace Agreement (CPA) between the SPLM and the Sudanese government in January 2005. One key outcome of the CPA was to catalyse a joint SPLA, UPDF and Sudanese army counter-insurgency against the LRA, whose main bases were in southern Sudan. This forced the LRA into Garamba National Park in north-eastern DRC and greatly disrupted Bigombe's communications with Otti and other LRA leaders.[75] While the ICC arrest warrants were not the primary reason Bigombe's talks broke down, Ocampo inaccurately ascribed the LRA's exodus to the threat of ICC prosecution. Once the warrants were issued, it then became almost impossible for Bigombe to restart the negotiations despite maintaining regular contact with Otti.

Several other factors undermined the Bigombe talks and carried into the Juba negotiations in 2006.[76] The main impediment was the LRA's distrust of Museveni and the Ugandan government. While Bigombe was trying to negotiate, the UPDF was busy attacking the LRA in southern Sudan, an act repeated at the beginning of the Juba process, which led to the killing of LRA commander and ICC suspect Raskia Lakwiya on 12 August 2006.[77] Kolo, the LRA's chief negotiator in the Bigombe talks who surrendered to the UPDF in February 2005, said, 'Even on the amnesty issue, the LRA doesn't trust the government...How can we trust Museveni when the government keeps attacking us?'[78]

---

[74] Author's interview, Ocampo, 22 March 2006.

[75] Senior UN sources claimed that Kony never travelled to the DRC but remained in Sudan and that Otti spent only limited time in the DRC, leaving some LRA units there before quickly rejoining Kony in Sudan. Author's interviews, UN officials, Kampala and Gulu, March 2006.

[76] For an excellent analysis of the corrosive impact of the LRA's distrust of the government over issues including amnesty – long before Juba and throughout the negotiations – see Schomerus, 'Even Eating You Can Bite Your Tongue'.

[77] Atkinson, '"The Realists in Juba"?', p. 214.

[78] Author's interview, Sam Kolo, former LRA commander, Gulu, 10 March 2006.

The Bigombe process was also severely hampered by divisions among international actors over whether to support peace talks, military action against the LRA or the ICC. Father Carlos Rodriguez from the Gulu Catholic Diocese and the ARLPI said, 'There needs to be big pressure on Sudan but there's little chance of influence there because currently the international community is reluctant. The US was involved in the early days of the peace process with Betty Bigombe but less so now. Later Norway, the Netherlands, the UK got involved and that's continuing somewhat.'[79] Magnhild Vasset, Resident Representative of the Norwegian Refugee Council (NRC), echoed these views regarding the US position: 'The US plays a double role here. They're involved in peace but they also support the UPDF [military campaign against the LRA]. You have these US marines staying at the Acholi Inn [in Gulu]. Meanwhile [US-funded] NUPI [the Northern Ugandan Peace Initiative] holds seminar after seminar about building peace.'[80]

Another key peace-related debate in northern Uganda concerns whether the ICC arrest warrants incited a violent backlash by the LRA and worsened the overall humanitarian situation in late 2005. This calls into question the ICC's asserted role of prosecuting atrocity suspects to help end conflict. Civil society and other interviewees in early 2006, especially in Acholiland, argued that the ICC actively encouraged the government's military campaign in the north by advocating the armed capture of the LRA leadership. They cited the fact that, within a week of the opening of the ICC's case in Uganda, the government announced that it would re-enter Sudan to find and arrest the LRA commanders.[81] Acholi political, cultural and religious leaders protested vehemently against the issuance of the LRA warrants. Kolo, the returned LRA commander, said, 'The ICC coming here to stop the LRA is like trying to beat a snake with a piece of paper. It doesn't kill the snake but just makes it wilder.'[82]

---

[79] Author's interview, Father Carlos Rodriguez, Gulu Catholic Diocese and ARLPI, Gulu, 10 March 2006.
[80] Author's interview, Magnhild Vasset, Resident Representative, NRC, Gulu, 13 March 2006.
[81] Author's interviews, ARLPI member and local government official, Gulu, 9–10 March 2006.
[82] Author's interview, Kolo, 10 March 2006.

Fears of increased LRA activity were confirmed by several rebel attacks on NGO personnel in northern Uganda. This coincided with the government's 'decongestion' programme in late 2005, which moved tens of thousands of IDPs from bigger to smaller camps, severely disrupting camp life but without substantially improving people's living conditions.[83] In late October and early November 2005, three international aid workers were killed in two LRA ambushes near the Sudan–Uganda border.[84] 'There's no question the ICC arrest warrants have jeopardised our security here', said Vasset from the NRC in Gulu:

LRA activity peaked in 2003 and 2004 but in early and mid-2005 things quietened down. Then there were the October attacks on the NGOs. This changed the whole perception of the security situation. There is no question this was related to the ICC arrest warrants. Suddenly it's become difficult to access the camps. We need escorts and many NGOs are reconsidering their presence here. MSF [Médecins sans Frontières] for example is considering leaving. Kitgum and Pader have quietened down but Gulu has worsened considerably. And of course there were the UN peacekeeper [murders by the LRA in Garamba National Park in January 2006], which frightened many people here. I was away in December and January and when I came back I could see all of these changes...CSOPNU [Civil Society Organisations for Peace in Northern Uganda] has been highly concerned about the ICC going public. Many groups here saw a link between the October attacks and the ICC announcements.[85]

Ocampo argued – with some justification – that, while the LRA had attacked some foreign NGO personnel, violence against civilians in northern Uganda had generally decreased after the issuance of the ICC warrants.[86] It is not clear, though, that a decrease in LRA attacks

[83] Author's interview, community sub-chief, Pabbo, 11 March 2006.
[84] IRIN News, 'Uganda–Sudan: Another International NGO Worker Killed by LRA Rebels', 7 November 2005, www.irinnews.org/news/2005/11/07/another-international-ngo-worker-killed-lra-rebels.
[85] Author's interview, Vasset, 13 March 2006.
[86] Author's interview, Ocampo, 22 March 2006. Various international legal commentators echo these claims regarding the ICC's contribution to peace in northern Uganda. A paradigmatic example is a bullish 2005 article by Payam Akhavan, whose role in advising the Ugandan government's self referral to the ICC was discussed in Chapter 3. Akhavan argues, 'Thus far, the empirical evidence suggests that international commitment to the [ICC] referral's success has contributed to the LRA's incapacitation. Sudan has been persuaded to end its support of the LRA...All of these developments are in sharp contrast to the

during this period resulted directly from the ICC's investigations. A key catalyst in this regard was undoubtedly the Sudanese government's reduced assistance to the LRA, as a result of the signing of the CPA between Khartoum and the government of southern Sudan and international pressure on Khartoum to ensure greater stability around the Sudan–Uganda border.[87] In sum, during this period, the ICC intervention led to the LRA targeting international NGO workers – to send a message to the international community about the arrest warrants – but the ICC was only a peripheral factor in the general environment of decreased violence against northern Ugandan civilians.

A major issue in the contestation over the Juba talks between 2006 and 2008 has been the impact of the ICC in pushing the LRA to negotiate for peace. Various senior ICC officials and academic commentators have argued that without the threat of ICC prosecution, the LRA would never have considered negotiating with the Ugandan government.[88] This argument is unconvincing in two key respects. As highlighted above, the signing of the CPA, which greatly weakened the LRA by threatening its bases in southern Sudan, occurred nine months before the ICC issued arrest warrants for the LRA leadership. While some LRA attacks continued in late 2005, the group's scope for violence was clearly curtailed by the CPA and the subsequent joint

---

period preceding the referral, during which LRA atrocities reached a new peak. This recent willingness to negotiate is linked to the LRA's political isolation and military containment – both of which are linked to the new context created by the ICC referral. In this respect at least, it would not be unreasonable to suggest that even without a single prosecution, the LRA referral has already been a success' (Akhavan, 'The Lord's Resistance Army Case', pp. 404–5). While the ICC referral was crucial in persuading the LRA to negotiate rather than continue fighting, Akhavan argues, negotiating with the LRA is futile. 'The view that dialogue with fanatical murderous leaders would somehow lead to a peaceful settlement is a chimera, often encouraged by an international community that is eager to insulate itself from genuine engagement in putting an end to the atrocities. It is time for the international community to transform the triumphalism of global justice into reality. Instead of holding Uganda hostage to never-ending, and potentially futile, negotiations, the international community. . .should focus on the arrest and prosecution of the perpetrators' (ibid., pp. 419–20).

[87] By early 2007, however, various Ugandan analysts claimed that Khartoum's support for the LRA had returned to previous levels (author's interviews, local journalists and academics, Kampala and Gulu, 19–27 February 2007).

[88] See, for example, Akhavan, 'The Lord's Resistance Army Case', p. 404; Chung, 'Punishment and Prevention', pp. 233–40.

counter-insurgency against the rebels. As Ron Atkinson argues, the signing of the CPA pushed the LRA toward peace talks by forcing the Sudanese government to halt its support for the LRA, dispersing the LRA from its bases and incentivising the newly autonomous government of southern Sudan to deal with 'foreign forces' including the LRA. This provided the grounds for the clandestine talks between the SPLM/A and the LRA mentioned above, which were central to the start of the Juba negotiations in 2006.[89]

The ICC arrest warrants may have provided an additional incentive for the LRA to negotiate. However, to frame the ICC as the only – or even the main – catalyst in this regard belies a series of more fundamental regional political developments months before the ICC arrest warrants. There is also a certain disingenuousness in Ocampo's and other ICC officials' argument that the warrants forced the LRA to negotiate at Juba, given that they vehemently opposed any attempts by the LRA to find a negotiated solution to the threat of ICC arrest. The ICC cannot justifiably take credit for catalysing the Juba talks when it subsequently challenged the basis on which the LRA supposedly joined the process.

Concerning the Juba talks themselves, debates have centred on whether blame for the collapse of the negotiations should ultimately rest with the ICC. Such a perspective is widespread among many northern Ugandan civil society and community-level actors as well as in the commentary on the Juba talks.[90] The ICC acknowledged these concerns over its impact and announced in December 2006 that it would launch a review into the matter, although it is unclear whether the review was ever conducted as no findings were ever publicised.[91]

The Juba talks officially began on 14 July 2006 and were structured around five agenda items: a cessation to hostilities; comprehensive political solutions to the conflict; accountability and reconciliation; DDR; and a permanent ceasefire. Hopes were raised with the signing of a cessation to hostilities agreement on 26 August 2006, which was

---

[89] Atkinson, '"The Realists in Juba"?', pp. 207–14.
[90] Author's interviews, civil society representatives, Gulu and Lira, 2008–15.
[91] International Criminal Court, Pre-Trial Chamber II, 'Order to the Prosecutor for the Submission of Additional Information on the Status of the Execution of the Warrants of Arrest in the Situation in Uganda', Situation in Uganda, *The Prosecutor v. Joseph Kony, Vincent Otti, Raska Lukwiya, Okot Odhiambo and Dominic Ongwen*, 30 November 2006.

renewed seven times throughout the duration of the talks.[92] From the outset, foremost among the LRA's demands was the withdrawal of the ICC arrest warrants against its commanders, allowing them to take up the government's amnesty, participate in cleansing and reintegration rituals in northern Uganda and, according to some observers, secure exile in southern Sudan or elsewhere.[93] The LRA's demand proved highly controversial, and the ICC stated shortly after that it would not withdraw the arrest warrants.[94] Meanwhile, the government – which had initially backed the LRA's request – then claimed to support the ICC's refusal to grant it.[95]

In response to the government's and the ICC's stance, in November 2006 Kony called three northern Ugandan political leaders – Norbert Mao, Walter Ochora and Alphonse Owiny-Dollo – to Garamba National Park to brief him on legal and political matters stemming from the ICC intervention. The three leaders travelled with Jan Egeland, UN head of humanitarian affairs. The day before leaving for Garamba, Owiny-Dollo, former Minister of State for the reconstruction of northern Uganda, told the author,

We've been called to Congo because Kony is seriously considering his options. Does he remain in the wilds of Congo or seek refuge elsewhere, for example in Sudan? Does he send his troops home and remain mobile or try to stay where he is now?...Kony is well aware of the situation with the ICC but he needs advice on the details. Our advice will be that there will be no easy removal of the ICC warrants.[96]

---

[92] Government of Uganda and the Lord's Resistance Army, 'Agreement on Cessation of Hostilities between the Government of the Republic of Uganda and the Lord's Resistance Army/Movement', 26 August 2006, p. 1.

[93] Author's interview, Alphonse Owiny-Dollo, Lira, 10 November 2006. The LRA also proposed that Uganda be governed under a federalist system that would afford northern districts greater autonomy (IRIN News, 'Uganda: Rebels Propose Federalist Solution at Juba Talks', 11 October 2006, www.irinnews.org/report.aspx?reportid=61303).

[94] International Criminal Court, Pre-Trial Chamber II, 'Submission of Information on the Status of the Execution of the Warrants of Arrest in the Situation in Uganda', Situation in Uganda, *The Prosecutor v. Joseph Kony, Vincent Otti, Raska Lukwiya, Okot Odhiambo and Dominic Ongwen*, 6 October 2006.

[95] Daily Monitor, 'Museveni Says ICC Indictments Will Stay Until Peace Agreement Signed', 27 October 2006, www.ugandacan.org/item/1781.

[96] Author's interview, Owiny-Dollo, 10 November 2006.

Owiny-Dollo reported after the meetings that Kony was willing to
stand trial in Uganda if it meant the ICC would remove the warrants.
'Kony made it clear that the ICC is biased, it has heard only one side of
the story and now he says he is willing to stand trial in Uganda',
Owiny-Dollo said. 'He mentioned Luzira and Lugore prisons which
means he is ready to face anything.'[97] The LRA announced in February
2007 that it would send a delegation of lawyers to The Hague to meet
Ocampo and petition directly for the removal of the ICC arrest
warrants.[98]

The Juba negotiations stalled between December 2006 and April
2007 after the LRA walked out, demanding a change of venue and
mediator.[99] Once the talks resumed – with Riek Machar remaining as
mediator but now supported by former President of Mozambique,
Joachim Chissano, who was appointed UN special envoy to the northern Ugandan conflict in December 2006 – the next year brought a
flurry of activity. This included the signing of the comprehensive
political solutions agreement on 2 May 2007, providing a roadmap
for addressing the root causes of the LRA rebellion; the accountability
and reconciliation agreement signed on 29 June 2007, with an implementation protocol signed on 19 February 2008; the agreement on a
permanent ceasefire signed on 23 February 2008; and the agreement
on DDR signed on 29 February 2008. The final peace agreement which
brought together all of the aforementioned agreements, however, was
never signed, meaning these protocols could never be fully
implemented.[100]

Blaming the ICC solely for the breakdown in the Juba talks belies the
fact that the negotiations lasted two full years and led to the

---

[97] Quoted in Daily Monitor, 'LRA Leader Kony Reportedly Willing to Face Trial
in Uganda, Not The Hague', 20 December 2006, www.ugandacan.org/archive/
1/2006-12.

[98] Daily Monitor, 'LRA High Command Hires Two International Lawyers to
Represent Kony and Others at ICC', 2 February 2007.

[99] Later, when the talks stalled over the final agreement, one proposal that the UN
considered – and for which some logistical arrangements were made through
Oxford Transitional Justice Research (OTJR) – was to move the negotiations to
a location with less media, NGO and diplomatic attention at Rhodes House,
University of Oxford (email correspondence, UN officials, Geneva, Juba, Gulu,
Kampala, March–April 2008).

[100] M. Tran, 'Ugandan Rebel Leader Fails to Sign Peace Deal', *Guardian*, 11 April
2008, www.theguardian.com/world/2008/apr/11/uganda.

agreements on these highly contentious issues, all while the ICC warrants hung over the LRA leadership. This equally counters the claim by Mark Kersten and others that the government and the LRA never took the talks seriously.[101] The ICC's intervention did nevertheless weaken the Juba process from the outset. A structural effect of the ICC warrants was the fact that none of the five LRA commanders charged by the Court – including Otti who had displayed an openness to negotiation during the previous process with Bigombe[102] – could lead the rebel delegation in Juba. Of the fifteen LRA delegates sent to Juba, only two, Col. Lubwe Bwone and Lt. Col. Santo Alit, were active commanders and had been present at failed LRA–government peace talks in 2004, thus bringing critical experience to the Juba process. A source of constant frustration for the mediation and advisory team to the talks was uncertainty over whether the LRA delegation spoke legitimately on behalf of the leadership in the bush and had the authority to enact the agreements signed in Juba, including the cessation to hostilities.[103] Regular changes to the leadership of the LRA delegation in Juba exacerbated this dynamic, as the did the murder of Otti – reportedly at the hands of Kony in early November 2007 – as he had maintained regular contact with the delegation.[104]

The ICC warrants also fundamentally shaped the tenor and substance of the Juba negotiations. During and after the two-year process, the LRA said repeatedly that it would neither sign the remaining sections of the final agreement nor countenance laying down its arms and demobilising its forces until the ICC warrants were withdrawn.[105] Particularly in the early stages of the talks, the issue of the arrest warrants was a major distraction to the five-point agenda. The first eighteen months of the talks, especially on the third agenda item of accountability and reconciliation, were dominated by discussions over modalities for removing the warrants or at least pausing the ICC

---

[101] Kersten, *Justice in Conflict*, pp. 101–4.
[102] Author's interviews, Bigombe, 10 March 2006, Kolo, 10 March 2006, and Lars Erik Skaansar, UN Representative to Northern Ugandan Peace Negotiations, Gulu, 8 March 2006.
[103] Author's interviews, members of Juba mediation team, Juba and Kampala, 10–21 February 2007.
[104] Ibid.
[105] Daily Monitor, 'LRA Leader Kony Reportedly Willing to Face Trial in Uganda, Not The Hague', 20 December 2006.

investigations for one year renewable under Article 16 of the Rome
Statute.[106]

A major complicating factor in the early stages of the talks was both
the Ugandan government's and the LRA delegation's weak grasp of the
Statute and what was considered permissible under international law.
The government of southern Sudan and UN mediation team, principally its chief legal advisor, Barney Afako, spent considerable time
educating both sides on the international legal parameters of the
negotiations, including the limitations imposed by the fact that the
ICC had already issued arrest warrants for the LRA leadership.[107]
Sandrine Perrot reports that even within the mediation team and

---

[106] ICC investigations and prosecutions can be halted in three ways. First,
according to Article 16 of the Rome Statute, the UN Security Council, acting
under Chapter VII of the UN Charter, may request a twelve-month pause to
investigations and prosecutions, which may be renewed at the end of that
period. This could enable, for example, peace talks to continue without the
threat of ICC prosecution of any of the parties involved or the state concerned
to reform its judiciary in order to justify domestic prosecutions. Second, under
Articles 17 and 19, an accused person or a state with jurisdiction over a
particular case can petition the PTC for the ICC to halt investigations or
prosecutions on the grounds that the state is willing and able to investigate and
prosecute the case. If the PTC believes that there are sufficient grounds for the
deferral of a case to the domestic jurisdiction, it will advise the Prosecutor to
suspend investigations. The Prosecutor may request a review of such a decision
and also regular updates on proceedings by domestic judiciaries that have
succeeded in reclaiming jurisdiction over the case in question. Third, under
Article 53, the Prosecutor may appeal to the PTC to halt an investigation or
prosecution if it 'is not in the interests of justice, taking into account all the
circumstances, including the gravity of the crime, the interests of victims and the
age or infirmity of the alleged perpetrator, and his or her role in the alleged
crime'. Paul Seils and Marieke Wierda argue that Article 53 shows that the ICC
does not support 'the view that justice must be done whatever the price' (P. Seils
and M. Wierda, 'The International Criminal Court and Conflict Mediation',
International Center for Transitional Justice, Occasional Paper Series, June
2005, p. 12). However, they also argue that the ICC 'cannot be seen to be a
hostage to threats to abandon a peace process (from either side)' (ibid., p. 13).
The Rome Statute does not clearly define 'the interests of justice' and whether
they may relate to the interests of peace or some other societal goal. The
International Crisis Group argues that a Prosecutor's request to suspend
investigations or prosecutions on the basis of Article 53 would be more feasible
if 'a genuine, robust and credible reconciliation and accountability process in is
prospect as part of a negotiated settlement' (International Crisis Group,
'Building a Comprehensive Peace Strategy for Northern Uganda', Africa
Briefing No. 27, 23 June 2005, p. 9).

[107] Author's interview, Barney Afako, legal advisor to Juba mediation team,
London, 2 March 2007.

among the various donors supporting the Juba process, there was substantial disagreement and confusion over how to balance the demands of the Rome Statute and the Ugandan Amnesty Act.[108]

Meanwhile, the ICC intervened routinely, often acerbically, in the negotiations with a series of public statements, supported by various UN agencies and international human rights organisations, stating that the ICC arrest warrants must be enacted.[109] These international interventions had two principal effects: first, to raise the temperature of the negotiations, framing various LRA proposals solely as attempts to extricate its leadership from the ICC warrants; and, second, to pressure all of the parties in Juba to narrow the parameters of substantive discussion. This amounted to significant over-reach by the ICC and its supporters and tainted the atmosphere and content of the Juba talks.[110] The barbed statements by the ICC Prosecutor and other senior Court officials – particularly as the third agenda item was being discussed in 2007 – complicated the mediators' task.[111] At a diplomatic briefing in October 2007, Ocampo described the entire Juba process as an attempt by the LRA to regroup and rearm while the world was distracted. 'The criminals have threatened to resume violence if the arrest warrants are not withdrawn', he said. 'They are setting conditions. It is blackmail. The international community has to ensure protection of those exposed to those threats...Those warrants must be executed. There is no excuse. There is no tension between peace and justice in Uganda: arrest the sought criminals today and you will have peace and justice tomorrow. Victims deserve both.'[112] After Ocampo's briefing, the Ugandan

---

[108] S. Perrot, 'Northern Uganda: A "Forgotten Conflict", Again? The Impact of the Internationalization of Conflict Resolution', in T. Allen and K. Vlassenroot (eds.), *The Lord's Resistance Army: Myth and Reality*, Zed Books, 2011, pp. 198–9. See also Kersten, *Justice in Conflict*, pp. 89–90.

[109] See, for example, ICC, OTP, 'Statement by the Chief Prosecutor Luis Moreno-Ocampo', 12 July 2006; Ocampo's quotes in Osike and Musaka, 'ICC Insists Kony Must Face Prosecution'; HRW, 'Benchmarks for Assessing Possible National Alternatives'; AI, 'Amnesty International Letter to Security Council'.

[110] For an analysis of the power imbalances around peace versus justice debates at Juba – highlighting that the more powerful actors were broadly on the 'justice' side and were largely successful at sidelining those on the 'peace' side – see K. Armstrong, 'Justice without Peace? International Justice and Conflict Resolution in Northern Uganda', *Development and Change*, 45, 3, 2014, pp. 589–607.

[111] Author's interviews, members of Juba mediation team, 10–24 February 2007.

[112] Quoted in Osike and Musaka, 'ICC Insists Kony Must Face Prosecution'.

state-owned newspaper, the *New Vision*, reported that the government supported Ocampo's criticisms:

Internal affairs minister, Dr. Ruhakana Rugunda, the leader of the Government delegation at the Juba talks, said Ocampo's statements were in order because he was carrying out the mandate of the ICC, to which Uganda is a member. The lifting of the arrest warrants would only be dealt with after the signing of a peace agreement, accountability has been carried out and impunity dealt with. [Only then] will the Government ask the ICC to review the indictments, [Rugunda] said.[113]

The variability of the Ugandan government's position on amnesty and prosecutions created further distrust among the LRA delegation.[114] On several occasions, Museveni announced that, if the LRA leaders would surrender, he would withdraw Uganda's referral to the ICC and the leaders would receive amnesties and pass through reconciliation rituals.[115] Following a visit to The Hague in July 2006 by Ugandan Minister for Security, Amama Mbabazi, however, Ocampo reported, 'The Government of Uganda did not ask for any withdrawal of the warrants of arrest. The arrest warrants remain in effect. It is the view of the Office of the Prosecutor and the Government of Uganda that justice and peace have worked together thus far and can continue to work together.'[116] The view that the state could unilaterally withdraw its referral to the ICC persisted, especially in Ugandan government and civil society circles. States, however, do not possess such capabilities. If a government withdraws its referral, the Prosecutor can still employ his or her *proprio motu* powers under Article 15 of the Rome Statute to proceed with investigations.

Finally, the ICC arrest warrants curtailed various options during the Juba process, especially concerning the third agenda item on

---

[113] Ibid.
[114] As Caroline Lamwaka and Sverker Finnström argue, the Ugandan government's changeability on issues of pardons and amnesties – and the subsequent distrust sowed with various negotiating parties, going back as far as the UPDA in the late 1980s – has undermined various peace processes in Uganda (C. Lamwaka, *The Raging Storm: A Reporter's Inside Account of the Northern Uganda War 1986–2005*, Fountain Publishers, 2016, ch. 7; and Finnström, 'An African Hell of Colonial Imagination?', pp. 79–80).
[115] See, for example, BBC, 'Uganda LRA Rebels Reject Amnesty', 7 July 2006, http://news.bbc.co.uk/2/hi/africa/5157220.stm.
[116] ICC, OTP, 'Statement by the Chief Prosecutor Luis Moreno-Ocampo', 12 July 2006.

accountability and reconciliation. As discussed above, the UN and other international actors with access to the Juba negotiators stressed consistently that the Amnesty Act could not legally apply to the LRA commanders. The Ugandan government claimed two months before the start of the Juba talks that the amendment to the Act denied amnesty to the LRA commanders or any other high-ranking suspects of international criminals. The May 2006 amendment to the Act, however, simply states, 'Notwithstanding the provisions of section 2 of the Act a person shall not be eligible for the grant of amnesty if he or she is declared not eligible by the Minister [of Internal Affairs] by the statutory instrument made with the approval of Parliament.'[117] This provision is much less restrictive than the changes proposed in an Amnesty Amendment Bill tabled in 2003 and gives the Minister of Internal Affairs the authority to deny amnesty to particular named suspects. At no point during or after the Juba process, however, did the Minister do this concerning the LRA or any other rebel leaders.[118]

The insistence by the government and various international actors that the Amnesty Act did not apply to the LRA leaders charged by the ICC caused anger among the LRA delegation and the Acholi civil society leadership that travelled to Juba.[119] Reflecting this, Machar's guidelines for government and LRA popular consultations on the accountability and reconciliation agenda item emphasised the need to consult widely on possible changes to the Amnesty Act and the links between traditional and formal justice mechanisms.[120] Afako also reported that the supposed prohibition against the amnesty stymied the discussions and gave the LRA delegation, their supporters and some members of the mediation team a sense that 'we did not own this process, that it was being curtailed by outside parties'.[121]

While the ICD of the Ugandan High Court, which emerged as a key mechanism from the Juba negotiations, was intended to construct a national prosecutorial mechanism that cohered with the Rome Statute, the LRA delegation viewed it as an attempt to steamroll their concerns

---

[117] Government of Uganda, 'Amnesty (Amendment) Act', 24 May 2006.
[118] See discussion with Justice Peter Onega, chairman of the Amnesty Commission, Radio Rhino International Afrika, 'Uganda News Summary', 5 July 2006.
[119] Author's interviews, civil society representatives, Juba and Gulu, June 2007–February 2008.
[120] R. Machar, 'Mediator's Guidelines', 28 June 2007, copy on file with author.
[121] B. Afako, comments at the 'Peace, Justice and the ICC in Africa' workshop.

about both domestic and international prosecutions. Simon Simonse, Willemijn Verkoren and Gerd Junne, who were part of the Pax Christi team that helped bring the government and LRA delegations to the negotiating table, argue that as the Juba process became more internationalised and legalistic – which they attribute both to the ICC and Chissano's mediation – the accountability and reconciliation options narrowed. They argue in particular that this excluded a range of mechanisms considered more legitimate by everyday northern Ugandans, particularly community-based rituals.[122]

Through the four phases of peace-related processes just outlined, the ICC contributed to the weakening of the Bigombe-led and Juba negotiations. While the Court was never the principal actor in decreasing violence or undermining peace processes, it stymied attempts to resolve peacefully the conflict between the LRA and the government. Consistent with the distance discourse, the ICC was rarely moved to consider its impact on peace negotiations, viewing itself as superior to such domestic efforts and regardless compatible with the broader pursuit of peace. The Court's capacity to evaluate fully its negative or positive impact on peace was also limited by its lack of deep contextual knowledge and the unwavering support of the ICC's epistemic community of international lawyers and international human rights organisations for the Court's prosecutions-at-all-costs approach.

Peace Negotiations in the DRC

The DRC has not generated the same 'peace versus justice' controversies as Uganda. Nonetheless, since the ICC launched investigations in the DRC in June 2004, the Court has overlapped with three major peace processes in which amnesty issues featured prominently: a series of informal peace negotiations with rebel groups mediated by the President of the Congolese TRC, Rev. Jean-Luc Kuye, in 2005 and 2006; the 2008 Goma talks which concerned primarily the CNDP rebel group; and the 2013 Kampala talks, focused on the M23 rebellion. The

---

[122] S. Simonse, W. Verkoren and G. Junne, 'NGO Involvement in the Juba Peace Talks: The Role and Dilemmas of IKV Pax Christi', in T. Allen and K. Vlassenroot (eds.), *The Lord's Resistance Army: Myth and Reality*, Zed Books, 2011, pp. 233–37.

ICC affected each of these processes differently, echoing some features of the Uganda case while diverging in several important ways.

First, the Congolese TRC incorporated an important element of peace mediation and negotiation. Article 5 of the TRC Statute broadened the commission's mandate to include active conflict resolution, described as 'the prevention or management of conflicts as they occur through mediation between divided communities.'[123] Kuye – the head of the Church of Christ in South Kivu, board member of Héretiers de la Justice, one of the largest Congolese human rights groups, and a civil society delegate to the Sun City talks in 2002 – and several TRC commissioners attempted to resolve conflict by travelling to Kisangani, Bukavu, Goma, Rutshuru and elsewhere to talk to protagonists.[124] Following RCD violence in North Kivu in January 2006, for example, Kuye and a delegation from the TRC travelled to meet with Laurent Nkunda, other RCD commanders and community leaders in Rutshuru and Goma.[125]

Kuye argued that the ICC hampered the TRC's efforts because belligerents refused to confess to crimes or cooperate with mediators for fear of evidence being used against them in criminal trials, either through the ICC or the domestic courts. 'The ICC came up forcefully in our discussions with several rebel leaders, including Nkunda', Kuye said. 'We would start talking to them, make good progress, then the conversation would stop. They didn't want to incriminate themselves, even when we stressed that the amnesty was in place.'[126] This situation echoes challenges in other countries such as Sierra Leone and Timor-Leste that have deployed trials and truth commissions simultaneously. Within such a structure, the former process typically addresses serious violations by high-ranking perpetrators while the latter addresses crimes by less senior actors. As various commentators have argued, however, the threat of prosecutions in such cases often deters even lower-ranking actors from appearing before truth commissions.[127]

---

[123] Government of the Democratic Republic of Congo, 'Loi No. 04/018 du 30 juillet 2004 Portant Organisation, Attributions et Fonctionnement de la Commission Vérité et Réconciliation', 30 July 2004, Article 5.

[124] Author's interview, Jean-Luc Kuye, President, TRC, Kinshasa, 24 January 2006.

[125] Ibid.   [126] Ibid.

[127] See, for example, K. Lanegran, 'Truth Commissions, Human Rights Trials and the Politics of Memory', *Comparative Studies of South Asia, Africa and the Middle East*, 25, 1, 2005, pp. 111–21.

While the ICC limited the TRC's mediation function, it should not be viewed as the main cause of the rapid collapse of the TRC in 2007, before it could hand down its final report. More fundamental catalysts of the breakdown included the fact that most of Kuye's fellow commissioners were themselves senior figures in rebel groups such as the MLC, RCD and various Mai Mai groups and therefore deterred most everyday Congolese from giving evidence to the commission[128]; the TRC lacked substantial financial and logistical support from the Congolese government[129]; and the commission ultimately buckled under the weight of its vast mandate (alongside its role in uncovering the truth about past atrocities, handing down amnesties and facilitating peace mediation, it was also expected to deliver victim reparations and hold reconciliation ceremonies between perpetrators and victims).[130] While the ICC undoubtedly weakened the TRC's efforts to pursue talks with the likes of Nkunda, from the outset the TRC displayed major structural flaws that it never overcame.

In January 2008, the Goma peace talks in January 2008 between the Congolese government and twenty-two rebel groups – but centring on the CNDP – began to show the more direct influence of the ICC, including flow-on effects from the concurrent Ugandan peace talks. The Goma talks comprised two parallel events, a large public

---

[128] A meeting of the International Human Rights Law Group (IHRLG), an umbrella body of local and international human rights organisations, in Kinshasa in July 2003 produced a document recommending that the TRC comprise thirty-five community leaders who are 'not members of office' (International Human Rights Law Group, 'Les Principes Clés d'une Commission Vérité et Réconciliation', July 2003, p. 14). Members of the IHRLG were dismayed when the government sanctioned that only the parties to the ICD could elect commissioners, nearly all of whom are political leaders, and before the National Assembly had even passed the TRC Law (author's interviews, local human rights workers, Kinshasa, 19–30 January 2006.) In 2006, a Munyamulenge member of the National Assembly said, 'The TRC has no credibility when those kinds of groups are represented. I am a Christian and I cannot confess to a priest if he is a thief. That is what the population asks about the TRC: how can I confess to those thieves?' (author's interview, member of National Assembly, Kinshasa, 19 January 2006). Much of the population claims that it is too fearful to give evidence to the TRC because of the presence of atrocity perpetrators on the Commission (author's interviews, general population, Kinshasa, Goma, Rutshuru, Bunia, Bukavu, 19 January–21 February 2006).

[129] Author's interviews, Kuye and TRC commissioners, Kinshasa and Goma, 24–30 January 2006.

[130] Ibid.

conference involving 1,200 members of civil society and rebel groups, which produced two working group reports on justice and related matters, and a smaller set of negotiations in a neighbouring hotel primarily between the government and the CNDP, facilitated by the UN, the US and the EU.[131] Ultimately, the talks did little to curb the CNDP's violence, which culminated in the massacre of 150 civilians in Kiwanja, North Kivu, in November 2008.[132]

The ICC had little impact on the government or rebel parties in Goma but influenced substantially the work of the international mediators. The CNDP pressed hard for a blanket amnesty that would include charges of genocide, war crimes and crimes against humanity, arguing that the 2005 amnesty law was too restrictive in this regard.[133] Despite strong civil society opposition to any form of amnesty for the rebels, Emmanuel Luzolo, the Congolese Minister of Justice and Human Rights, wrote to the Attorney-General, Tshimanga Mukeba, soon after the signing of the Goma agreement, stating that no criminal proceedings should be carried out against any members of the rebel groups that had signed the agreement.[134] Several observers who interviewed the EU and other international mediators in Goma, however, underline the 'invisible presence'[135] of the ICC during the negotiations, principally on the legality of amnesties for international crimes. In particular, the mediators wanted to avoid the heated contestation over amnesties and international prosecutions that dominated the Ugandan peace talks. For this reason, EU Special Representative for the Great Lakes Region, Roeland van de Geer, tabled guidelines designed to avoid amnesties for crimes within the ICC's jurisdiction.[136]

The UN, however, found itself in a more complicated position, having supported through MONUC the use of blanket amnesties for

[131] L. Davis and P. Hayner, 'Difficult Peace, Limited Justice: Ten Years of Peacemaking in the DRC', International Center for Transitional Justice, March 2009, pp. 18–19.
[132] Human Rights Watch, 'Killings in Kiwanja: The UN's Inability to Protect Civilians', 11 December 2008.
[133] L. Davis, 'Case Study: Democratic Republic of Congo', International Justice and the Prevention of Atrocities project, European Council on Foreign Relations, November 2013, p. 4; Government of the Democratic Republic of Congo, 'Peace Agreement between the Government and the CNDP', Goma, 23 March 2009, Article 3.
[134] Davis, 'Case Study: Democratic Republic of Congo', p. 4.
[135] Davis, 'Power Shared and Justice Shelved', p. 9.
[136] Davis and Hayner, 'Difficult Peace, Limited Justice', p. 11.

the Ituri rebel leaders in 2006, discussed in the previous section, while supporting the EU opposition to amnesties for international crimes during the Goma process. Tatiana Carayannis observes that the UN found it an 'embarrassment' that the final Goma agreement involved a peace deal with CNDP deputy leader, Bosco Ntaganda.[137] At the time of the Goma talks, a sealed ICC arrest warrant for Ntaganda was in place (issued on 22 August 2006, it was unsealed soon after the Goma talks on 28 April 2008).[138] Laura Davis argues that rumours of the ICC warrant against Ntaganda abounded in Goma and reinforced the EU's and UN's stringent opposition to amnesties for international crimes. They did not want to jeopardise possible ICC moves against Ntaganda in the way that they perceived the Ugandan Amnesty Act to have done in the ICC cases against the LRA leaders.[139]

Despite these mediators' attempts, Ntaganda became an even more powerful political and military actor after the Goma process. In early 2009, he declared his leadership of the CNDP and cooperated with Rwanda in arresting his predecessor, Nkunda. Soon after, 6,000 CNDP troops were integrated into the Congolese army as part of a separate peace agreement between the government and the CNDP on 23 March 2009. Ntaganda was reinstated as a colonel in the FARDC. Two months later he became deputy commander of the Kimia II joint operations between the Congolese and Rwandan armed forces against the FDLR throughout North and South Kivu. Ntaganda remained a colonel in the Congolese army until he and other integrated CNDP leaders mutinied and formed the M23 in April 2012.[140]

The government's opposition to prosecutions for the rebel leaders involved in the Goma talks – compounded by its military promotion of Ntaganda despite the ICC arrest warrant against him – shows that, while prohibitions against amnesties for international crimes can be secured on paper, pursuing prosecutions for such crimes is an

---

[137] T. Carayannis, 'The Challenge of Building Sustainable Peace in the DRC', Centre for Humanitarian Dialogue, Background Paper, July 2009, p. 13.

[138] International Criminal Court, 'Ntaganda Case', Situation of the Democratic Republic of Congo, *The Prosecutor v. Bosco Ntaganda*.

[139] L. Davis, 'The EU and Post-conflict Interventions: Supporting Reform or Business as Usual? The Democratic Republic of Congo', conference paper, 2011, p. 9, www.gu.se/digitalAssets/1349/1349860_conf-2011-davis.pdf.

[140] For further discussion of Ntaganda's role in Kimia II and the build-up to the M23 rebellion, see M. Deibert, *The Democratic Republic of Congo: Between Hope and Despair*, Zed Books, 2013, ch. 8.

altogether separate matter. As argued earlier, this underscores the variability of both the Ugandan and the Congolese governments on questions of amnesties and prosecutions and, more broadly, their fluctuating cooperation with the ICC. The Court, however, did influence the behaviour of international mediators who succeeded in ensuring amnesties did not extend to international crimes (although this task was made considerably easier by the fact that previous amnesty laws in the DRC also did not apply in such cases). Meanwhile, the impact of the amnesty and prosecutions debates in Juba on the simultaneous negotiations in Goma highlights the vital intertwining of the Uganda and DRC cases.

Throughout 2013, the Kampala peace talks between the Congolese government and the M23 rebels – precipitated by the M23 capture of Goma in November 2012 – again showed the varied influence of the ICC. The stop–start negotiations, hosted by the Ugandan government under the auspices of the International Conference on the Great Lakes Region and observed by the UN, the AU and the US, lasted between December 2012 and December 2013. The talks were punctuated by a split in the M23, discussed in Chapter 1, between forces loyal to Ntaganda and Sultani Makenga, who had been a close ally of the now deposed Nkunda; Ntaganda's fleeing to Kigali in March 2013, which led to his transfer to the ICC; and a Peace, Security and Cooperation Framework for the DRC signed in Addis Ababa by the AU, UN and various regional governments, which paved the way for the more robustly mandated UN FIB against the M23 and other rebel groups in North and South Kivu.

Echoing the 2008 Goma talks between the Congolese government and the M23's predecessor organisation, the CNDP, the rebel leaders pressed hard for a blanket amnesty that would cover international crimes as well as a favourable reintegration into the Congolese army. The talks collapsed several times but the M23 leaders were eventually forced back to the negotiating table in September 2013 as the FIB severely weakened the rebel ranks and dispersed most of their fighters across the border into Rwanda and Uganda. The parties refused to sign a joint agreement and instead issued two separate declarations in Nairobi in December 2013. As a result of the talks, an amnesty law was passed in January 2014 that covered 'insurrectional acts' but not genocide, war crimes or crimes against humanity. Only twenty-nine M23 fighters were granted amnesty under the law, while the Congolese government deemed seventy-eight M23 members ineligible for reintegration into the FARDC and issued arrest warrants for nineteen M23 officials at large in Rwanda and Uganda.[141]

Despite the inevitable structural similarities between the Goma and Kampala talks, given that many of the key players were the same, some important differences over amnesty and ICC issues emerged. The early phases of the Kampala talks were dominated by debates over the scope of any amnesty. Crucial to these discussions was the fact that the ICC warrant against Ntaganda was now unsealed, increasing international pressure on the Congolese government to eschew amnesties for international crimes committed by the M23 and to hand Ntaganda over to the ICC. Interviews with observers to the talks indicate that the ICC was a much stronger force in the Kampala negotiations than in Goma because of the unsealing of the Ntaganda warrant and the perception that the ICC could turn its gaze toward other M23 leaders, including Makenga.[142] This pressure – coupled with the Congolese government's desire to avoid reintegrating the M23 leadership into the FARDC, given the failure of a similar move with the CNDP in 2008 – led to a more restricted amnesty policy after the Kampala process and, most tellingly, to arrest warrants for nineteen high-ranking M23 figures.

Similar to the behaviour of the LRA at the Juba talks, Ntaganda saw the Kampala process as a way to protect himself from ICC prosecution through the kind of senior military position he had secured through the Goma negotiations. Rumours were rife in Goma, Kigali and London throughout 2011 and 2012 that Ntaganda was seeking experienced defence counsel, given the likelihood that he would one day find himself in The Hague.[143] Jason Stearns argues that the ICC's conviction of Ntaganda's former UPC compatriot, Thomas Lubanga, in March 2012 rattled Ntaganda and was a key factor in his leading the M23 mutiny the following month.[144] This implies that Ntaganda no longer saw his senior rank in the Congolese army as insulation from

---

[141] Social Science Research Council, 'Consolidating the Peace: Closing the M23 Chapter', paper prepared on behalf of the DRC Affinity Group, December 2014, p. 8.

[142] Author's interviews, observers to Kampala peace talks, Kampala, 4 April 2015.

[143] Author's interviews, diplomats, lawyers and civil society representatives, Goma, Kigali, London, 2011–12.

[144] J. Stearns, 'Strongman of the Eastern DRC: A Profile of General Bosco Ntaganda', Rift Valley Institute, 12 March 2013, p. 3.

ICC prosecution, no doubt having witnessed what happened to Mathieu Ngudjolo.

Conclusion

Viewed side by side, the Ugandan and DRC cases highlight the crucial but diverse ways in which the ICC impinges on national amnesties and peace processes. Throughout peace negotiations in the two countries, the ICC was one – but never the decisive – barrier to peace, often exacerbating more fundamental challenges. The claims by the ICC and its backers that criminal investigations and prosecutions inevitably contribute to peace diverge from the deontological justifications for international justice discussed in Chapter 2, which view justice as an inherent good irrespective of its outcomes. Crucially, these consequentialist arguments ring hollow when assessed through the various phases of peace processes in the two countries. Participating in peace talks also encouraged the Ugandan and Congolese governments to use amnesties, while claiming simultaneously to support fully the ICC. This once again highlights the pitfalls of the ICC's reliance on cooperation with states which themselves display a wavering allegiance to the Court and a willingness, when required, to revert to amnesties for high-ranking suspects, including those charged by the ICC.

That these governments, the UN and other international bodies that ostensibly support the ICC so regularly advocate the use of amnesties – when confronted with the need to facilitate peace talks, DDR, SSR and TRCs – shows the continued utility of amnesty as a means to resolve mass conflict. While the ICC has rendered the Rome Statute an unavoidable touchstone in debates over amnesty and the conduct of peace talks today, these actors are reluctant to jettison amnesty entirely and to embrace international prosecutions fully. The ICC's conception of distance insists that justice should not bow to contextual calculations regarding peace-related outcomes. The Court's attempts to influence peace negotiations and strident opposition to amnesties (seen most vividly during the Juba talks), however, risk alienating actors who are directly embroiled in attempts to mitigate conflict and do not have the luxury of ignoring context and consequences.

7 | The ICC and Community-Based Responses to Atrocity

Introduction

International criminal law today continues to draw inspiration from the experience of the Nuremberg and Tokyo trials following the Second World War. Underpinning those trials was a belief that punishing elite perpetrators of grave crimes was necessary to condemn their actions publicly and to deter similar atrocities in the future.[1] The resonances of Nuremberg and Tokyo, especially the emphasis on prosecuting senior political and military officials, can be seen in all current international justice institutions. Serious questions arise, however, over the applicability of the Nuremberg model of international law when confronted with new forms of decentralised conflict since the end of the Cold War. Modern warfare – including the last thirty years in northern Uganda and eastern DRC, as highlighted by the popular perceptions examined in Chapter 4 – involves a wide range of state and non-state perpetrators, including political and military elites, rebel, militia and paramilitary groups and everyday citizens, with varying degrees of cohesive orchestration of violence.[2] Whereas the Nuremberg model assumes top-down crimes and therefore focuses on small numbers of elite perpetrators, modern conflict is often more diffuse, which necessitates new thinking on appropriate legal remedies. Furthermore, decentralised conflict and its impact on civilian populations raise important questions about the most effective non-legal responses, including pursuing broader social and economic objectives such as

[1] See, for example, C. Tomuschat, 'The Legacy of Nuremberg', *Journal of International Criminal Justice*, 4, 2006, pp. 830–44; and K. J. Heller, 'Retreat from Nuremberg: The Leadership Requirement in the Crime of Aggression', *European Journal of International Law*, 18, 3, 2007, pp. 477–97.
[2] See, for example, S. Kalyvas, *The Logic of Violence in Civil War*, Cambridge University Press, 2006; S. Straus, *The Order of Genocide: Race, Power, and War in Rwanda*, Cornell University Press, 2006; L. A. Fujii, *Killing Neighbors: Webs of Violence in Rwanda*, Cornell University Press, 2009.

truth recovery, psychosocial healing, economic development and rec-onciliation. These objectives highlight the multiple forms of harm that individuals and groups suffer following mass conflict and extend far beyond the remit of conventional court processes.

Responding to these two concerns – that accountability for non-elite perpetrators is also required and international trials alone will not address adequately the complex needs of transitional societies – an important challenge to the Nuremberg paradigm has emerged recently in the form of 'local' or 'community-based' responses to conflict. It is becoming increasingly common, particularly in various parts of Africa, to employ forms of local, customary or traditional justice and dispute resolution following mass atrocity. Two of the most prominent examples of this approach are the state-orchestrated *gacaca* courts in Rwanda, where 11,000 community-level jurisdictions between 2002 and 2012 prosecuted around 400,000 genocide suspects, and a range of northern Ugandan reintegration and reconciliation rituals, which have been used in the context of LRA combatants returning from the bush.[3] The impetus for community-level transitional justice emanates from various sources, including the need for faster, cheaper mechanisms to handle enormous backlogs of community-level perpet-rators; a frustration with expensive, often detached international approaches to transitional justice, especially war crimes tribunals, which focus only on high-level suspects; and a desire for local owner-ship in situations where a wide range of external interventions have historically constrained domestic sovereignty.

At the same time, a growing body of scholarship and practice criticises local approaches to transitional justice, which are often pathologised as inherently antagonistic, retributive, patriarchal, open to manipulation by national and community elites and responsible for some of the fiercest causes of mass violence.[4] As Nicola Palmer shows

---

[3] See, for example, P. Clark, *The Gacaca Courts, Post-Genocide Justice and Reconciliation in Rwanda: Justice without Lawyers*, Cambridge University Press, 2010; L. Waldorf, 'Mass Justice for Mass Atrocity: Rethinking Local Justice as Transitional Justice', *Temple Law Review*, 1, 55, 2006, pp. 1–80; B. Ingelaere, *Inside Rwanda's Gacaca Courts: Seeking Justice after Genocide*, University of Wisconsin Press, 2016; and T. Harlacher, F. Okot, C. Obonyo, M. Balthazard and R. Atkinson, *Traditional Ways of Coping in Acholi: Cultural Provisions for Reconciliation and Healing from War*, Caritas Gulu Archdiocese, 2007.

[4] See, for example, Amnesty International, 'Rwanda – Gacaca: A Question of Justice', AI Index AFR 47/007/2002, December 2002; Waldorf, 'Mass Justice for

in her study of the interactions among the ICTR, the Rwandan national courts and *gacaca*, a major impediment to the coordination of these institutions is their profound mutual miscomprehension and distrust. This includes a widespread view among ICTR personnel that the *gacaca* courts, overseen by lay judges elected by local communities and barring professional judges and lawyers, do not constitute a legitimate legal remedy after genocide.[5]

This chapter argues that such critiques of local approaches too easily dismiss the impetus for, and virtues of, these practices. They also fail to recognise that most of these criticisms apply just as equally – if not more so – to international criminal law, which itself is highly patriarchal, retributive, open to manipulation by various parties and capable of fomenting rather than resolving violent conflict. While it is imperative to highlight the various shortcomings of community-based transitional justice, to dismiss it out of hand means failing to grapple sufficiently with a widespread practice and its multifaceted consequences in central Africa and elsewhere.

This chapter focuses on the intersections between the ICC and these community 'spaces of justice'[6] in Uganda and the DRC. Specifically, it explores the overlaps among the ICC and a range of local rituals in northern Uganda and two important community-level mediation processes in eastern DRC, the *Barza Inter-Communautaire* in North and South Kivu and the RHA in Ituri. While recent scholarship has focused extensively on multi-institutional transitional justice responses to mass atrocity, most commentators have focused on connections between the international and national levels, with little examination of links between the international and community levels. This chapter argues that the ICC has often complicated the vital – although inevitably imperfect – work of community-level responses to conflict in Uganda

Mass Atrocity'; Allen, *Trial Justice*, especially ch. 6; E. Drexler, 'Addressing the Legacies of Mass Violence and Genocide in Indonesia and East Timor', in A. Hinton and K. O'Neill (eds.), *Genocide: Truth, Memory and Representation*, Duke University Press, 2009, pp. 219–45; Human Rights Watch, 'Justice Compromised: The Legacy of Rwanda's Community-Based Gacaca Courts', 31 May 2011; T. Allen and L. Storm, 'Quests for Therapy in Northern Uganda: Healing at Laropi Revisited', *Journal of Eastern African Studies*, 6, 1, 2012, pp. 22–46.
[5] Palmer, *Courts in Conflict*.
[6] C. Butler and E. Mussawir (eds.), *Spaces of Justice: Peripheries, Passages, Appropriations*, Routledge, 2017.

and the DRC. These local processes represent fundamentally different understandings of the causes of mass conflict and necessary responses to violence (including different conceptions of justice) from those espoused by the ICC. While the international level's scepticism of the 'local' is pronounced when relating to national actors and processes – consistent with the distance discourse – it is even more extreme regarding the community level.[7]

Community-Based Practices in Northern Uganda

This section focuses on a range of community-based rituals in northern Uganda designed to cleanse and reintegrate former combatants and reconcile them with conflict-affected communities. The analysis here examines the controversy over the LRA's proposal during the Juba talks to use community-based rituals rather than the ICC to address crimes by the LRA, including its leaders. These parties argued that local (especially Acholi) rituals constituted a crucial alternative to ICC prosecutions.[8] This section, as well as the next one on the DRC, is organised in three parts: first, some brief background to the practices under examination here; second, a discussion of the popularly perceived virtues and pitfalls of local processes; and, third a critical examination of the ICC's intersections with these community-based practices.

Background to Community-Based Mechanisms
in Northern Uganda

Echoing the debates over the Amnesty Act in Juba, those concerning community-based mechanisms in northern Uganda have tended to ignore the longer historical context of these approaches. Beyond the particular claims by the LRA delegation in Juba, considerations of localised responses to mass conflict reflect national constitutional

---

[7] See, for example, Nouwen's discussion of the OTP's outright rejection of 'traditional reconciliation mechanisms' as relevant for admissibility calculations in the Darfur situation (Nouwen, *Complementarity in the Line of Fire*, p. 301).

[8] Lord's Resistance Army Delegation to the Juba Talks, 'LRA Position Paper on Accountability and Reconciliation in the Context of Alternative Justice System for Resolving the Northern Ugandan and Southern Sudan Conflicts', August 2006, p. 1.

provisions and a longer history of community-level mediation and governance structures in Uganda. The Ugandan Constitution enshrines the concurrence of common and customary law.[9] As discussed further below, some government officials believe this legal arrangement may pave the way for the codification of northern rituals to handle serious criminal cases in the current conflict.[10] The creation and reform of traditional practices, particularly by national elites, is not a new phenomenon in Uganda, as shown by the history of the current LCs. Designed initially as fora for communal decision-making on day-to-day community issues, the LCs have evolved into the primary local-level political and judicial institution throughout Uganda.[11] The LCs, as they became known after Museveni's election victory in 1996, grew out of Resistance Councils (RCs) established by the National Resistance Army during the bush war to maintain law and order in rebel-held regions and to gather intelligence and mobilise recruitment in areas held by Milton Obote's government forces. Soon after the NRM's rise to power, Museveni proclaimed that 'popular justice' could help overcome the rampant corruption of political and judicial structures inherited from Idi Amin and Obote and reinvigorate Ugandan community life.[12] In 1987, the RCs and Committees Statute afforded the RCs the role of hearing low-level civil cases, as a means to overcoming the congestion of the Magistrates Courts and to making

---

[9] Republic of Uganda, *Constitution of the Republic of Uganda*, 1995, Preamble (Section XXIV) and Article 126.

[10] Author's interviews, Ugandan government officials, Kampala, 3–4 March 2006.

[11] Holly Porter – also drawing on Paul Gready's theorisation outlined in Chapter 2 – describes the LCs as an example of distanced state-based justice that has became embedded at the community level, albeit often without securing substantial popular legitimacy (H. Porter, 'Justice and Rape on the Periphery: The Supremacy of Social Harmony in the Space between Local Solutions and Formal Judicial Systems in Northern Uganda', *Journal of Eastern African Studies*, 6, 1, 2012, p. 89). Adam Branch meanwhile discusses widespread northern opposition to the establishment of first the RCs and later the LCs because of their perceived use by the NRM as a tool of surveillance and control and close links to violence perpetrated by local defence units (Branch, 'Exploring the Roots of LRA Violence', pp. 39–40). See also L. Khadiagala, 'The Failure of Popular Justice in Uganda: Local Councils and Women's Property Rights', *Development and Change*, 32, 2001, p. 60.

[12] Y. Museveni, *Sowing the Mustard Seed: The Struggle for Freedom and Democracy in Uganda*, MacMillan, 1997, p. 30.

justice more accessible – physically and culturally – to local populations.[13] Six years later, the Local Government (Resistance Councils)
Statute created the LCs, which maintained the RCs' jurisdiction and
procedures and rationalised a five-tier governance structure, with LC1s
responsible for villages in rural areas or urban neighbourhoods and
LC5s overseeing entire districts.[14] In 2011, the Ugandan parliament
also passed the Traditional and Cultural Leaders Act, which formalised the role of customary governance structures within the broader
apparatus of the state by legislating the scope of their powers and
paying customary leaders a government salary.[15]

A key issue surrounding the use of local rituals to address mass
violence is the role of Ugandan traditional leaders in their administration. The increased interest in the use of the rituals in this context
coincides with attempts to revitalise the traditional leadership. Between
the start of the nineteenth century and the beginning of the British
colonial era, around seventy chiefdoms (comprising more than 350
clans) existed in the central and northern regions of Uganda most
affected by mass conflict.[16] Colonial policy weakened the chieftancies
by installing proxy chiefs and setting them against each other politically. The regimes of Obote and Amin almost destroyed customary
structures entirely. In 1995, the new Ugandan Constitution reinstated
the Acholi traditional leadership known as Ker Kwaro Acholi (KKA).
An influential 1997 report by Dennis Pain, entitled 'The Bending of the
Spears', called for a community-based approach to resolving conflict in
northern Uganda.[17] Spurred by the findings of the report, the Belgian
government in 1999 funded research conducted by the Gulu-based
organisation ACORD into Acholi traditional leadership. Subsequently,
in 2000 Acholi traditional chiefs known as *rwodi* were elected and the

---

[13] B. Baker, 'Popular Justice and Policing from Bush War to Democracy: Uganda,
1981–2004', *International Journal of the Sociology of Law*, 32, 4, 2004, p. 336.
[14] Government of Uganda, 'Local Government (Resistance Councils)
Statute', 1997.
[15] Government of Uganda, 'Traditional and Cultural Leaders Act', 2011.
[16] Atkinson, *The Roots of Ethnicity*, p. 261.
[17] D. Pain, 'The Bending of the Spears: Producing Consensus for Peace and
Development in Northern Uganda', International Alert and Kacoke Madit,
1997. For detailed critiques of this report, see C. Dolan, 'Inventing Traditional
Leadership? A Critical Assessment of Dennis Pain's "The Bending of the
Spears"', COPE Working Paper 31, April 2000; and M. Bradbury, 'An
Overview of Initiatives for Peace in Acholi, Northern Uganda', Reflecting on
Peace Practice Project, October 1999.

Rwot of Payira in Gulu district was named the Acholi Paramount
Chief, leader of the KKA, a position that Tim Allen claims had never
before existed.[18] Soon traditional leaders, most notably then-Acholi
Paramount Chief Elect Rwot David Acana II, began advocating the use
of local rituals, particularly *mato oput*, to hold Joseph Kony and other
LRA commanders accountable for their crimes and to help reconcile
them with affected communities.[19] Members of the ARLPI, founded
the year before ACORD's research into traditional leadership, also
strongly supported the use of local rituals, emphasising their embedded
notions of forgiveness, atonement and mercy.

A vital international dimension also impinges on community-based
practices in the Ugandan context. The concurrent emergence of
organised traditional and religious leadership in northern Uganda
and support for this process from foreign governments and NGOs
are crucial to any analysis of the capacity of local rituals to address
mass conflict. Several Western NGOs, principally NUPI, an inter-
agency US government initiative, have actively supported the reinvig-
oration of local rituals, particularly in Gulu district. NUPI and other
organisations have helped identify traditional leaders and run programmes 'introducing' them to the population, mainly to Acholi
youth groups and IDP communities.[20] This has led some observers
to claim that an 'industry' has emerged, in which the rituals carry
more meaning for their foreign proponents and donor agencies than
for the local communities from which they supposedly derive.[21]
These external actors have been instrumental in creating new customary structures and elevating individual leaders, many of them
largely unknown in the community. In one incident observed by the
author, NUPI organised a ceremony in Pabbo IDP camp to 'introduce' the newly appointed customary leader of the district to the

---

[18] Allen, *Trial Justice*, p. 149. See also, T. Allen, 'Ritual (Ab)use? Problems with
Traditional Justice in Northern Uganda', in N. Waddell and P. Clark (eds.),
Courting Conflict? Justice, Peace and the ICC in Africa, Royal African Society,
2008, pp. 47–54.

[19] Author's interview, Rwot David Acana II, Acholi Paramount Chief, Gulu, 27
February 2007.

[20] Ker Kwaro Acholi and the Northern Uganda Peace Inititiave, 'Report on Acholi
Youth and Chiefs Addressing Practices of the Acholi Culture of Reconciliation',
USAID, June 2005.

[21] Author's interviews, UN official, Kampala, 3 March 2006; international
humanitarian worker, Gulu, 13 March 2006.

local population. A NUPI representative holding a megaphone on the back of a truck extolled the virtues of the visibly unsettled man standing beside him. One Acholi man exclaimed to the crowd around him, 'I know who that white man is. He comes here often. But who is the man next to him?'[22]

Having explored the historical context in which debates over local Ugandan practices occur, it is now necessary to explore some of these practices in depth. Central to Acholi rituals and conflict resolution mechanisms is an explicit Acholi emphasis on the spiritual dimensions of conflict.[23] Just as a view of the spirit world shapes the LRA's motivations for fighting, so it is vital to understanding Acholi remedies to violence. Father Joseph Okumu, Director of the Catechetical Training Centre in Gulu and a member of the ARLPI, describes Acholi rituals as 'religious act[s] of profound acknowledgement of the spiritual existence of a human...created by a Supreme Being' and 'the expression of a fabric that keeps the Acholi people in harmony with the forces of life around'.[24] Joseph Kony claimed that attacks on the Acholi civilian population were necessary to purify them of *cen* – the threat of 'ghostly vengeance'[25] – produced by their refusal to rise up and confront Museveni's forces in northern Uganda. Similarly, Acholi cultural leaders claim that certain rituals are necessary to purify former combatants or anyone directly or indirectly involved in killings and to help rebuild social relations after conflict.[26]

Different Acholi rituals fulfil different purposes but all relate to three primary aims: to cleanse and purify those affected by violence; to

---

[22] Author's field notes, Pabbo, 16 March 2006.
[23] For a full discussion of the importance of the spiritual realm for understanding many northern Ugandan communities' understandings of conflict and of the necessary responses to violence, see E. Baines, 'Spirits and Social Reconstruction after Mass Violence: Rethinking Transitional Justice', *African Affairs*, 109, 436, 2010, pp. 409–30.
[24] J. Okumu, 'Acholi Rites of Reconciliation', *The Examiner*, Human Rights Focus, 2, 2005, p. 15.
[25] O. p'Bitek, *Religion of the Central Luo*, Uganda Literature Bureau, 1980.
[26] Author's interviews, Acholi cultural leaders, Gulu, 8–10 March 2006. It should also be noted that historically Acholi rituals have been used to cleanse individuals from *cen* in preparation for battle – particularly by the Holy Spirit Movement and the LRA – as well as to purify them after conflict and to prepare them for reintegration into the community (H. Behrend, *Alice Lakwena and the Holy Spirits: War in Northern Uganda, 1986–97* (2nd edition), trans. M. Cohen, James Currey, 2004, pp. 43–6).

appease the spirits; and to restore social harmony. In the current literature, the most useful description and delineation of relevant Acholi rituals comes from Thomas Harlacher et al. in their book, *Traditional Ways of Coping in Acholi: Cultural Provisions for Reconciliation and Healing from War.*[27] Drawing on two years' community-level research by the Caritas Gulu Archdiocese, the authors explore eleven Acholi rituals and their interlinkages. The rituals encompass four main processes: receiving returned combatants into their home communities; conflict resolution and reconciliation; cleansing geographical areas affected by violence; and individual healing. The remainder of this section focuses on the second type of Acholi rituals – those for conflict resolution and reconciliation – which are most relevant to the question of how best to respond to mass violence, and specifically to two rituals within that category, *mato oput* and *gomo tong*. The other categories of rituals are also important in this context but primarily in support of these two main rituals.

In Luo, '*mato oput*' means literally 'drinking *oput*', a bitter beverage used in the reconciliation ceremony between parties after a premeditated or accidental killing. It is not a stand-alone practice but follows lengthy negotiations. As Harlacher et al. explain, 'the actual ritual marks the peak, and successful conclusion, of a reconciliation process between two clans in the aftermath of a killing'.[28] Following a murder, the two clans involved cease all social and economic interactions, necessitating mediation and a ceremony to symbolise a return to good relations. *Mato oput* also serves a spiritual function, warding off the *cen* that would otherwise haunt the killer and his or her family, manifesting in disease or other misfortune.

Preceding *mato oput*, traditional elders, usually from neutral clans, are called to mediate. When the elders determine that emotions have sufficiently cooled and the parties are ready to communicate, they facilitate a discussion about culpability for the murder in question and the appropriate compensation. Restitution usually involves the transfer of cattle and goats from the offender's clan to the victim's. This process may take many years, as some clans are not immediately prepared to negotiate or may need time to raise the required compensation.

---

[27] Harlacher et al., *Traditional Ways of Coping in Acholi.*   [28] Ibid., p. 80

Many cultural and political leaders, particularly in Acholiland, argue that *mato oput* should be used to reconcile clans of LRA offenders and their victims, after lengthy mediation by elders. '*Mato oput* gives us a way to accept back our sons and daughters who were abducted and have committed murder while they were in the bush', argues Angelo Banya, coordinator of the Office of the Paramount Chief in Gulu district.

We won't hang them. Instead, the elders will come and mediate...There will be an acceptance of guilt, an apology, the victim's acceptance of the request for forgiveness, as our tradition dictates. Then there is the compensation aspect, which varies according to guilt and the severity of the crime...There must be compensation and accountability. This way, we can wash away the pains of the clans involved and allow them to forgive and reconcile.[29]

The second major Acholi ritual relevant to the current conflict is *gomo tong*, a ceremony traditionally performed to mark the end of violence between different clans or neighbouring ethnic groups. The meaning of '*gomo tong*' – the bending of spears – refers to the belief that, once the ceremony is performed, if either side again threatens violence against the other, the point of the spear will be turned back against the perpetrator. The process of *gomo tong* is more straightforward than that of *mato oput*, involving elders from warring clans invoking 'the living dead' and vowing to cease their fighting. *Gomo tong*, which focuses on collective conflict, can be practised with or without *mato oput*, which follows a single case of killing. The two rituals are often combined when one side believes they deserve compensation for an initial killing that sparked wider violence. In such cases, neutral elders mediate between the parties, as outlined above, leading to the *mato oput* ceremony, followed by *gomo tong* later the same day. *Gomo tong* has also been practised without *mato oput*, in cases involving conflicts between Acholi and clans from neighbouring ethnic groups.

In all cases of *gomo tong*, elders from the two groups meet to discuss the causes of the conflict, resolve to end the fighting and command their people to cease all violence. Sometimes the elders literally bend or break a spear to symbolise the end of violence, and the *gomo tong*

---

[29] Author's interview, Angelo Banya, coordinator, office of the Acholi Paramount Chief, Gulu, 13 March 2006.

ceremony closes with the slaughter of a bull, which the elders eat. The anthropologist Sverker Finnström reports that *gomo tong* has not been practised since 1986, when the Acholi and groups from West Nile performed the ceremony to symbolise the end to their conflict, which had decimated both groups following the overthrow of Amin in 1979.[30] An Acholi NGO worker explained that many Acholi nonetheless believe *gomo tong* would be useful in dealing with recent conflict in northern Uganda: 'Gomo tong is crucial because this is a conflict between groups. It's the LRA against other Acholi and the LRA against other groups, like the Iteso or Langi. If these groups can bend spears, it can end this conflict and ensure things don't flare up again. *Gomo tong* could be very important for us.'[31]

Popularly Perceived Virtues and Pitfalls of Community-Based Mechanisms in Northern Uganda

Before examining the ICC's impact on these community-based practices in northern Uganda, it is important to analyse popular perceptions of these processes. Research across northern Uganda – not just in Acholiland – highlights a wide range of popular responses to these local rituals. Drawing on the author's empirical research and the findings of the 2007 OHCHR study into popular perceptions on transitional justice in northern Uganda, this section highlights three principal virtues of these processes that are overlooked in international legal approaches to transitional justice: their reflection of diffuse, multi-level conflict and the need for accountability for community-level perpetrators; their capacity to pursue broader transitional objectives, including truth and reconciliation; and their proximity and presence among affected communities.

Northern Ugandan respondents broadly emphasise the importance of local rituals as comprehensive responses to the particular form of conflict they have experienced and the central role of intimate actors in perpetrating violence. This highlights a key shortcoming of the Nuremberg model of accountability favoured by many human rights and legal advocates, which focuses on only a handful of elite suspects. As

---

[30] S. Finnström, *Living with Bad Surroundings: War, History and Everyday Moments in Northern Uganda*, Duke University Press, 2008, p. 291.
[31] Author's interview, local human rights worker, Lira, 10 November 2006.

discussed in Chapter 4, in many interviews with atrocity survivors in northern Uganda, when asked whom they view as the principal perpetrators in the conflict, they also cite the specific neighbour who wielded the machete or threw the grenade and not only the faceless government or military official who may have ordered the attack. Given the intimacy of violence across northern Uganda, the widespread desire for accountability for individuals at the community level is not surprising and echoes Holly Porter's finding that a deep desire for 'social harmony' underpins many Acholis' pursuit of justice.[32] 'These people coming back from the bush have done terrible things', said Babra in Amuru. 'We know who they are because they used to live here. They killed many people here and chased others away. They should face justice now. They should come back to the places where they did these things and go through *mato oput*. Then they should apologise and their clans should pay compensation.'[33]

The local rituals also respond to another perceived shortcoming in international criminal justice by seeking to contribute to broader social objectives than punitive accountability for crimes. Diffuse forms of violence affect societies in political, social, economic and psychosocial terms at regional, national, provincial, communal, inter-personal and individual levels. Underpinning the northern Ugandan rituals is a view that community-based transitional processes are required to address these myriad dimensions of conflict. A widely expressed concern throughout interviews over a decade in northern Uganda was how victims, perpetrators and other groups would coexist given the extreme harm people had suffered during the war. 'We must live together', said Bale, a victim of LRA violence in Lamwo. 'We have no choice in that. We need the fighters to come back to help work on the farms. Now that people are back from the camps, we have regained our land. Everyone must work so that we can survive.'[34]

The intimacy of victim–perpetrator relations before, during and after conflict, including the immense challenges of peaceful coexistence today, underpin a regular emphasis on the need for intimate engagement between parties during transitional justice processes. This

---

[32] See Porter, 'Justice and Rape on the Periphery', p. 81; Porter, *After Rape*.
[33] Author's interview, Babra, Amuru, 12 March 2006.
[34] Author's interview, Bale, Lamwo, 28 February 2007.

explains the widespread support for local rituals expressed by inter-viewees across northern Uganda and their linkage of the rituals with objectives such as truth-telling, material compensation and reconcili-ation. As discussed in Chapter 4, this insistence on presence and proximity contrasts starkly with the distanced form of justice delivered by the national judiciary, the ICC and other international courts and tribunals. During the same interview cited above, Babra said, 'When [the returned combatants] go through *mato oput*, everyone can watch how they behave. Are they respectful of the elders, are they sincere when they ask for forgiveness from the victims?'[35] Akello, a victim of LRA violence in Pader, said, 'The traditional rituals are important because, when we see the perpetrators standing here in the yard, we can demand compensation from them and their clans. They can't avoid us.'[36]

For all of these reasons, many respondents report having directly participated in local rituals. Overall use of key Acholi rituals has increased in recent years, although precisely to what extent remains unclear. Based on limited surveys, usually of several hundred respond-ents, several commentators report that between 28 per cent and 50 per cent of returned rebel combatants have participated in some form of ritual, usually welcoming or cleansing ceremonies.[37] The majority of the author's combatant interviewees stated that they had participated in at least one local ritual. Godfrey, a twenty-one-year-old man in the Bobi IDP camp, who had fought with the LRA and returned from the bush in early 2006, said, 'I went through a cleansing ceremony when I first came back. About 30 of us who came back went through the

---

[35] Author's interview, Babra, 12 March 2006.

[36] Author's interview, Pader, 24 February 2007.

[37] Tim Allen and Mareike Schomerus found that 28 per cent of the 248 formerly abducted persons they surveyed in 2005 had been through some form of ritual (Allen and Schomerus, 'A Hard Homecoming', p. 18.), compared to 50 per cent of the 506 formerly abducted persons surveyed in 2005 by the Liu Institute for Global Issues, Gulu District NGO Forum, Ker Kwaro Acholi and Northern Ugandan Peace Initiative (*Roco Wat I Acoli: Restoring Relationships in Acholi-land – Traditional Approaches to Justice and Reintegration*, September 2005, p. 39), and 50 per cent of the 186 abductees interviewed in 2002 by the ARLPI, Caritas Gulu and the Gulu Justice and Peace Commission (C. Rodriguez, K. Smith-Derksen and S. J. Akera, 'Seventy Times Seven: The Impact of the Amnesty Law in Acholi', Acholi Religious Leaders Peace Initiative, Women's Desk of Caritas Gulu, and Justice and Peace Commission of Gulu Archdiocese, 2002, p. 5).

ceremony. Many people from the community attended. It made us feel welcome – we feel like we can live with our people again.'[38]

Crucially, the majority of interviewees who had participated in local rituals said they avoided the spectacular ceremonies organised by KKA, NUPI or other formal groups, preferring more localised rituals mediated by *ajok* or other customary or clan leaders. Respondents critiqued the performative element of many of the more formal rituals as well as their entanglement with international NGOs and local and national politics. Numerous interviewees expressed distrust of the KKA because of its increasingly close relationship with the government after the passing of the 2011 Act, which altered the legal status of KKA and customary structures across the country. 'I avoid those big ceremonies', said Achen, whose son was abducted by the LRA and had recently returned from the bush and received an amnesty. 'Those are just for show, for the foreigners. When we hold the rituals in our homesteads, it's much calmer and people can talk freely. The only people who come are the ones who committed the crimes or the victims and their families.'[39] LRA commander Sam Kolo, who had participated in a large ritual organised by KKA and NUPI in the centre of Gulu, echoed these views in 2006:

The way KKA and the donors are talking about *mato oput* at the moment, I'm not sure it can help much...*Mato oput* is supposed to be for the individuals concerned, not for groups. That is the main issue. Atrocities were committed broadly but the one-to-one experience is what really matters. At the moment, the way people describe *mato oput*, it generalises things. It could be more effective if it happens between individuals, in their homes, but that means identifying each individual involved, the perpetrator and the victim, and that isn't easy...So, for reconciliation and peacebuilding, I'm not sure how effective these big *mato oput* ceremonies can be.[40]

Much of the scholarly critique of northern Ugandan rituals focuses on these high-profile ceremonies conducted by KKA and local and international NGOs. Adam Branch, for example, categorises them as an 'externally funded ethnojustice project'[41] that reifies recently

---

[38] Author's interview, general population, Bobi, 13 March 2006.
[39] Author's interview, Achen, Pader, 25 April 2013.
[40] Author's interview, Kolo, 10 March 2006.
[41] Branch, *Displacing Human Rights*, p. 174. See also Allen, *Trial Justice*; and T. Allen, 'Bitter Roots: The "Invention" of Acholi Traditional Justice', in

invented modes of traditional (especially male) authority such as KKA, while entrenching donor and state influence and shrouding the role of these actors in perpetuating the northern conflict. Despite these valid criticisms, the evidence presented here shows that the local Ugandan rituals, particularly when they are conducted outside of the KKA and NGO context – a category largely overlooked by the majority of commentators – enjoy substantial legitimacy and widespread use among everyday citizens. Writing in 2003 before the ICC intervention in northern Uganda, Finnström argued that local practices 'far from being dislocated in a past that no longer exists, have always continued to be situated socially. They are called upon to address present concerns. Of course, like any culturally informed practice, with time they shift in meaning and appearance.'[42] An ICTJ survey in 2007 showed that 57 per cent of Acholi and non-Acholi believed that returning LRA combatants should go through some form of traditional ceremony.[43] This stems from their proximity, resonance with local norms and values and a lack of other trusted responses to mass conflict. While a great deal of scholarly and practitioner attention has been paid to the more formal rituals overseen by foreign actors and customary leaders, the majority of respondents who claim to have participated in rituals eschew these practices for more intimate rituals that facilitate confessions, apologies and compensation from former combatants and their clans.

The ICC's Intersections with Community-Based Mechanisms in Northern Uganda

The ICC affected the public discourse and practice of community-based rituals in northern Uganda in diverse ways before, during and after the Juba peace negotiations. After the issuance of the ICC warrants for the LRA leadership but before the start of the Juba process, the ICC catalysed debates in northern Uganda about the possible use of

T. Allen and K. Vlassenroot, *The Lord's Resistance Army: Myth and Reality*, Zed Books, 2010, pp. 242–60.

[42] Finnström, *Living with Bad Surroundings*, p. 299.

[43] ICTJ, 'When the War Ends', p. 40; See also J. Quinn, 'Beyond Truth Commissions: Indigenous Reconciliation in Uganda', *Review of Faith and International Affairs*, 4, 1, 2006, pp. 31–7, on the 'staying power' of traditional practices as 'socially accepted mechanisms' across northern Uganda.

local rituals to deal with the LRA. As discussed above, these debates have a much longer history but they became more energised and widespread after the ICC's intervention. The year before the Juba talks, an Acholi leaders' delegation to The Hague, including Rwot Acana and various members of the ARLPI, told the ICC Prosecutor of the import- ance of local cleansing and reconciliation rituals for addressing LRA crimes.[44] For actors such as the ARLPI, local rituals were seen as a crucial support for – and the ICC as an impediment to – the nationwide amnesty process and a means to the reintegration and reconciliation of a wide range of rebel groups.[45] Two prominent international NGOs that supported the Acholi traditional leadership, the Liu Institute for Global Issues and NUPI, published reports framing local rituals as superior to the ICC in resolving the LRA conflict and achieving long- term peace and reconciliation in northern Uganda.[46]

At the same time, Rwot Acana and KKA began to hold large public *mato oput* ceremonies for returned LRA combatants, including a high- profile ceremony mentioned earlier for the rebel commanders Kolo, Banya and others in Gulu in April 2005[47] and another for Charles Otim, which was widely publicised in an article by Marc Lacey from the *New York Times*.[48] Field interviews indicate that many local

---

[44] International Criminal Court, Office of the Prosecutor, 'Press Release: Statements by ICC Chief Prosecutor and the Visiting Delegation of Acholi Leaders from Northern Uganda', 18 March 2005.

[45] Author's interviews, Rodriguez, 10 March 2006; Bishop Macleod Baker Ochola II, ARLPI, Gulu, 11 March 2006.

[46] Liu Institute for Global Issues, 'Pursuing Peace and Justice: International and Local Initiatives', May 2005; Liu Institute for Global Issues, Gulu District NGO Forum, KKA and NUPI, *Roco Wat I Acoli*.

[47] Pax Christi, 'Justice and Peace News: A Newsletter from the Justice and Peace Commission of Gulu Archdiocese', May 2005, p. 7, www.paxchristi.net/sites/ default/files/documents/MO154E06.pdf; author's interview, Kolo, 10 March 2006.

[48] M. Lacey, 'Atrocity Victims in Uganda Choose to Forgive', *The New York Times*, 18 April 2005, www.nytimes.com/2005/04/18/world/africa/atrocity- victims-in-uganda-choose-to-forgive.html. The article, however, conflates the Acholi ritual of *nyono tonggweno* or 'stepping on the egg' with *mato oput*, especially its emphasis on compensation and reconciliation. *Nyono tonggweno* is performed to welcome home members of the clan (such as former LRA combatants) who have been away for long periods and to cleanse them of any malevolent spirits they may have encountered on their travels. While *mato oput* occurs after lengthy mediation and concerns individual murders, *nyono tonggweno* is performed soon after clan members return to the community and whenever they have been away for a long time, not only when they have

communities had for several years before the ICC's intervention used local rituals to help reintegrate returning LRA combatants.[49] The ICC appears to have had little influence on this type of more private ritual. The main effect of the ICC in this period was to catalyse much greater activity by KKA in the hosting and publicising of rituals – shifting practices typically held within homesteads among the parties most directly affected by acts of violence in the public domain. The ICC therefore tapped into febrile local dynamics around the revival of traditional leadership in Acholi and catalysed Rwot Acana and other Acholi leaders to legitimise themselves as a bulwark against the Court's interference in local conflict resolution.

All of these issues flowed into the Juba talks, where the ICC and its supporters substantially altered the ways in which community-based transitional justice approaches were discussed. These actors succeeded in limiting local rituals within the Juba agreements and future government policy in two key respects: circumscribing these practices for low-ranking LRA combatants only; and laying the groundwork for the government to formalise, codify and nationalise local rituals, in the process restricting the agency of local communities in northern Uganda.

From the outset at Juba, both the LRA delegation and northern Ugandan civil society – especially KKA – advocated the use of local rituals for all members of the LRA, including the leaders charged by the ICC. The LRA viewed local rituals as 'alternative mechanisms' to the Court.[50] Many northern Ugandan civil society actors meanwhile viewed support for local rituals in Juba as an important riposte to the perceived overly cosy relationship between Museveni and the ICC. In this view, the ICC was doing the government's bidding by charging only LRA suspects and continuing Museveni's subjugation of northern ethnic groups. 'Local justice is a way of taking back control', said Michael Otim, who led the Acholi civil society delegation to the peace talks. 'In the north, there is lots of grassroots support for using rituals to handle the LRA. It's a form of justice that people understand. But

---

committed crimes. Furthermore, *nyono tonggweno* is often used to cleanse groups of returnees, in a ceremony known as *nyono tonggweno lumuku*, while *mato oput* involves only individuals.

[49] Author's interviews, local population, Acholi, Lango and Teso sub-regions, 2006–2015.

[50] LRA, 'Position Paper on Accountability and Reconciliation', op. cit.

the government and the ICC are trying to limit the ability of northern Ugandans to decide for themselves how the LRA should be tackled.'[51] Barney Afako, the legal advisor to the mediation team in Juba, confirmed the importance of this sentiment: 'There were various motivations behind the arguments for local mechanisms. But a major one was a desire for self-determination and autonomy among northern Ugandans.'[52]

The argument that local rituals should replace the ICC as a means of dealing with the LRA leadership raised the ire of the ICC's supporters in the international human rights community. The linkage of local Ugandan rituals with notions of amnesty and forgiveness in particular proved highly controversial.[53] Groups such as HRW and AI and various legal commentators stated that local rituals could not deliver the degree of accountability necessary for perpetrators of egregious crimes; a task, they argued, that should be the sole purview of the ICC or another form of conventional court.[54] The polarised 'peace versus justice' debate explored in the previous chapter therefore spawned a further binary argument over 'traditional/informal/restorative' versus 'Western/formal/retributive' justice.[55] The critique of community-based rituals by groups such as HRW and AI overlooked the local context, discussed in Chapters 4 and 6, namely that popular concerns

---

[51] Author's interview, Michael Otim, Leader of Acholi Civil Society Delegation to Juba Peace Talks, Gulu, 26 February 2007.

[52] Author's interview, Afako, op. cit. See also Z. Lomo and J. Otto, 'Not a Crime to Talk: Give Peace a Chance in Northern Uganda', Refugee Law Project and Human Rights Focus press release, 24 July 2006.

[53] For a broader discussion of connections between local understandings of forgiveness and amnesty in northern Uganda, see Refugee Law Project, 'Forgiveness: Unveiling an Asset for Peacebuilding', 2015.

[54] See, for example, AI, 'Proposed National Framework'; Human Rights Watch, 'Trading Justice for Peace Won't Work', 2 May 2007.

[55] See, for example, T. McConnell, 'Uganda: Peace versus Justice?', openDemocracy, 13 September 2006, www.opendemocracy.net/democracy-africa_democracy/uganda_peace_3903.jsp; L. Parrott, 'The Role of the International Criminal Court in Uganda: Ensuring that the Pursuit of Justice Does Not Come at the Price of Peace', *Australian Journal of Peace Studies*, 1, 2006, pp. 8–29; *The Economist*, 'Hunting Uganda's Child-Killers: Justice versus Reconciliation', 7 May 2007, p. 57; A. Branch, 'Uganda's Civil War and the Politics of ICC Intervention', *Ethics and International Affairs*, 21, 2, 2007, pp. 179–98; and Justice and Reconciliation Project, "Abomination': Local Belief Systems and International Justice', Liu Institute for Global Issues and the Gulu District NGO Forum, Field Notes No. 5, September 2007.

over amnesty were one of the key factors motivating popular support for the rituals. In particular, many northern Ugandans view the local rituals as filling two gaps in the Amnesty Act, truth-telling and compensation. Viewing the ICC as the sole legitimate transitional justice response to the Ugandan conflict, HRW and AI ignored these more complex debates occurring within Ugandan society. Crucially, they ignored the fact that much of the impetus for local rituals comes from a desire for greater – not less – accountability than the previous amnesty process, given the rituals' focus on confession, apology and compensation.

The ICC, for its part, expressed similar views to these international organisations, albeit more diplomatically. Invoking the principle of complementarity, the Court argued that it posed no threat to the use of community-based practices, provided they did not apply to the LRA commanders. A September 2007 OTP policy paper on Article 53 of the Rome Statute and the 'interests of justice' provision that can trigger a withdrawal of ICC arrest warrants advocated 'the complementary role that can be played by domestic prosecutions, truth seeking, reparations programs, institutional reform and traditional justice mechanisms in the pursuit of a broader justice'.[56] This echoed Ocampo's statement three months earlier, in an interview with the *New Vision*, that '[t]his case in Uganda is to show how traditional mechanisms to reconcile people can work together with investigation and prosecution…Basically we are doing a case on four people, all the others could be handled using different mechanisms.'[57]

Increasingly, as the Juba talks progressed, the Ugandan government internalised the ICC's complementarity discourse regarding the local rituals, in particular the stipulation that community-based practices should not apply to high-ranking atrocity suspects. Recognising that local rituals were central to the LRA's demands, while wanting to work within the strictures of the Rome Statute, the government proposed the codification of the northern Ugandan rituals to produce a system capable of addressing LRA crimes. Some Ugandan government sources in Juba and Kampala suggested that this included creating a formalised version of local rituals that could facilitate an admissibility challenge to

---

[56] ICC, OTP, 'Policy Paper on the Interests of Justice', p. 8.
[57] F. Osike, 'Uganda: Here Is ICC Prosecutor Luis Ocampo in his Office in The Hague', *New Vision*, 16 July 2007, http://allafrica.com/stories/200707160105.html.

the ICC and this had been proposed to the LRA behind the scenes.[58] The LRA delegation's position paper on accountability and reconciliation supports this process: 'Because of the apparent difficulty encountered in persuading the [W]estern countries to accept [a] traditional justice system as sufficient to meet the standards of international criminal justice, it is strongly proposed that a specific provision in our law, setting some standards, should be made to cater for alternative justice to address such situations as the present one.'[59]

This view also gained some currency among Acholi civil society actors and customary leaders. At a conference organised by the International Bar Association (IBA) in Lira in November 2006, an Acholi executive member of the Gulu NGO Forum argued that, on the basis of Article 126 of the Constitution, the government should codify and nationalise *mato oput* and create a 'Mato Oput Act', similar to Rwanda's *Gacaca* Law, to facilitate compensation and reconciliation.[60] A cyclical genealogy of ideas emerged, as the Ugandan government considered the post-genocide version of *gacaca* in Rwanda (which was partly inspired by the transfer of concepts from the RCs and LCs, which RPF leaders had observed while fighting with the NRM in Uganda[61]) as a model for its own considerations of community-based processes. In 2006, a Ugandan parliamentary committee was established to consider whether local (particularly Acholi) rituals could be codified and nationalised, similar to Rwanda's reform and formalisation of the *gacaca* courts. 'We are considering whether something like *gacaca* in Rwanda provides a model for us here in Uganda', a Ugandan government official said. 'There are pros and cons to the use of traditional practices and we have to weigh up what the best approach is. But certainly we believe traditional methods can teach us a lot about dealing with the current situation.'[62]

---

[58] Author's interviews, Ugandan Government officials, Juba and Kampala, 10–21 February 2007.
[59] LRA Delegation to the Juba Talks, 'Position Paper', p. 3.
[60] Author's notes, 'Traditional Justice in the Northern Ugandan Conflict' workshop, IBA, Lira, 10 November 2006.
[61] For detailed discussion of these issues, see Clark, *The Gacaca Courts*, ch. 2.
[62] Author's interview, Ugandan government official, Kampala, 3 March 2006. The language of 'gacaca' has also gained significant currency in Ugandan public discussions. In an article in the Ugandan state-owned *New Vision* newspaper, one commentator characterised the 'free and fair' elections in Uganda in 1989, which he described as exhibiting little executive interference, as a 'gacaca

KKA meanwhile viewed the issue of codification of local rituals as a means to shore up its relationship with the government and to bolster its political and cultural role in Acholiland. In December 2007, KKA facilitated a large consultation meeting in Gulu, in the middle of the Juba debates over the accountability and reconciliation agreement, which a KKA background document described as 'the stickiest part of the Juba Peace Talks'.[63] After the meeting, representatives from the customary leadership of seven northern Ugandan groups (including the Acholi, Langi and Iteso) stated that the 'cultural leaders of the wider north' should be responsible for implementing this agreement. The document also argued that local rituals should be codified, with parliamentary oversight, and that it was the government's responsibility to 'strengthen and facilitate community level structures' such as KKA.[64] These developments reinforce the concerns raised above by Branch and Allen about the extent to which KKA used discussions of community-based rituals during Juba to further its own narrow agenda.

Even more so than with the Amnesty Act, the accountability and reconciliation agreement signed by the government and the LRA in June 2007 gave mixed messages regarding the use of community-based practices, including in the cases of the LRA commanders charged by the ICC. The agreement stated that '[t]raditional justice mechanisms...shall be promoted, with necessary modifications, as a central part of the framework for accountability and reconciliation'.[65] It also specified that individuals 'alleged to bear particular responsibility for the most serious crimes, especially crimes amounting to international crimes' will be prosecuted through 'formal courts provided for under the Constitution'.[66] The agreement appears to meld the functions of

---

(community) exercise devoid of vertical civic...discourse' (A. Bisika, 'Otunnu Is Not Obama because Uganda Is Not USA', *New Vision*, 2 September 2009).

[63] Ker Kwaro Acholi Gulu Conference, 'Background Document', December 2007, p. 1, copy on file with author. The document also claims, 'To ensure significant participation and comprehensive ownership of the Juba Peace Talks proceedings by the real victims of the conflicts, the Institutions of the Traditional Leaders of Northern Uganda are deemed appropriate to provide such a platform; that would provide balanced, apolitical and significant contributions to the Juba Peace Talks' (ibid., p. 1).

[64] Ker Kwaro Acholi Gulu Conference, 'Cultural Leaders Statement', December 2007, p. 2.

[65] Government of Uganda and the Lord's Resistance Army, 'Agreement on Accountability and Reconciliation', 29 June 2007, section 5.4.

[66] Ibid., section 6.1.

the formal courts and traditional mechanisms by establishing 'a regime of alternative penalties and sanctions which shall apply, and replace existing penalties, with respect to serious crimes and human rights violations committed by non-state actors in the course of the conflict'.[67] These alternative penalties must 'reflect the gravity of the crimes or violations; promote reconciliation between individuals and within communities; promote the rehabilitation of offenders; take into account an individual's admissions or other cooperation with proceedings; and, require perpetrators to make reparations to victims'.[68]

The principal impact of the ICC overall therefore was to narrow the Juba discussions of community-based rituals to their use only for low-level rebel combatants and to encourage a legalistic discourse regarding their codification and legislation. These trends continued after Juba with the bolstering of JLOS in 2008 and the passing of the ICC Bill in 2010, discussed in Chapter 5. The ICC maintained pressure on the government to thwart community level attempts to use local rituals for high-ranking LRA suspects. At an event in Kampala in June 2009 to debate the ICC Bill then before the Ugandan parliament, ICC Judge Daniel Nsereko, a Ugandan, said,

Crimes against humanity, genocide, aggression against other states and war crimes are internationally condemned and cannot be tried by traditional courts but by the ICC...You cannot expect someone who caused the death of 100 people to be tried in a traditional court if you are looking for justice to be done...You must convince the international community that justice was done and that the punishment is proportionate with the crime.[69]

The impact of the ICC in this regard was, along with international donor pressure, to strengthen the government's attempts to bring community-based practices within the purview of the state through legislation and codification. The JLOS National Transitional Justice Strategy, buttressed by the 2011 Traditional and Cultural Leaders Act, includes codification of local rituals.[70] Similarly to the ICD of the High Court and the Amnesty Act, the Ugandan government used the ICC's legalist framework and the agreements signed in Juba to construct a

---

[67] Ibid., section 6.3.   [68] Ibid., section 6.4.

[69] Quoted in J. Maseruka, 'Traditional Justice Not Applicable to War Suspects', *New Vision*, 30 June 2009.

[70] Government of Uganda, Justice, Law and Order Sector, 'National Transitional Justice Strategy', sixth draft, 2017.

prosecutions-focused system designed to target rebel actors and to increase state control.

A range of northern Ugandan actors have vociferously contested the government's proposal to codify local rituals and thus subsume them into the national criminal legal framework. In Acholiland, many actors view this as a further attempt by the state to co-opt traditional practices – echoing a dynamic from the colonial era through all post-independence regimes – and to legalise and make rigid community-based approaches, whose flexibility and non-state oversight are considered among their principal strengths.[71] 'We don't support this idea of writing down the rituals in law and following rules', said Alur, a clan elder in Odek district. 'We use the rituals like *mato oput* to reconcile people, as we have always done. We don't need the government or Ker Kwaro Acholi for this.'[72]

Crucially, respondents in Lango and Teso view the proposed codification as preferencing Acholi rituals, neglecting the diversity of community-based principles and practices deployed across northern Uganda. In his opening address to the IBA workshop in Lira mentioned earlier, Franco Ojur, LC5 chairman of Lira district, expressed the concerns of many non-Acholi:

Discussions about traditional justice have emerged because of mass conflict and because of our Acholi brothers. Here in Lango, we consider all of this something new, something foreign to us...We don't understand *mato oput* and traditional justice. We believe that if Kony is pardoned, it should happen unconditionally, without putting him through traditional justice. If he is punished, it should be more than traditional justice, something stronger...There are many questions about *mato oput*, such as which of Kony's crimes it refers to. Is it only for Kony's crimes against Acholi or against other groups as well? What about his crimes in the DRC and Sudan? Can there be *mato oput* for those cases?[73]

---

[71] See, for example, F. Nsibambi, 'Paying for Cultural Leaders' Upkeep against the Constitution', *Daily Monitor*, 17 June 2013, www.monitor.co.ug/OpEd/ Commentary/Paying-for-cultural-leaders–upkeep-against-the-Constitution/ 689364-1884998-342lue/index.html.

[72] Author's interview, Alur, Odek, 26 April 2013.

[73] F. Ojur, 'Opening Remarks', 'Traditional Justice in the Northern Ugandan Conflict' workshop. For further discussion of Langi and Iteso scepticism about the dominance of Acholi rituals in these debates, see, OHCHR, 'Making Peace Our Own', p. 53.

Groups such as the Langi and Iteso that have suffered greatly at the hands of the LRA and the UPDF and view the conflict as essentially driven by animosity between the Acholi and the government are unlikely to view Acholi rituals codified by the state as legitimate responses to violence.

In northern Uganda, the ICC intersected with, and magnified, a range of national and community-level dynamics around the use of community-based rituals to address serious crimes. Before, during and after the Juba talks, the ICC insisted that local rituals should be used only for low-level combatants and should not hamper efforts to prosecute the LRA commanders. The general legalism of the ICC's approach to complementarity that so dominated the Juba process, as discussed in the previous chapter, gave the government and KKA the pretext to pursue an agenda of codifying and rigidifying local practices. Critically, however, many northern Ugandans have continued to use informal rituals – far beyond the view of state and civil society actors – to respond to the legacies of mass conflict, especially for the peaceful reintegration of combatants. If the government's codification proposals, currently contained in the JLOS draft Transitional Justice Bill, ever materialise, these may undermine the informal practices that have become vital tools for a significant proportion of the northern Ugandan population.

Community-Based Practices in Eastern DRC

This section explores two community-based conflict mediation processes in eastern DRC that have intersected with the ICC over the last decade, the *Barza Inter-Communautaire* in North Kivu and the RHA in Ituri. Unlike the Ugandan case where the local rituals were explicitly framed as an alternative to the ICC, the Congolese processes examined here fulfil very different functions to the ICC and thus have a less antagonistic relationship with the Court. These processes have nevertheless overlapped with the ICC's work, sometimes with negative consequences both for the community-based practices and for the ICC. This section begins with a brief discussion of the history of customary law and local approaches to conflict mediation in the DRC before moving to a detailed examination of the *Barza*, the RHA and their interactions with the Court.

Background to Community-Based Mechanisms in Eastern DRC

Similar to the Ugandan case, the background to the use of community-based practices to address mass violence in the DRC is the concurrence of common and customary law, which derives from the colonial era. Belgian civil law, as summarised in the *Codes et Lois du Congo Belge*,[74] proscribed the procedures and limits of customary law. The Belgians vested in customary authorities the responsibility for resolving the kinds of everyday disputes that the colonials associated with the 'natives', over issues such as marriage, land ownership, inheritance and basic misdemeanours in rural communities.[75] Mahmood Mamdani argues that this system of Belgian indirect rule created a 'bifurcated form of the state'[76] in which civil law, applying only to urban dwellers, conveyed rights on the basis of their civic identity as Congolese citizens, while customary law, which applied only to rural inhabitants, ruled according to custom and on the basis of individuals' ethnic identity. The concentration of civil law in a handful of cities and towns, in a country where the bulk of the population lives in rural areas, means that customary law wields greater influence over the daily lives of most Congolese. Historically, civic law was heavily racialised until independence, favouring whites over blacks and those considered indigenous over *non-indigènes*, while customary law was ethnicised, favouring certain ethnic groups over others. After independence, civic law was deracialised but customary law continued to operate along ethnic lines.[77] This system did not result in a single customary legal regime but rather a proliferation of customary laws for each ethnic group across the country, with each jurisdiction overseen by a separate Native Authority. 'What holds Congo together', argues Mamdani, 'is not as much the civic power in Kinshasa and Kisangani and so on, but the hundreds of Native Authorities that control the bulk of the population in the name of enforcing "custom".'[78]

---

[74] P. Piron and G. Devos (eds.), *Codes et Lois du Congo Belge* (8th edition), Larcier, 1961.

[75] W. MacGaffey, 'The Policy of National Integration in Zaire', *Journal of Modern African Studies*, 20, 1, March 1982, p. 87.

[76] M. Mamdani, 'Preliminary Thoughts on the Congo Crisis', *Social Text*, 17, 3, 1999, p. 54.

[77] W. Breytenbach, D. Chilemba, T. Brown and C. Plantive, 'Conflicts in the Congo: From Kivu to Kabila', *African Security Review*, 8, 5, 1999, pp. 33–42.

[78] Mamdani, 'Preliminary Thoughts', p. 54.

Against this back-drop, between 1998 and 2005 the *Barza Inter-Communautaire* assembled leaders from North Kivu's nine major ethnic groups – the Hunde, Hutu, Kano, Kumu, Nande, Nyanga, Tembo, Tutsi and Twa – to discuss issues central to community life and to help resolve low-level conflicts before they escalated to violence. *Barza* members were elected by community leaders in each ethnic group: twenty-five candidates from each group were initially chosen, from whom three per group – a total of twenty-seven – were elected to the *Barza*. Two attempts were made to establish the *Barza* in South Kivu but, for reasons explored elsewhere, both failed.[79] The *Barza* was therefore exclusively a North Kivu phenomenon. The word *Barza* derives from the Swahili word *baraza*, meaning 'verandah' or a meeting place, usually outside a hut in the centre of a village or under a large tree, for local elders to assemble and discuss problems in the community, providing 'a framework for giving directions as to the way of life inside and around the villages.'[80] Among many groups in North Kivu, the *baraza* is traditionally where local inhabitants bring their disputes for their elders' resolution and where visitors first call to receive the elders' blessing on their stay in the community.

Between 1998 and early 2004, a period of major instability and armed conflict in many parts of eastern DRC – including severe disruption to customary structures[81] – the *Barza* generally succeeded in resolving ethnic disputes in North Kivu, particularly those concerning land ownership, before they sparked mass violence. The primary purpose of the *Barza* was to 'prevent, resolve, and heal wounds after, conflict'.[82] This required countering what its leaders call 'negative values' in the community, such as incendiary attitudes and statements

---

[79] For further discussion of this point, see P. Clark, 'Ethnicity, Leadership and Conflict Mediation in the Eastern Democratic Republic of Congo: The Case of the *Barza Inter-Communautaire*', *Journal of Eastern African Studies*, 2, 1, 2008, pp. 1–17.

[80] E. Kisa Kalobera, quoted in Pole Institute, 'Inter-Congolese Dialogue: The Experience of the Intercommunal *Barza* and the Pacification Commission of North Kivu', *The Inter-Congolese Dialogue 2: Intercommunal Peace Work in North Kivu*, Regards Croisés no. 2, May 2000, p. 4.

[81] For an excellent discussion of this issue, see J. Verweijen, 'The Disconcerting Popularity of Popular In/justice in the Fizi/Uvira Region, Eastern Democratic Republic of the Congo', *International Journal on Minority and Group Rights*, 22, 2015, pp. 335–59.

[82] Author's interview, Safi Adili, Tutsi community leader and President of *Barza Inter-Communautaire*, Goma, 17 February 2006.

against other ethnic groups, before they lead to conflict.[83] Thus, the *Barza* often denounced politicians who stirred up ethnic hatred for political gain. The *Barza* encouraged all inhabitants of North Kivu to bring their personal and collective disputes to the members of the *Barza* who represented their particular ethnic group. The *Barza* as a whole considered these matters, formulated solutions and oversaw their implementation, for example by sending leaders to help negotiate between parties to a particular dispute. Issues that were commonly addressed by the *Barza* included conflicts over land and property, the distribution of ethnically discriminatory literature, cases of hate speech, social disturbance resulting from the influx of refugees into North Kivu (particularly since the Rwandan genocide in 1994), and the regular nocturnal arrests, kidnap and illegal detention of civilians by the police or rebel groups. On two occasions, the *Barza* sent delegates to Kampala to raise concerns with President Museveni over crimes committed by Ugandan-backed rebels in North Kivu.[84] Evaluating the overall contribution of the *Barza*, an EU mission to the DRC in 2001 reported:

Together with other complementary initiatives in North Kivu, the *Barza* [has] been able to find peaceful and sustainable solutions to some conflicts and to promote peaceful coexistence. There has been no 'ethnic' violence in the *Barza* sphere of influence since 1997, despite regular attempts by one or another authority or armed group to spark new clashes. Moreover, partly as a result of the *Barza*['s] work, there is now a trend among the displaced people to settle in multi-ethnic rather than mono-ethnic villages in North Kivu. Despite repeated requests to donors, the *Barza* has not received any financial support.[85]

As discussed further below, by the end of 2004, however, the *Barza*'s ability to mitigate ethnic tensions had weakened considerably, and by the end of 2005 the *Barza* had collapsed altogether. During fieldwork after 2005, the *Barza* remained disbanded, although some of its leaders continued to meet informally to resolve conflicts among their respective communities.

---

[83] Kalobera, quoted in Pole Institute, 'Inter-Congolese Dialogue', p. 4.

[84] F. Ndyanabo Buundo, quoted in ibid., pp. 6–7.

[85] European Union, 'The European Union's Political and Development Response to the Democratic Republic of Congo', July 2001, p. 29.

Meanwhile, the RHA, which continues to operate in the five administrative territories of Ituri district (Aru, Mahagi, Djugu, Irumu and Mambasa), displays some key similarities to the *Barza* in North Kivu but also some important differences. The RHA focuses on resolving land and other community disputes before they escalate into wider violence, as occurred between the mainly pastoralist Hema and agriculturalist Lendu in Djugu and Irumu in 1999. In February 2003, as violence among various militias raged throughout Ituri, the Dutch NGO Pax Christi organised a conference in Arua, Uganda, on the proliferation and illegal trafficking of small arms in the border region between the DRC, Uganda and Sudan. One outcome of the conference was the formation of the RHA in 2004, comprising various church-based Justice and Peace Commissions, women's networks and local human rights groups, with support from Pax Christi and later from Cordaid, the Interchurch Organization for Development Cooperation, International Alert and Trocaire.

Initially, the RHA focused on organising local *baraza* (in the original Swahili meaning and not to be confused with the *Barza*) among local customary and militia leaders in violence-affected communities but expanded to establish 500 initiatives locales de paix (ILPs). These comprise committees of twelve people elected by local authorities and civil society organisations, which engage in conflict resolution and mediation whenever local disputes arise and assist the return of populations displaced by violence. The ILPs focus on conflicts within communities but also between communities and state actors, including the Congolese army.[86] Whenever solutions are found to these local disputes, the ILPs deliver a report to both the RHA and the relevant government bodies, providing an important source of information on causes of conflict and approaches to conflict resolution. In turn, the RHA provides training to the ILPs and can be called on to provide direct mediation in local disputes or to organise community *baraza*

---

[86] R. Willems, *Security and Hybridity after Armed Conflict: The Dynamics of Security Provision in Post-Civil War States*, Routledge, 2015, p. 130. See also E. Mongo, A. Nkoy Elela and J. van Puijenbroe, 'Conflits Fonciers en Ituri: Poids du Passé et Défis pour l'Avenir de la Paix', IKV Pax Christi and Réseau Haki na Amani, December 2009.

where needed.[87] The RHA is also increasingly involved in community-level consultations around natural resource management and the role of international corporations. In July 2014, for example, the RHA published with International Alert a human rights and conflict risk assessment on behalf of Total E&R, the French oil and gas company, regarding the possible effects on the local population and environment of oil exploration around Lake Albert, which straddles the border between the DRC and Uganda.[88]

Unlike the *Barza* in North Kivu, the RHA has received extensive financial and other forms of support from international actors such as the five foreign NGOs mentioned above.[89] Recently, this has included funding from the ICC through the TFV, which lists the RHA as one of its thirteen 'implementing partners' in northern Uganda and eastern DRC.[90] Between November 2008 and September 2014, the RHA received nearly $1.5 million from the TFV[91], principally for its Caravan of Peace initiative, mentioned in Chapter 4. The project provides psychosocial, socio-economic and medical support to 'victims of crimes under the jurisdiction of the ICC'[92] in Ituri as well as collecting victims' testimonies as a contribution to community-level reconciliation. As a TFV document describes,

Aware of the fact that peace-building and reconciliation processes cannot proceed without truth-telling, RHA designed a methodology combining sociological and anthropological approaches to collect and document the

---

[87] F. Nsengimana, E. van Kemenade and A. Tobie, 'Strengthening Local Mediation Efforts: Lessons from Eastern DRC', Initiative for Peacebuilding, International Alert, 2010, p. 12.

[88] International Alert and Réseau Haki na Amani, 'Oil Exploration in Ituri: A Human Rights and Conflict Risk Assessment in Block III', July 2014.

[89] Because three of those organisations receive substantial funding from the Dutch government, the RHA is subject to project evaluations by Dutch consultants such as the following: C. Jacobs and B. Weijs, 'Capacity Development and Civil Society Strengthening Report – Réseau Haki na Amani, Final Report MFS II Evaluation', 2015, http://mfs2.partos.nl/documents/DRC-CSS-RHA.pdf.

[90] International Criminal Court, The Registry, 'Trust Fund for Victims – Implementing Partners', www.trustfundforvictims.org/en/where-we-work/implementing-partners.

[91] International Center for Research on Women, 'External Evaluation of the Trust Fund for Victims Programmes'. Most of the funding for this project came from the Republic of Estonia (ibid., p. 58).

[92] International Criminal Court, The Registry, 'Earmarked Support at the Trust Fund for Victims', Programme Progress Report, Winter 2011, p. 25.

stories of 500 beneficiaries. The aim of the so-called 'Histoire Réconciliée' (reconciled stories) is to determine the root causes of the conflicts and propose solutions to address them and avoid the reoccurrence of violence. This compilation of true stories will serve as a tool to preserve the communities' historical memory.[93]

Popularly Perceived Virtues and Pitfalls of Community-Based Mechanisms in Eastern DRC

As with the Ugandan rituals, it is important to analyse popular perceptions of these two conflict mediation practices in eastern DRC before examining their intersections with the ICC. The *Barza* successfully facilitated an inter-ethnic dialogue in North Kivu between 1998 and early 2004. As a result, local respondents routinely praised it for its ability to respond quickly to conflicts before they escalated, including visiting the sites and key parties involved in violence. Justine, a farmer in Masisi, described one example in 2004:

The *Barza* leaders came here because Hunde and Nande families were fighting over land. It was very tense, lots of anger, lots of squabbling. Some of the young men were fighting. We were all very scared because you know what happens when young men fight...When the *Barza* arrived, they took the family elders and the chief to the church building over there and they talked for the whole week until things calmed down. The *Barza* made a big difference here.[94]

The *Barza*, however, increasingly faced two main problems that led to its eventual breakdown in 2005: fraught connections to local political leaders; and an inability to resolve disputes among *Barza* representatives' communities and within the *Barza* leadership itself. The *Barza* continually allied itself with local administrators in North Kivu, especially the RCD leadership, fuelling a perception that it was little more than an RCD mouthpiece. The emergence of the *Barza* during a period when the RCD gained political and military control over much of North Kivu and set about dismantling customary authority led to accusations by observers and the general population that the *Barza* was simply a means for the rebels to ensconce sympathetic leadership

---

[93] Ibid., p. 26. [94] Author's interview, Justine, Masisi, 13 February 2006.

at the grassroots level.[95] Louis, a trader in Rutshuru, expressed a common view on this issue: 'The *Barza* has a big presence in the different [ethnic] communities but people do not know if they can trust them. Many people think the *Barza* just does what the authorities in Goma tell them to do.'[96]

Relations between ethnic groups also deteriorated significantly in North Kivu after 2004, further complicating the *Barza*'s work. The *Barza* was unable to resolve inter-ethnic disputes and manifested many of the same divisions among its own members. Many human rights observers in North Kivu accused the *Barza* leaders of 'blatant hypocrisy',[97] as the leaders denounced others' manipulation of ethnicity while continuing to fuel ethnic antagonisms themselves. On 12 December 2005, the *Barza* officially suspended operations in North Kivu because fractious relations among its leaders – particularly between Banyarwanda and non-Banyarwanda – had rendered meaningful dialogue impossible.

The *Barza* came to mirror the broader divisions between Banyarwanda and non-Banyarwanda in the province, which reached a climax in late 2004. Non-Banyarwanda members of the *Barza* accused Hutu and Tutsi leaders of knowing about, yet failing to do anything to stop, the mass import and distribution of arms among Hutu in North Kivu. These weapons were used to attack non-Banyarwanda civilians in Rutshuru and Masisi in 2004. A local lawyer in Goma explained:

It is no surprise that the *Barza Inter-Communautaire* has broken down. The biggest issue is the weapons coming over the border from Rwanda. Those weapons are being used to kill non-Banyarwanda civilians. We say in our culture: you cannot talk to a man while he is holding a spear. If Hutu and Tutsi put down their weapons, maybe people can talk again and the *Barza* can function. Until then, there will be no dialogue.[98]

In contrast to the *Barza*, the RHA has functioned continuously in Ituri for twelve years and has generated sustained legitimacy among the local population. Interviews with local citizens who interacted with the RHA, including victims of violence in Ituri, indicate that the RHA

---

[95] Author's interviews, local human rights workers and general population, Goma and Rutshuru, 1–10 February 2006.
[96] Author's interview, Louis, Rutshuru, 8 February 2006.
[97] Author's interviews, local human rights workers, Goma, 1–10 February 2006.
[98] Author's interview, lawyer, Goma, 10 February 2006.

is widely perceived as politically and ethnically non-partisan and, similar to the *Barza*, able to travel quickly to conflict hotspots to address communal discord. 'We trust *Haki na Amani* here', said Joubert, a trader in Djugu. 'They come here often and get people talking about their problems. When people talk, it means they don't pick up *pangas*.'[99] Numerous interviewees expressed the view that the RHA was more effective at dealing with local belligerents than political, military or rebel leaders. 'All of these other leaders say they can help us resolve our conflicts', said Marcel, a trader in Irumu. 'But when people start fighting about land or something else, they ask how quickly *Haki na Amani* can come.'[100]

In his study of the RHA, Rens Willems similarly found that his respondents generally preferred resolving their disputes through the RHA rather than local chiefs or the police because those actors are corrupt and invariably asked for money.[101] In contrast, the RHA – often because they comprised local religious leaders who were well known and trusted in the community – was widely believed to deliver honest outcomes. Willems argues, 'When the RHA becomes involved in a conflict between two communities, they do not necessarily intervene but rather provide support to the two communities in the mediation process. As a result, the outcome of the process is not one that is imposed from the outside but one that is very much owned by the communities themselves.'[102] Based on a similar study to Willems', Louise Anten argues,

[The RHA's] consistent activities over the years have contributed to increased stability, and the network has gained substantial credibility among the population. Even leaders have started to realize that they need to work with RHA on the resolution of conflicts if they are to retain support among the population. Deputies [members of the National Assembly at the district level] have recently sought contact with RHA to discuss a conference on peacebuilding in Ituri.[103]

---

[99] Author's interview, Joubert, Djugu, 16 April 2013.
[100] Author's interview, Marcel, Irumu, 17 April 2013.
[101] Willems, *Security and Hybridity*, p. 131.   [102] Ibid., p. 131.
[103] L. Anten, 'Strengthening Governance in a Post-Conflict District of the Democratic Republic of Congo: A Study of Ituri', paper for the Conflict Research Unit, Netherlands Institute for International Relations, July 2010, p. 24.

The ICC's Intersections with Community-Based Mechanisms in Eastern DRC

The ICC's intersections with community-based mechanisms in eastern DRC are more varied than in the Ugandan case, exemplified by its indirect interactions with the *Barza* in North Kivu and direct relations with the RHA in Ituri. While the *Barza* was operating, its leaders stated that the start of ICC investigations in the DRC disrupted some of their community-level mediation. Echoing Kuye's comments about the TRC in the previous chapter, Safi Adili, the Tutsi representative and President of the *Barza*, said, 'We met some resistance after the ICC started investigations [in 2004]. Some armed actors didn't want to talk because talking meant producing evidence for the courtroom. We had to assure them that nothing they said would ever be shared with the ICC.'[104] Alexis Kalinda, the Nyanga representative of the *Barza*, confirmed this perspective: 'Mediation becomes harder when people think they could be prosecuted – or if others close to them could be prosecuted...Suddenly there were rumours of the ICC coming to North Kivu to look for evidence, so many people went quiet.'[105] What is telling about these statements is that, in 2004 and 2005, the ICC was not investigating crimes in North Kivu. Regardless, the prospect of ICC investigations was enough to disrupt some of the *Barza*'s mediation efforts in the province because actors involved in conflict viewed criminal investigations as anathema to open dialogue.

Interviews with *Barza* leaders in 2011, six years after the collapse of the institution, highlighted a different effect of the ICC. By this time, two important ICC developments had taken place regarding North Kivu: the unsealing of the arrest warrant for Bosco Ntaganda, who was based in Goma; and the start of investigations into alleged crimes committed in both North and South Kivu by the FDLR leaders, Callixte Mbarushimana and Sylvestre Mudacumura. When discussing whether the *Barza* could ever be revived to play the key mediation role it had fulfilled between 1997 and 2004, the *Barza* leaders emphasised the presence of the ICC as one barrier to the group's revival. Kalinda said,

---

[104] Author's interview, Adili, 17 February 2006.
[105] Author's interview, Alexis Kalinda, Nyanga representative and treasurer of the *Barza Inter-Communautaire*, Goma, 17 February 2006.

There was already a Hutu-Tutsi problem in the *Barza*. It was one of the main reasons the whole process fell apart, because the Hutu and Tutsi leaders kept blaming each other for crimes...Then the ICC came along and became part of this ethnic picture. They went after Ntaganda, a Tutsi. They went after Mbarushimana, a Hutu. Each side saw the ICC as the enemy and blamed the other side for giving evidence to the ICC. How could anyone talk peacefully in this situation?[106]

Again, much of this scenario was based on rumour rather than reality, as Ntaganda was being investigated only for crimes in Ituri and the OTP's evidence against Mbarushimana, as discussed earlier, was obtained primarily through third-party sources such as international human rights reports. Scant on-the-ground OTP investigations against these two suspects were conducted in North Kivu in the period described by Kalinda. The mere presence of the ICC in eastern DRC nevertheless was enough to disrupt the function and potential renewal of the *Barza*. This also shows the ICC's embeddedness within local political and ethnic dimensions, despite the insistence of the distance discourse that the Court can and should insulate itself from the domestic arena.

The case of the RHA involves more direct ICC relations and therefore more direct consequences for the community-based practice and for the Court. In particular, the RHA – and its wider work in the community – has benefited substantially from the support of the TFV. This support, however, has also drawn the RHA into the wider remit of the ICC and forced it to explain the Court's objectives to an often sceptical, even hostile, local population, echoing some of the sentiments expressed by the OTP's intermediaries in Ituri. The experience of the RHA mirrors that of many grassroots organisations in Africa that over time attract international funding. One RHA leader in Djugu said,

The funding is obviously a very good thing because we've been able to expand all of our work across the district. But it comes with a cost. We work with international partners and they limit what we can do. They help set our priorities and we are accountable to them because of the funding. For example, we now do less conflict mediation work than before. We used to do this constantly around land conflicts. Because of the funding, we now do more medical and psychosocial work. This is of course very important but

---

[106] Author's interview, Alexis Kalinda, Goma, 21 August 2011.

the mediation work is what we've always done. It's what the community expects from us and now some people are confused about what we do.[107]

Eric Mongo, the RHA President based in Bunia, highlighted the significant benefits stemming from the ICC's funding of the organisation:

We use [the Trust Fund resources] mainly for our Caravan of Peace, which is a process of reconciliation and transitional justice. The Caravan provides psychosocial assistance to victims, especially to help them deal with trauma. The ICC funding also helps with economic and reintegration issues, creating microfinance opportunities and providing medical assistance for victims. We've also been collecting stories of the conflict. These are highly politicised but it's still a worthwhile process. There's a great need for local versions of history for the sake of future generations. So in all of these ways the ICC has contributed to local peace processes and assisting victims, while also helping with the reintegration of combatants. This shows there has been some positive impact of international justice. But it's still very far away, very distant from most people and their daily problems.[108]

Mongo also emphasised major problems the RHA faced because it was considered the ICC's local representative. '[The ICC's] type of justice hasn't generally gained the confidence of the people', Mongo said.

They say our leaders always manipulate the ICC and use it politically. Lubanga is still a hero in his community. The ICC hasn't changed this because he sacrificed himself for his community...There's a problem of the ICC seeing Lubanga as a chief. There are many others, including many higher than him. The child soldier charges against him were also seen as laughable. This was a major error by the Prosecutor. There have also been problems with witnesses working with intermediaries and the fact that many people have lied. They've been hoping for money and a trip to The Hague. The Prosecutor blamed a Congolese mafia mentality but he created many of his own problems. He needed to be better at judging the quality of witnesses...We hear all of these complaints about the ICC when we work with communities. Sometimes people ask us to share their complaints with the Prosecutor. Sometimes they actively blame us because they think we're an arm of the ICC.[109]

---

[107] Author's interview, member of *Réseau Haki Na Amani*, Djugu, 26 August 2011.
[108] Author's interview, Eric Mongo, President, *Réseau Haki na Amani*, Bunia, 25 August 2011.
[109] Ibid.

Community-level participants in RHA activities echoed many of these concerns. 'We've been helping with *Haki na Amani* programmes here for many years', said Loic, a Catholic priest in Mahagi. 'They do very good work, bringing people together and encouraging a community dialogue...*Haki na Amani* working with the ICC, though, is a difficult issue. Not everyone here likes the Court. Most people either know little about it or think it does whatever Kabila wants. *Haki na Amani* is with them now, which creates problems for [the RHA].'[110]

As discussed in Chapter 4, the RHA has absorbed popular criticisms of the ICC in two further respects: its narrow interpretation of who qualifies as a victim of crimes within its jurisdiction in Ituri, which shapes the Court's reparations policies; and the seeming incompatibility between the version of mediation and reconciliation conducted by the RHA and the ICC's distanced model of international justice. These issues point to important divisions within the ICC, between the more trial-focused branches such as the Chambers, OTP and Defence on the one hand and the Registry (which oversees the TFV) on the other. Such vagaries regarding the inner workings of the Court, though, are of little concern to participants in community-based processes such as the RHA, who view the ICC as a single institution and question how the RHA's approaches – with their emphasis on open dialogue and mediation by known local actors[111] – comport with those of the ICC, with its focus on criminal investigations, close working relations with the Congolese government and justice delivered from afar.

Conclusion

The examples of the *Barza* and the RHA highlight the ICC's complex intersections with community-based approaches to resolving mass conflict. The threat of ICC prosecutions can hamper attempts at dialogue and mediation through local practices, even when the Court is not investigating within their direct realm. In the case of the RHA, which the TFV has actively supported, the ICC has diverted the community-based institution from some of its core mediation work

---

[110] Author's interview, Loic, Catholic priest, Mahagi, 27 August 2011.

[111] E. Mongo, 'Evaluation des Mécanismes des Résolutions des Conflits Utilisés par le RHA jusqu'à ces Jours', *Réseau Haki na Amani* and IVK Pax Christi, powerpoint presentation, 2009.

to more Court-driven activities such as psychosocial and medical support. Coupled with popular concerns over how the ICC's distanced approach to justice meshes with the RHA's more localised methods, this causes confusion – and sometimes outright criticism – among community actors. The geographical, personnel and attitudinal distancing of the ICC from the local terrain, discussed throughout this book, limit the Court's ability to gauge these highly specific consequences at the village level in Uganda and the DRC.

In the early years of the ICC's operations, it was clear that Court personnel had not generally considered the possibility that it would overlap with community-based transitional justice and conflict mediation processes such as *mato oput, gomo tong*, the *Barza Inter-Communautaire* or the RHA.[112] Once the ICC intervened in Uganda and the DRC, it quickly found itself sharing the conflict mitigation terrain with these local actors and approaches, which sometimes clashed directly with the conception and modalities of justice delivered from The Hague. In Uganda, the Juba talks led to a direct contestation between the ICC and local rituals, which ultimately precipitated an attempt by the Ugandan government – deploying the ICC's legalist framework and supported by foreign donors – to co-opt local rituals for its own political purposes. In the DRC, meanwhile, the ICC's operations inadvertently undermined some mediation efforts and the possibility of reviving the *Barza* in North Kivu. In Ituri, the focus of ICC investigations in the DRC, the Court has become directly embroiled with community-based peacebuilding through the TFV's support for the RHA. While this has broadened the scope of the RHA's work, it has also made it vulnerable to reflected critiques and suspicion of the ICC.

These various intersections highlight the profound impact of the ICC on community-based practices, whether they occur far from sites of direct ICC operation or in cases where the ICC purposely coordinates with local institutions. A recurring theme through all of these examples is the apparent clash between the responses to conflict represented by community-based practices – with their emphasis on dialogue, mediation, engagement, agency and presence – and the ICC's focus on gathering local testimony for the purposes of criminal investigations

---

[112] Author's interviews, ICC staff, The Hague and Amsterdam, 22–4 March 2006, 5–7 May 2011 and 7–8 January 2016.

and prosecutions conducted at great distance from local communities. The Ugandan and Congolese cases show that, when The Hague intersects with African villages in these ways, the result is highly problematic both for the ICC and community-based approaches, but most acutely for the latter.

8 | Continental Patterns
Assessing the ICC's Impact in the Remaining African Situations

Introduction

This chapter surveys the ICC's operations in the six other African situations – CAR, Sudan, Kenya, Libya, Côte d'Ivoire and Mali – highlighting important similarities with the Uganda and DRC cases. This examination shows the extent to which key features of the ICC's first two situations have recurred throughout its work in Africa. While the Ugandan and Congolese examples elicit some unique features, because of the in-depth contextual factors explored earlier, the broader survey approach in this chapter illuminates structural aspects of the ICC, routinised behaviour by Court agents and the unavoidable complexities of African conflict environments. At a deeper level, these issues show the embeddedness of the principle of distance in all aspects of the ICC's operations.

This chapter unearths a range of consistent issues that we have already witnessed in Uganda and the DRC: challenges of dealing with fragmented states, including interim and transitional governments, some of which have come to power after coups and manipulated elections; the lack of prosecution of government crimes; fluctuating cooperation with the ICC by states and other key actors; prosecutorial opportunism rather than a clear strategy for selecting situations, cases and suspects; the decision to hibernate cases because of lack of prosecutorial progress; challenges to the admissibility of cases before the ICC; the pitfalls of distanced investigations, particularly in dealing with local witnesses; and generally poor relations with affected populations. The recurrence of these problems suggests deep structural and ideological characteristics of the ICC rather than passing matters of policy that can be remedied without substantial reform. This includes challenging the oft-stated view that many of the ICC's shortcomings to date should be seen either as the inevitable teething problems of a new global institution[1] or the idiosyncrasies of the Ocampo era which will be easily addressed under Bensouda and future prosecutors.[2] This chapter examines the six other African situations in the chronological order of the opening of ICC investigations. Rather than dissecting each case exhaustively, the focus here is on select developments and intersections with domestic actors and processes that reinforce the common themes emerging from the ICC's interventions in Uganda and the DRC.

Central African Republic

The CAR government referred the conflict situation across the whole country to the ICC in December 2004 and the Court opened investigations in May 2007. As discussed earlier, the first phase of those investigations concerned alleged crimes in 2002 and 2003 committed by Jean-Pierre Bemba's MLC rebels after they responded to calls from CAR President Ange-Félix Patassé to help suppress a coup mounted by Gen. François Bozizé.[3] In May 2014, the transitional government of CAR, led by newly ensconced President Catherina Samba-Panza, referred to the ICC a separate conflict since 1 August 2012 between Séléka rebels and anti-balaka forces (known as the CAR II situation).[4] In March 2016, ICC Trial Chamber III found Bemba guilty of command responsibility over two counts of crimes against humanity (murder and rape) and three counts of war crimes (murder, rape and pillage). The same Chamber sentenced him to eighteen years' imprisonment in June 2016.

---

[1] See, for example, A. Cassese, 'Is the ICC Still Having Teething Problems?', *Journal of International Criminal Justice*, 4, 3, 2006, pp. 434–41; L. Carter, M. Ellis and C. Jalloh, *The International Criminal Court in an Effective Global Justice System*, Edward Elgar Publishing, 2016, p. 256.

[2] See, for example, A. Hirsch, 'Fatou Bensouda: The Woman Who Could Redeem the International Criminal Court', *Guardian*, 14 June 2012, https://www.theguardian.com/law/2012/jun/14/fatou-bensouda-international-criminal-court; M. Kersten, 'A Brutally Honest Confrontation with the ICC's Past: Thoughts on "The Prosecutor and the President"', Justice in Conflict blog, 23 June 2016, https://justiceinconflict.org/2016/06/23/a-brutally-honest-confrontation-with-the-iccs-past-thoughts-on-the-prosecutor-and-the-president/.

[3] International Criminal Court, Office of the Prosecutor, 'Central African Republic', Situation in the Central African Republic, ICC-01/05.

[4] International Criminal Court, Office of the Prosecutor, 'Central African Republic II', Situation in the Central African Republic II, ICC-01/14.

Three main issues concerning the ICC's operations in CAR parallel the Uganda and DRC situations and highlight key issues stemming from the Court's distance from the domestic arena. First, the CAR case highlights fraught relations between the ICC and domestic governments around state referrals and the prosecutorial focus on rebel rather than state actors. The ICC's interventions in CAR coincide not only with an ongoing civil war but major political upheaval, with no fewer than six presidents holding office in thirteen years. Both of the CAR state referrals were made by newly ensconced governments against their recently defeated military opponents. Bozizé's referral in December 2004 followed his coming to power through a coup in March 2003, while Samba-Panza's referral in May 2014 followed her appointment as interim President in January 2014. Before Samba-Panza, the presidency was held by Séléka leader, Michel Djotodia, who overthrew Bozizé in March 2013 but, after pressure by regional leaders, relinquished the presidency to acting head of state, Alexandre-Ferdinand Nguendet, who presided for two weeks before Samba-Panza's appointment. In March 2016, Faustin-Archange Touadéra was elected President.[5]

These rapidly changing political developments have shaped all aspects of the ICC's work in CAR and drawn it into a complex and dynamic political terrain, contrary to the expectations of a distanced and apolitical Court. The OTP's investigations into Bemba's crimes were aided by Bozizé's lengthy period as President, his consistent cooperation with investigations into the crimes of Patassé's principal backer and the cooperation of Kabila's government in the DRC, which shows the important overlap of ICC cases in contiguous situations.[6] Bemba's defence counsel argued on several occasions that the OTP was focusing singularly on his responsibility for MLC crimes because of its close working relationship with Kabila, Bemba's main political rival.[7] This included an accusation by the Defence that some Prosecution

---

[5] For an excellent analysis of this conflict period in CAR, see L. Lombard, *State of Rebellion: Violence and Intervention in the Central African Republic*, Zed Books, 2016.

[6] See, for example, S. Roper and L. Barria, 'State Cooperation and International Criminal Court Bargaining Influence in the Arrest and the Surrender of Suspects', *Leiden Journal of International Law*, 22, 2008, pp. 467–9.

[7] International Criminal Court, Trial Chamber III, 'Public Redacted Version of Closing Brief of Mr. Jean-Pierre Bemba Gombo', Situation in the Central African Republic, *The Prosecutor v. Jean-Pierre Bemba Gombo*, para. 6.

witnesses against Bemba were Congolese government spies who had given false testimony and coerced other witnesses into testifying against Bemba.[8]

Investigations in the CAR II situation meanwhile have not enjoyed the same political stability and state cooperation as the case against Bemba.[9] This highlights a key challenge for the ICC: while newly ensconced governments may have a significant incentive to refer situations to the ICC to distance themselves categorically from the crimes of their predecessors, those same governments may be short-lived and incoming governments may not have the same incentives to cooperate with the Court. To respond to such machinations requires the ICC to possess a degree of in-depth knowledge of national politics that is unlikely given the distanced avoidance of country-specific expertise throughout the Court.

Echoing the Ugandan and Congolese cases, the ICC's investigations to date in CAR have focused solely on rebel actors – Bemba's MLC in the first situation and Séléka and anti-balaka forces in CAR II – while eschewing government crimes, which have been widespread since 2002. This has generated substantial criticism within CAR and beyond.[10] Further highlighting the ICC's reliance on cooperation with states and other actors in January 2015, it secured the custody of LRA commander Dominic Ongwen through his capture by Séléka, the same rebel force that was subject to ICC investigations in the CAR II situation opened the previous year.

Second, the CAR situation raises similar issues regarding admissibility and complementarity as witnessed in the ICC's relations with domestic courts in Uganda and the DRC. Mirroring the Katanga and Ngudjolo cases in particular, Bemba's defence team contested the admissibility of his case before the ICC on the grounds that the domestic courts were already handling it. A key difference, though, was that in Bemba's case the Defence argued that an order on 16 September 2004 by the Bangui Regional Court's Senior Investigating

---

[8] Ibid., para. 7.
[9] Author's interviews, ICC personnel, Amsterdam, 7 January 2016.
[10] For lengthy discussion of CAR civil society reactions in this regard, see M. Glasius, '"We Ourselves, We Are Part of the Functioning": The ICC, Victims and Civil Society in the Central African Republic', *African Affairs*, 108, 430, 2008, pp. 56–9. See also Human Rights Watch, 'Unfinished Business: Closing Gaps in the Selection of ICC Cases', 15 September 2011, pp. 31–4.

Judge constituted a 'decision not to prosecute' under Article 17(1)(b) of the Rome Statute.[11] According to this Article, a case should be determined inadmissible if domestic courts have conducted an investigation into the same crimes charged by the ICC and subsequently decided not to prosecute, provided this was not due to the state's unwillingness or inability to prosecute.

In June 2010, Trial Chamber III found that the order by the Bangui judge was not the final decision in the case against Bemba, as it was appealed the following day by the CAR Deputy Prosecutor.[12] As noted by the ICC Appeals Chamber, however, on 23 November 2004 the First Advocate-General of the Bangui Court of Appeal argued that the cases of Bemba and Patassé should be handled by the CAR national courts. The following day, the Public Prosecutor of the Bangui Court of Appeal filed a request to transfer these cases to the ICC, a request amplified in the government's referral to the ICC on 11 December 2004.[13] This situation has important parallels to the cases of the Ituri warlords, exhibiting key divisions within the state, including within the national judiciary itself, and the need for the ICC to possess context-specific knowledge to fathom these complicated domestic dynamics. As in the DRC, ultimately the will of the executive prevailed and President Bozizé referred the CAR situation to the ICC.

Third, the CAR example highlights the difficulties of witness protection especially when the ICC is located so far from witnesses' home communities. The CAR cases involve the most substantial victim participation of any ICC situation to date, with around 5,000 victims participating through a common legal counsel.[14] On 30 November 2013, as the defence team in the Bemba case was preparing its final arguments, the ICC issued five arrest warrants against Bemba, two

---

[11] International Criminal Court, Appeals Chamber, 'Corrigendum to Judgment on the Appeal of Mr Jean-Pierre Bemba Gombo against the Decision of Trial Chamber III of 24 June 2010 Entitled "Decision on the Admissibility and Abuse of Process Challenges"', Situation in the Central African Republic, *The Prosecutor v. Jean-Pierre Bemba Gombo*, 19 October 2010, para. 51.

[12] International Criminal Court, Trial Chamber III, 'Decision on the Admissibility and Abuse of Process Challenges', Situation in the Central African Republic, *The Prosecutor v. Jean-Pierre Bemba Gombo*, para. 7.

[13] ICC, Appeals Chamber, 'Corrigendum to Judgment on the Appeal of Mr Jean-Pierre Bemba Gombo', para. 40.

[14] W. Wakabi, 'Another 777 Victims to Participate in Bemba Trial', International Justice Monitor, 14 November 2012, www.ijmonitor.org/2012/11/another-777-victims-to-participate-in-bemba-trial/.

senior members of his defence team, a Congolese member of parliament and a defence witness for forging documents and bribing witnesses.[15] At the time of writing, the case against these five accused is ongoing. It underscores the ability of powerful suspects to manipulate various aspects of their trials from prison cells in The Hague, including their reach into victim communities in the countries where crimes are alleged to have been committed. While the ICC's distance from the national arena greatly impedes its ability to protect witnesses, powerful suspects such as Bemba routinely overcome the challenges of distance to continue wielding substantial influence 'on the ground'.

Sudan

The Darfur situation in Sudan provided a series of firsts for the ICC: the first referral by the UN Security Council; the first investigations on the territory of – and into alleged crimes committed by – a non-signatory state to the Rome Statute; the first arrest warrant issued for a sitting head of state; and the first warrant to include the charge of genocide. For these reasons, the Darfur situation has stirred considerable controversy and, as discussed earlier, provoked the still barbed relationship between the ICC and the AU.[16]

The Darfur situation displays three main resonances with the ICC's operations in Uganda and the DRC. First, the ICC's investigations in Darfur highlight that, even when the Security Council refers a situation, the Court depends heavily on cooperation by the state in which crimes were allegedly committed. From the outset, Bashir's government barred ICC investigators from gathering on-the-ground evidence and refused any form of cooperation with the Court.[17] Both Ocampo

---

[15] International Criminal Court, Pre-Trial Chamber II, 'Warrant of Arrest for Jean-Pierre Bemba Gombo, Aimé Kilolo Musamba, Jean-Jacques Mangenda Kabongo, Fidèle Babala Wandu and Narcisse Arido', Situation in the Central African Republic, *The Prosecutor v. Jean-Pierre Bemba Gombo, Aimé Kilolo Musamba, Jean-Jacques Mangenda Kabongo, Fidèle Babala Wandu and Narcisse Arido*, 20 November 2013.

[16] See, for example, J. Flint and A. de Waal, 'Case Closed: A Prosecutor without Borders', *World Affairs*, Spring 2009, pp. 23–38; and C. Chung, 'Letters to the Editor: A Prosecutor without Borders', *World Affairs*, Summer 2009, p. 104.

[17] For further discussion of the impact of the Sudanese government's refusal to cooperate with the ICC, see G. Barnes, 'The International Criminal Court's Ineffective Enforcement Mechanisms: The Case of President Omar al Bashir', *Fordham International Law Journal*, 34, 6, 2011, pp. 1585–619; Chatham

and Bensouda have reported the Sudanese government annually to the Security Council for its non-cooperation and expressed deep frustration at the UN's inability to compel Sudan to cooperate.[18] This situation forced the ICC to gather evidence from more distanced sources such as satellite imagery and testimony from Darfurian refugees in Chad and further afield.[19] A member of the OTP investigative team for Darfur said that one piece of evidence in the cases against President Bashir and then-Minister of State for Humanitarian Affairs, Ahmed Haroun, was a collection of pictures drawn by Darfurian children depicting Janjaweed attacks on their villages, which had been gathered by an international NGO based in Darfur.[20]

The Darfur situation underscores the ICC's severe limitations given its lack of enforcement mechanism. Not only has it failed to secure any form of meaningful cooperation by the Sudanese state but both the UN and international NGOs, with a physical presence in Darfur and other parts of Sudan, have provided limited assistance to the Court.[21] On 4 March 2009, the ICC issued an arrest warrant for Bashir. The same day, the Sudanese government revoked the licences of ten international humanitarian organisations, accusing them of 'espionage' on behalf of the ICC.[22] Shortly after, the government expelled three more international NGOs and disbanded three Sudanese humanitarian organisations. Several groups including the IRC – which had been singled out by the government as a primary collaborator with the ICC – stated that they had considered cooperating with the Court but decided otherwise

House, 'The ICC at a Crossroads: The Challenges of Kenya, Darfur, Libya and Islamic State', International Law Programme Meeting Summary, 11 March 2015.

[18] See, for example, M. Nichols, 'ICC Prosecutor Pleads for UN Security Council Act on Darfur Case', Reuters, 29 June 2015, www.reuters.com/article/us-sudan-darfur-court-idUSKCN0P92S420150629.

[19] Author's interview, ICC investigator, The Hague, 22 March 2006.   [20] Ibid.

[21] See, for example, F. Weissman, 'Humanitarian Aid and the International Criminal Court: Grounds for Divorce', Centre de Réflexion sur l'Action et les Savoirs Humanitaires (CRASH), Médecins sans Frontières, July 2009, www.msf-crash.org/sites/default/files/2017-06/7d9b-fw-2009-humanitarian-aid-and-international-criminal-court-grounds-for-divorce.-_fr-art-p._.pdf.

[22] X. Rice and T. Branigan, 'Sudanese President Expels Aid Agencies', *Guardian*, 5 March 2009, www.theguardian.com/world/2009/mar/05/sudan-aid-agencies-expelled.

because it could jeopardise their relief efforts.[23] At a September 2009 seminar in London, senior MSF officials debated the long-term consequences of the Darfur expulsions for their and other international organisations' cooperation with the ICC. At the event, some MSF staff echoed statements by UN and NGO actors in Ituri that the ICC often pressured international actors on the ground to assist the Court even if it would potentially undermine their own humanitarian work.[24]

As a result of these investigative shortcomings, the ICC has had little tangible effect on the Sudanese government's behaviour in Darfur and other parts of the country, where government crimes have persisted right up to the present.[25] After the opening of ICC investigations in Darfur, the Sudanese government expanded immunities for national officials through the Armed Forces Act in 2007 and an amnesty established in the 2011 Doha agreement between the government and seven Darfuri rebel groups.[26] Meanwhile, Bashir and other senior officials charged by the ICC have travelled freely to numerous African states, most notably to an AU summit in South Africa in June 2015, which led to a legal challenge in the South African courts to compel the South African government to arrest Bashir and transfer him to The Hague.[27] Bashir's travel to similar summits in Uganda and the DRC, however, garnered more muted criticism from the Court and its supporters, probably because these host states were seen to be broadly cooperating with the ICC in their own conflict situations.[28]

---

[23] L. Charbonneau, 'NGO Expelled from Darfur Considered ICC Cooperation', Reuters, 16 March 2009, www.reuters.com/article/us-sudan-warcrimes-ngo-idUSTRE52F6SX20090316.

[24] These discussions, in which the author participated, were summarised in Médecins sans Frontières, 'International Justice – Pragmatism or Principle?', MSF Dialogue 9, 27 July 2010, www.msf.org.uk/sites/uk/files/MSF_Dialogue_No9__International_Justice_201007270041.pdf.

[25] See, for example, J. Rothwell, 'Darfur Conflict: "Hundreds of Children Gassed to Death since January by Government in Sudan"', *Daily Telegraph*, 29 September 2016, www.telegraph.co.uk/news/2016/09/29/darfur-conflict-sudanese-government-has-gassed-hundreds-of-child/.

[26] Nouwen, *Complementarity in the Line of Fire*, p. 317.

[27] For a full discussion of these issues and South Africa's subsequent attempt to withdraw from the Rome Statute, see M. du Plessis and G. Mettraux, 'South Africa's Failed Withdrawal from the Rome Statute: Politics, Law, and Judicial Accountability', *Journal of International Criminal Justice*, 15, 2, 2017, pp. 361–70.

[28] See, for example, P. Clottey, 'International Court Urges Uganda to Arrest Sudan President Bashir', Voice of America, 12 May 2006, www.voanews.com/a/

Echoing the Ugandan case until Ongwen's arrest in 2015, the ICC has failed to secure the arrest and transfer of any Sudanese government officials. To date, only three Sudanese suspects – all rebel leaders – have appeared before the ICC following summonses: Bahr Abu Garda and Abdallah Banda from the Justice and Equality Movement; and Saleh Jerbo, a commander in the Sudan Liberation Movement. In February 2010, Pre-Trial Chamber I ruled that the charges against Abu Garda would not be confirmed. In September 2014, Trial Chamber IV replaced the summons for Banda with an arrest warrant and suspended the case until he appears in court. In April 2013, Jerbo was killed on the battlefield.[29]

These rebel cases highlight the recurring challenges confronting the ICC when operating from a distance. The weakness of the Prosecution's evidence, which led to the dropping of charges against Abu Garda, underlines the difficulty in gathering effective evidence from afar. The case of Banda also highlights the ICC's lack of enforcement: while Banda appeared at his initial hearing in June 2010, he and Jerbo (his co-accused) were permitted to return to Sudan. Since the issuance of the arrest warrant against Banda in September 2014, he has refused to attend his trial in The Hague. Such is the Sudanese government's antipathy toward the ICC, it has refused to cooperate in arresting and transferring Banda to the Court, despite his role in leading one of the main armed opposition groups against the Sudanese state. In August 2014, the ICC Registry reported that an envelope containing a formal request for the government's cooperation in the Banda case had been returned unopened.[30]

In December 2014, Bensouda officially hibernated the Darfur situation[31], as she had previously done with the situation in northern

sudanese-president-bashir-defies-international-arrest-warrant-with-trip-to-uganda/3327216.html.

[29] International Criminal Court, Office of the Prosecutor, 'Darfur, Sudan', Situation in Darfur, Sudan, ICC-02/05.

[30] Radio Dabanga, 'ICC Arrest Warrant for Darfur Rebel', 11 September 2014, www.dabangasudan.org/en/all-news/article/icc-arrest-warrant-for-darfur-rebel.

[31] United Nations Security Council, 'Reports of the Secretary-General on the Sudan and South Sudan', 12 December 2014, pp. 2–3. For further discussion of the ICC's hibernation of cases, see T. Weatherall, 'The Evolution of "Hibernation" at the International Criminal Court: How the World Misunderstood Prosecutor Bensouda's Darfur Announcement', *American Society of International Law* online series, 20, 10, 2016, www.asil.org/insights/volume/20/issue/10/evolution-hibernation-international-criminal-court-how-world.

Uganda between 2012 and Ongwen's arrest in 2015.[32] She told the UN Security Council, 'Given this Council's lack of foresight on what should happen in Darfur, I am left with no choice but to hibernate investigative activities in Darfur as I shift resources to other urgent cases...What is needed is a dramatic shift in this Council's approach to arresting Darfur suspects.'[33] Bensouda also said that allegations that Sudanese government forces raped 200 women and girls in a Darfur village in late October 2014 'should shock this Council into action'.[34] Bashir responded triumphantly to the hibernation of the Darfur case: 'They wanted us to kneel before the international criminal court but the ICC raised its hands and admitted that it had failed...The Sudanese people have defeated the ICC and have refused to hand over any Sudanese to the colonialist courts.'[35]

Second, the case of the senior Janjaweed commander, Ali Kushayb, echoes the cases of the Ituri warlords in generating fraught admissibility issues that hinge on the 'same person, same conduct' test. Like Lubanga and Katanga, Kushayb had been detained by the national authorities when the Pre-Trial Chamber ruled on the OTP's request to issue his summons to appear before the Court.[36] The Sudanese judicial system was investigating Kushayb for crimes committed during five separate incidents involving looting, burning houses, murder and forced displacement. The OTP argued that the case was admissible before the ICC because the domestic authorities were not investigating Kushayb for the same attacks as those investigated by the OTP and for the specific conduct of 'rape or other inhumane treatment'.[37] As Nouwen argues, 'In short, the Prosecutor submitted that the "same conduct" test required domestic proceedings to involve not merely the same acts, generally speaking, but also the same *incidents*; that is, the

---

[32] International Criminal Court, Pre-Trial Chamber II, 'Public Redacted Version of "Prosecution's Application for Postponement of the Confirmation Hearing", 10 February 2015, ICC-02/04-01/15-196-Conf-Exp', Situation in Uganda, *The Prosecutor v. Dominic Ongwen*, 12 February 2015, para. 1.

[33] Ibid., p. 2. [34] Ibid., p. 2.

[35] Quoted in D. Smith, 'ICC Prosecutor Shelves Darfur War Crimes Probe', *Guardian*, 14 December 2014, www.theguardian.com/world/2014/dec/14/icc-darfur-war-crimes-fatou-bensouda-sudan.

[36] Nouwen, *Complementarity in the Line of Fire*, pp. 320–1.

[37] International Criminal Court, Pre-Trial Chamber I, 'Prosecutor's Application under Article 58(7)', Situation in Darfur, Sudan, 27 February 2007, para. 265.

same factual allegations.'[38] In this very narrow interpretation of the 'same conduct' test – ultimately upheld by the PTC, which ruled the case admissible before the ICC – the domestic system is expected to replicate almost all of the specific elements of the OTP's charges to maintain domestic jurisdiction over a case.

Third, issues of distance have greatly undermined the ICC's relations with affected communities in Darfur, including victims who have expressed a willingness to testify in ICC cases. In October 2015, a group of victims assured of their right to participate in the Bashir case withdrew their participation from the proceedings because the Prosecutor had hibernated the Darfur investigations a year before.[39] Nick Kaufman, the legal representative for the Darfur victims, accused the Prosecutor of 'grandstanding' to force the UN Security Council to act on the Court's behalf and failing to consult victims about hibernating the Darfur cases.[40] This situation underscores many victims' concerns over the slowness of ICC investigations, their perceived vulnerability during drawn-out proceedings and their inability to influence the nature of investigations. With no subpoena powers to compel witnesses to testify,[41] the ICC relies on the goodwill and cooperation of witnesses, which is difficult to secure without a strong presence within local communities to help build confidence. As seen in the Ugandan and Congolese situations, a key tension for the ICC is how to balance the necessary cooperation with both states and witnesses, given that many of the latter view suspiciously the Court's close relationship with the former.

Kenya

The Kenya situation, which focuses on violence following the 27 December 2007 presidential election, echoes key features of the other situations examined so far: the challenges of state non-

---

[38] Nouwen, *Complementarity in the Line of Fire*, p. 47.
[39] International Criminal Court, Pre-Trial Chamber II, 'Victims' Notification of Withdrawal from the Case against Omar Hassan Ahmed al-Bashir', Situation in Darfur, Sudan, *The Prosecutor v. Omar Hassan Ahmed al-Bashir*, 19 October 2005.
[40] Quoted in Smith, 'ICC Prosecutor Shelves Darfur War Crimes Probe'.
[41] G. Sluiter, 'The Problematic Absence of Subpoena Powers at the ICC', *New Criminal Law Review*, 12, 2009, pp. 590–608.

cooperation; judicial interventions during fraught national elections; dropping cases for lack of evidence; problematic relations with victims and witnesses; and complex intersections between the ICC and domestic transitional justice mechanisms. Perhaps the greatest difference, though, between the ICC's operations in Kenya and those elsewhere in Africa has been the OTP's ability – principally due to Ocampo's lobbying – to build widespread support among Kenyan civil society, especially Nairobi-based human rights organisations that advocate trial-based approaches to justice.[42]

This section examines two features of the Kenyan situation that reinforce dimensions witnessed in Uganda and the DRC: the ICC's deep entanglement in national politics; and, as a consequence, its difficult relations with affected communities. The ICC's relations with the Kenyan state have been equally as controversial as those with the Sudanese government. As with Sudan, Kenya did not refer its situation to the Court; rather, this represented the Prosecutor's first use of his *proprio motu* powers. In October 2008, the Waki commission's report into the post-electoral violence recommended that Kenya establish a special tribunal to investigate and prosecute those responsible for the violence but stated that, if the government failed to do so, it would forward a list of names of senior suspects to the ICC Prosecutor. A month later, the Kenyan parliament passed the Truth, Justice and Reconciliation Commission (TJRC) Bill, which mandated the TJRC to investigate but not prosecute crimes from Kenya's independence in 1963 to the post-election violence in 2008.[43] By July 2009, a lack of progress on the special tribunal led Kofi Annan to deliver the list to Ocampo, who four months later sought the PTC's approval to launch investigations.[44]

---

[42] See, for example, S. Brown and C. Sriram, 'The Big Fish Won't Fry Themselves: Criminal Accountability for Post-Election Violence in Kenya', *African Affairs*, 111, 443, 2012, pp. 244–60.

[43] For an excellent discussion of the TJRC, see L. K. Bosire and G. Lynch, 'Kenya's Search for Truth and Justice: The Role of Civil Society', *International Journal of Transitional Justice*, 8, 2, 2014, pp. 256–76.

[44] For further discussion of these aspects of the ICC's operations in Kenya, see L. Nichols, *The International Criminal Court and the End of Impunity in Kenya*, Springer, 2015; C. Sriram and S. Brown, 'Kenya in the Shadow of the ICC: Complementarity, Gravity and Impact', *International Criminal Law Review*, 12, 2, 2012, pp. 219–44.

Again mirroring the Sudan situation, the Kenyan government's non-cooperation and active interference have dominated the ICC's investigations and further highlighted the Court's inability to deter the crimes of powerful political actors.[45] Crucial to these dynamics are the changing political fortunes of the principal suspects charged by the ICC, Uhuru Kenyatta and William Ruto. Before the 2007 election, Kenyatta and Ruto were on opposite political sides, the former with Mwai Kibaki's Party of National Unity (PNU) and the latter with Raila Odinga's Orange Democratic Movement (ODM). The power-sharing arrangement mediated by Annan following the electoral violence, however, brought both Kenyatta and Ruto into the cabinet as Deputy Prime Minister and Minister for Agriculture, respectively. When the ICC issued arrest warrants for six Kenyan suspects, including Kenyatta and Ruto, on 8 March 2011, some commentators praised the Prosecutor for not destabilising the coalition government by pursuing either President Kibaki or his deputy Odinga and targeting instead a lower rung of political elites.[46] Kenyatta and Ruto (and their four co-accused, Henry Kosgey, Francis Muthaura, Joshua Arap Sang and Mohammed Hussein Ali) subsequently attended the initial and confirmation of charges hearings in The Hague in 2011.

These second tier leaders, however, quickly rose to much greater political prominence. In January 2013, Kenyatta and Ruto joined forces to form the Jubilee Alliance, which won the general election in March 2013, along with Kenyatta's election as President and Ruto as Deputy President. During the election campaign, Kenyatta and Ruto portrayed themselves as the victims of the neo-colonialist ICC which, along with interference by foreign donors, was trying to manipulate the outcome of the vote. The fact that the pair had been charged by the ICC seemingly increased their popularity among the electorate.[47] The

---

[45] See, for example, Chatham House, 'The ICC at a Crossroads'; Y. Dutton and T. Alleblas, 'Lessons from Kenya: Unpacking the ICC's Deterrent Effect', openDemocracy, 5 July 2016, www.opendemocracy.net/openglobalrights/yvonne-m-dutton-tessa-alleblas/lessons-from-kenya-unpacking-icc-s-deterrent-effect.

[46] For further discussion of this point, see Nichols, *The International Criminal Court and the End of Impunity in Kenya*, pp. 82–108.

[47] See, for example, S. Mueller, 'Kenya and the International Criminal Court (ICC): Politics, the Election and the Law', *Journal of Eastern African Studies*, 8, 1, 2014, pp. 25–42; G. Lynch and M. Zgonec-Rožej, 'The ICC Intervention in Kenya', Africa/International Law Programmes, Chatham House, February 2013.

ICC found itself further enmeshed in Kenyan domestic politics after the al-Shabaab terrorist attack on the Westgate shopping mall in Nairobi on 21 September 2013. At the time, Ruto was in The Hague for his trial, which had begun on 10 September. The ICC judges allowed him to return to Kenya for one week to deal with the aftermath of the Westgate attack.[48]

Over time, however, all of the Kenya cases before the ICC collapsed.[49] In January 2012, the charges were not confirmed against Kosgey and Ali. In March 2013, the Prosecutor was forced to withdraw the charges against Muthaura for lack of evidence. The same occurred with Kenyatta in December 2014 and Ruto and Sang in April 2016. The Prosecutor argued that Kenyatta and Ruto in particular had manipulated the process through the destruction and withholding of evidence and the murder and intimidation of witnesses.[50] In October 2013, the ICC unsealed an arrest warrant for Walter Barasa,[51] followed by arrest warrants for Paul Gicheru and Philip Bett in September 2015, all accused of corrupting Prosecution witnesses.[52] Such was the extent of the Kenyan government's attempts to undermine the Court, it hired a London-based public relations company, BTP Advisers, to develop an extensive media campaign framing the Court as a foreign meddler in Kenya's domestic affairs.[53]

---

[48] International Criminal Court, Trial Chamber V, 'Status Conference', Situation in the Republic of Kenya, *The Prosecutor v. William Samoei Ruto and Joshua Arap*, 23 September 2013.

[49] International Criminal Court, 'Situation in the Republic of Kenya', ICC-01/09.

[50] See BBC, 'Kenya's William Ruto's Case Dismissed by ICC', 5 April 2016, www.bbc.co.uk/news/world-africa-35965760; M. Makokha, 'Interview with Fatou Bensouda', The Hague Trials Kenya, 20 June 2016, https://neveragain .co.ke/bensouda-speaks-why-kenya-cases-icc-collapsed/article.

[51] International Criminal Court, Office of the Prosecutor, 'Statement of the Prosecutor of the International Criminal Court, Fatou Bensouda, on the Warrant of Arrest issued against Walter Barasa', Situation in the Republic of Kenya, *The Prosecutor v. Walter Barasa*, 2 October 2013.

[52] International Criminal Court, Pre-Trial Chamber II, 'Order Unsealing the Warrant of Arrest and Other Documents', Situation in the Republic of Kenya, *The Prosecutor v. Paul Gicheru and Philip Kipkoech Bett*, 10 September 2015.

[53] A. Rowell, 'Former Tory PR Advises Kenyan Facing Hague Trial', *Independent*, 13 October 2012, www.independent.co.uk/news/uk/politics/former-tory-pr-advises-kenyan-facing-hague-trial-8210442.html. On 3 September 2012, the author declined an email invitation to contribute to a documentary produced by Gizmo Films, working with BTP Advisers, as part of Kenyatta's overall public relations campaign against the Court (email on file with author).

Because of the collapse of the cases against the six Kenyan suspects, the ICC has suffered fraught relations with affected communities. The routine harassment of Prosecution witnesses in particular highlighted the inability of the ICC to protect witnesses in the face of a powerful state. In April 2016, following the collapse of the Ruto and Sang cases, Fergal Gaynor, legal representative for the victims in the Kenyatta case, wrote,

In 2013 and 2014, I held 49 days of meetings with 839 [post-election violence] victims of the crimes charged in the Kenyatta case in the Nyanza, Western and Rift Valley regions of Kenya. In 2015, following the withdrawal of charges against Kenyatta, I met approximately 700 of those victims in another series of meetings to discuss the termination of the case and associated issues. They made abundantly clear to me their total lack of faith in their own government's willingness to deliver justice, decried its repeated promises to deliver fair compensation, and many expressed deep anger at the ICC's inability to stand up to the Kenyan government's bullying.[54]

In October 2014, ICC Judge Andrew Fulford highlighted a further problem concerning witnesses in the Kenya situation, which he believed departed from the approach taken to witnesses in the Lubanga case, over which he had presided. Fulford argued that the use of the common legal representative for victims, based in Kenya, meant that victims' views were being filtered through this individual, followed by an Office of the Public Counsel for Victims advocate in the courtroom. This resulted in a 'real element of distance' with victims' perspectives 'represented, in the main if not exclusively, by court-based lawyers who frequently will have no connection with or personal knowledge of the events in question'.[55]

Libya

The Libya situation results from the first unanimous UN Security Council referral to the ICC on 26 February 2011 and concerns crimes

---

[54] The Hague Trials Kenya, 'Victims Lawyer Reveals Dark Tactics Kenya Used to End ICC Cases', 1 December 2016, www.jfjustice.net/uhurur-kenyatta-case-status-conference-trial-chamber-vb-09-july-2014/icc-cases/gaynor-reveals-dark-tactics-kenya-used-to-end-icc-cases.

[55] Lord Justice Fulford, 'Sir Richard May Memorial Lecture The International Criminal Court: Progress Made, Progress Needed', International Law Programme Meeting Summary, Chatham House, 29 October 2014, p. 4.

committed during the Gaddafi regime's crackdown against demonstrators from 15 February 2011. To date, this represents the ICC's only intervention stemming from the 'Arab Spring' uprisings, after Russia and China blocked an attempt by the Security Council to refer the Syria situation to the ICC in March 2014. On 27 June 2011, the OTP issued arrest warrants for three senior Libyan government officials – President Muammar Gaddafi, who was head of the armed forces; Saif al-Islam Gaddafi, the President's son and Libya's de facto Prime Minister; and Abdullah al-Senussi, a colonel in the army and the head of military intelligence – followed by a fourth warrant on 24 April 2017 for the arrest of former Libyan head of internal security, al-Tuhamy Mohamed Khaled.[56] Highlighting a wider trend that flows from the ICC's regular involvement in situations of ongoing conflict, Muammar Gaddafi was killed on 20 October 2011 before he could be arrested and transferred to the Court;[57] the same fate as four other ICC suspects, Otti, Lukwiya and Odhiambo in Uganda and Jerbo in Darfur.

Two connected aspects of the Libya situation pertain to the broader analysis here. First, the ICC's relations with the current Libyan government echo dynamics witnessed in Uganda, the DRC and several of the other situations examined in this chapter. To date, the OTP has issued arrest warrants only for members of Gaddafi's deposed government, ignoring alleged crimes committed by the anti-Gaddafi rebels who formed the National Transitional Council (NTC) and claimed to have 'liberated' Libya in October 2011. The OTP has also ignored alleged crimes by the North Atlantic Treaty Organisation (NATO), which conducted a military campaign against Gaddafi's forces between 19 March and 31 October 2011. This fuels perceptions of the ICC as an accompanying international intervention to that of NATO,[58] a theme of major overlap between external judicial and military endeavours examined further below and already seen in Uganda.

Echoing the CAR and DRC situations in particular, the ICC has confronted a highly fragmented Libyan state, which is unable to control its entire national territory. In August 2012, the NTC handed power to an elected parliament, the General National Congress (GNC), which was replaced in June 2014 by a new parliament, the

---

[56] International Criminal Court, 'Situation in Libya', ICC-01/11.
[57] Al Jazeera, 'Muammar Gaddafi Killed as Sirte Falls', 21 October 2011, www.aljazeera.com/news/africa/2011/10/20111020111520869621.html.
[58] See, for example, the discussion of this issue in Kersten, *Justice in Conflict*, ch. 8.

Council of Representatives (CoR). Soon after, the CoR relocated to the eastern city of Tobruk, leaving the capital city Tripoli controlled by various militias. Fighting between forces loyal to the ousted GNC and the newly elected CoR allowed the Islamic State (IS) to capitalise on the situation and capture control of several coastal cities, including Gaddafi's birthplace and former stronghold, Sirte. In October 2015, the UN helped broker a new 'unity' government, the Presidential Council (PC), although both the Tripoli and Tobruk administrations opposed its establishment. Four months later, the PC headed by Prime Minister Fayez al-Sarraj, set up its headquarters in Tripoli. At present, Libya is in effect ruled by three governments – al-Sarraj's PC, the former GNC headed by Khalifa Ghwell and the CoR in Tobruk – and a range of militias, including IS, Libya Dawn and the Benghazi Defence Brigade.[59]

The lack of a coherent state has greatly hampered the ICC's operations, evidenced by the three administrations' refusal to hand over Saif Gaddafi which – as with the Darfur situation – has led the ICC Prosecutor constantly to lobby the UN Security Council for support in enforcing his arrest warrant.[60] As with the Darfur situation, the Prosecutor's entreaties to the Security Council have fallen on deaf ears.[61] Saif Gaddafi was captured in November 2011 by a militia that later became part of the Libyan National Army. The militia held Gaddafi in the north-western town of Zintan, until his reported release in June 2017.[62] Highlighting the severe security challenges for ICC staff, a four-person defence team that visited Gaddafi, headed by Melinda

---

[59] For detailed discussions of these conflict and political dynamics in post-2011 Libya, see M. Eriksson, 'A Fratricidal Libya: Making Sense of a Conflict Complex', *Small Wars and Insurgencies*, 27, 5, 2016, pp. 817–36; R. Lefèvre, 'High Stakes for the Peace Process in Libya', *Journal of North African Studies*, 20, 1, 2016, pp. 1–6; I. Constantini, 'Conflict Dynamics in Post-2011 Libya: A Political Economy Perspective', *Conflict, Security and Development*, 16, 5, 2016, pp. 405–22.

[60] United Nations Security Council, 'Meetings Coverage: State Cooperation with International Criminal Court Vital to Ensure Justice for Victims of Atrocity Crimes in Libya, Prosecutor Tells Security Council', 8 May 2017.

[61] For a full discussion of this issue, see. V. Peskin and M. Boduszynski, 'The Rise and Fall of the ICC in Libya and the Politics of International Surrogate Enforcership', *International Journal of Transitional Justice*, 10, 2, 2016, pp. 272–91.

[62] C. Stephen, 'Gaddafi Son Saif al-Islam Freed by Libyan Militia', *Guardian*, 11 June 2017, www.theguardian.com/world/2017/jun/11/gaddafi-son-saif-al-islam-freed-by-libyan-militia.

Taylor, was detained for four weeks in Zintan in June 2012. Since the team's detention, almost no ICC personnel have travelled to Libya and the OTP has stated in two of its budgets – consistently the smallest allocated to any of the situations under ICC investigation[63] – that there would be no travel to Libya for those particular years.[64] For these same security reasons, the Registry has conducted almost no outreach to affected communities, greatly undermining popular understanding and the legitimacy of the Court.[65]

Second, similar to the Ituri cases, the Libya situation highlights key problems for the ICC over interpretations of complementarity and admissibility. The Libyan government challenged the admissibility of both the Saif Gaddafi and al-Senussi cases before the ICC. The defence teams for both suspects, however, argued for prosecution in The Hague because of Libya's continued use of the death penalty.[66] On 31 May 2013, the PTC rejected Libya's challenge in the case against Gaddafi, partly on the grounds that the government could not secure the transfer of Gaddafi from his place of detention in Zintan. This decision was upheld by the Appeals Chamber on 21 May 2014. Conversely, on 11 October 2013, the Pre-Trial Chamber ruled the case against al-Senussi inadmissible before the ICC because he was subject to ongoing judicial proceedings by Libyan authorities that covered the same alleged crimes as those before the ICC. On 24 July 2014, the Appeals Chamber rejected an appeal by al-Senussi's defence team and upheld the Pre-Trial Chamber's decision that al-Senussi should be tried in Libya – the first ever finding of inadmissibility by the ICC.[67]

[63] T. Ebbs and E. Saudi, 'The ICC in Libya – Justice Delayed and Denied', openDemocracy, 25 February 2015, www.opendemocracy.net/openglobalrights/thomas-ebbs-elham-saudi/icc-in-libya-%E2%80%93-justice-delayed-and-denied.
[64] International Criminal Court, Assembly of States Parties, 'Proposed Programme Budget for 2017 of the International Criminal Court', 17 August 2016, para. 131; International Criminal Court, Assembly of States Parties, 'Report on the Activities of the International Criminal Court', 9 November 2016, Annex.
[65] Ibid.
[66] International Criminal Court, Pre-Trial Chamber I, 'Decision on the Admissibility of the Case against Saif al-Islam Gaddafi', Situation in Libya, *The Prosecutor v. Saif al-Islam Gaddafi and Abdullah al-Senussi*, 31 May 2013, para. 159.
[67] International Criminal Court, Appeals Chamber, 'Judgment on the Appeal of Mr Abdullah al-Senussi against the Decision of Pre-Trial Chamber I of 11 October 2013 entitled "Decision on the Admissibility of the Case against

Several commentators have critiqued the apparent inconsistencies in the admissibility determinations regarding Gaddafi and al-Senussi.[68] While these observers identify different problems in the two domestic cases, they concur that a central issue was the government's supposed ability to obtain the accused in al-Senussi's, as opposed to Gaddafi's, case. At the time of the Pre-Trial Chamber rulings, the Libyan government exercised control over the Al-Hadba prison where al-Senussi was held but could not secure the custody of Gaddafi. Valid concerns have been raised about the standard of justice these suspects would face within the Libyan legal system,[69] a point reinforced by the handing down of the death penalty against both suspects in July 2015 after a trial in which al-Senussi appeared in person and Gaddafi by video-link from Zintan.[70] Since the verdict, Gaddafi has reportedly received an amnesty while al-Senussi's death sentence remains in place.[71]

Questions arise over the ICC judges' reasoning that a suspect who is in government custody should be prosecuted by that state, while a suspect over whom the state cannot gain custody should be prosecuted by the ICC, which is even further afield and relies on that same state for

Abdullah al-Senussi''', Situation in Libya, *The Prosecutor v. Saif al-Islam Gaddafi and Abdullah al-Senussi*, 24 July 2014.

[68] See, for example, K. Fisher, 'Libya, the ICC and Security Post-Conflict Justice', Middle East Institute, 16 December 2013, www.mei.edu/content/libya-icc-and-securing-post-conflict-justice; K. J. Heller, 'The ICC Fiddles while Libya Burns', *Opinio Juris*, 24 March 2014, http://opiniojuris.org/2014/03/24/30477/; Chatham House, 'The International Criminal Court and Libya: Complementarity in Conflict', International Law Programme Meeting Summary, 22 September 2014; M. Tedeschini, 'Complementarity in Practice: The ICC's Inconsistent Approach in the Gaddafi and al-Senussi Admissibility Decisions', *Amsterdam Law Forum*, 7, 1, 2015, pp. 76–97.

[69] See, for example, J. O'Donoghue and S. Rigney, 'The ICC Must Consider Fair Trial Concerns in Determining Libya's Application to Prosecute Saif al-Islam Gaddafi Nationally', *EJIL: Talk!* blog, 8 June 2012, www.ejiltalk.org/the-icc-must-consider-fair-trial-concerns-in-determining-libyas-application-to-prosecute-saif-al-islam-gaddafi-nationally/; A. Bishop, 'Failure of Complementarity: The Future of the International Criminal Following the Libyan Admissibility Challenge', *Minnesota Journal of International Law*, 22, 2, 2013, pp. 388–421; J. Trahan, 'A Complementarity Challenge Gone Awry: The ICC and the Libya Warrants', *Opinio Juris*, 30 August 2015, http://opiniojuris.org/2015/09/04/guest-post-a-complementarity-challenge-gone-awry-the-icc-and-the-libya-warrants/.

[70] Reuters, 'Libyan Court Sentences Gaddafi Son Saif, Eight Other Ex-Officals to Death', 28 July 2015, www.reuters.com/article/us-libya-security-idUSKCN0Q20UP20150728.

[71] Stephen, 'Gaddafi Son Saif al-Islam Freed by Libyan Militia'.

the arrest and transfer of the suspect. Repeating the situation encountered in northern Uganda, where the determination of admissibility of the LRA cases hinged on the inability of the Ugandan authorities to capture the five LRA commanders in question, the ICC has even less capacity than the Libyan state to secure the custody of suspects such as Gaddafi and al-Senussi. Furthermore, it is unclear why the ICC judges (both at the Pre-Trial and Appeals stages) have afforded the Libyan state – in its present fragmented condition – the opportunity to prosecute al-Senussi domestically, while denying similar requests by judicial actors in the DRC, CAR and (as discussed below) Côte d'Ivoire. A key factor in the al-Senussi case is the domestic courts' mirroring of ICC investigations in overcoming the 'same person, same conduct' test, which highlights the centrality of the narrow legalist interpretation of the complementarity – which is most consistent with the principle of distance – that predominates within the Court.

Côte d'Ivoire

The OTP opened investigations in Côte d'Ivoire on 3 October 2011. From the outset, it focused on crimes allegedly committed by forces loyal to former President Laurent Gbagbo before and after the 2010 presidential election; the ICC's second situation, after Kenya, concerning post-election violence. The vote on 31 October 2010 did not produce a clear-cut winner between Gbagbo and Alassane Ouattara, requiring a second round on 28 November 2010. On 2 December 2010, the Electoral Commission declared Ouatarra the winner but was overridden by the Gbagbo-aligned Constitutional Council. Both candidates nominated their own governments. This sparked armed attacks against each other's forces and civilian supporters, during which an estimated 3,000 people were killed.[72] Ouattara was backed by most international actors and Guillaume Soro, leader of the Forces Nouvelles (FN), an insurgency that had controlled the northern half of the country since late 2002. Ouattara's forces prevailed and, supported by French and UN troops, captured Laurent Gbagbo and his wife Simone in the presidential compound in Abidjan on 11 April 2011.

---

[72] United Nations Human Rights Council, 'Report of the Independent, International Commission of Inquiry on Côte d'Ivoire', 6 June 2011, p. 2.

After the ICC failed to land two sitting heads of state in the dock, Bashir in Sudan and Gaddafi in Libya, Gbagbo afforded the Court its first prosecution of a former President. The Côte d'Ivoire situation also represents, after Kenya, the second use of the ICC Prosecutor's *proprio motu* powers. The Ivorian case differs from the Kenyan one, however, in that the Ivorian government asked the Prosecutor on 14 December 2010 to initiate a *proprio motu* investigation, given that at the time Côte d'Ivoire was not a signatory to the Rome Statute.[73] This renders the Côte d'Ivoire situation an example of the Prosecutor launching an investigation independently but with many of the state referral dynamics seen in Uganda, the DRC, CAR and Mali.

The OTP initiated its investigations in Côte d'Ivoire on 23 June 2011 and received Pre-Trial Chamber authorisation on 3 October 2011. The OTP requested authorisation to investigate crimes after the 28 November 2010 vote but this was later expanded to cover crimes since 19 September 2002, the date of a mutiny against President Gbagbo by northerners within the national army, which sparked a civil war that lasted until a peace agreement between Gbagbo's government and the FN in March 2007.[74] To date, the ICC has launched three cases in Côte d'Ivoire against Laurent and Simone Gbagbo and Charles Blé Goudé, the youth minister under Gbagbo, who is being prosecuted in a joint case with the former President. All three are charged with crimes against Ouattara's supporters in the context of the 2010 election.

Three aspects of the Côte d'Ivoire situation are relevant for the broader analysis here. First, this situation echoes that in Uganda, the DRC, CAR, Libya and Mali by focusing only on non-state actors or members of the deposed regime. Crucially, the OTP has not opened cases against troops allied to Ouatarra, the current President, despite findings by national and international bodies that implicate his forces in atrocities.[75] The OTP has also focused on crimes surrounding the

---

[73] Ouattara, 'Confirmation de la Déclaration de Reconnaissance'.

[74] International Criminal Court, Pre-Trial III, 'Request for Authorisation of an Investigation Pursuant to Article 15', Situation in the Republic of Côte d'Ivoire, 23 June 2011.

[75] See, for example, Human Rights Watch, 'Côte d'Ivoire: Ouattara Forces Kill, Rape Civilians during Offensive', 9 April 2011; Amnesty International, 'Ivory Coast: Both Sides Responsible for War Crimes and Crimes against Humanity', 25 May 2011.

2010 election and specifically within Abidjan, eschewing cases during the civil war starting in late 2002 and in other parts of the country – factors that, if taken into account, could potentially implicate forces loyal to Ouattara as well as a wider range of actors on the Gbagbo side.

With Gbagbo currently on trial in The Hague, the political landscape in Côte d'Ivoire has been completely transformed, mirroring the impact of the prosecution of Bemba in the DRC. Highlighting Ouattara's dominance of the political domain with Gbagbo now out of the way, in October 2015 he secured another presidential term with 84 per cent of the national vote. None of the other candidates registered double digits.[76] As Sophie Rosenberg argues, however, despite Gbagbo's imprisonment, he continued to loom large over the 2015 elections:

Although Gbagbo tried to ostensibly remove himself from the political scene, opposition candidates used his imprisonment as a rallying call during their campaigns. The promise to bring Gbagbo home became a cheap way to score political points and cast aspersions on Ouattara's record in reconciling Ivorians. Even independent candidates, like Kouadio Konan Bertin, were heard stating, 'As soon as I am elected, the next day, I will jump in a plane to free Gbagbo.'...Disagreements over Gbagbo's continued political role also contributed to a split in the main opposition party. The *Front Populaire Ivoirien* (FPI) – the party founded by Gbagbo that has historically served as a foil for Ouattara's *Rassemblement des Républicains* (RDR) – fractured in part due to disagreements over how to move forward without Gbagbo at the helm.[77]

The OTP's close working relationship with Ouattara's government, coupled with its focus on investigating only Gbagbo-related crimes and only in Abidjan, plays into volatile divisions in Ivorian national life. Echoing the relationship between northern and southern Uganda, several country experts highlight a widespread popular perception of the ICC as favouring Ouattara and northern groups (which are often depicted as some combination of Muslim, Dioula ethnicity and originating from neighbouring countries, principally Burkina Faso, a point

[76] S. Rosenberg, 'How Did the ICC Trial of Laurent Gbagbo Impact the Elections in Côte d'Ivoire?', Democracy in Africa blog, 13 November 2015, http://democracyinafrica.org/how-did-the-icc-trial-of-laurent-gbagbo-impact-the-elections-in-cote-divoire/.
[77] Ibid.

that taps into highly divisive debates over national identity, *ivoirité* and foreignness).[78] Reflecting this, in December 2016 a reported 26 million Ivorians in the country and the diaspora signed a petition calling for the ICC to release Gbagbo.[79]

Second, these same issues impinge on the ICC's relations with affected Ivorian communities, especially those – mainly in the south of the country – that remain sympathetic to Gbagbo. Compounding these problems, the ICC Registry did not deploy a full-time member of the Outreach Unit until October 2014, three years after the start of investigations, by which time critical narratives about the Court – not least the perception of anti-Gbagbo bias – had already taken hold.[80] Until the arrival of the full-time outreach official, the Registry focused on 'disseminating information to victims of the specific incidents contained in the prosecution's charges through a network of civil society organizations'[81], extending the local intermediaries trend discussed in Chapter 3.

Third, the Ivorian government has challenged the admissibility of the Simone Gbagbo case before the ICC, raising similar issues regarding complementarity, the criteria for genuine domestic proceedings and the ICC's difficult relations with national judiciaries, as witnessed in the DRC, CAR and Libya. The ICC issued an arrest warrant against Simone Gbagbo in February 2012, charging her with crimes against humanity, including murder and rape. In October 2013, the Ivorian government submitted a claim of inadmissibility before the ICC, arguing that national proceedings against Gbagbo were already underway. In late 2014, the Pre-Trial Chamber rejected Côte d'Ivoire's claim on the grounds that the national proceedings were unconvincing, and reminded the government of its obligation to transfer her to The Hague.[82] The government responded that, as a state emerging from a

---

[78] Ibid. See also, comments by Mike McGovern in K. Kotarski, 'Ivory Coast: Calls for More Prosecutions', Institute for War and Peace Reporting, 14 December 2011, https://iwpr.net/global-voices/ivory-coast-calls-more-prosecutions.

[79] BBC, '26 millions de Signatures pour la Libération de Gbagbo', 29 December 2016, www.bbc.com/afrique/region-38460089.

[80] Human Rights Watch, 'Making Justice Count: Lessons from the ICC's Work in Côte d'Ivoire', 4 August 2015.

[81] Human Rights Watch, 'ICC: Côte d'Ivoire Case Highlights Court's Missteps', 4 August 2015.

[82] International Criminal Court, Pre-Trial Chamber I, 'Decision on Côte d'Ivoire's Challenge to the Admissibility of the Case against Simone Gbagbo', Situation in the Republic of Côte d'Ivoire, *The Prosecutor v. Simone Gbagbo*, 11 December 2014.

major conflict and therefore lacking 'considerable material and human resources',[83] it could not investigate Gbagbo's case more quickly. It stressed nevertheless that investigations were underway and a trial was expected within months.[84]

In March 2015, the national courts convicted Simone Gbagbo and eighty-two supporters of various crimes relating to the 2010 post-election violence and sentenced her to twenty years in jail for endangering state security. Shortly after, Ouattara stated that no further suspects would be transferred to the ICC and all future trials would take place domestically.[85] Some commentators argue that this reflects Ouattara's fear that the ICC may soon turn its attention to him or his followers.[86] In May 2015, the ICC Appeals Chamber upheld the admissibility of the Gbagbo case on the grounds that she was being prosecuted domestically for different crimes from those with which she was charged at the ICC – the 'same person, same conduct' test discussed in the DRC and Darfur situations.[87] The Ivorian authorities responded by initiating new proceedings against Gbagbo and charging her with the same crimes against humanity as those alleged by the ICC. Her trial in Abidjan on these charges began in May 2016, with the ICC insisting that she should still be transferred to The Hague. She was acquitted of all charges in March 2017.[88]

---

[83] International Criminal Court, Appeals Chamber, 'Judgment on the Appeal of Côte d'Ivoire against the Decision of Pre-Trial Chamber I of 11 December 2014 Entitled "Decision on Côte d'Ivoire's Challenge to the Admissibility of the Case against Simone Gbagbo"', Situation in the Republic of Côte d'Ivoire, *The Prosecutor v. Simone Gbagbo*, 27 May 2015, para. 120.

[84] For further discussion of admissibility and complementarity issue surrounding the Simone Gbagbo case, see K. J. Heller, 'Radical Complementarity', *Journal of International Criminal Justice*, 14, 3, 206, pp. 637–65.

[85] BBC, 'Alassane Ouattara: No More Ivorians Will Go to ICC', 5 February 2016, www.bbc.co.uk/news/world-africa-35502013.

[86] See, for example, A. Vines, 'Does the International Criminal Court Help to End Conflict or Exacerbate It?', *Guardian*, 22 February 2016, www.theguardian .com/global-development/2016/feb/22/international-criminal-court-help-to-end-conflict-or-exacerbate-it.

[87] ICC Appeals Chamber, 'Judgment on the Appeal of Côte d'Ivoire against the Decision of Pre-Trial Chamber I of 11 December 2014'.

[88] Deutsche Welle, 'Ex-Ivory Coast First Lady Simone Gbagbo Acquitted of War Crimes', 28 March 2017, www.dw.com/en/ex-ivory-coast-first-lady-simone-gbagbo-acquitted-of-war-crimes/a-38174997.

The Simone Gbagbo case exhibits several problems observed in Uganda, the DRC and elsewhere. Principally, it highlights the problematic insistence on the 'same person, same conduct' test, which is heavily skewed towards prosecution by the ICC, even when domestic proceedings have commenced. Again, this underscores the predominance of the legal conception of complementarity over the political, relational and developmental interpretations and the broader emphasis on maintaining the Court's distance from the domestic realm. Given that Gbagbo was convicted by the national courts and sentenced to a longer jail term than the ICC has given any of its convicts, there would have been little benefit to the post-conflict society in seeing her prosecuted in The Hague as opposed to Abidjan.

The Ivorian government's argument following the PTC's initial rejection of its admissibility challenge also underlines the inevitable material and logistical barriers for any state emerging from mass conflict that wishes to investigate and prosecute its own nationals. The PTC judges appeared to expect unreasonable progress in domestic investigations to trigger an admissibility challenge; a degree of progress that the ICC itself has failed to achieve in the majority of its cases, most of which have spanned many years.

Finally, it is unclear whether the second trial of Simone Gbagbo – constructed explicitly to ward off intervention by the ICC – will be of significant benefit to the domestic population, which has already witnessed her prosecution by the national courts. The catalytic effect of the ICC in this case has not contributed substantially to the domestic delivery of justice. While Ouattara's government has shown a marked dedication to prosecuting members and supporters of Laurent Gbagbo's regime, it has shown little willingness to address atrocities committed by its own allies.[89] The ICC would greatly increase its popular legitimacy by focusing on cases that are not being addressed by the domestic authorities, including against Ouattara's side. The ICC's decision to avoid these cases substantially weakens its grounds for intervention in Côte d'Ivoire and highlights its inability to hover objectively and apolitically above the fray, contrary to the expectations of the distance principle.

---

[89] For further discussion of this point, see A. Kobi, 'Can Gbagbo's ICC Trial Help Quench Côte d'Ivoire's Thirst for Justice?', Institute for Security Studies, 9 March 2016, www.issafrica.org/iss-today/can-gbagbos-icc-trial-quench-cote-divoires-thirst-for-justice.

Mali

The Malian government referred the conflict situation in its territory to the ICC in June 2012 after various Islamist rebel groups captured control of the north of the country in January 2012 and a coup on 21 March 2012 toppled the government of Amadou Toumani Touré. This represented the first new situation opened during Bensouda's tenure as ICC Prosecutor. Mali's referral followed sustained pressure by high-level Economic Community of West African States (ECOWAS) mediators in the Malian conflict.[90] The OTP opened investigations in Mali in January 2013, focusing on crimes committed in the northern regions of Gao, Kidal and Timbuktu. To date, the ICC has launched only one case in Mali, which led to the conviction in September 2016 of Ahmad al Faqi al Mahdi, an affiliate of al-Qaeda in the Islamic Maghreb. Al Mahdi confessed to the war crime of attacking historic and religious monuments – specifically nine mausoleums and a mosque – in the UNESCO world heritage city of Timbuktu in June and July 2012. The al Mahdi case represents the first confession by an ICC suspect and the first ICC prosecution of war crimes concerning cultural destruction.[91]

Three features of the Mali situation echo those in Uganda and DRC, as well as several of the other situations examined in this chapter. First, in Mali the OTP once again found itself negotiating with an interim government in a highly fluid political environment. After the March 2012 coup, the military junta – under pressure from ECOWAS – handed control to an interim President, Dioncounda Traoré, who remained in power until September 2013. Mali's state referral to the ICC came during Traoré's interim presidency, a combustible political period. In May 2012, Traoré was attacked in his office by pro-junta demonstrators, who knocked him unconscious and stripped him naked.[92] In August 2012, a new government of national unity was

---

[90] Al Jazeera, 'ECOWAS Call on ICC over "War Crimes" in Mali', 7 July 2012, www.aljazeera.com/news/africa/2012/07/201277194319595934.html.

[91] International Criminal Court, Trial Chamber VIII, 'Judgment and Sentence', Situation in the Republic of Mali, *The Prosecutor v. Ahmad al Faqi al Mahdi*, 27 September 2016.

[92] A. Nossiter, 'Mali Mob Assaults President after Pact', *The New York Times*, 21 May 2012, www.nytimes.com/2012/05/22/world/africa/mali-protesters-attack-interim-president-dioncounda-traore.html.

formed, led by Prime Minister Cheick Modibo Diarra and a new cabinet of thirty-one ministers, including several seen as close to the coup leader, Amadou Sanogo. On 10 December 2012, Sanogo led a second coup attempt. Soldiers arrested Diarra, who immediately resigned and was succeeded as Prime Minister by Django Sissoko. The June 2013 peace deal between the Malian government and northern rebels paved the way for presidential elections in July and August 2013, which were won by Ibrahim Boubacar Keita.[93]

Both the state referral and the OTP's opening of investigations in Mali occurred during Traoré's interim presidency, in which the legitimacy of the government was heavily contested. Ottilia Anna Maunganidze and Antoinette Louw argued in July 2012, 'The self-referral [by Mali] could...be characterised as an attempt by the interim government – which is weak and in search of support and legitimacy both locally and abroad – to put down the rebellion in the north, and eliminate opposition from those who might seek to destabilise a new government.'[94] This situation raises critical questions about the legitimacy of the ICC acting on state referrals by interim or unelected governments, as it has done in CAR, Libya and Mali, or through *proprio motu* action in cases of narrow and highly controversial electoral victories, as in Kenya and Côte d'Ivoire. In CAR, Libya and Mali, interim or unelected governments have used state referrals, among other mechanisms, as a means of bolstering their claims to statehood. In practical terms, the prevailing atmosphere of political instability in Mali also stymied the ICC's investigations on the ground, leading to an effective hibernation of the Mali situation soon after the OTP opened investigations in January 2013 until the unexpected transfer of al Mahdi from Niger in September 2016, discussed in more detail below.

Second, the Mali situation raises key questions about the ICC's broad prosecutorial approach, principally its opportunism – rather than systematic strategy – in selecting crimes and suspects for prosecution. The OTP focused on crimes committed by al Mahdi largely

---

[93] For a useful analytical overview of this conflict period in Mali, see S. Wing, 'Mali: Politics of a Crisis', *African Affairs*, 112, 448, 2013, pp. 476–85.

[94] O. Maunganidze and A. Louw, 'The Decision by the Government of Mali to Refer the Situation in the Country Has Several Implications for the Country, Africa and the ICC', Institute for Security Studies, 24 July 2012, www.issafrica.org/iss-today/implications-of-another-african-case-as-mali-self-refers-to-the-icc.

because he was available, having been captured and detained by Niger authorities (with strong parallels to the Ongwen and Ntaganda cases, where unanticipated surrender or capture caught the OTP unawares, although in those two cases the suspects had already been charged by the ICC). When France launched a military intervention in northern Mali in early 2013 to oust Islamist rebels, al Mahdi fled Timbuktu. In October 2014, he was part of a convoy transporting weapons from Libya to Mali via Algeria. Al Mahdi was captured along the Niger–Algeria border during the anti-terrorist Opération Barkhane, which comprised 3,000 troops from France and five former French colonies in the Sahel, Burkina Faso, Mali, Mauritania, Chad and Niger.[95] Imprisoned in Niamey, he was charged with terrorism by a local court. On 18 September 2015, the ICC issued an arrest warrant for al Mahdi, and eight days later the Niger authorities transferred him to The Hague.[96]

The al Mahdi case echoes those of Lubanga, Katanga and Ngudjolo in the DRC, who were charged by the ICC principally because they were available for prosecution, having been arrested by the Congolese authorities. It is not clear whether the Prosecution's investigations had identified al Mahdi as an actor considered most responsible for serious crimes before he was captured by Niger forces or whether the OTP pursued him because he was in custody. What is clear, however, is that the OTP focused only on the set of charges for which it already had trial-ready evidence – namely those concerning cultural destruction – while ignoring arguably more serious crimes such as rape, of which substantial evidence has emerged.[97] This echoes the controversies over the narrow charges in the Lubanga and Katanga cases in particular.

[95] B. Dürr, '*Ahmad al Mahdi: Who is the First Alleged Islamist at the ICC?*', *Justice Hub, 29 February 2016*, https://justicehub.org/article/ahmad-al-mahdi-who-first-alleged-islamist-icc.

[96] International Criminal Court, Pre-Trial Chamber I, 'Mandat d'arrêt à l'encontre d'Ahmad Al Faqi al Mahdi', Situation in the Republic of Mali, *The Prosecutor v. Ahmad al Faqi al Mahdi*, 28 September 2015.

[97] For further discussion of this issue, see International Federation for Human Rights, 'Q&A: The Al Mahdi Case at the ICC', 17 August 2016, www.fidh.org/en/region/Africa/mali/q-a-the-al-mahdi-case-at-the-icc; M. Forestier, 'ICC to War Criminals: Destroying Shrines Is Worse than Rape', *Foreign Policy*, 22 August 2016, http://foreignpolicy.com/2016/08/22/icc-to-war-criminals-destroying-shrines-is-worse-than-rape-timbuktu-mali-al-mahdi/.

During the one-week trial of al Mahdi in The Hague – the shortest at the ICC to date because of his confession – the OTP's heavy reliance on distanced sources of evidence, particularly video footage, became apparent. The OTP's lack of more extensive on-the-ground evidence, which would be necessary to pursue charges regarding sexual violence, for example, highlights the inherent challenges of investigating violent and politically volatile situations from a distance.[98] On 6 March 2015, the FIDH along with fourteen Malian human rights organisations filed a complaint before the High Court of Commune 3 of Bamako, on behalf of thirty-three victims, accusing al Mahdi and fourteen others of war crimes and crimes against humanity, including torture and sexual and gender-based crimes.[99] While some commentators praised the OTP for pursuing the most available suspect for crimes based on the available evidence and casting a spotlight on the international crime of destruction of heritage sites,[100] others criticised this approach as too narrow and pursuing crimes arguably less grave than those affecting the bodily integrity of victims.[101] Following al Mahdi's conviction, the FIDH issued a statement calling on the OTP to investigate other serious crimes against him in light of the OTP's recent policy on pursuing sexual and gender-based crimes, discussed in Chapter 3.[102]

[98] On the extent to which the OTP relied on video footage of al Mahdi's destruction of shrines and public sermons, see International Criminal Court, Pre-Trial Chamber I, 'Confirmation of Charges: Public Transcript', Situation in the Republic of Mali, *The Prosecutor v. Ahmad al Faqi al Mahdi*, 1 March 2016; International Criminal Court, Trial Chamber VIII, 'Trial Hearings: Public Transcripts', Situation in the Republic of Mali, *The Prosecutor v. Ahmad al Faqi al Mahdi*, 22–4 August 2016; ICC, Trial Chamber VIII, 'Judgment and Sentence', Situation in the Republic of Mali, *The Prosecutor v. Ahmad al Faqi al Mahdi*.

[99] International Federation for Human Rights, 'Mali: The Hearing of Al Mahdi before the ICC is a Victory, But Charges Must Be Expanded', 30 September 2015, www.fidh.org/en/issues/international-justice/international-criminal-court-icc/mali-the-hearing-of-abou-tourab-before-the-icc-is-a-victory-but.

[100] See, for example, A. Whiting, 'The Significance of the ICC's First Guilty Plea', Just Security blog, 23 August 2016, www.justsecurity.org/32516/significance-iccs-guilty-plea/.

[101] See, for example, Forestier, 'ICC to War Criminals'.

[102] International Federation for Human Rights, 'First Step on the Path to Justice: ICC Sentences Al Mahdi to 9 Years', 27 September 2016, www.fidh.org/en/region/Africa/mali/first-step-on-the-path-to-justice-icc-sentences-al-mahdi-to-9-years.

Finally, the Mali situation displays the problematic linkage of the ICC and international military interventions, as witnessed in Uganda, Libya and Côte d'Ivoire. In particular, some observers have questioned the influence of France over the ICC's operations in Mali. The ICC Prosecutor launched investigations in Mali only five days after the start of France's military intervention in the north of the country. Leslie Vinjamuri argues that this 'reinforces the ICC's emerging (if informal) role as an instrument of coercive diplomacy', following the ICC's intervention in Libya soon after the NATO aerial bombing campaign. Vinjamuri highlights that Bensouda herself suggested such a role by stating, in relation to the Mali situation, 'Justice can play its part in supporting the joint efforts of ECOWAS, the AU and the entire international community to stop the violence and restore peace to the region.'[103] Similarly, Mark Kersten argues that the ICC's effective hibernation of the Mali situation – with little progress between the launch of investigations in January 2013 and the unexpected capture of al Mahdi in September 2015 – may have stemmed from pressure by the French government not to unsettle the delicate peace process between the Malian government and Tuareg rebels.[104] While this may represent a more laudably circumspect role than the ICC played during the Ugandan peace talks, it raises important questions about the influence of a powerful foreign state and member of the Security Council, France, in key aspects of the ICC's operations.

Conclusion

Examining the six situations above alongside those of Uganda and the DRC shows that the ICC, in its first fifteen years of operation, has struggled with the complexity of investigating and prosecuting serious crimes in Africa. Some of the issues examined in the Uganda and DRC

---

[103] L. Vinjamuri, 'Is the International Criminal Court Following the Flag in Mali?', Political Violence @ a Glance blog, 22 January 2013, https://politicalviolenceataglance.org/2013/01/22/is-the-international-criminal-court-following-the-flag-in-mali/. See also P. Schmitt, 'France, Africa and the ICC: The Neocolonialist Critique and the Crisis of Institutional Legitimacy', in K. Clarke, A. Knottnerus and E. de Volder (eds.), *Africa and the ICC: Perceptions of Justice*, Cambridge University Press, 2016, pp. 138–43.

[104] M. Kersten, 'What Happened to the ICC in Mali?', Justice in Conflict blog, 29 May 2015, https://justiceinconflict.org/2015/05/29/what-happened-to-the-icc-in-mali/.

situations in earlier chapters are specific to those contexts. Many of the most pressing challenges, however, are consistent across most – and sometimes all – of the ICC's eight situations in Africa to date. Four connected structural challenges in particular recur throughout these situations.

First, because of the Court's temporal mandate, it routinely finds itself investigating and prosecuting cases during recent or ongoing conflict. This causes insecurity for ICC personnel on the ground as well as local victims and witnesses. This has also resulted in the battle deaths of several ICC suspects in the Uganda and Darfur situations before they could be brought to trial.

Second, the ICC's relatively scant resources have shaped all of its interventions in Africa so far. This has influenced the limited time spent *in situ* by most ICC personnel as well as the OTP's decision to focus on contiguous African states where investigators can be used across borders in multiple situations (for example, in Kenya/Uganda/DRC/ CAR, CAR/Darfur/Libya and Mali/Côte d'Ivoire).[105] Cross-border factors have impinged on various ICC cases, for example the OTP's decision to overlook Ugandan government crimes in Ituri; the Defence's claim of undue influence by the Congolese government over the prosecutorial strategy in CAR; and the Ugandan government's increased criticisms of the ICC because of its intervention in Kenya, one of Uganda's key regional allies.

Third, because of insecurity and limited resources, the ICC has been forced to cooperate extensively with domestic states for the security of ICC personnel, sharing of evidence and the transport of suspects and witnesses to The Hague. The last issue has led to a high degree of opportunism on the part of the OTP, which has in several instances selected crimes and suspects for prosecution because particular individuals had been arrested by state authorities, for example in the DRC and Mali situations. The ICC has also cooperated with powerful Western states – mainly because of the ICC's lack of its own police and military to enforce arrest warrants – which has drawn the Court into controversial foreign military interventions in Libya, Côte d'Ivoire and Mali and the regional military response to the LRA.

---

[105] Author's interviews, ICC staff, The Hague and Amsterdam, 22–4 March 2006, 5–7 May 2011 and 7–8 January 2016.

Fourth, often because of recent or ongoing conflict, the ICC has intervened in – and exacerbated – situations of immense political volatility. A crucial challenge for the Court has been determining how best to engage with interim governments, some of which comprise former rebel groups and other actors who have emerged victorious from the same conflicts the Court is attempting to investigate, or in cases of post-election violence in which government actors have come to power following highly contentious votes. The ICC has often made these situations more volatile by substantially altering the political landscape, for example removing key presidential contenders such as Bemba and Gbagbo (after state referrals or invitations to intervene by the political opponents of those suspects) or bolstering the election campaigns of Bashir, Kenyatta and Ruto (who have framed the ICC's involvement through either UN Security Council referrals or use of the Prosecutor's *proprio motu* powers as an egregious form of external interference in domestic affairs).

Across these African situations, these structural factors have had two principal effects. First, the ICC has shown itself unable to deal effectively with cases involving sitting members of government because of the Court's fundamental reliance on state cooperation. When the Court has pursued current government actors – in the Darfur and Kenya situations – those cases have faltered, with the Prosecutor forced to hibernate all cases in the former and drop all charges against the suspects in the latter. While it is highly problematic for the ICC to focus only on non-state suspects, as it has in Uganda, the DRC, CAR, Côte d'Ivoire and Mali, it has so far proven incapable of doing otherwise.

Second, in the cases that have reached The Hague, the quality of both Prosecution and Defence evidence has often been called into question, not least by the Pre-Trial and Trial judges. Evidentiary problems led to two pauses in the Lubanga trial, while the charges against two suspects, Mbarushimana in the DRC and Abu Garda in Darfur, have not been confirmed because of lack of evidence. The judges were also forced to amend the charges in the Katanga, Ngudjolo and Bemba cases based on the preliminary evidence submitted.[106]

---

[106] For further discussion of this issue, see V. Nerlich, 'The Confirmation of Charges Procedure at the International Criminal Court: Advance or Failure?', *Journal of International Criminal Justice*, 10, 5, 2012, pp. 1339–56; S. Rigney, '"The Words Don't Fit You": Recharacterisation of the Charges, Trial Fairness,

In response to the challenges above, the ICC has persisted with a broadly distanced approach to the African situations analysed here. Prosecution and Defence investigators have spent limited time on the ground in all eight situations, while ICC outreach programmes through the Registry have often begun years after the launch of investigations and sometimes not at all. While the Court lauds victim participation as a central feature of its operations,[107] this has also increasingly taken a distant form through the use of common legal counsel, designed to aggregate victim perspectives, as opposed to giving individual victims a voice in the courtroom, as occurred in the early ICC cases in the DRC. The Prosecution has been particularly energetic in both limiting victim participation in trials and arguing against *in situ* trials, which would bring the ICC's work closer to affected populations. All of these factors, coupled with perennial weaknesses in ICC witness protection, have greatly undermined the Court's relations with local communities.

A final recurring feature of the ICC's distanced approach has been its inconsistent – and sometimes dismissive – response to admissibility challenges by domestic judiciaries. Nearly all of the eight African situations have generated such challenges but only the al-Senussi case in Libya has led the ICC to cede jurisdiction to national courts. As argued earlier, the Lubanga, Katanga, Ngudjolo and Simone Gbagbo cases provided an equally, if not more, compelling basis to challenge the ICC's admissibility on the grounds of ensuing domestic investigations into these individuals. A key outcome of these issues concerning admissibility and complementarity is the weakening of relations between the ICC and domestic courts, with lasting consequences for the reform of national judiciaries in several of the African situations within the ICC's purview.

and Katanga', *Melbourne Journal of International Law*, 15, 2, 2014, pp. 1–18; E. Fry, 'Legal Recharacterisation and the Materiality of Facts at the International Criminal Court: Which Changes are Permissible?', *Leiden Journal of International Law*, 29, 2, 2016, pp. 577–97. For a critique of the OTP's and the judges' refusal to amend the charges against Lubanga, even when evidence that substantially exceeded the charges emerged during trial, see C. Ferstman, 'Limited Charges and Limited Judgments by the International Criminal Court – Who Bears the Greatest Responsibility?', *International Journal of Human Rights*, 16, 5, 2012, pp. 796–813.

[107] See International Criminal Court, 'Victims', www.icc-cpi.int/about/victims.

Taken together, the first fifteen years of the ICC's work – with its singular focus on situations, crimes and suspects in Africa – shows a Court that, in key respects, is ill-equipped to fulfil its mandate of addressing serious crimes in contexts that are geographically removed and foreign to most of its staff. Attempting to distance itself from domestic politics, it has become embroiled in – and has profoundly shaped – the politics of African states. Compounding these problems is the Court's insistence on its superiority to domestic responses to mass atrocity and its failure to live up to its own principle of complementarity. The final chapter in this book provides some insights into ways to make the Court more effective by returning it to this core principle.

9 Conclusion
Narrowing the Distance

This book has argued that, while the ICC prefers to describe its work in terms of complementarity with domestic institutions and actors, in practice it has maintained a fundamental and problematic distance from the domestic arena. This highlights the complacency of complementarity as a principle and set of practices. The analysis in the preceding chapters shows that, as the ICC has intervened in African states and encountered national governments, local populations and domestic responses to mass atrocity, it has actively undermined the four expressions of complementarity outlined in Chapter 2. Meanwhile, the ICC's insistence on distance has led to the enactment of a highly particularist, rather than universal, mode of prosecutorial justice that is consistently intolerant of different responses to mass atrocity and has generated a range of negative consequences for African societies.

The legal conception of complementarity – with its emphasis on the idea of the ICC as a back-stop to national judiciaries – has been weakened by the ICC's tendency actively to chase cases and to provide legally narrow and often dismissive responses to admissibility challenges by African states. The ICC has contravened the political conception of complementarity – and its attendant notions of deference to states and respect for national sovereignty – by intervening in situations where domestic judiciaries were already investigating and prosecuting cases. Furthermore, the ICC has undermined national sovereignty by pressuring domestic institutions to mimic its mode of international justice and publicly criticising national approaches that are perceived to diverge from this norm. These practices have also contradicted the relational understanding of complementarity, which stresses partnership and interdependence with domestic actors, along with the tendency of the Court to view itself as the most important response to atrocity, always equipped to handle cases in any jurisdiction, and to expect a range of actors to assist it, often with little reciprocity. Finally, the ICC has undermined the developmental conception of complementarity, which ascribes a catalytic or multiplier effect to the Court, by refusing to cooperate with national legal systems on issues such as evidence-sharing and by collaborating with national executives in actively undermining these judiciaries.

Instead, the ICC has manifested the political and philosophical conceptions of distance, discussed in Chapter 2, by framing itself as superior to national institutions, which are viewed as infected by political, social and cultural influences from which the ICC claims to be insulated. Seeking to safeguard its objectivity and impartiality, the ICC has also actively distanced itself from the domestic terrain through its mainly non-African personnel spending very limited time in investigation sites, performing many of its core investigative functions through intermediaries and conducting delayed and often unresponsive forms of outreach to local communities.

In Uganda, the DRC and the other African states analysed here, the impact of this distanced approach has been extensive. Particularly where states have been encouraged to refer their situations to the ICC, the Court's lack of political expertise in domestic contexts has allowed it to be instrumentalised by states, while failing to deter national governments from repressive practices against their own citizens. This includes encouraging armed campaigns against ICC suspects, increasing militarisation and reducing incentives for peace negotiations and other remedies predicated on amnesties. Paradoxically, the ICC's claim to objectivity through its distanced practices has exacerbated its vulnerabilities to political manipulation.

Meanwhile, at the community level, everyday citizens suffer the effects of continued violence, foreign and alienating forms of justice, the ICC's flawed witness protection mechanisms, bolstered and repressive governments, the removal of key opposition political actors from the national arena and, in some cases, the perpetuation rather than resolution of armed conflict. The Court's distanced approach has undermined its relations with affected communities and therefore its ability to build trust with potential witnesses and to gather high-quality evidence for the purpose of effective trials. This jeopardises the fundamental role of the ICC in investigating and prosecuting those considered most responsible for the gravest crimes around the world, including sitting government officials, a category that the ICC to date has shown a structural inability to prosecute. This further delegitimises the ICC in the eyes of local populations – which view state crimes as especially grave – compounding the Court's difficult relations with these communities. This is critical because it shows that the emphasis on distance weakens the Court on its own terms. The ICC's focus on distance has also thwarted African national judiciaries, some of which are currently undergoing major reforms, and strengthened executive branches that have a direct interest in limiting the capacity of the national courts to handle cases of international crimes, especially those involving state perpetrators.

The African cases examined in this book highlight the ICC's confrontation with the stark realities of delivering justice – and pursuing the principle of complementarity – in complex parts of the world that are alien to most of its personnel, have a long history of fraught foreign interventions and often manifest different conceptions of conflict and justice from its own. This book's focus on the ICC's intersections with domestic actors and processes thus elucidates some key reasons behind increased scepticism – even among previously supportive sources[1] – of the ICC's model of justice when applied to these far-flung contexts. Much of that scepticism stems from the numerous crises the ICC has experienced during its first fifteen years – which in turn flow from the Court's fundamental weddedness to distance. These crises include the near collapse of the Prosecution's case against Thomas Lubanga on the opening day of his trial because of poor evidence gathering and witness selection; the expulsion of international humanitarian agencies from Sudan following the genocide charges against President Bashir; the 'peace versus justice' controversies around the Ugandan peace talks; the dropping of all charges against the Kenyan suspects and the hibernation of various situations due to lack of investigative progress; the threats of a mass AU exodus from the Court; the withdrawal of several African states from the Rome Statute; and various member states' (including Uganda's and the DRC's) decision to host ICC suspects such as Bashir at domestic summits.

Despite the ICC's political and practical shortcomings, some commentators have continued to speak soothingly to the Court, attributing its problems to the Machiavellian behaviour of African states, resource

---

[1] See, for example, Human Rights Watch, 'ICC: Course Correction', 16 June 2011; and P. Akhavan, 'Rise, and Fall, and Rise of International Criminal Justice', *Journal of International Criminal Justice*, 11, 3, 2013, pp. 527–36.

limitations or the fact that, as a new institution, the ICC is still finding its feet and will soon prove more effective.[2] The consistency of the ICC's missteps and weaknesses across all eight African situations, however, suggests that these cannot be so easily wished away or blamed on other parties. The critiques in this book show the ICC to be highly imperfect rather than an ideal mode of justice to which all national institutions should aspire. Demystifying the ICC and its inherent reliance on domestic governments and other actors shows that it is not the 'fail-safe remedy' that Christine Chung predicted in the Court's early years, which should be contrasted with the inevitable shortcomings of domestic courts. These critiques also highlight that the ICC's approach to justice does not involve a universal 'view from nowhere' but rather derives from a particular legalist conception of trial-based justice with deep roots in a Western individualist Enlightenment tradition. The ICC represents categorically a 'view from somewhere' and an often highly contested, contradictory and counter-productive one at that.

The remainder of this final chapter explores the consequences of the ICC's elevation of distance over complementarity for broader theoretical debates about appropriate responses to mass atrocity. It concludes with some practical recommendations for the reform of the ICC to reinvigorate its self-stated core principle of complementarity and thus to make it a more effective intervention in African conflict zones, with greater benefits for African polities.

Theoretical Insights from the ICC's Practice of Distance over Complementarity

The ICC's claimed pursuit of complementarity but practical manifestation of distance elicits broader theoretical insights into these two key terms. This section highlights some ramifications of the ICC's trajectory so far for debates over the role of international criminal law in addressing mass crimes and other liberal interventions – such as

---

[2] See, for example, Akhavan, 'Rise, and Fall, and Rise'; D. Orentlicher, 'Owning Justice and Wrestling with Its Complexity', *Journal of International Criminal Justice*, 11, 3, 2013, pp. 517–26; Roth, 'Africa Attacks the International Criminal Court'; A. Whiting, 'Finding Strength within Constraints', International Criminal Justice Today project, American Bar Association-International Criminal Court, 23 November 2016.

peacekeeping missions and humanitarian aid – that confront similar tensions between independence and interdependence. The ICC's inexorable shift from complementarity to distance highlights its weak adherence to the former principle. Within liberalism more broadly – the philosophical realm that underpins complementarity – various commentators argue that international actors will tolerate only 'foreign' practices they consider completely consistent with liberal norms.[3] In effect, this does not constitute toleration at all, as it fails to wrestle with practices that international actors may find objectionable or that challenge their jurisdiction. The ICC's practice of complementarity to date shows a willingness to recognise and cooperate only with those domestic practices that conform to the Court's conception of justice and pose no jurisdictional threat. When confronted with different conceptions of justice and claims of ownership and national sovereignty – for example, the proposal during the Ugandan peace talks to use amnesty or community-based rituals to deal with the LRA commanders or the Bunia courts' desire to prosecute the cases of the Ituri warlords – the ICC has retreated to the principle of distance, invoking its superiority over the domestic realm and reasserting its jurisdiction.

The ICC's practices so far indicate that, despite the Court's claims, complementarity breaks down in the face of the national and local particularities of African societies. Not only do these often represent very different conceptions of justice and other post-conflict objectives but, given many African states' damaging experiences of colonialism and other external interventions, they are often deliberately framed antagonistically toward international processes. Compounding this problem, the ICC's lack of Africa-specialist staff, including nationals of the situations under investigation, and lack of time spent in the field undermine its ability to get to grips with these practices and concerns in African states. The ICC has displayed competitiveness even toward processes that are arguably similar to itself, such as national prosecutions, as witnessed in its treatment of the admissibility challenges in the DRC, CAR, Côte d'Ivoire and Libya. Even where these institutions have reformed themselves according to international prescriptions, including mimicking the ICC through domestication of the Rome

---

[3] See, for example, C. Kukathas, 'The Mirage of Global Justice', *Social Philosophy and Policy*, 23, 1, January 2006, including an explicit discussion of the ICC in this regard (pp. 10–11).

Statute and other (often donor-driven) procedures, they have rarely secured jurisdiction. This stems from pressure on the ICC to bring cases to trial soon after its inauguration – a key factor behind the chasing of cases in Uganda and the DRC – but also an ingrained scepticism of, and sense of pre-eminence over, the domestic realm.

A major challenge for the ICC in this respect is that it is a relative latecomer in terms of responses to mass atrocity in the African states in question. As Antony Anghie argues, 'non-European societies are often assumed to be lacking in legal personality'[4] or even entirely lawless, providing a blank canvas for external actors to display their technical artistry. On the contrary, as the African cases examined in this book show, a wide range of national and community-level actors were already responding to mass atrocity in manifold ways long before the ICC intervened. Once the Court became involved and intersected with domestic processes, it expressed its predominant status and actively undercut these more established approaches, despite experiencing numerous failures of its own.

Moreover, the ICC, with its global mandate, is by definition itinerant, a short-term institution that will move on to address criminal cases elsewhere. The roving Court thus displays key parallels to management consultancy firms, called in as supposedly neutral experts to intervene briefly in the affairs of corporate entities but without having to contend with the full impact of their prescriptions. Domestic actors and processes, by contrast, remain in place long after the ICC has departed the scene, must live with the consequences of their and any external interventions and, in the case of state institutions, are directly accountable to their citizens in the long term. These features of all liberal interventions demand that we pay closer attention to their lasting impact on the domestic realm.

While the ICC has displayed a weak adherence to complementarity, its embodiment of distance has proven highly unconvincing and ineffective. This shows that notions of distance provide a poor basis for other types of interventions in conflict-affected societies. Returning to the view of distance underpinning the ICC, as outlined in Chapter 2,

---

[4] A. Anghie, 'The Evolution of International Law: Colonial and Postcolonial Realities', in R. Falk, B. Rajagopal and J. Stevens, *International Law and the Third World: Reshaping Justice*, Routledge-Cavendish, 2008 p. 40. For an example of this perspective in practice, see Human Rights Watch, 'Congo: Bringing Justice to the Heart of Darkness', 6 February 2006.

the Court's practice in Africa to date casts doubt on the various theoretical components of this concept. Not only has distance superseded complementarity as the ICC's core operating principle, it has also failed to deliver its assumed practical virtues.

The fundamental scepticism of state power that underpins the discourse of distance belies the ICC's deep reliance on state cooperation, as well as the Court's ability to boost state capacity, including its repressive tendencies, as witnessed in Uganda and the DRC. While the ICC may wish to supersede state influence, it has routinely shown itself incapable of doing so. This pertains to all international interventions in conflict-affected societies that self-identify as 'neutral and impartial'. As argued earlier, however, the 'distancing' approach of legal institutions is even more forceful than that of other external interventions such as humanitarian aid delivery and peacekeeping because the law, unlike these other practices, views distance as an inherent virtue.

Problems concerning state cooperation also undermine the expectation within the distance discourse that the ICC can improve the practice of domestic politics, including the relations between states and between states and their citizens. The ICC's essential reliance on governments has produced two key dynamics, either an overly cosy relationship with some states (especially those that self-refer situations to the Court, as in Uganda and the DRC) or outright hostility toward others (most acutely in the Sudan and Kenya situations). The former dynamic does not encourage states to improve their political behaviour because they do not feel threatened by the prospect of ICC prosecution but are rather emboldened in their repression of domestic populations, as Uganda and the DRC have been in the context of national elections. In the latter category, governments' antagonism toward the ICC has generated further state repression and interference to stymie the ICC's work or to frame the ICC's intervention as a form of external meddling that warrants a strong nationalistic response by the government. In both cases, the ICC's capacity to improve state behaviour is extremely limited and relies on the ICC fulfilling its basic legal function of conducting effective investigations and prosecutions which, as discussed at length, it has often failed to do because of a recurring failure to grapple sufficiently with the complexity of African conflict zones.

The third component of the political conception of distance – namely the ICC's claimed universality and application of consistent rules as opposed to the volatile and often unprincipled particularities of the domestic political realm – is also unconvincing. Rather than a form of 'global justice' as Teitel and others have pronounced,[5] the ICC has proven to be a highly particularist mode of justice that cannot easily accommodate or coexist with other conceptions of justice or entirely different modes of responding to mass crimes. The claimed universality of the ICC because of the democratic moment of the Rome conference also has not manifested in practice. States' ratifications of the Rome Statute, and even their cooperation with the ICC, have been motivated by a range of principled and less principled factors, rather than some automatic reflection of their adherence to the rule of law and willingness to be regulated by the ICC's framework. As evidenced in the early negotiations between the OTP and the Ugandan and Congolese governments, states also did not necessarily recognise what they had signed up to when they ratified the Statute or grasp all of the intricacies of the Statute and its impact on their own behaviour.

The ICC's operations to date also contest the philosophical conception of distance – which is much stronger in international law than other liberal interventions – namely that delivering justice for international crimes requires a deontological rather than consequentialist approach if it is to remain neutral and even-handed. Connected to the discussion of the political conception of distance above, this view presupposes that the ICC can ever attain this detached and impartial position, an assumption that does not hold when examining the Court's operations in Africa to date. Rather than remaining above the fray, the ICC has quickly become part of the domestic political, social and cultural arena, crucially influenced by and influencing local dynamics. As a profoundly politically embedded institution, the ICC's operations have wide-ranging consequences for domestic environments, irrespective of the Court's claim that it should ignore consequentialist calculations. That the ICC has such significant effects on the domestic sphere requires it to consider these factors – to achieve what Rodman calls 'politically grounded legalism'[6] or Weiner terms 'prudent politics'[7] – including for its own efficacy. Such consideration is

---

[5] Teitel, 'Global Transitional Justice'.

[6] Rodman, 'Justice as a Dialogue between Law and Politics', p. 463.

[7] A. Weiner, 'Prudent Politics: The International Criminal Court, International Relations and Prosecutorial Independence', *Washington University Global Studies Law Review*, 12, 2013, pp. 545–62.

not deterministic. For example, analysing the probable impact of the ICC during peace talks does not mean that in every case the ICC should relinquish jurisdiction for the purposes of negotiations. However, a careful and reasoned calculation of the ICC's impact is required for the sake of the societies in question and the Court itself.

Another major challenge for the ICC's weddedness to the discourse of distance as critical detachment has been its confrontation with very different conceptions of justice in many local communities in northern Uganda, eastern DRC and elsewhere. Many of these local perspectives emphasise the need for justice to be understood and imparted contextually, weighing the effects on justice of geography, politics and sentiments and in turn its impact on interpersonal and communal relations, all the while underscoring the importance of presence – in terms of the location of proceedings and direct involvement of those most affected by crimes – rather than distance.

For all of these reasons, the idea of basing justice on political and philosophical notions of distance is found wanting when analysed in the context of the ICC's interventions in Uganda, the DRC and elsewhere. This also calls into question Gready's argument, outlined in Chapter 2, for a 'correct balance' between distanced and embedded forms of justice, seeking to combine the best of international and more localised responses to mass atrocity. Gready's view underestimates the desire to dominate that is embedded in the distance perspective. Achieving the proposed balance would require the international level to quell its hegemonic impulses and to view itself as an equal among very different types of actors and processes.[8] The ICC, for example, would have to become more flexible and to show a greater reluctance to intervene in cases where domestic proceedings are either underway or are very likely to commence. Gready's 'correct balance' also belies the likelihood that, in some instances, different responses to conflict will prove incommensurate because the espoused conceptions of justice and other objectives fundamentally clash. This becomes increasingly likely as the 'global' model of justice through the ICC is applied in more and more foreign contexts, a task that has proven highly controversial when applied to a single but diverse continent such as Africa

---

[8] For a powerful critique of liberal institutions' desire to dominate African polities, see Young, 'A Project to Be Realised'.

before countenancing the effects when (if ever) the Court launches fully fledged investigations and prosecutions on other continents.

Clashes between the ICC and a wide range of domestic actors and institutions that are also geared toward remedying atrocity are highly likely wherever the Court seeks to intervene. A key means to addressing this challenge is to return to Ocampo's initial depiction of an 'independent and interdependent' ICC in his inaugural speech as Prosecutor and the more modest representation of the Court as a back-stop to domestic institutions. This understanding of complementarity, which has been greatly diluted as the ICC has begun to operate across Africa, offers a critical starting point for determining how best to deliver international justice in the diverse and complex situations analysed in this book. The foundational principle in this respect should be deference to local practices,[9] regardless of their flaws, because they have several inherent advantages over international approaches, namely understanding of local context and challenges, sustained operation within the states in question and greater presence and visibility among local populations, including those most affected by violence.[10]

This view of complementarity approaches the question of the most appropriate responses to conflict from the standpoint of imperfection and the need for innovation, recognising that no perfect or 'fail-safe' response exists and the complexity of mass conflict and its consequences will require creative and tailormade remedies. This includes taking a risk on domestic practices that may not completely fulfil expectations but nevertheless have the inherent value of maintaining domestic sovereignty, autonomy, longevity, contextual understanding and presence. The ICC's travails in Africa so far should lower its status

---

[9] For comprehensive discussions of the justifiable degree of deference the ICC should show domestic institutions, see M. Drumbl, *Atrocity, Punishment and International Law*, Cambridge University Press, 2007, ch. 7; M. Drumbl, 'Policy through Complementarity: The Atrocity Trial as Justice', in C. Stahn and M. El Zeidy (eds.), *The International Criminal Court and Complementarity: From Theory to Practice*, vol. II, Cambridge University Press, 2011, pp. 222–32; M. Newton, 'The Complementarity Conundrum: Are Watching Evolution or Evisceration?', *Santa Barbara Journal of International Law*, 8, 1, 2010, pp. 115–64; L. Keller, 'The Practice of the International Criminal Court: Comments on "The Complementarity Conundrum"', *Santa Barbara Journal of International Law*, 8, 1, 2010, pp. 199–231.

[10] On this point, see also F. Mégret and N. Samson, 'Holding the Line on Complementarity in Libya', *Journal of International Criminal Justice*, 11, 3, 2013, p. 577.

to one approach among many, whose virtues may be more marked in some situations than others – although even this will require a substantial improvement on the ICC's work to date – and whose involvement may be required in some settings but not in others. Part of determining if, when and how the ICC should intervene involves a deep and sustained dialogue with domestic actors (who are more than members of state executives), with a high degree of openness and friction, rather than the rigid imposition of rules and judgments from The Hague, as has occurred so far.[11] This scenario involves placing the ICC more appropriately within the range of possible responses to conflict, establishing more equal relations among the Court, national and community-level actors and providing a stronger basis for an appropriate and well coordinated set of approaches.

Reinvigorating Complementarity: Practical Recommendations for Reform of the ICC

This book concludes with some practical recommendations to enable the ICC to embody more fully the spirit and modalities of complementarity just outlined. This requires radical thinking because of the deep embeddedness of distance within the ICC in legal, philosophical, cultural, attitudinal and geographical terms. Fully grasping the ICC's shortcomings to date and the necessary reforms may require a second Rome conference, located in Bunia or Gulu or another town at the epicentre of the ICC's work and more inclusive than the 2010 review conference in Kampala, in which the ICC and its close supporters dominated discussions and critical voices were systematically marginalised.[12] The recommendations here concern legal, personnel and geographical reforms to the operation of the Court.

First, as argued above, the ICC must return to Ocampo's original depiction of the ICC as a subsidiary institution that engages only in the most exceptional circumstances and only when the Court can show that it is genuinely capable of conducting effective investigations and prosecutions. This requires humility and caution on the ICC's part and an ideological shift away from viewing international criminal law as

---

[11] This echoes arguments made in Palmer, *Courts in Conflict*, ch. 6.

[12] See, for example, Bosco, *Rough Justice*, pp. 166 and 182–83; Branch, *Displacing Human Rights*, pp. 199, 212–13.

inherently superior to, and separable from, the domestic political arena.[13] This also requires some fundamental changes to the Rome Statute and the ways in which it is currently interpreted by the OTP and Chambers in particular. At present, the threshold for states to maintain jurisdiction over particular situations, crimes and suspects is too high, requiring fully fledged domestic investigations to be underway and for these to mirror closely the type of criminal justice delivered by the ICC. After the Pre-Trial judges refused to confirm the charges against Callixte Mbarushimana and various other setbacks for the Prosecution, former OTP coordinator of investigations and later of prosecutions, Alex Whiting, lamented,

Given all of the variables and the OTP's limited tools to control and manage all of the different moving parts, an overly rigid and formalistic approach that insists that the investigation be 'complete' before arrest or confirmation is unwise. The procedures and process must account for the realities of practice at the ICC. Although the prosecution cannot investigate its case forever, and the rights of the defense require that it know the case that it must answer, there must be some flexibility in allowing the prosecution to continue its investigations even after confirmation in order to insure that it fulfill its obligation to uncover the truth.[14]

This statement exhibits a clear double standard. As the Ituri cases show, the OTP believes domestic investigations must be 'complete' to challenge admissibility before the ICC and no comparable 'flexibility'

---

[13] This includes jettisoning views such as Kai Ambos's and Rod Rastan's that domestic non-prosecutorial alternatives to the ICC should never be seen as a substitute, but rather only a complement, to criminal prosecutions (Ambos, 'The Legal Framework of Transitional Justice', p. 40; Rastan, 'Complementarity: Contest or Collaboration?', pp. 106–17). Ambos also argues that such 'alternatives' are only legitimate if they involve victims fundamentally in their design and execution; arguably, a much higher standard than that applied to the ICC (Ambos, 'The Legal Framework of Transitional Justice', p. 40). As Drumbl, McEvoy, Palmer and others argue, this would involve coaxing international criminal legal scholars and practitioners from their sociological weddedness to particular notions of the criminal trial (Drumbl, *Atrocity, Punishment and International Law*, ch. 5; McEvoy, 'Beyond Legalism'; Palmer, *Courts in Conflict*, chs. 2 and 6). See also Sekhon, 'Complementarity and Postcoloniality', p. 820; and K. Campbell, 'The Making of Global Legal Culture and International Criminal Law', *Leiden Journal of International Law*, 26, 1, March 2013, pp. 161–70.

[14] A. Whiting, 'Dynamic Investigative Practice at the International Criminal Court', *Law and Contemporary Problems*, 76, 3/4, 2013, p. 189.

should be afforded the domestic judicial system. Whiting's statement assumes unjustifiably that the ICC deserves every opportunity to display its capacity to prosecute, rather than the spirit of caution and deference to the domestic realm first espoused (though rarely practised) by Ocampo. In this view, the 'burden-sharing' or 'division of labour' aspect of the relational conception of complementarity would not simply relegate national institutions to dealing with cases perceived to be 'lower level' and would not automatically incorporate the ICC.

The emphasis instead should be on domestic actors showing a dedication genuinely to confront past atrocities through whichever means and according to whichever contextually specific norms and values they deem appropriate. International prosecutions of a small number of elite suspects are only one conceivable response to mass conflict. As this book has highlighted, international trials are often highly flawed and can produce lasting and damaging effects. There should therefore be no inherent impediment to Uganda, for example, deciding to use *mato oput*, another local ritual or an amnesty conditional on locally determined goods such as public confessions and compensation to address the crimes of Joseph Kony and other LRA commanders, if affected communities and other relevant domestic actors deem this an appropriate mode of accountability according to local needs and norms. A critical shortcoming of the ICC's practice of complementarity to date has been to consider only ICC-like national prosecutions when determining whether cases should be addressed by the Court or domestic institutions. This ignores the much more varied range of actors and practices that address mass atrocity in African contexts, including non-prosecutorial approaches at the community level. The ICC has compounded this problem by engaging primarily – and sometimes exclusively – with members of national executives, who may not fully grasp community-level concerns and values or wish to use legalistic frameworks for their own political advantage.

This more contextually attuned approach does not amount to a freewheeling form of cultural relativism. The ICC and the ASP can still play an important role in assessing the genuineness of these domestic efforts, in consultation with country nationals and experts on specific situations. Crucially, though, the ICC and the ASP must not be the sole arbiters of domestic judicial activity. As argued earlier, this scenario gives the ICC too much latitude in deciding the admissibility of cases before the Court, which necessitates the involvement of other international and regional actors. For the Court to participate in such adjudications, it should alter the mandate and personnel profile of the Jurisdiction, Complementary and Cooperation Division of the OTP, requiring it not only to judge admissibility in narrow legal terms – according to the technical legal checklist that currently prevails – but more broadly according to the contextual 'genuineness' of cases. This would also entail jettisoning the 'same person, same conduct' test to determine whether a case is being investigated or prosecuted domestically, which in effect guarantees that the ICC can claim jurisdiction even when national proceedings are underway against particular suspects.

Second, there should be a fundamental change in the profile of personnel throughout the ICC. The complexities and nuances of the settings in which the ICC intervenes require deep contextual, as well as more general technical and legal, expertise. On a case by case basis, the ICC should hire nationals from the states where it is considering intervening and specialists on the political, social, cultural, linguistic and economic specifics of situations. Their role should be to advise on whether the Court should intervene, the consequences of doing so and the best way to approach any investigations and prosecutions so that they benefit the domestic arena and advance the reputation of the Court. These national actors would also greatly improve the degree of consultation between the ICC and domestic judicial personnel that Nicola Palmer argues is central to fruitful cooperation between the international and national levels and to the effective enactment of complementarity.[15] A singular reliance on generalist staff who can apply their skills and knowledge to any possible situation across the globe is a key cause of the ICC's missteps to date. Contact with country nationals and situation experts should be maintained throughout proceedings in a particular situation, not only in the early stages when the ICC is considering intervention. Context impinges heavily on every facet of the ICC's work from the launch of investigations to the passing of judgments against suspects and beyond, as the ramifications of these interventions continue to play out. Bolstering the expertise of the Court is also a key matter for the ASP, which will be required to fund this endeavour.

[15] N. Palmer, 'The Place of Consultation in the International Criminal Court's Approach to Complementarity and Cooperation', in O. Bekou and D. Birkett (eds.), *Cooperation and the International Criminal Court: Perspectives from Theory and Practice*, Brill Nijhoff, 2016, pp. 210–26.

Finally, in geographical terms, the ICC must increase its presence in the communities where it operates and decentralise control over its operations, which currently rests almost exclusively in The Hague. Following the recent lead of AI and other human rights and humanitarian organisations, which have maintained their headquarters in London or New York while opening regional hubs in places like Nairobi, Johannesburg, Mexico City, Beirut and Bangkok, the ICC should open regional offices staffed with nationals who, as argued above, can advise on every aspect of the Court's work.[16] These regional offices can absorb more localised insights and critiques of the ICC and channel these to key ICC actors to make the work of the Court more responsive and effective. There is some momentum within the ICC already for this kind of reform, given attempts to open an ICC liaison office close to the AU headquarters in Addis Ababa, which were stymied by opposition from the AU.[17] Had such a move occurred at the start of ICC investigations in Africa, rather than after relations between the Court and the AU had already soured, this could have greatly improved the situation. This geographical shift would open the Court up to new influences and audiences, help it to context-ualise its own work better and communicate more effectively with local communities. These regional hubs should then liaise with the in-country outreach teams, which at present have much of their work dictated by principals in The Hague, advising on how best to communicate the Court's work to heterogeneous populations in a responsive rather than didactic manner. Outreach personnel must spend more time in the exact locations where atrocities were committed and investigations are being conducted, rather than in capital cities such as Kampala and Kinshasa, to communicate more clearly with those most affected by violence and by the ICC's work.

This geographical reorientation should also involve the holding of ICC trials *in situ*, as close as possible to communities affected by violence. Actors within the Court, especially the OTP but also

---

[16] For broad discussion of these issues, see S. Hopgood, *Keepers of the Flame: Understanding Amnesty International*, Cornell University Press, 2006; S. Hopgood, *The Endtimes of Human Rights*, Cornell University Press, 2013, especially ch. 5.

[17] M. Maru, 'The Future of the ICC and Africa: The Good, the Bad and the Ugly', Al Jazeera, 11 October 2013, www.aljazeera.com/indepth/opinion/2013/10/future-icc-africa-good-bad-ugly-20131011143130881924.html.

Chambers, have consistently opposed attempts to do this in Uganda and the DRC[18], although there is some evidence of a change of view on this issue within the OTP.[19] The prevalence of community-based responses to atrocity in central Africa, such as the local rituals in northern Uganda, the mobile gender units, the *Barza Inter-Communautaire* and RHA in eastern DRC and *gacaca* in Rwanda, highlights the importance that many local communities ascribe to the holding of trials, ceremonies and rituals close to atrocity sites and locations where affected communities currently live.

Vital lessons for the ICC, seeking to operate in these environments, can be learnt from Finland's prosecution of Rwandan genocide suspect, François Bazaramba, in 2009. As part of the trial in a Finnish district court, proceedings were held in Kigali and all judges and lawyers participating in the case travelled to the Rwandan villages where Bazaramba allegedly committed crimes.[20] In the Barazamba case, the suspect was not transported to Rwanda for the trial but rather appeared by videolink. For maximum visibility, suspects should appear in person *in situ* but if this is deemed impossible for security or other reasons, the videolink option should be considered. Interviews with witnesses involved in the Bazaramba trial and everyday citizens who attended some of the hearings highlighted the enormous societal value of holding these proceedings as close as possible to communities affected by conflict.[21]

Together these legal, personnel and geographical reforms would enable the ICC to embody complementarity fully, avoid the pitfalls of

---

[18] For a revealing interview on these issues with President of the ICC, Sang-Hyun Song, including a discussion of Song's one trip to the DRC to visit Thomas Lubanga's village in Ituri, see L. Barber, 'Lunch with the FT: Sang-Hyun Song', *Financial Times*, 13 March 2015, www.ft.com/content/e9fc4382-c89f-11e4-8617-00144feab7de?mhq5j=e2. Song states that his staff in Chambers strongly opposed his Ituri trip.

[19] International Criminal Court, Pre-Trial Chamber II, 'Prosecution's Submissions on Conducting the Confirmation of Charges Hearing In Situ', Situation in Uganda, *The Prosecutor v. Dominic Ongwen*, 10 July 2015.

[20] BBC, 'Finnish Genocide Trial in Rwanda', 16 September 2009, http://news.bbc.co.uk/1/hi/uk/8258113.stm. See also discussion in Palmer and Clark, 'Testifying to Genocide', pp. 12–13.

[21] Helsingin Sanomat, 'Prosecutor in Genocide Case Takes Court on Tour of Rwanda Village', 17 September 2009. For further discussion of the use of videolink in such cases, see Palmer and Clark, 'Testifying to Genocide', pp. 12–19.

distance and, in the process, become a more legitimate and effective actor in Africa and beyond. As expressed by a Congolese investigator in Bunia, who was gathering evidence for a domestic trial of Germain Katanga and Mathieu Ngudjolo before they were transferred to The Hague, 'We don't want the ICC above us because it can't help us there. We want it alongside us. And if the ICC isn't willing to do that, it should get out of our way.'[22]

[22] Author's interview, Congolese Investigator, Bunia, 16 February 2006.

Bibliography

Aas, K., '(In)security-at-a-Distance: Rescaling Justice, Risk and Warfare in a Transnational Age', *Global Crime*, 13, 4, 2012, pp. 235–53.

Adamson, F., 'Spaces of Global Security: Beyond Methodological Nationalism', *Journal of Global Security Studies*, 1, 1, 2016, pp. 19–35.

Afako, B., 'Reconciliation and Justice: "Mato Oput" and the Amnesty Act', in O. Lucima (ed.), *Protracted Conflict, Elusive Peace: Initiatives to End the Violence in Northern Uganda*, Conciliation Resources/ Accord, 2002.

Agence France-Presse, 'DRC Soldiers, Serial Rapists, Jailed for "Crimes against Humanity"', 12 April 2006, www.reliefweb.int/rw/RWB.NSF/ db900SID/ABES-6NSRRL?OpenDocument.

Agger, K., 'The End of Amnesty in Uganda: Implications for LRA Defections', Enough Project, August 2012.

Ainley K., 'The Responsibility to Protect and the International Criminal Court: Counteracting the Crisis', *International Affairs*, 91, 1, 2015, pp. 37–54.

Akhavan, P., 'The Lord's Resistance Army Case: Uganda's Submission of the First State Referral to the International Criminal Court', *American Journal of International Law*, 99, 2, April 2005, pp. 403–21.

'The Rise, and Fall, and Rise, of International Criminal Justice', *Journal of International Criminal Justice*, 11, 3, 2013, pp. 527–36.

Al Jazeera, 'ECOWAS Call on ICC over "War Crimes" in Mali', 7 July 2012, www.aljazeera.com/news/africa/2012/07/201277194319595934 .html.

'Germany Latest to Suspend Rwanda Aid', 29 July 2012, www.aljazeera .com/news/africa/2012/07/20127281579389961.html.

'Muammar Gaddafi Killed as Sirte Falls', 21 October 2011, www.aljazeera.com/news/africa/2011/10/20111020111520869621.html.

'Uganda Opposition Leader "Under House Arrest"', 16 May 2011, www.aljazeera.com/news/africa/2011/05/20115169413805969.html.

Allen, T., 'Bitter Roots: The "Invention" of Acholi Traditional Justice', in T. Allen and K. Vlassenroot (eds.), *The Lord's Resistance Army: Myth and Reality*, Zed Books, 2010, pp. 242–60.

'Ritual (Ab)use? Problems with Traditional Justice in Northern Uganda', in N. Waddell and P. Clark (eds.), *Courting Conflict? Justice, Peace and the ICC in Africa*, Royal African Society, 2008, pp. 47–54.

Trial Justice: The International Criminal Court and the Lord's Resistance Army, Zed Books, 2006.

Allen, T. and M. Schomerus, 'A Hard Homecoming: Lessons Learned from the Reception Center Process in Northern Uganda – An Independent Study', report commissioned by USAID and UNICEF for Management Systems International, June 2006.

Allen, T. and L. Storm, 'Quests for Therapy in Northern Uganda: Healing at Laropi Revisited', *Journal of Eastern African Studies*, 6, 1, 2012, pp. 22–46.

Ambos, K., 'The Legal Framework of Transitional Justice: A Systematic Study with a Specific Focus on the ICC', in K. Ambos, J. Large and M. Wierda (eds.), *Building a Future on Peace and Justice: Studies on Transitional Justice*, Springer, 2014, pp. 19–102.

Amnesty International, 'Amnesty International Letter to Security Council', AI Index: AFR 59/003/2008, 1 April 2008.

'Ivory Coast: Both Sides Responsible for War Crimes and Crimes against Humanity', 25 May 2011.

'Rwanda – Gacaca: A Question of Justice', AI Index AFR 47/007/2002, December 2002.

'Uganda: Fear for Safety/Fear of Torture or Ill-Treatment/Possible Extra-judicial Execution, Twenty Prisoners in Northern Uganda', 19 September 2002.

'Uganda: Violence against Women in Northern Uganda', 16 July 2005.

Anderson, D., 'Vigilantes, Violence and the Politics of Public Order in Kenya', *African Affairs*, 101, 405, 2002, pp. 531–55.

Anderson, J., 'ICC Enters Uncharted Territory', Institute for War and Peace Reporting, 24 March 2006, https://iwpr.net/global-voices/icc-enters-uncharted-territory.

'World Court Faces Biggest Challenge', Institute for War and Peace Reporting, 16 June 2006, https://iwpr.net/global-voices/world-court-faces-biggest-challenge.

Anghie, A., 'The Evolution of International Law: Colonial and Postcolonial Realities', in R. Falk, B. Rajagopal and J. Stevens (eds.), *International Law and the Third World: Reshaping Justice*, Routledge-Cavendish, 2008, pp. 35–50.

Anten, L., 'Strengthening Governance in a Post-Conflict District of the Democratic Republic of Congo: A Study of Ituri', paper for the Conflict Research Unit, Netherlands Institute for International Relations, July 2010.

Apps, P., 'ICC Hopes for Uganda Trial in 6 Months, Then Congo', Reuters, 26 January 2005, www.globalpolicy.org/component/content/article/164/28492.html.

Apuuli, K., 'Peace over Justice: The Acholi Religious Leaders Peace Initiative vs. the International Criminal Court in Northern Uganda', *Studies in Ethnicity and Nationalism*, 11, 1, 2011, pp. 116–29.

Arbia, S. and G. Bassy, 'Proactive Complementarity: A Registrar's Perpsective and Plans', in C. Stahn and M. El Zeidy (eds.), *The International Criminal Court and Complementarity*, vol. I, Cambridge University Press, 2011, pp. 52–68.

Armstrong, K., 'Justice without Peace? International Justice and Conflict Resolution in Northern Uganda', *Development and Change*, 45, 3, 2014, pp. 589–607.

Arnould, V., 'Transitional Justice in Peacebuilding: Dynamics of Contestation in the DRC', *Journal of Intervention and Statebuilding*, 10, 3, 2016, pp. 321–38.

Arsanjani, M. and M. Reisman, 'Developments at the International Criminal Court: The Law-in-Action of the International Criminal Court', *American Journal of International Law*, 99, 2005, pp. 385–403.

Atieno, A., 'Mungiki, "Neo-Mau Mau" and the Prospects for Democracy in Kenya', *Review of African Political Economy*, 34, 113, September 2007, pp. 526–31.

Atkinson, R., '"The Realists in Juba"? An Analysis of the Juba Peace Talks', in T. Allen and K. Vlassenroot (eds.), *The Lord's Resistance Army: Myth and Reality*, Zed Books, 2011, pp. 205–21.

The Roots of Ethnicity: The Origins of the Acholi of Uganda, Fountain Publishers, 1999.

et al., 'Do No Harm: Assessing a Military Approach to the Lord's Resistance Army', *Journal of Eastern African Studies*, 6, 2, 2012, pp. 371–82.

Atri, S. and S. Cusimano, 'Perceptions of Children Involved in War and Transitional Justice in Uganda', Trudeau Centre for Peace and Conflict Studies, University of Toronto, 2012.

Australian Red Cross, 'The OTP vs. Thomas Lubanga Dyilo: The Challenges of Using "Intermediaries" in the International Criminal Court', Humanitarian Law Perspectives Project, July 2011.

Autesserre, S., 'Dangerous Tales: Dominant Narratives on the Congo and their Unintended Consequences', *African Affairs*, 111, 443, 2012, pp. 202–22.

Peaceland: Conflict Resolution and the Everyday Politics of International Intervention, Cambridge University Press, 2014.

Avocats sans Frontières, 'Analyse de Verdict: Condamnation des Militaires de la 1ere Brigade Integrée pour Crimes de Guerre, Tribunal Militaire de

Garnison de Bunia, RD Congo – 19.02.2007', 23 March 2007, www.congoforum.be/fr/nieuwsdetail.asp?subitem=2&newsid=26121& Actualiteit=selected.

Baines, E., 'Spirits and Social Reconstruction after Mass Violence: Rethinking Transitional Justice', *African Affairs*, 109, 436, 2010, pp. 409–30.

Baker, B., 'Popular Justice and Policing from Bush War to Democracy: Uganda, 1981–2004', *International Journal of the Sociology of Law*, 32, 4, 2004, pp. 333–48.

Barber, L., 'Lunch with the FT: Sang-Hyun Song', *Financial Times*, 13 March 2015, www.ft.com/content/e9fc4382-c89f-11e4-8617-00144feab7de?mhq5j=e2.

Barnes, G., 'The International Criminal Court's Ineffective Enforcement Mechanisms: The Case of President Omar al Bashir', *Fordham International Law Journal*, 34, 6, 2011, pp. 1585–619.

Bayart, J. F., 'Africa in the World: A History of Extraversion', *African Affairs*, 99, 2000, pp. 217–67.

The State in Africa: The Politics of the Belly (2nd edition), *Polity*, 2009.

BBC, '26 Millions de Signatures pour la Libération de Gbagbo', 29 December 2016, www.bbc.com/afrique/region-38460089.

'Alassane Ouattara: No More Ivorians Will Go to ICC', 5 February 2016, www.bbc.co.uk/news/world-africa-35502013.

'Bosco Ntaganda: Wanted Congolese in US Mission in Rwanda', 18 March 2013, www.bbc.co.uk/news/world-africa-21835345.

'DR Congo Colonel Kibibi Mutware Jailed for Mass Rape', 21 February 2011, www.bbc.co.uk/news/world-africa-12523847.

'DR Congo Militias Lay Down Arms', 27 July 2006, http://news.bbc.co.uk/1/hi/world/africa/5219076.stm.

'Finnish Genocide Trial in Rwanda', 16 September 2009, http://news.bbc.co.uk/1/hi/uk/8258113.stm.

'Girls Escape Ugandan Rebels', 25 June 2003, http://news.bbc.co.uk/1/hi/world/africa/3018810.stm.

'Interpol Push for Uganda Arrests', 2 June 2006, http://news.bbc.co.uk/1/hi/world/africa/5039620.stm.

'Kenya's William Ruto's Case Dismissed by ICC', 5 April 2016, www.bbc.co.uk/news/world-africa-35965760.

'LRA's Dominic Ongwen "Capture": Séléka Rebels Want $5m Reward', 9 January 2015, www.bbc.co.uk/news/world-africa-30743647.

'LRA Rebel Dominic Ongwen Surrenders to US Forces in CAR', 7 January 2015, www.bbc.co.uk/news/world-africa-30705649.

'Milosevic Found Dead in his Cell', 11 March 2006, http://news.bbc.co.uk/1/hi/world/europe/4796470.stm.

'Uganda LRA Rebels Reject Amnesty', 7 July 2006, http://news.bbc.co.uk/2/hi/africa/5157220.stm.

Behrend, H., *Alice Lakwena and the Holy Spirits: War in Northern Uganda, 1986–97* (2nd edition), trans. M. Cohen, James Currey, 2004.

Bensouda, F., 'The International Criminal Court: A New Approach to International Relations', transcript of speech to Council for Foreign Relations, Washington DC, 21 September 2012, www.cfr.org/event/international-criminal-court-new-approach-international-relations-0.

'International Justice and Diplomacy', *New York Times*, 19 March 2013, www.nytimes.com/2013/03/20/opinion/global/the-role-of-the-icc-in-international-justice-and-diplomacy.html?_r=0.

'Prosecuting Sexual and Gender-Based Violence: New Directions in International Criminal Justice', speech to Council for Foreign Relations, Washington DC, 11 December 2014, www.cfr.org/event/fatou-bensouda-international-criminal-court-and-gender-based-crimes-0.

'R2P in 2022', speech to the Stanley Foundation, Iowa, 18 January 2012, http://library.fora.tv/2012/01/18/R2P_in_2022.

Beyond Juba Project, 'Tradition in Transition: Drawing on the Old to Develop a New Jurisprudence for Dealing with Uganda's Legacy of Violence', Working Paper No. 1, July 2009.

Bishop, A., 'Failure of Complementarity: The Future of the International Criminal Following the Libyan Admissibility Challenge', *Minnesota Journal of International Law*, 22, 2, 2013, pp. 388–421.

Bisiika, A., 'Museveni's Bashir Arrest Dilemma', *The East African*, 27 July 2009, http://mobile.theeastafrican.co.ke/News/-/433842/629636/-/format/xhtml/item/2/-/3dorasz/-/index.html.

'Otunnu Is Not Obama because Uganda Is Not USA', *New Vision*, 2 September 2009.

Blattman, C. and J. Annan, 'On the Nature and Causes of LRA Abduction: What the Abductees Say', in T. Allen and K. Vlassenroot (eds.), *The Lord's Resistance Army: Myth and Reality*, Zed Books, 2010, pp. 132–54.

Blumenson, E., 'The Challenge of a Global Standard of Justice: Peace, Pluralism and Punishment at the International Criminal Court', *Columbia Journal of Transnational Law*, 44, 2006, pp. 797–867.

Bogner, A. and D. Neubert, 'Negotiated Peace, Denied Justice? The Case of West Nile (Northern Uganda)', *Africa Spectrum*, 48, 3, 2013, pp. 55–84.

Boraine, A., 'Transitional Justice: A Holistic Interpretation', *Journal of International Affairs*, 60, 1, Fall/Winter 2006, pp. 17–27.

Borello, F., 'A First Few Steps: The Long Road to a Just Peace in the Democratic Republic of Congo', International Center for Transitional Justice, 2004.

Bosco, D., *Rough Justice: The International Criminal Court in a World of Power Politics*, Oxford University Press, 2014.

Bosire, L. K., 'Judicial Statecraft in Kenya and Uganda: Explaining Transitional Justice Choices in the Age of the International Criminal Court', D.Phil thesis, University of Oxford, 2013.

Bosire, L. K. and G. Lynch, 'Kenya's Search for Truth and Justice: The Role of Civil Society', *International Journal of Transitional Justice*, 8, 2, 2014, pp. 256–76.

Bouwknegt, T., 'How Did the DRC Become the ICC's Pandora's Box?', African Arguments blog, Royal African Society, 5 March 2014, http://africanarguments.org/2014/03/05/how-did-the-drc-become-the-iccs-pandoras-box-by-thijs-b-bouwknegt/.

Bradbury, M., 'An Overview of Initiatives for Peace in Acholi, Northern Uganda', Reflecting on Peace Practice Project, October 1999.

Branch, A., *Displacing Human Rights: War and Intervention in Northern Uganda*, Oxford University Press, 2011.

  'Exploring the Roots of LRA Violence: Political Crisis and Ethnic Politics in Acholiland', in T. Allen and K. Vlassenroot (eds.), *The Lord's Resistance Army: Myth and Reality*, Zed Books, 2010, pp. 25–44.

  'Neither Peace nor Justice: Political Violence and the Peasantry in Northern Uganda, 1986–1998', *African Studies Quarterly*, 8, 2, 2005, pp. 1–31.

  'Uganda's Civil War and the Politics of ICC Intervention', *Ethics and International Affairs*, 21, 2, 2007, pp. 179–98.

Brewer, J., *Peace Processes: A Sociological Approach*, Polity, 2010.

Breytenbach, W., D. Chilemba, T. Brown and C. Plantive, 'Conflicts in the Congo: From Kivu to Kabila', *African Security Review*, 8, 5, 1999, pp. 33–42.

Brown, S. and C. Sriram, 'The Big Fish Won't Fry Themselves: Criminal Accountability for Post-Election Violence in Kenya', *African Affairs*, 111, 443, 2012, pp. 244–60.

Brubacher, M., 'The ICC Investigation of the Lord's Resistance Army: An Insider's View', in T. Allen and K. Vlassenroot (eds.), *The Lord's Resistance Army: Myth and Reality*, Zed Books, 2010, pp. 262–78.

  'The ICC, National Governments and Judiciaries', presentation at Royal African Society workshop, London, 8 March 2007.

Budget and Finance Team of the Coalition for the International Criminal Court, 'Submission to the 3rd Meeting of the Assembly of States Parties: The Report of the Committee on Budget and Finance', 26 August 2004.

'Building a Future on Peace and Justice', Nuremberg conference, June 2007, www.jordanembassy.de/nuremberg_conference_on_peace_an.htm.

Burke, J., 'Clashes in Kinshasa Leave 50 Dead, Say DRC Opposition Groups', *Guardian*, 20 September 2016, www.theguardian.com/world/2016/sep/19/democratic-republic-congo-demonstrations-banned-police-killed-joseph-kabila-etienne-tshisekedi.

'DRC Minister Says Country "Can't Afford" to Hold Election This Year', *Guardian*, 16 February 2017, www.theguardian.com/world/2017/feb/16/delayed-drc-elections-could-be-put-back-further-by-cash-shortage.

Burke-White, W., 'Complementarity in Practice: The International Criminal Court as Part of a System of Multi-level Global Governance', *Leiden Journal of International Law*, 18, 3, 2005, pp. 557–90.

'Reframing Positive Complementarity', in C. Stahn and M. El Zeidy (eds.), *The International Criminal Court and Complementarity*, vol. I, Cambridge University Press, 2011, pp. 341–60.

Burr, J. and R. Collins, *Revolutionary Sudan: Hasan al-Turabi and the Islamist State, 1989–2000*, Brill, 2003.

Butler, C. and E. Mussawir (eds.), *Spaces of Justice: Peripheries, Passages, Appropriations*, Routledge, 2017.

Butt, R., 'Briton Killed as Uganda Rebels Attack Tourists', *The Guardian*, 9 November 2005, www.theguardian.com/uk/2005/nov/09/world.travelnews.

Campbell, K., 'The Making of Global Legal Culture and International Criminal Law', *Leiden Journal of International Law*, 26, 1, March 2013, pp. 151–72.

Carter, L., M. Ellis and C. Jalloh, *The International Criminal Court in an Effective Global Justice System*, Edward Elgar Publishing, 2016.

Carayannis, T., 'The Challenge of Building Sustainable Peace in the DRC', Centre for Humanitarian Dialogue, Background Paper, July 2009.

Caryannis, T., 'Elections in the DRC: The Bemba Surprise', United States Institute of Peace, February 2008.

Cassese, A., 'Is the ICC Still Having Teething Problems?', *Journal of International Criminal Justice*, 4, 3, 2006, pp. 434–41.

Chapman, Terrence L. and S. Chaudoin, 'Ratification Patterns and the International Criminal Court', *International Studies Quarterly*, 57, 2, 2012, pp. 400–9.

Charbonneau, L., 'NGO Expelled from Darfur Considered ICC Cooperation', Reuters, 16 March 2009, www.reuters.com/article/us-sudan-war crimes-ngo-idUSTRE52F6SX20090316.

Chatham House, 'The ICC at a Crossroads: The Challenges of Kenya, Darfur, Libya and Islamic State', International Law Programme Meeting Summary, 11 March 2015.

'The International Criminal Court and Libya: Complementarity in Conflict', International Law Programme Meeting Summary, 22 September 2014.

Chazal, N., *The International Criminal Court and Global Social Control: International Criminal Justice in Late Modernity*, Routledge, 2016.

Chung, C., 'Letters to the Editor: A Prosecutor without Borders', *World Affairs*, Summer 2009, p. 104.

'The Punishment and Prevention of Genocide: The International Criminal Court as a Benchmark of Progress and Need', *Case Western Reserve Journal of International Law*, 40, 1, 2007–8, pp. 227–42.

Clark, P., 'Bringing Them All Home: The Challenges of DDR and Transitional Justice in Contexts of Displacement in Rwanda and Uganda', *Journal of Refugee Studies*, 27, 2, 2014, pp. 234–59.

'Ethnicity, Leadership and Conflict Mediation in the Eastern Democratic Republic of Congo: The Case of the *Barza Inter-Communautaire*', *Journal of Eastern African Studies*, 2, 1, 2008, pp. 1–17.

The Gacaca Courts, Post-Genocide Justice and Reconciliation in Rwanda: Justice without Lawyers, Cambridge University Press, 2010.

'Law, Politics and Pragmatism: The ICC and Case Selection in the Democratic Republic of Congo and Uganda', in N. Waddell and P. Clark (eds.), *Courting Conflict: Justice, Peace and the ICC in Africa*, Royal African Society, 2008, pp. 37–45.

Clark, P., N. Palmer, D. Matthee and D. Matthee et al., 'Finding it within Ourselves: Forgiveness, Reconciliation and Rescue in Post-Atrocity Rwanda and Uganda (Luo version)', 2014, www.youtube.com/watch?v=xu7nmqJLurk.

Clarke, K., A. Knottnerus and E. de Volder, 'Africa and the ICC: An Introduction', in K. Clarke, A. Knottnerus and E. de Volder (eds.), *Africa and the ICC: Perceptions of Justice*, Cambridge University Press, 2016, p. 14.

Clarke, K., A. Knottnerus and E. de Volder (eds.), *Africa and the ICC: Perceptions of Justice*, Cambridge University Press, 2016.

Clifford, L., 'Uganda: ICC Policy under Scrutiny', Institute of War and Peace Reporting, 13 April 2007, https://iwpr.net/global-voices/uganda-icc-policy-under-scrutiny.

Clottey, P., 'International Court Urges Uganda to Arrest Sudan President Bashir', Voice of America, 12 May 2006, www.voanews.com/a/sudanese-president-bashir-defies-international-arrest-warrant-with-trip-to-uganda/3327216.html.

Coalition for the International Criminal Court, 'Interview with International Criminal Court Deputy Prosecutor and Prosecutor-Elect H. E. Ms. Fatou Bensouda', June 2012, www.iccnow.org/documents/Fatou_Bensouda_Full_Interview_eng.pdf.

The Monitor: Journal of the Coalition for the International Criminal Court, 36, May–October 2008.

Coffey, K., 'Why Sub-Saharan African States Supported the ICC: Equality and Exceptionalism in International Law', August 2014.

Coghlan, B., R. Brennan, P. Ngoy et al., 'Mortality in the Democratic Republic of Congo: A Nationwide Survey', *The Lancet*, 367, 9504, 2006, pp. 44–51.

Collinson, S., M. Duffield et al., 'Paradoxes of Presence: Risk Management and Aid Culture in Challenging Environments', Humanitarian Policy Group, Overseas Development Institute, March 2013.

Conciliation Resources, 'A People Dispossessed: The Plight of Civilians in Areas of the Democratic Republic of Congo Affected by the Lord's Resistance Army', July 2014, www.c-r.org/downloads/People_dispos sessed_report_2014.pdf.

Constantini, I., 'Conflict Dynamics in Post-2011 Libya: A Political Economy Perspective', *Conflict, Security and Development*, 16, 5, 2016, pp. 405–22.

Critical Investigations into Humanitarianism in Africa blog, www.cihablog .com/category/home/.

Cronin-Furman, K., 'Managing Expectations: International Criminal Trials and the Prospects of Deterrence of Mass Atrocity', *International Journal of Transitional Justice*, 7, 2013, pp. 434–54.

Crowder, G., 'Pluralism and Liberalism', *Political Studies*, 42, 1994, pp. 293–305.

Daily Monitor, 'LRA High Command Hires Two International Lawyers to Represent Kony and Others at ICC', 2 February 2007.
'LRA Leader Kony Reportedly Willing to Face Trial in Uganda, Not The Hague', 20 December 2006, www.ugandacan.org/archive/1/2006-12.
'Museveni Says ICC Indictments Will Stay Until Peace Agreement Signed', 27 October 2006, www.ugandacan.org/item/1781.

Daily Nation, 'Uganda's President Museveni Calls for Africa to Review Its Ties with ICC', 9 October 2014, www.nation.co.ke/news/Africa-should-review-ties-with-ICC–Museveni/-/1056/2480492/-/138otwdz/-/index .html.

Dancy, G., K. Sikkink et al., 'The ICC's Deterrent Impact – What the Evidence Shows', openDemocracy, 3 February 2015, www.opendemocracy .net/openglobalrights/geoff-dancy-bridget-marchesi-florencia-montal-kathryn-sikkink/icc%E2%80%99s-deterrent-impac.

Davis, L., 'Case Study: Democratic Republic of Congo', International Justice and the Prevention of Atrocities project, European Council on Foreign Relations, November 2013.

Davis, L., 'The EU and Post-conflict Interventions: Supporting Reform or Business as Usual? The Democratic Republic of Congo', conference paper, 2011, www.gu.se/digitalAssets/1349/1349860_conf-2011-davis.pdf.

'Power Shared and Justice Shelved: the Democratic Republic of Congo', *International Journal of Human Rights*, 17, 2, 2013, pp. 289–306.

Davis, L. and P. Hayner, 'Difficult Peace, Limited Justice: Ten Years of Peacemaking in the DRC', International Center for Transitional Justice, March 2009.

deGuzman, M., 'Bensouda on ICC Prosecutions', 31 March 2011, www.intlawgrrls.com/2011/03/bensouda-on-icc-prosecutions.html.

Deibert, M., *The Democratic Republic of Congo: Between Hope and Despair*, Zed Books, 2013.

Democratic Republic of Congo, Military Tribunal of Ituri, 'Military Prosecutor v. Massaba (Blaise Bongi), Criminal Trial Judgment and Accompanying Civil Action for Damages', RP No 018/2006, RMP No 242/PEN/06, ILDC 387 (CD 2006), 24 March 2006.

'Projet de Loi Modifiant et Complétant la Loi Organique No 13/011-B of April 11, 2013 portant Organisation, Fonctionnement, et Compétences des Juridictions de l'Ordre Judiciaire en Matière de Répression des Crimes de Génocide, des Crimes contre l'Humanité et des Crimes de Guerres', April 2014.

Deprez, C., 'Foundations and Scope of the Human Rights Obligations of the International Criminal Court: Brief Overview of an Unsettled Question', *Revue de la Faculté de Droit de l'Université de Liège*, 3, 2014, pp. 475–93.

Dersso, S., 'The ICC's Africa Problem: A Spotlight on the Politics and Limits of International Criminal Justice', in K. Clarke, A. Knottnerus and E. de Volder (eds.), *Africa and the ICC: Perceptions of Justice*, Cambridge University Press, 2016, pp. 61–76.

Deutsche Welle, 'Ex-Ivory Coast First Lady Simone Gbagbo Acquitted of War Crimes', 28 March 2017, www.dw.com/en/ex-ivory-coast-first-lady-simone-gbagbo-acquitted-of-war-crimes/a-38174997.

De Vos, C., 'All Roads Lead to Rome: Implementation and Domestic Politics in Kenya and Uganda', in C. De Vos, S. Kendall and C. Stahn (eds.), *Contested Justice: The Politics and Practice of International Criminal Court Interventions*, Cambridge University Press, 2015, pp. 379–406.

'Investigating from Afar: The ICC's Evidence Problem', *Leiden Journal of International Law*, 26, 4, December 2013, pp. 1009–24.

Dixon, P., 'Reparations and the Politics of Recognition', in C. De Vos, S. Kendall and C. Stahn (eds.), *Contested Justice: The Politics and Practice of International Criminal Court Interventions*, Cambridge University Press, 2015, pp. 326–50.

Dixon, P. and C. Tenove, 'International Criminal Justice as a Transnational Field: Rules, Authority and Victims', *International Journal of Transitional Justice*, 7, 2013, pp. 393–412.

Dolan, C., 'Inventing Traditional Leadership? A Critical Assessment of Dennis Pain's "The Bending of the Spears"', COPE Working Paper 31, April 2000.

Social Torture: The Case of Northern Uganda, 1986–2006, Berghahn Books, 2009.

Drexler, E., 'Addressing the Legacies of Mass Violence and Genocide in Indonesia and East Timor', in A. Hinton and K. O'Neill (eds.), *Genocide: Truth, Memory and Representation*, Duke University Press, 2009, pp. 219–45.

Drumbl, M., *Atrocity, Punishment, and International Law*, Cambridge University Press, 2007.

'Policy through Complementarity: The Atrocity Trial as Justice', in C. Stahn and M. El Zeidy (eds.), *The International Criminal Court and Complementarity: From Theory to Practice*, vol. II, Cambridge University Press, 2011, pp. 222–32.

Reimagining Child Soldiers in International Law and Policy, Oxford University Press, 2012.

Duffield, M., 'From Immersion to Simulation: Remote Methodologies and the Decline of Area Studies', *Review of African Political Economy*, 41, 1, 2014, pp. S75–S94.

'Risk-Management and the Fortified Aid Compound: Everyday Life in Post-Interventionary Society', *Journal of Intervention and Statebuilding*, 4, 4, 2010, pp. 453–74.

du Plessis, M. and G. Mettraux, 'South Africa's Failed Withdrawal from the Rome Statute: Politics, Law, and Judicial Accountability', *Journal of International Criminal Justice*, 15, 2, 2017, pp. 361–70.

Dürr, B., 'Ahmad al Mahdi: Who is the First Alleged Islamist at the ICC?', *Justice Hub, 29 February 2016*, https://justicehub.org/article/ahmad-al-mahdi-who-first-alleged-islamist-icc.

Dutton, Y. and T. Alleblas, 'Lessons from Kenya: Unpacking the ICC's Deterrent Effect', openDemocracy, 5 July 2016, www.opendemocracy.net/openglobalrights/yvonne-m-dutton-tessa-alleblas/lessons-from-kenya-unpacking-icc-s-deterrent-effect.

The East African, 'Museveni to Move Motion for Africa to Withdraw from the ICC', 13 December 2014, www.theeastafrican.co.ke/news/Museveni-to-move-motion-for-Africa-to-withdraw-from-the-ICC/-/2558/2555174/-/ilne4k/-/index.html.

Ebbs, T. and E. Saudi, 'The ICC in Libya – Justice Delayed and Denied', openDemocracy, 25 February 2015, www.opendemocracy.net/openglobalrights/thomas-ebbs-elham-saudi/icc-in-libya-%E2%80%93-justice-delayed-and-denied.

The Economist, 'Hunting Uganda's Child-Killers: Justice versus Reconcili-
    ation', 7 May 2007, p. 57.
Electoral Commission of Uganda, www.ec.or.ug/.
El Zeidy, M., 'The Genesis of Complementarity', in C. Stahn and M. El
    Zeidy (eds.), *The International Criminal Court and Complementarity*,
    vol. I, Cambridge University Press, 2011, pp. 71–141.
Enough Project, 'Completing the Mission: US Special Forces Are Essential
    for Ending the LRA', October 2013, www.enoughproject.org/files/Com
    pleting-The-Mission-US-Special-Forces-Essential-to-Ending-LRA.pdf.
Eriksson, M., 'A Fratricidal Libya: Making Sense of a Conflict Complex',
    Small Wars and Insurgencies, 27, 5, 2016, pp. 817–36.
Eslava, L., *Local Space, Global Life: The Everyday Operation of Law and
    Development*, Cambridge University Press, 2015.
European Commission, 'Press Release; The European Commission Contrib-
    utes to the Restoration of Justice in the East of the Democratic Republic
    of Congo', Doc. IP/06/845, 26 June 2006.
European Union, 'The European Union's Political and Development
    Response to the Democratic Republic of Congo', July 2001.
Evans-Pritchard, B. and S. Jennings, 'ICC to Unveil New Investigation
    Strategy', Institute for War and Peace Reporting, 21 October 2013,
    https://iwpr.net/global-voices/icc-unveil-new-investigation-strategy.
Ferstman, C., 'Limited Charges and Limited Judgments by the International
    Criminal Court – Who Bears the Greatest Responsibility?', *Inter-
    national Journal of Human Rights*, 16, 5, 2012, pp. 796–813.
Finnström, S., 'An African Hell of Colonial Imagination? The Lord's Resist-
    ance Army in Uganda, Another Story', in T. Allen and K. Vlassenroot
    (eds.), *The Lord's Resistance Army: Myth and Reality*, Zed Books,
    2010, pp. 74–91.
    'In and Out of Culture: Fieldwork in War-Torn Uganda', *Critique of
    Anthropology*, 21, 3, 2001, pp. 247–58.
    *Living with Bad Surroundings: War, History and Everyday Moments in
    Northern Uganda*, Duke University Press, 2008.
Fisher, J., 'Reproducing Remoteness? States, Internationals and the
    Co-Constitution of Aid: 'Bunkerization' in the East African Periphery',
    Journal of Intervention and Statebuilding, 11, 1, 2017, pp. 98–119.
Fisher, K., 'Libya, the ICC and Security Post-Conflict Justice', Middle East
    Institute, 16 December 2013, www.mei.edu/content/libya-icc-and-secur
    ing-post-conflict-justice.
Flint, J., and A. de Waal, 'Case Closed: A Prosecutor without Borders',
    World Affairs, Spring 2009, pp. 23–38.

Foreign and Commonwealth Office, 'Strategy Paper on the International Criminal Court', July 2013, www.gov.uk/government/uploads/system/uploads/attachment_data/file/223702/ICC_Strategy_Final.pdf.

Forestier, M., 'ICC to War Criminals: Destroying Shrines Is Worse than Rape', *Foreign Policy*, 22 August 2016, http://foreignpolicy.com/2016/08/22/icc-to-war-criminals-destroying-shrines-is-worse-than-rape-timbuktu-mali-al-mahdi/.

Fouladvand, S., 'Complementarity and Cultural Sensitivity: Decision-Making by the ICC Prosecutor in Relation to the Situations in the Darfur Region of the Sudan and the Democratic Republic of the Congo (DRC)', D.Phil thesis, University of Sussex, 2012.

Freeland, V., 'Rebranding the State: Uganda's Strategic Use of the International Criminal Court', *Development and Change*, 46, 2, 2015, pp. 293–319.

Freeman, M., *Necessary Evils: Amnesties and the Search for Justice*, Cambridge University Press, 2011.

Freeman, M. and M. Pensky, 'The Amnesty Controversy in International Law', in F. Lessa and L. Payne (eds.), *Amnesty in the Age of Human Rights Accountability: Comparative and International Perspectives*, Cambridge University Press, 2012, pp. 42–65.

Fry, E., 'Legal Recharacterisation and the Materiality of Facts at the International Criminal Court: Which Changes are Permissible?', *Leiden Journal of International Law*, 29, 2, 2016, pp. 577–97.

Fujii, L. A., *Killing Neighbors: Webs of Violence in Rwanda*, Cornell University Press, 2009.

Fulford, Lord Justice, 'Sir Richard May Memorial Lecture The International Criminal Court: Progress Made, Progress Needed', International Law Programme Meeting Summary, Chatham House, 29 October 2014.

Gargarella, R., '"Too Far Removed from the People" Access to Justice for the Poor: The Case of Latin America', UNDP Issue Paper, Christian Michelsen Institute, 2002.

Gettleman, J., 'An Interview with Joseph Kabila', *New York Times*, 3 April 2009, www.nytimes.com/2009/04/04/world/africa/04kabilatranscript.html.

Gladstone, R., 'A Lifelong Passion Is Now Put to Practice in The Hague', *New York Times*, 19 January 2013, www.nytimes.com/2013/01/19/world/africa/challenging-start-for-bensouda-as-chief-prosecutor-in-the-hague.html?pagewanted=1&_r=1&ref=todays paper&.

Glasius, M., *The International Criminal Court: A Global Civil Society Achievement*, Routledge, 2006.

'"We Ourselves, We Are Part of the Functioning": The ICC, Victims and Civil Society in the Central African Republic', *African Affairs*, 108, 430, 2008, pp. 56–9.

Glassborow, K., 'ICC Investigative Strategy under Fire', Institute for War and Peace Reporting, 27 October 2008, https://iwpr.net/global-voices/icc-investigative-strategy-under-fire.

Global Rights, 'S.O.S. Justice: Assessment of the Justice Sector in North and South Kivu, Maniema and North Katanga', August 2005.

Global Witness, '"Faced with a Gun, What Can You Do?" War and the Militarisation of Mining in Eastern Congo', July 2009.

Goodfellow, T., 'Legal Manoeuvres and Violence: Law Making, Protest and Semi-Authoritarianism in Uganda', *Development and Change*, 45, 4, 2014, pp. 753–6.

Gouby, M., 'On Home Ground, Lubanga Verdict Falls Flat', Institute for War and Peace Reporting, 15 March 2012, https://iwpr.net/global-voices/home-ground-lubanga-verdict-falls-flat.

Gourevitch, P., 'Justice in Exile', *New York Times*, 24 June 1996, A15.

Government of the Democratic Republic of Congo, 'Amnesty Decree-Law', *Journal Officiel de la République Démocratique du Congo*, No. 03–001, 15 April 2003.

'The Constitution of the Democratic Republic of Congo', 2005.

'Loi No. 04 Portant Amnistie Pour Faits de Guerre, Infractions Politiques et d'Opinion', 30 November 2005.

'Loi No. 04/018 du 30 juillet 2004 Portant Organisation, Attributions et Fonctionnement de la Commission Vérité et Réconciliation', 30 July 2004.

'Loi No. 09/003 du 7 mai 2009 portant Amnistie pour Faits de Guerre et Insurrectionnels Commis dans les Provinces du Nord-Kivu et du Sud-Kivu', 7 May 2009.

'Loi No. 14/006 du 11 février 2014 portant Amnistie pour Faits Insurrectionnels, Faits de Guerre et Infractions Politiques', 11 February 2014.

'Peace Agreement between the Government and the CNDP', Goma, 23 March 2009.

'Referral of the Situation in the Democratic Republic of Congo', 19 April 2004.

Government of Uganda, 'Amnesty (Amendment) Act', 24 May 2006.

Justice, Law and Order Sector, 'National Transitional Justice Strategy', sixth draft, 2017.

'Local Government (Resistance Councils) Statute', 1997.

'Referral of the Situation concerning the Lord's Resistance Army Submitted by the Republic of Uganda', 16 December 2003.

'Traditional and Cultural Leaders Act', 2011.

Government of Uganda and the Lord's Resistance Army, 'Agreement on Accountability and Reconciliation', 29 June 2007.

'Agreement on Cessation of Hostilities between the Government of the Republic of Uganda and the Lord's Resistance Army/Movement', 26 August 2006.

Government of the United Kingdom, Foreign and Commonwealth Office, 'International Criminal Court Strategy Paper', London, 17 July 2013, p. 2, www.gov.uk/government/publications/international-criminal-court-strategy-paper.

Gready, P., 'Reconceptualising Transitional Justice: Embedded and Distanced Justice', *Conflict, Security and Development*, 5, 1, 2005, pp. 3–21.

Greenawalt, A., 'Complementarity in Crisis: Uganda, Alternative Justice, and the International Criminal Court', *Virginia Journal of International Law*, 50, 1, 2009, pp. 107–62.

Grono, N. and A. O'Brien, 'Justice in Conflict? The ICC and Peace Processes', in N. Waddell and P. Clark (eds.), *Courting Conflict: Justice, Peace and the ICC in Africa*, Royal African Society, 2008, pp. 13–20.

Guardian, 'African Leaders Plan Mass Withdrawal from the International Criminal Court', 31 January 2017, www.theguardian.com/law/2017/jan/31/african-leaders-plan-mass-withdrawal-from-international-criminal-court.

Gulf Times, 'Defeated Congo Rebels Surrender', 16 March 2013, www.gulf-times.com/story/345710/Defeated-Congo-rebels-surrender.

Hague, W., 'International Law and Justice in a Networked World', The Hague, 9 July 2012, www.gov.uk/government/speeches/international-law-and-justice-in-a-networked-world.

The Hague Trials Kenya, 'Victims Lawyer Reveals Dark Tactics Kenya Used to End ICC Cases', 1 December 2016, www.jfjustice.net/uhurur-kenyatta-case-status-conference-trial-chamber-vb-09-july-2014/icc-cases/gaynor-reveals-dark-tactics-kenya-used-to-end-icc-cases.

Harlacher, T., F. Okot, C. Obonyo, M. Balthazard and R. Atkinson, *Traditional Ways of Coping in Acholi: Cultural Provisions for Reconciliation and Healing from War*, Caritas Gulu Archdiocese, 2007.

Heller, K. J., 'The ICC Fiddles while Libya Burns', *Opinio Juris*, 24 March 2014, http://opiniojuris.org/2014/03/24/30477/.

'Radical Complementarity', *Journal of International Criminal Justice*, 14, 3, 2016, pp. 637–65.

'Retreat from Nuremberg: The Leadership Requirement in the Crime of Aggression', *European Journal of International Law*, 18, 3, 2007, pp. 477–97.

Helsingin Sanomat, 'Prosecutor in Genocide Case Takes Court on Tour of Rwanda Village', 17 September 2009.

Hemedi, C., 'Thomas Lubanga Dyilo's Arrest: Survey on the Ground Indicates an Overall Positive Reaction', *Insight on the International Criminal Court: Newsletter of the NGO Coalition for the ICC*, 8, July 2006.

Hirsch, A., 'Fatou Bensouda: The Woman Who Could Redeem the International Criminal Court', *Guardian*, 14 June 2012, https://www.theguardian.com/law/2012/jun/14/fatou-bensouda-international-criminal-court.

Holmes, J., 'The Principle of Complementarity', in R. Lee (ed.), *The International Criminal Court: The Making of the Rome Statute*, Kluwer Law International, 1999, pp. 41–78.

Hopgood, S., *Keepers of the Flame: Understanding Amnesty International*, Cornell University Press, 2006.

The Endtimes of Human Rights, Cornell University Press, 2013.

Hopwood, J., 'Women's Land Claims in the Acholi Region of Northern Uganda: What Can be Learnt from What Is Contested', *International Journal on Minority and Group Rights*, 22, 2015, pp. 387–409.

Horovitz, S., 'Uganda: Interactions between International and National Responses to Mass Atrocities', DOMAC project, Paper No. 18, January 2013, DOMAC Project, 'Project Final Report', 30 June 2011.

Hovil, L., 'A Poisoned Chalice? Local Civil Society and the International Criminal Court's Engagement in Uganda', International Refugee Rights Initative, Discussion Paper No. 1, October 2011.

Hoyle, C. and L. Ullrich, 'New Court, New Justice? The Evolution of "Justice for Victims" at Domestic Courts and at the International Criminal Court', *Journal of International Criminal Justice*, 12, 14, 2014, pp. 681–703.

Human Rights Watch, 'Army and Rebels Commit Atrocities in the North: International Criminal Court Must Investigate Abuses on Both Sides', 20 September 2005.

'Benchmarks for Assessing Possible National Alternatives to International Criminal Court Cases against LRA Leaders: A Human Rights Watch Memorandum', May 2007.

'Congo: Bringing Justice to the Heart of Darkness', 6 February 2006.

'Côte d'Ivoire: Ouattara Forces Kill, Rape Civilians during Offensive', 9 April 2011.

'Democratic Republic of Congo (DRC): Events of 2008', *HRW World Report*, 2009, pp. 61–6.

'ICC: Côte d'Ivoire Case Highlights Court's Missteps', 4 August 2015.

'ICC: Course Correction', 16 June 2011.

'ICC/DRC: Second War Crimes Suspect to Face Justice in The Hague', 18 October 2007.

'Justice Compromised: The Legacy of Rwanda's Community-Based Gacaca Courts', 31 May 2011.

'Killings in Kiwanja: The UN's Inability to Protect Civilians', 11 December 2008.

'Making Justice Count: Lessons from the ICC's Work in Côte d'Ivoire', 4 August 2015.

'Soldiers Who Rape, Commanders Who Condone: Sexual Violence and Military Reform in the Democratic Republic of Congo', July 2009.

'Trading Justice for Peace Won't Work', 2 May 2007.

'Trail of Death: LRA Atrocities in Northeastern Congo', March 2010.

'Uganda: Electoral Irregularities Require Judicial Probe', 2 March 2006.

'Unfinished Business: Closing Gaps in the Selection of ICC Cases', 15 September 2011.

'World Report 2011: Uganda – Events of 2010', *HRW World Report*, 2011, pp. 185–94.

'"You Will Be Punished": Attacks on Civilians in Eastern Congo', December 2009.

Huyse, L. and M. Salter (eds.), *Traditional Justice and Reconciliation after Violent Conflict: Learning from African Experiences*, International Institute for Democracy and Electoral Assistance (IDEA), 2008.

Ingelaere, B., *Inside Rwanda's Gacaca Courts: Seeking Justice after Genocide*, University of Wisconsin Press, 2016.

International Alert and *Réseau Haki na Amani*, 'Oil Exploration in Ituri: A Human Rights and Conflict Risk Assessment in Block III', July 2014.

International Bar Association, 'Judicial Independence Undermined: A Report on Uganda', September 2007.

International Center for Research on Women, 'External Evaluation of the Trust Fund for Victims Programmes in Northern Uganda and the Democratic Republic of Congo: Towards a Perspective of Upcoming Interventions', November 2013, www.icrw.org/publications/external-evaluation-of-the-trust-fund-for-victims-programmes-in-northern-uganda-and-the-democratic-republic-of-congo-towards-a-perspective-for-upcoming-interventions/.

International Center for Transitional Justice and the Human Rights Center, University of California, Berkeley, 'Forgotten Voices: A Population-Based Survey of Attitudes about Peace and Justice in Northern Uganda', July 2005.

International Center for Transitional Justice and Human Rights Center, University of California, Berkeley, 'Living with Fear: A Population-Based Survey on Attitudes about Peace, Justice, and Social Reconstruction in Eastern Democratic Republic of Congo', August 2008.

University of California, Berkeley, 'When the War Ends: A Population-Based Survey on Attitudes about Peace, Justice and Social Reconstruction in Northern Uganda', December 2007.

International Court of Justice, 'Armed Activities on the Territory of Congo', Judgment in *Democratic Republic of Congo vs. Rwanda*, 3 February 2006.

'Armed Activities on the Territory of Congo', Judgment in *Democratic Republic of Congo vs. Uganda*, 19 December 2005.

'Case concerning Armed Activities on the Territory of the Congo: *Democratic Republic of Congo v. Uganda*', Judgment of 19 December 2005.

International Criminal Court, 'Ntaganda Case', Situation of the Democratic Republic of Congo, *The Prosecutor v. Bosco Ntaganda*.

'President of the European Parliament Visits ICC', 12 November 2003.

'Press Release: Lubanga Case: Trial Chamber II Orders Trust Fund for Victims to Add Information to the Reparations Plan', Situation in the Democratic Republic of Congo, *The Prosecutor vs. Thomas Lubanga Dyilo*, 9 February 2016.

'The Prosecutor v. Bosco Ntaganda', ICC-01/04-02/06, www.icc-cpi.int/drc/ntaganda.

'The Prosecutor v. Jean-Pierre Bemba Gombo, Aimé Kilolo Musamba, Jean-Jacques Mangenda Kabongo, Fidèle Babala Wandu and Narcisse Arido', 29 September 2015.

'Prosecutor's Application for Warrant of Arrest under Article 58 of Omar Hassan Ahmad al Bashir', Situation in Darfur, the Sudan, 17 April 2008.

Rome Statute of the International Criminal Court, 1998.

'Situation in Central African Republic II', ICC-01/14, www.icc-cpi.int/carII.

'Situation in Libya', ICC-01/11.

'Situation in the Republic of Kenya', ICC-01/09.

'Situation in Uganda', ICC-02/04, www.icc-cpi.int/uganda.

'Situations under Investigation', www.icc-cpi.int/pages/situations.aspx.

'States Parties to the Rome Statute', https://asp.icc-cpi.int/en_menus/asp/states%20parties/pages/the%20states%20parties%20to%20the%20rome%20statute.aspx.

'Victims', www.icc-cpi.int/about/victims.

Appeals Chamber, 'Corrigendum to Judgment on the Appeal of Mr Jean-Pierre Bemba Gombo against the Decision of Trial Chamber III of 24 June 2010 Entitled "Decision on the Admissibility and Abuse of Process Challenges"', Situation in the Central African Republic, *The Prosecutor v. Jean-Pierre Bemba Gombo*, 19 October 2010.

Appeals Chamber, 'Judgment on the Appeal of Côte d'Ivoire against the Decision of Pre-Trial Chamber I of 11 December 2014 Entitled "Decision on Côte d'Ivoire's Challenge to the Admissibility of the Case against Simone Gbagbo"', Situation in the Republic of Côte d'Ivoire, *The Prosecutor v. Simone Gbagbo*, 27 May 2015.

Appeals Chamber, 'Judgment on the Appeal of Mr. Germain Katanga against the Oral Decision of Trial Chamber II of 12 June 2009 on the Admissibility of the Case', Situation in the Democratic Republic of Congo, *The Prosecutor v. Germain Katanga and Mathieu Ngudjolo Chui*, 25 September 2009.

Appeals Chamber, 'Judgment on the Appeal of Mr Abdullah al-Senussi against the Decision of Pre-Trial Chamber I of 11 October 2013 entitled "Decision on the Admissibility of the Case against Abdullah al-Senussi"', Situation in Libya, *The Prosecutor v. Saif al-Islam Gaddafi and Abdullah al-Senussi*, 24 July 2014.

Assembly of States Parties, 'Proposed Programme Budget for 2017 of the International Criminal Court', 17 August 2016.

Assembly of States Parties, 'Report on the Activities of the International Criminal Court', 9 November 2016, Annex.

Assembly of States Parties, 'Retreat on the Future of the ICC', 18 October 2011, https://asp.icc-cpi.int/en_menus/asp/press%20releases/press%20releases%202011/Pages/pr732.aspx.

Office of the Prosecutor, 'Central African Republic', Situation in the Central African Republic, ICC-01/05.

Office of the Prosecutor, 'Central African Republic II', Situation in the Central African Republic II, ICC-01/14.

Office of the Prosecutor, 'Ceremony for the Solemn Undertaking of the Chief Prosecutor of the International Criminal Court', The Hague, 16 June 2003, p. 2, www.iccnow.org/documents/MorenoOcampo16June03.pdf.

Office of the Prosecutor, 'Darfur, Sudan', Situation in Darfur, Sudan, ICC-02/05.

Office of the Prosecutor, 'The Investigation in Northern Uganda: ICC OTP Press Conference', 14 October 2005.

Office of the Prosecutor, 'Mudacumura Case', Situation in the Democratic Republic of Congo, *The Prosecutor v. Sylvestre Mudacumura*.

Office of the Prosecutor, 'Paper on Some Policy Issues before the Office of the Prosecutor', September 2003.

Office of the Prosecutor, 'Policy Paper on the Interests of Justice', September 2007.

Office of the Prosecutor, 'Press Release: Communications Received by the Office of the Prosecutor of the ICC', 16 July 2003.

Office of the Prosecutor, 'Press Release: President of Uganda Refers Situation concerning the Lord's Resistance Army (LRA) to the ICC', 29 January 2004.

Office of the Prosecutor, 'Press Release: Statements by ICC Chief Prosecutor and the Visiting Delegation of Acholi Leaders from Northern Uganda', 18 March 2005.

Office of the Prosecutor, 'Prosecutorial Strategy, 2009–2012', 1 February 2010.

Office of the Prosecutor, 'Regulations of the Office of the Prosecutor', ICC-BD/05-01-09, 23 April 2009.

Office of the Prosecutor, 'Second Assembly of States Parties to the Rome Statute of the International Criminal Court, Report of the Prosecutor of the ICC', 8 September 2003.

Office of the Prosecutor, 'Statement by the Chief Prosecutor, Luis Moreno-Ocampo', The Hague, 14 October 2005.

Office of the Prosecutor, 'Statement by the Chief Prosecutor Luis Moreno-Ocampo', 12 July 2006.

Office of the Prosecutor, 'Statement by the Chief Prosecutor on the Uganda Arrest Warrants', 14 October 2005.

Office of the Prosecutor, 'Statement by Luis Moreno Ocampo', 6 July 2006.

Office of the Prosecutor, 'Statement by the Prosecutor, Luis Moreno Ocampo, to Diplomatic Corps, The Hague, Netherlands', 12 February 2004.

Office of the Prosecutor, 'Statement by the Prosecutor Related to Crimes Committed in Barlonyo Camp in Uganda', 23 February 2004.

Office of the Prosecutor, 'Statement of the Prosecutor of the International Criminal Court, Fatou Bensouda, on the Warrant of Arrest Issued against Walter Barasa', Situation in the Republic of Kenya, *The Prosecutor v. Walter Barasa*, 2 October 2013.

Office of the Prosecutor, 'Strategic Plan, June 2012–2015', 11 October 2013.

Office of the Prosecutor, 'Strategy Paper on Sexual and Gender-Based Crimes', June 2014.

The Presidency, 'Decision pursuant to Article 108(1) of the Statute', Situation in the Democratic Republic of Congo, *The Prosecutor v. Germain Katanga*, 7 April 2016.

Pre-Trial Chamber I, 'Confirmation of Charges: Public Transcript', Situation in the Republic of Mali, *The Prosecutor v. Ahmad al Faqi al Mahdi*, 1 March 2016.

Pre-Trial Chamber I, 'Decision concerning Pre-Trial Chamber I's Decision of 10 February 2006 and the Incorporation of Documents into the Case against Mr. Thomas Lubanga Dyilo, Annex I: Decision on the Prosecutor's Application for a Warrant of Arrest, Article 58', 27 February 2006.

Pre-Trial Chamber I, 'Decision on the Admissibility of the Case against Saif al-Islam Gaddafi', Situation in Libya, *The Prosecutor v. Saif al-Islam Gaddafi and Abdullah al-Senussi*, 31 May 2013.

Pre-Trial Chamber I, 'Decision on the Confirmation of Charges', Situation in the Democratic Republic of Congo, *The Prosecutor v. Germain Katanga and Mathieu Ngudjolo Chui*, 30 September 2008.

Pre-Trial Chamber I, 'Decision on the Confirmation of Charges', Situation in the Democratic Republic of Congo, *The Prosecutor v. Thomas Lubango Dyilo*, 29 January 2007.

Pre-Trial Chamber I, 'Decision on the Confirmation of Charges – *The Prosecutor v. Callixte Mbarushimana*', 16 December 2011.

Pre-Trial Chamber I, 'Decision on Côte d'Ivoire's Challenge to the Admissibility of the Case against Simone Gbagbo', Situation in the Republic of Côte d'Ivoire, *The Prosecutor v. Simone Gbagbo*, 11 December 2014.

Pre-Trial Chamber I, 'Decision on the Evidence and Information Provided by the Prosecution for the Issuance of a Warrant of Arrest for Mathieu Ngudjolo Chui', Situation in the Democratic Republic of Congo, *The Prosecutor v. Germain Katanga and Mathieu Ngudjolo Chui*, 6 July 2007.

Pre-Trial Chamber I, 'Mandat d'arrêt à l'encontre d'Ahmad Al Faqi al Mahdi', Situation in the Republic of Mali, *The Prosecutor v. Ahmad al Faqi al Mahdi*, 28 September 2015.

Pre-Trial Chamber I, 'Redacted Version of the Transcript of the Hearing Held on 2 February 2006 and Certain Materials Presented during That Hearing', Situation in the Democratic Republic of Congo, *The Prosecutor v. Thomas Lubango Dyilo*, 22 March 2006.

Pre-Trial Chamber I, '*The Prosecutor v. Thomas Lubanga Dyilo* – Decision on the Confirmation of Charges', 5 February 2007.

Pre-Trial Chamber I, '*The Prosecutor vs. Thomas Lubanga Dyilo* – Prosecutor's Information on Further Investigation', 28 June 2006.

Pre-Trial Chamber I, 'Prosecutor's Application under Article 58(7)', Situation in Darfur, Sudan, 27 February 2007.

Pre-Trial Chamber I, 'Public Document: Decision on the Schedule of the Confirmation Hearing', Situation in the Democratic Republic of Congo, *The Prosecutor v. Callixte Mbarushimana*, 12 August 2011, www.icc-cpi.int/CourtRecords/CR2011_12170.PDF.

Pre-Trial Chamber I, 'Public Redacted Version: Decision on the Confirmation of Charges', Situation in the Democratic Republic of Congo, *The*

Prosecutor v. Germain Katanga and Mathieu Ngudjolo Chui, 30 September 2008.

Pre-Trial Chamber I, 'Situation in the Democratic Republic of Congo in the Case of the Prosecutor vs. Thomas Lubanga Dyilo: Decision on the Applications for Participation in the Proceedings Submitted by VPRS1 to VPRS6 in the Case of of the Prosecutor vs. Thomas Lubanga Dyilo', Doc. ICC-01/04-01/06-172-tEN, 29 June 2006.

Pre-Trial Chamber I, 'Situation in the Democratic Republic of Congo: Decision on the Applications for Participation in the Proceedings of VPRS1, VPRS2, VPRS3, VPRS4, VPRS5, VPRS6', Doc. ICC-01/04-101-tEN-Corr, 17 January 2006.

Pre-Trial Chamber II, 'Dissenting Opinion by Judge Hans-Peter Kaul to Pre-Trial Chamber II's "Decision on the Prosecutor's Application for Summonses to Appear for Francis Kirimi Muthaura, Uhuru Muigai Kenyatta and Mohammed Hussein Ali"', 15 March 2011, Situation in the Republic of Kenya, *The Prosecutor v. Francis Kirimi Muthaura and Uhuru Muigai Kenyatta and Mohammed Hussein Ali*, 15 March 2011.

Pre-Trial Chamber II, 'Order to the Prosecutor for the Submission of Additional Information on the Status of the Execution of the Warrants of Arrest in the Situation in Uganda', Situation in Uganda, *The Prosecutor v. Joseph Kony, Vincent Otti, Raska Lukwiya, Okot Odhiambo and Dominic Ongwen*, 30 November 2006.

Pre-Trial Chamber II, 'Order Unsealing the Warrant of Arrest and Other Documents', Situation in the Republic of Kenya, *The Prosecutor v. Paul Gicheru and Philip Kipkoech Bett*, 10 September 2015.

Pre-Trial Chamber II, 'Prosecution's Submissions on Conducting the Confirmation of Charges Hearing In Situ', Situation in Uganda, *The Prosecutor v. Dominic Ongwen*, 10 July 2015.

Pre-Trial Chamber II, 'Public Redacted Version of "Prosecution's Application for Postponement of the Confirmation Hearing", 10 February 2015, ICC-02/04-01/15-196-Conf-Exp', Situation in Uganda, *The Prosecutor v. Dominic Ongwen*, 12 February 2015.

Pre-Trial Chamber II, 'Situation in the Republic of Kenya: Request for Authorisation of an Investigation Pursuant to Article 15', 26 November 2009.

Pre-Trial Chamber II, 'Situation in Uganda: Prosecutor's Application to Disclose to Internal Auditor Certain Information relating to the Amended Application for Warrants', 13 June 2005.

Pre-Trial Chamber II, 'Situation in Uganda: Warrant of Arrest for Joseph Kony Issued on 8 July 2005 as Amended on 27 September 2005', 27 September 2005

Pre-Trial Chamber II, 'Submission of Information on the Status of the Execution of the Warrants of Arrest in the Situation in Uganda', Situation in Uganda, *The Prosecutor v. Joseph Kony, Vincent Otti, Raska Lukwiya, Okot Odhiambo and Dominic Ongwen*, 6 October 2006.

Pre-Trial Chamber II, 'Victims' Notification of Withdrawal from the Case against Omar Hassan Ahmed al-Bashir', Situation in Darfur, Sudan, *The Prosecutor v. Omar Hassan Ahmed al-Bashir*, 19 October 2005.

Pre-Trial Chamber II, 'Warrant of Arrest for Jean-Pierre Bemba Gombo, Aimé Kilolo Musamba, Jean-Jacques Mangenda Kabongo, Fidèle Babala Wandu and Narcisse Arido', Situation in the Central African Republic, *The Prosecutor v. Jean-Pierre Bemba Gombo, Aimé Kilolo Musamba, Jean-Jacques Mangenda Kabongo, Fidèle Babala Wandu and Narcisse Arido*, 20 November 2013.

Pre-Trial Chamber III, 'Public Redacted Version: Amended Document containing the Charges', Situation in the Democratic Republic of Congo, *The Prosecutor v. Jean-Pierre Bemba Gombo*, 17 October 2008.

Pre-Trial Chamber III, 'Request for Authorisation of an Investigation Pursuant to Article 15', Situation in the Republic of Côte d'Ivoire, 23 June 2011.

The Registry, 'Assistance and Reparations: Achievements, Lessons Learnt and Transitioning', TFV, Programme Progress Report, 2015, www.legal-tools.org/doc/370265/pdf/.

The Registry, 'Draft Implementation Plan for Collective Reparations to Victims', Situation in the Democratic Republic of Congo, *The Prosecutor v. Thomas Lubanga Dyilo*, 3 November 2015.

The Registry, 'Earmarked Support at the Trust Fund for Victims', Programme Progress Report, Winter 2011.

The Registry, 'Outreach Report 2007', Outreach Unit, 2007.

The Registry, 'Strategic Plan for Outreach of the International Criminal Court', Doc. ICC/ASP/5/12, 29 September 2006, pp. 22–3.

The Registry, 'Transmission par le Greffier des observations écrites des autorités congolaises telles que présentées à l'audience du 1er juin 2009', 4 June 2009.

The Registry, 'Transmission to Pre-Trial Chamber II of the Observations Submitted by the Democratic Republic of Congo Pursuant to the "Decision Requesting Observations on Omar al-Bashir's Visit to the Democratic Republic of Congo" dated 3 March 2014', 17 March 2004.

The Registry, 'Trust Fund for Victims – Implementing Partners', www.trustfundforvictims.org/en/where-we-work/implementing-partners.

Trial Chamber I, 'Deposition of Witness DRC-OTP-WWWW-0582 in *The Prosecutor v. Thomas Lubanga Dyilo*', 16 November 2010.

Trial Chamber I, '*The Prosecutor v. Thomas Lubanga Dyilo* – Decision on the Consequences of Non-Disclosure of Exculpatory Materials Covered by Article 54(3)(e) Agreements and the Application to Stay the Prosecution of the Accused, together with Certain Other Issues Raised at the Status Conference on 10 June 2008', 13 June 2008.

Trial Chamber I, '*The Prosecutor v. Thomas Lubanga Dyilo* – Redacted Decision on the Prosecution's Urgent Request for Variation of the Time Limit to Disclose the Identity of Intermediary 143 or Alternatively to Stay Proceedings Pending Further Consultations with the VWU', 8 July 2010.

Trial Chamber II, 'Dissenting Opinion of Christine Van den Wyngaert', Situation in the Democratic Republic of Congo, *The Prosecutor v. Germain Katanga*, 20 May 2013.

Trial Chamber II, 'Judgment pursuant to Article 74 of the Rome Statute – *The Prosecutor v. Mathieu Ngudjolo*', 18 December 2012.

Trial Chamber II, 'Motion Challenging the Admissibility of the Case by the Defence of Germain Katanga, Pursuant to Article 19 (2) (a) of the Statute', Situation in the Democratic Republic of Congo, *The Prosecutor v. Germain Katanga and Mathieu Ngudjolo Chui*, 11 March 2009.

Trial Chamber II, 'Order Approving the Proposed Plan of the Trust Fund for Victims in Relation to Symbolic Collective Reparations', Situation in the Democratic Republic of Congo, *The Prosecutor v. Thomas Lubanga Dyilo*, 21 October 2016.

Trial Chamber II, 'Order of Reparations under Article 75 of the Statute', Situation in the Democratic Republic of Congo, *The Prosecutor v. Germain Katanga*, 24 March 2017.

Trial Chamber II, 'Reason for the Oral Decision on the Motion Challenging the Admissibility of the Case (Article 19 of the Statute)', Situation in the Democratic Republic of Congo, *The Prosecutor v. Germain Katanga and Mathieu Ngudjolo Chui*, 16 June 2009.

Trial Chamber III, 'Decision on the Admissibility and Abuse of Process Challenges', Situation in the Central African Republic, *The Prosecutor v. Jean-Pierre Bemba Gombo*.

Trial Chamber III, 'Public Redacted Version of Closing Brief of Mr. Jean-Pierre Bemba Gombo', Situation in the Central African Republic, *The Prosecutor v. Jean-Pierre Bemba Gombo*.

Trial Chamber V, 'Status Conference', Situation in the Republic of Kenya, *The Prosecutor v. William Samoei Ruto and Joshua Arap*, 23 September 2013.

Trial Chamber VIII, 'Judgment and Sentence', Situation in the Republic of Mali, *The Prosecutor v. Ahmad al Faqi al Mahdi*, 27 September 2016.

Trial Chamber VIII, 'Trial Hearings: Public Transcripts', Situation in the Republic of Mali, *The Prosecutor v. Ahmad al Faqi al Mahdi*, 22–4 August 2016.

International Crisis Group, 'Building a Comprehensive Peace Strategy for Northern Uganda', Africa Briefing No. 27, 23 June 2005.

'Congo Crisis: Military Intervention in Ituri', 2003.

'Congo: Five Priorities for a Peacebuilding Strategy', Africa Report No. 150, 11 May 2009.

'Katanga: The Congo's Forgotten Crisis', 9 January 2006.

International Federation for Human Rights, 'First Step on the Path to Justice: ICC Sentences Al Mahdi to 9 Years', 27 September 2016, www.fidh.org/en/region/Africa/mali/first-step-on-the-path-to-justice-icc-sentences-al-mahdi-to-9-years.

'Mali: The Hearing of Al Mahdi before the ICC is a Victory, But Charges Must Be Expanded', 30 September 2015, www.fidh.org/en/issues/international-justice/international-criminal-court-icc/mali-the-hearing-of-abou-tourab-before-the-icc-is-a-victory-but.

'Q&A: The Al Mahdi Case at the ICC', 17 August 2016, www.fidh.org/en/region/Africa/mali/q-a-the-al-mahdi-case-at-the-icc.

International Human Rights Law Group, 'Les Principes Clés d'une Commission Vérité et Réconciliation', July 2003.

International Refugee Rights Initative and Open Society Initiative, 'Commentary on the ICC Draft Guidlelines for Intermediaries', 18 August 2011.

Invisible Children, 'Kony2012', www.youtube.com/watch?v=Y4MnpzG5Sqc.

IRIN News, 'DRC: Amnesty Law Passed without MPs from Kabila's Party', IRIN, 30 November 2005, www.irinnews.org/report/57408/drc-amnesty-law-passed-without-mps-kabilas-party.

'DRC: Ex-Militiamen Get Life for Murdering UN Soldiers', 21 February 2007, www.irinnews.org/report/70288/drc-ex-militiamen-get-life-murdering-un-soldiers.

'DRC: Summary of Lusaka Accord', 21 July 1999, www.irinnews.org/news/1999/07/21/summary-lusaka-accord.

'The ICC and the Northern Uganda Conflict', 9 June 2005, www.irinnews.org/fr/node/222384.

'No More Amnesty Certificates for Rebels', 1 June 2012, www.irinnews.org/report/95569/uganda-no-more-amnesty-certificates-rebels.

'Uganda: Rebels Propose Federalist Solution at Juba Talks', 11 October 2006, www.irinnews.org/report.aspx?reportid=61303.

'Uganda: Senior LRA Commander Captured by the Army', 15 July 2004, www.irinnews.org/news/2004/07/15/senior-lra-commander-captured-army.

'Uganda–Sudan: Another International NGO Worker Killed by LRA Rebels', 7 November 2005, www.irinnews.org/news/2005/11/07/ another-international-ngo-worker-killed-lra-rebels.

'War Crimes Trial May Affect LRA Defections – Analysts', 29 July 2011, http://reliefweb.int/report/uganda/war-crimes-trial-may-affect-lra-defec tions-analysts.

Izama, A., 'Secret Dealings that Got LRA before World Court', *Daily Monitor*, 18 May 2008, http://allafrica.com/stories/200805190624.html

Jacobs, C. and B. Weijs, 'Capacity Development and Civil SocietyStrengthening Report – Réseau Haki na Amani, Final Report MFS II Evaluation', 2015, http://mfs2.partos.nl/documents/DRC-CSS-RHA.pdf.

Jacobs, D., 'The Lubanga Trial Is Stayed, the Slapstick Comedy Continues...But Isn't the Joke Wearing a Little Thin?', Spreading the Jam blog, 9 July 2010, https://dovjacobs.com/2010/07/09/the-lubanga-trial-is-stayed-the-slapstick-comedy-continues-but-isnt-the-joke-wearing-a-little-thin/.

Johnson, D., *The Root Causes of Sudan's Civil Wars*, James Currey, 2003.

Johnson, D. and D. Anderson, 'Revealing Prophets', in D. Johnson and D. Anderson (eds.), *Revealing Prophets: Prophecy in Eastern African Studies*, James Currey, 1995, p. 14.

Joireman, S., A. Sawyer and J. Wilhoit, 'A Different Way Home: Resettlment Patterns in Northern Uganda', *Political Geography*, 31, 4, May 2012, pp. 197–204.

Joppke, C., 'The Retreat Is Real – But What Is the Alternative? Multiculturalism, Muscular Liberalism and Islam', *Constellations*, 21, 2, June 2014, pp. 286–95.

Jones, J., 'The Implications of the Peace Agreement for the International Criminal Tribunal for the Former Yugoslavia', *European Journal of International Law*, 7, 1996, pp. 226–44.

Justice, Law and Order Sector, 'JLOS Strategic Investment Plan II 2006/7 – 2010/11', www.laspnet.org/index.php?view=document&alias=267-jlos-strategic-investment-plan-ii-20067-201011&category_slug=strategic-plans&layout=default&option=com_docman&Itemid=837.

Justice and Reconciliation Project, "Abomination': Local Belief Systems and International Justice', Liu Institute for Global Issues and the Gulu District NGO Forum, Field Notes No. 5, September 2007.

'Complicating Victims and Perpetrators in Uganda: On Dominic Ongwen', JRP Field Note 7, July 2008, http://justiceandreconciliation.com/ wp-content/uploads/2008/07/JRP_FN7_Dominic-Ongwen.pdf.

Kabungulu Ngoy-Kangoy, H., 'Parties and Political Transition in the Democratic Republic of Congo', Election Institute of Southern Africa, Research Report No. 20, 2006.

Kagwanja, P., 'Facing Mount Kenya or Facing Mecca? The Mungiki, Ethnic Violence and the Politics of the Moi Succession in Kenya, 1987–2002', *African Affairs*, 102, 406, 2003, pp. 25–49.

Kalyvas, S., *The Logic of Violence in Civil War*, Cambridge University Press, 2006.

Kambale, P., 'The ICC and Lubanga: Missed Opportunities', Social Science Research Council, 16 March 2012, http://forums.ssrc.org/african-futures/2012/03/16/african-futures-icc-missed-opportunities/.

'A Story of Missed Opportunities: The Role of the International Criminal Court in the Democratic Republic of Congo', in C. de Vos, S. Kendall and C. Stahn (eds.), *Contested Justice: The Politics and Practice of International Criminal Court Interventions*, Cambridge University Press, 2015, pp. 171–96.

Kastner, P., *International Criminal Justice in Bello? The ICC between Law and Politics in Darfur and Northern Uganda*, Martinus Nijhoff, 2012.

Kaul, H.-P., 'Ten Years of the International Criminal Court', speech at the experts' discussion, '10 Years: International Criminal Court and the Role of the United States in International Justice', Berlin, 2 October 2012, www.icc-cpi.int/NR/rdonlyres/FB16B529-3A60-441D-8DBE-5D6A768 CA6FF/284995/02102012_Berlin_DGAP_THEICCatTen_Final.pdf.

Keller, L., 'The Practice of the International Criminal Court: Comments on "The Complementarity Conundrum"', *Santa Barbara Journal of International Law*, 8, 1, 2010, pp. 199–231.

Kelsall, T., *Culture under Cross-Examination: International Justice and the Special Court for Sierra Leone*, Cambridge University Press, 2009.

Kendall, S., 'Beyond the Restorative Turn: The Limits of Legal Humanitarianism', in C. de Vos, S. Kendall and C. Stahn (eds.), *Contested Justice: The Politics and Practice of International Criminal Court Interventions*, Cambridge University Press, 2015, pp. 352–75.

Kersten, M., 'A Brutally Honest Confrontation with the ICC's Past: Thoughts on "The Prosecutor and the President"', Justice in Conflict blog, 23 June 2016, https://justiceinconflict.org/2016/06/23/a-brutally-honest-confrontation-with-the-iccs-past-thoughts-on-the-prosecutor-and-the-president/.

Justice in Conflict: The Effects of the International Criminal Court's Interventions on Ending Wars and Building Peace, Oxford University Press, 2016.

'What Happened to the ICC in Mali?', Justice in Conflict blog, 29 May 2015, https://justiceinconflict.org/2015/05/29/what-happened-to-the-icc-in-mali/.

Ker Kwaro Acholi Gulu Conference, 'Background Document', December 2007.

'Cultural Leaders Statement', December 2007.

Ker Kwaro Acholi and the Northern Uganda Peace Inititiave, 'Report on Acholi Youth and Chiefs Addressing Practices of the Acholi Culture of Reconciliation', USAID, June 2005.

Khadiagala, G., 'The Role of the Acholi Religious Leaders Peace Initiative (ARLPI) in Peace Building in Northern Uganda', Appendix in USAID/ Management Systems International, 'The Effectiveness of Civil Society Initiatives in Controlling Violent Conflicts and Building Peace: A Study of Three Approaches in the Greater Horn of Africa', March 2001.

Khadiagala, L., 'The Failure of Popular Justice in Uganda: Local Councils and Women's Property Rights', *Development and Change*, 32, 2001, pp. 55–76.

Kobi, A., 'Can Gbagbo's ICC Trial Help Quench Côte d'Ivoire's Thirst for Justice?', Institute for Security Studies, 9 March 2016, www.issafrica .org/iss-today/can-gbagbos-icc-trial-quench-cote-divoires-thirst-for-justice.

Kotarski, K., 'Ivory Coast: Calls for More Prosecutions', Institute for War and Peace Reporting, 14 December 2011, https://iwpr.net/global-voices/ ivory-coast-calls-more-prosecutions.

Krever, T., 'Dispensing Global Justice', *New Left Review*, 85, January– February 2014, pp. 67–97.

Kukathas, C., 'The Mirage of Global Justice', *Social Philosophy and Policy*, 23, 1, January 2006.

Labuda, P., 'Applying and "Misapplying" the Rome Statute in the Democratic Republic of Congo', in C. De Vos, S. Kendall and C. Stahn (eds.), *Contested Justice: The Politics and Practice of International Criminal Court Interventions*, Cambridge University Press, 2015, pp. 408–31.

'The ICC in the Democratic Republic of Congo: A Decade of Partnership and Antagonism', in K. Clarke, A. Knottnerus and E. de Volder (eds.), *Africa and the ICC: Perceptions of Justice*, Cambridge University Press, 2016, pp. 277–99.

'The International Criminal Court and Perceptions of Sovereignty, Colonialism and Pan-African Solidarity', *African Yearbook of International Law Online/Annuaire Africain de Droit International Online*, 20, 1, 2014, pp. 289–321.

Lacey, M., 'Atrocity Victims in Uganda Choose to Forgive', *New York Times*, 18 April 2005, www.nytimes.com/2005/04/18/world/africa/ atrocity-victims-in-uganda-choose-to-forgive.html.

Lamwaka, C., *The Raging Storm: A Reporter's Inside Account of the Northern Uganda War 1986–2005*, Fountain Publishers, 2016.

Lanegran, K., 'Truth Commissions, Human Rights Trials and the Politics of Memory', *Comparative Studies of South Asia, Africa and the Middle East*, 25, 1, 2005, pp. 111–21.

Lefèvre, R., 'High Stakes for the Peace Process in Libya', *Journal of North African Studies*, 20, 1, 2016, pp. 1–6.

Lindemann, S., 'The Ethnic Politics of Coup Avoidance: Evidence from Zambia and Uganda', *Africa Spectrum*, 2, 2011, pp. 3–41.

Lipscomb, R., 'Structuring the ICC Framework to Advance Transitional Justice: A Search for a Permanent Solution in Sudan', *Columbia Law Review*, 106, 1, 2006, pp. 182–212.

Liu Institute for Global Issues, Gulu District NGO Forum, Ker Kwaro Acholi and Northern Ugandan Peace Initiative, *Roco Wat I Acoli: Restoring Relationships in Acholi-land – Traditional Approaches to Justice and Reintegration*, September 2005.

'Pursuing Peace and Justice: International and Local Initiatives', May 2005.

Lombard, L., *State of Rebellion: Violence and Intervention in the Central African Republic*, Zed Books, 2016.

Lomo, Z. and J. Otto, 'Not a Crime to Talk: Give Peace a Chance in Northern Uganda', Refugee Law Project and Human Rights Focus press release, 24 July 2006.

Lord's Resistance Army Delegation to the Juba Talks, 'LRA Position Paper on Accountability and Reconciliation in the Context of Alternative Justice System for Resolving the Northern Ugandan and Southern Sudan Conflicts', August 2006.

LRA Crisis Tracker, www.lracrisistracker.com/.

Luban, D., 'After the Honeymoon: Reflections on the Current State of International Criminal Justice', *Journal of International Criminal Justice*, 11, 2013, pp. 505–15.

Lynch, G. and M. Zgonec-Rožej, 'The ICC Intervention in Kenya', Africa/International Law Programmes, Chatham House, February 2013.

McAuliffe, P., 'From Watchdog to Workhouse: Explaining the Emergence of the ICC's Burden-Sharing Policy as an Example of Creeping Cosmopolitanism', *Chinese Journal of International Law*, 13, 2014.

McEvoy, K., 'Beyond Legalism: Towards a Thicker Understanding of Transitional Justice', *Journal of Law and Society*, 34, 4, December 2007, pp. 411–40.

McConnell, T., 'Measures to Keep Peace in Congo Draw Fire', *Christian Science Monitor*, 5 September 2006, www.csmonitor.com/2006/0905/p04s02-woaf.html.

'Uganda: Peace versus Justice?', openDemocracy, 13 September 2006, www.opendemocracy.net/democracy-africa_democracy/uganda_peace_3903.jsp.

Macdonald, A., 'Justice in Transition? Transitional Justice and Its Discontents', PhD thesis, King's College London, 2016.

'Local Understandings and Experiences of Transitional Justice: A Review of the Evidence', Justice and Security Research Programme, London School of Economics, July 2013.

McEwan, I., *The Children Act*, Jonathan Cape, 2014.

MacGaffey, W., 'The Policy of National Integration in Zaire', *Journal of Modern African Studies*, 20, 1, March 1982, pp. 87–105.

Machar, R., 'Mediator's Guidelines', 28 June 2007, copy on file with author.

Makokha, M., 'Interview with Fatou Bensouda', The Hague Trials Kenya, 20 June 2016, https://neveragain.co.ke/bensouda-speaks-why-kenya-cases-icc-collapsed/article.

Mallinder, L., *Amnesty, Human Rights and Political Transitions: Bridging the Peace and Justice Divide*, Hart Publishing, 2008.

Mallinder, L. and K. McEvoy, 'Rethinking Amnesties: Atrocity, Accountability and Impunity in Post-Conflict Societies', *Contemporary Social Science*, 6, 1, 2011, pp. 107–28.

Mamdani, M., 'Beware Human Rights Fundamentalism!', *Mail & Guardian*, 20 March 2009, https://mg.co.za/article/2009–03–20-beware-human-rights-fundamentalism.

'Darfur, ICC and the New Humanitarian Order: How the ICC's "Responsibility to Protect" Is Being Turned into an Assertion of Neocolonial Domination', *Pambazuka News*, 396, 17 September 2008, www.pambazuka.org/governance/darfur-icc-and-new-humani tarian-order.

'Preliminary Thoughts on the Congo Crisis', *Social Text*, 17, 3, 1999, pp. 53–62.

Manson, K., 'Tea with The Terminator: The Day I Met Bosco Ntaganda', *Financial Times*, 23 March 2013, http://blogs.ft.com/the-world/2013/03/tea-with-the-terminator-the-day-i-met-bosco-ntaganda/.

Maru, M., 'The Future of the ICC and Africa: The Good, the Bad and the Ugly', Al Jazeera, 11 October 2013, www.aljazeera.com/indepth/opin ion/2013/10/future-icc-africa-good-bad-ugly-20131011143130881924 .html.

Maseruka, J., 'Traditional Justice Not Applicable to War Suspects', *New Vision*, 30 June 2009.

Maunganidze, O., and A. Louw, 'The Decision by the Government of Mali to Refer the Situation in the Country Has Several Implications for the Country, Africa and the ICC', Institute for Security Studies, 24 July 2012, www.issafrica.org/iss-today/implications-of-another-african-case-as-mali-self-refers-to-the-icc.

Maupas, S., 'Le Procureur de la Cour Pénale Internationale Veut Inculper Deux Chefs Rebelles Ougandais', *Le Monde*, 12 June 2005, www .lemonde.fr/international/article/2005/06/11/le-procureur-de-la-cour-

penale-internationale-veut-inculper-deux-chefs-rebelles-ougandais_6609
80_3210.html.

Mazlish, B., 'The Global and the Local', *Current Sociology*, 35, 1, 2005,
pp. 93–111.

Médecins sans Frontières, 'International Justice – Pragmatism or Principle?',
MSF Dialogue 9, 27 July 2010, www.msf.org.uk/sites/uk/files/MSF_
Dialogue_No9__International_Justice_201007270041.pdf.

Mégret, F., 'Beyond "Fairness": Understanding the Determinants of International Criminal Procedure', *UCLA Journal of International Law and
Foreign Affairs*, 14, 2010, pp. 37–71.

Mégret F., 'Cour Pénale Internationale et Néocolonialisme: Audelà des Evidences', *Revue Études Internationales*, 45, 1, March 2014, pp. 27–50.

'In Whose Name? The ICC and the Search for Constituency', in C. De
Vos, S. Kendall and C. Stahn (eds.), *Contested Justice: The Politics and
Practice of International Criminal Court Interventions*, Cambridge
University Press, 2015, pp. 23–45.

Mégret, F. and N. Samson, 'Holding the Line on Complementarity in Libya',
Journal of International Criminal Justice, 11, 3, 2013, pp. 571–90.

Mergelsberg, B., 'Between Two Worlds: Former LRA Soldiers in Northern
Uganda', in T. Allen and K. Vlassenroot (eds.), *The Lord's Resistance
Army: Myth and Reality*, Zed Books, 2010, pp. 156–75.

Meron, T. and F. Bensouda, 'Twenty Years of International Criminal Law:
From the ICTY to the ICC and Beyond', *Proceedings of the Annual
Meeting (American Society of International Law)*, 107, 2013, pp. 407–20.

Mgbeoji, I., 'The Civilised Self and the Barbaric Other: Imperial Delusions of
Order and the Challenges of Human Security', in R. Falk, B. Rajagopal
and J. Stevens (eds.), *International Law and the Third World: Reshaping Justice*, Routledge-Cavendish, 2008, pp. 151–65.

Mills, K., *International Responses to Mass Atrocities in Africa: Responsibility to Protect, Prosecute and Palliate*, University of Pennsylvania
Press, 2015.

Mission of the United States to Switzerland, 'Press Briefing with Stephen
J. Rapp, Ambassador-at-Large for War Crimes Issues', 22 January
2010, https://webcache.googleusercontent.com/search?q=cache:3RlA8
TYqWm4J:https://geneva.usmission.gov/2010/01/22/stephen-rapp/+&
cd=1&hl=en&ct=clnk&gl=tr.

Mnookin, R., 'Rethinking the Tension between Peace and Justice: The
International Criminal Prosecutor as Diplomat', *Harvard Negotiation
Law Review*, 18, 2013, pp. 145–72.

Monageng, S. M., 'Africa and the International Criminal Court: Then and
Now', in G. Werle et al. (eds.), *Africa and the International Criminal
Court*, T. M. C. Asser Press, 2014, pp. 13–20.

Mongo, E., 'Evaluation des Mécanismes des Résolutions des Conflits Utilisés par le RHA jusqu'à ces Jours', RHA and IVK Pax Christi, powerpoint presentation, 2009.

Mongo, E., A. Nkoy Elela and J. van Puijenbroe, 'Conflits Fonciers en Ituri: Poids du Passé et Défis pour l'Avenir de la Paix', IKV Pax Christi and Réseau Haki na Amani, December 2009.

Morris, M., 'The Trials of Concurrent Jurisdiction: The Case of Rwanda', *Duke Journal of Comparative and International Law*, 7, 1997, pp. 349–74.

Moyn, S., 'Judith Shklar versus the International Criminal Court', *Humanity: An International Journal of Human Rights, Humanitarianism and Development*, 4, 3, 2013, pp. 473–500.

Mueller, S., 'Kenya and the International Criminal Court (ICC): Politics, the Election and the Law', *Journal of Eastern African Studies*, 8, 1, 2014, pp. 25–42.

Mukasa, H., 'Withdraw ICC Bill, Former Minister Pleads', *New Vision*, 17 December 2006, www.newvision.co.ug/new_vision/news/1134759/withdraw-icc-minister-pleads.

Museveni, Y., *Sowing the Mustard Seed: The Struggle for Freedom and Democracy in Uganda*, MacMillan, 1997.

Mutagwera, F., 'Détentions et Poursuites Judiciaires au Rwanda', in J.-F. Dupaquier (ed.), *La Justice Internationale Face au Drame Rwandais*, Karthala, 1996, pp. 17–36.

Mutua, M., 'Africans and the ICC', in K. Clarke, A. Knotterus and E. Volder (eds.), *Africa and the ICC: Perceptions of Justice*, Cambridge University Press, 2016, pp. 39–46.

Nagy, R., 'Transitional Justice as Global Project: Critical Reflections', *Third World Quarterly*, 29, 2, 2008, pp. 275–89.

Namutebi, J. and J. Odyek, 'International Criminal Court Bill Out', *New Vision*, 5 December 2006, www.newvision.co.ug/new_vision/news/1135544/international-criminal-court.

Ndahinda, F., 'The Bemba–Banyamulenge Case before the ICC: From Individual to Collective Criminal Responsibility', *International Journal of Transitional Justice*, 7, 2013, pp. 476–96.

Nerlich, V., 'The Confirmation of Charges Procedure at the International Criminal Court: Advance or Failure', *Journal of International Criminal Justice*, 10, 5, 2012, pp. 1339–56.

Newton, M., 'A Synthesis of Community-Based Justice and Complementarity', in C. De Vos, S. Kendall and C. Stahn (eds.), *Contested Justice: The Politics and Practice of International Criminal Court Interventions*, Cambridge University Press, 2015, pp. 131–8.

'The Complementarity Conundrum: Are Watching Evolution or Eviscer-ation?', *Santa Barbara Journal of International Law*, 8, 1, 2010, pp. 115–64.

Nichols, L., *The International Criminal Court and the End of Impunity in Kenya*, Springer, 2015.

Nichols, M., 'ICC Prosecutor Pleads for UN Security Council Act on Darfur Case', Reuters, 29 June 2015, www.reuters.com/article/us-sudan-darfur-court-idUSKCN0P92S420150629.

Nino, C., 'The Duty to Punish Past Abuses of Human Rights Put into Context: The Case of Argentina', *Yale Law Journal*, 100, 8, 1991, pp. 2619–40.

Nossiter, A., 'Mali Mob Assaults President after Pact', *The New York Times*, 21 May 2012, www.nytimes.com/2012/05/22/world/africa/mali-protest ers-attack-interim-president-dioncounda-traore.html.

Nouwen, S., *Complementarity in the Line of Fire: The Catalysing Effect of the International Criminal Court in Uganda and Sudan*, Cambridge University Press, 2013.

Nouwen, S. and W. Werner, 'Monopolizing Global Justice: International Criminal Law as Challenge to Human Diversity', *Journal of International Criminal Justice*, 13, 2015, pp. 157–76.

Nsengimana, F., E. van Kemenade and A. Tobie, 'Strengthening Local Mediation Efforts: Lessons from Eastern DRC', Initiative for Peace-building, International Alert, 2010.

Nsibambi, F., 'Paying for Cultural Leaders' Upkeep against the Constitution', *Daily Monitor*, 17 June 2013, www.monitor.co.ug/OpEd/Commentary/Paying-for-cultural-leaders–upkeep-against-the-Constitution/689364-1884998-342lue/index.html.

Ocampo, L. M., 'Building a Future on Peace and Justice', speech at Nurem-berg conference, 24–5 June 2007, www.icc-cpi.int/NR/rdonlyres/4E466EDB-2B38-4BAF-AF5F-005461711149/143825/LMO_nuremberg_20070625_English.pdf.

'The International Criminal Court and Prospects for Peace in Africa', expert roundtable on Peace, Justice and the Dilemmas of the ICC in Africa, London School of Economics, 2 March 2007, notes on file with author.

'Keynote Address: Integrating the Work of the ICC into Local Justice Initiatives', *American University International Law Review*, 21, 4, 2005, pp. 497–503.

'Review Conference – General Debate Statement', Kampala, 31 May 2010.

Ochola II, M.B., 'Hope in the Storm: Experience of ARLPI in Conflict Resolution of the Northern Ugandan Armed Conflict', paper delivered at 'Seminar on Northern Uganda', Mission Church of Uppsala, Sweden, 15 April 2004.

Odokonyero, M., 'Ugandans Edgy over US Move against LRA', Institute for War and Peace Reporting, 22 July 2010, https://iwpr.net/global-voices/ugandans-edgy-over-us-move-against-lra.

O'Donoghue, J. and S. Rigney, 'The ICC Must Consider Fair Trial Concerns in Determining Libya's Application to Prosecute Saif al-Islam Gaddafi Nationally', *EJIL: Talk!* blog, 8 June 2012, www.ejiltalk.org/the-icc-must-consider-fair-trial-concerns-in-determining-libyas-application-to-prosecute-saif-al-islam-gaddafi-nationally/.

Office of the United Nations High Commissioner for Human Rights, 'Making Peace Our Own: Victims' Perceptions of Accountability, Reconciliation and Transitional Justice', Geneva: OHCHR, 2007, www.uganda.ohchr.org/Content/publications/Making%20Peace%20Our%20Own.pdf.

O'Kadameri, B., 'Protracted Conflict, Elusive Peace: Initiatives to End the Violence in Northern Uganda', Accord Issue 11, Conciliation Resources, 2002.

Okafor, O. and U. Ngwaba, 'The International Criminal Court as a "Transitional Justice" Mechanism in Africa: Some Critical Reflections', *International Journal of Transitional Justice*, 9, 1, 2015, pp. 90–108.

Okumu, J., 'Acholi Rites of Reconciliation', *The Examiner*, Human Rights Focus, 2, 2005, p. 15.

Olsen, T., L. Payne and A. Reiter, *Transitional Justice in Balance: Comparing Processes, Weighing Efficacy*, United States Institute of Peace, 2010.

Oola, S., 'In the Shadow of Kwoyelo's Trial: Complementarity in Practice in Uganda', in C. De Vos, S. Kendall and C. Stahn (eds.), *Contested Justice: The Politics and Practice of International Criminal Court Interventions*, Cambridge University Press, 2015, pp. 147–69.

Open Society Foundations, 'Justice in DRC: Mobile Courts Combat Rape and Impunity in Eastern Congo', 14 January 2014.

Open Society Justice Initiative, 'Factsheet: ICC Katanga Reparations', March 2017.

Orentlicher, D., 'Owning Justice and Wrestling with Its Complexity', *Journal of International Criminal Justice*, 11, 3, 2013, pp. 517–26.

'A Reply to Professor Nino', *Yale Law Journal*, 100, 8, 1991, pp. 2641–3.

'Settling Accounts: The Duty to Prosecute Human Rights Violations of a Prior Regime. *Yale Law Journal*, 100, 8, 1991, pp. 2537–615.

Osike, F., 'Uganda: Here Is ICC Prosecutor Luis Ocampo in his Office in The Hague', *New Vision*, 16 July 2007, http://allafrica.com/stories/200707160105.html.

Osike, F. and H. Musaka, 'ICC Insists Kony Must Face Prosecution', *New Vision*, 11 October 2007, www.newvision.co.ug/new_vision/news/1217697/icc-insists-kony-prosecution.

Otim, M. and S. Kasande, 'On the Path to Vindicate Victims' Rights in Uganda: Reflections on the Transitional Justice Process since Juba', International Center for Transitional Justice, June 2015.

Otto, A., 'Top LRA Commanders, Returnees Undergo Ritual Cleansing', Uganda Radio Network, 9 March 2015, http://ugandaradionetwork .com/story/top-lra-commanders-returnees-undergo-ritual-cleansing.

Ouattara, A., 'Confirmation de la Déclaration de Reconnaissance', 14 December 2010, www.icc-cpi.int/NR/rdonlyres/498E8FEB-7A72-4005-A209-C14BA374804F/0/ReconCPI.pdf.

Paet, U., 'The Complex Relationship between R2P and the ICC: Can it Succeed?', speech at human rights conference in Reyjavik, Iceland, 10 April 2013, www.vm.ee/en/news/complex-relationship-between-r2p-and-icc-can-it-succeed.

Pain, D., 'The Bending of the Spears: Producing Consensus for Peace and Development in Northern Uganda', International Alert and Kacoke Madit, 1997.

Palmer, N., *Courts in Conflict: Interpreting the Layers of Justice in Post-Genocide Rwanda*, Oxford University Press, 2015.

'The Place of Consultation in the International Criminal Court's Approach to Complementarity and Cooperation', in O. Bekou and D. Birkett (eds.), *Cooperation and the International Criminal Court: Perspectives from Theory and Practice*, Brill Nijhoff, 2016, pp. 210–26.

Palmer, N. and P. Clark, 'Testifying to Genocide: Victim and Witness Protection in Rwanda', REDRESS Trust, 2012.

Papenfuss, A., '"We Should at All Costs Prevent the ICC from Being Politicized": Interview with Fatou Bensouda', *Vereinte Nationen* (German Review on the United Nations), 62, 1, 2014, pp. 16–21, www.dgvn.de/fileadmin/user_upload/DOKUMENTE/English_Documents/Interview_Fatou_Bensouda.pdf.

Paris, R., 'Saving Liberal Peacebuilding', *Review of International Studies*, 36, 2, 2010, pp. 337–65.

Parrott, L., 'The Role of the International Criminal Court in Uganda: Ensuring that the Pursuit of Justice Does Not Come at the Price of Peace', *Australian Journal of Peace Studies*, 1, 2006, pp. 8–29.

Pax Christi, 'Justice and Peace News: A Newsletter from the Justice and Peace Commission of Gulu Archdiocese', May 2005, www.paxchristi .net/sites/default/files/documents/MO154E06.pdf.

'Peace, Justice and the ICC in Africa' workshop, Royal African Society, London, 8 March 2007.

p'Bitek, O., *Religion of the Central Luo*, Uganda Literature Bureau, 1980.

Pensky, M., 'Amnesty on Trial: Impunity, Accountability and the Norms of International Law', *Ethics and Global Politics*, 1, 1–2, 2008, pp. 1–40.

Perrot, S., 'Northern Uganda: A "Forgotten Conflict", Again? The Impact of the Internationalization of Conflict Resolution', in T. Allen and K. Vlassenroot (eds.), *The Lord's Resistance Army: Myth and Reality*, Zed Books, 2011, pp. 187–203.

Peskin, V., *International Justice in Rwanda and the Balkans: Virtual Trials and the Struggle for State Cooperation*, Cambridge University Press, 2008.

Peskin, V. and M. Boduszynski, 'The Rise and Fall of the ICC in Libya and the Politics of International Surrogate Enforcership', *International Journal of Transitional Justice*, 10, 2, 2016, pp. 272–91.

Phillips, A., 'Equality, Pluralism, Universality: Current Concerns in Normative Theory', *British Journal of Politics and International Relations*, 2, 2, 2000, pp. 237–55.

Piron, P. and G. Devos (eds.), *Codes et Lois du Congo Belge* (8th edition), Larcier, 1961.

Pole Institute, 'Inter-Congolese Dialogue: The Experience of the Intercommunal *Barza* and the Pacification Commission of North Kivu', *The Inter-Congolese Dialogue 2: Intercommunal Peace Work in North Kivu*, Regards Croisés no. 2, May 2000.

Porter, E., *Connecting Peace, Justice and Reconciliation*, Lynne Rienner, 2015.

Porter, H., *After Rape: Violence, Justice and Social Harmony in Uganda*, Cambridge University Press, 2017.

'Justice and Rape on the Periphery: The Supremacy of Social Harmony in the Space between Local Solutions and Formal Judicial Systems in Northern Uganda', *Journal of Eastern African Studies*, 6, 1, 2012, pp. 81–97.

Porter, H. and A. Macdonald, 'The Trial of Thomas Kwoyelo: Opportunity or Spectre? Reflections from the Ground on the First LRA Prosecution', *Africa*, 86, 4, pp. 698–722.

Porter, N., *The Elusive Quest: Reconciliation in Northern Ireland*, The Blackstaff Press, 2003.

Quinn, J., 'Beyond Truth Commissions: Indigenous Reconciliation in Uganda', *Review of Faith and International Affairs*, 4, 1, 2006, pp. 31–7.

Radio Dabanga, 'ICC Arrest Warrant for Darfur Rebel', 11 September 2014, www.dabangasudan.org/en/all-news/article/icc-arrest-warrant-for-darfur-rebel.

'"Prospects of Arrests in Darfur Case Bleak": ICC Prosecutor', 31 March 2015, www.dabangasudan.org/en/all-news/article/prospect-of-arrests-in-darfur-case-bleak-icc-prosecutor.

Radio Netherlands Worldwide, 'ICC's First Trial at Risk as Prosecutor Ignores Judges' Orders', 14 July 2010, www.rnw.org/archive/iccs-first-trial-risk-prosecution-ignores-judges-orders.

Radio Rhino International Afrika, 'Uganda News Summary', 5 July 2006.

Rastan, R., 'Complementarity: Contest or Collaboration?', in M. Bergsmo (ed.), *Complementarity and the Exercise of Universal Jurisdiction for Core International Crimes*, Forum for International and Humanitarian Law, 2010, www.toaep.org/ps-pdf/7-bergsmo.

'What is "Substantially the Same Conduct?": Unpacking the ICC's "First Limb" Complementarity Jurisprudence', *Journal of International Criminal Justice*, 15, 1, 2017, pp. 1–29.

Rawls, J., *A Theory of Justice*, revised edition, Harvard University Press, 1999.

Refugee Law Project, 'Forgiveness: Unveiling an Asset for Peacebuilding', 2015.

'Negotiating Peace: Resolution of Conflicts in Uganda's West Nile Region', Working Paper No. 12, June 2004.

'Ongwen's Justice Dilemma: Perspectives from Northern Uganda', 26 January 2015.

'A Renewed Promise for Peace and Justice: The Reinstatement of Uganda's Amnesty Act 2000', 29 May 2013.

'War as Normal: The Impact of Violence on the Lives of Displaced Communities in Pader District, Northern Uganda', Working Paper No. 5, June 2002.

'Whose Justice? Perceptions of Uganda's Amnesty Act 2000', Working Paper No. 15, 28 February 2005.

Republic of Uganda, 'The Amnesty Act', 2000.

Constitution of the Republic of Uganda, 1995.

Resolve LRA Crisis Initative, 'The Kony Crossroads: President Obama's Chance to Define his Legacy on the LRA Crisis', August 2015, www.theresolve.org/wp-content/uploads/2015/08/The-Kony-Crossroads-August-2015.pdf.

Reuters, 'Libyan Court Sentences Gaddafi Son Saif, Eight Other Ex-Officals to Death', 28 July 2015, www.reuters.com/article/us-libya-security-idUSKCN0Q20UP20150728.

'UN Council Deplores Congo Violence, Urges Talks', 4 April 2007, www.alertnet.org/thenews/newsdesk/N03244140.htm.

Rice, X. and T. Branigan, 'Sudanese President Expels Aid Agencies', *Guardian*, 5 March 2009, www.theguardian.com/world/2009/mar/05/sudan-aid-agencies-expelled.

Richmond, O., 'A Post-Liberal Peace: Eirenism and the Everyday', *Review of International Studies*, 35, 2009, pp. 557–80.

'Becoming Liberal, Unbecoming Liberalism: Liberal-Local Hybridity via the Everyday as a Response to the Paradoxes of Liberal Peacebuilding', *Journal of Intervention and Statebuilding*, 3, 3, 2009, pp. 324–44.

Rigney, S., '"The Words Don't Fit You": Recharacterisation of the Charges, Trial Fairness, and Katanga', *Melbourne Journal of International Law*, 15, 2, 2014, pp. 1–18.

Roach, S., 'Justice of the Peace? Future Challenges and Prospects for a Cosmopolitan Court', in S. Roach (ed.), *Governance, Order and the International Criminal Court: Between Realpolitik and a Cosmopolitan Court*, Oxford University Press, 2009.

Politicizing the International Criminal Court: The Convergence of Politics, Ethics, and Law, Rowman and Littlefield, 2006.

Robinson, D., 'The Identity Crisis of International Criminal Law', *Leiden Journal of International Law*, 21, 2008, pp. 925–63.

'Inescapable Dyads: Why the International Criminal Court Cannot Win', *Leiden Journal of International Law*, 28, 2015, pp. 323–47.

'The Mysterious Mysteriousness of Complementarity', *Criminal Law Forum*, 21, 2010, pp. 67–102.

'Serving the Interests of Justice: Amnesties, Truth Commissions and the International Criminal Court', *European Journal of International Law*, 14, 3, 2003, pp. 481–505.

Rodman, K., 'Justice as a Dialogue between Law and Politics: Embedding the International Criminal Court within Conflict Management and Peacebuilding', *Journal of International Criminal Justice*, 12, 3, 2014, pp. 437–69.

'The Peace versus Justice Debate at the ICC: The Case of the Ituri Warlords in the Democratic Republic of the Congo', workshop paper, March 2016, http://web.colby.edu/karodman/files/2016/03/ICCWorkshop_DRC.pdf.

Rodriguez, C., K. Smith-Derksen and S. J. Akera, 'Seventy Times Seven: The Impact of the Amnesty Law in Acholi', Acholi Religious Leaders Peace Initiative, Women's Desk of Caritas Gulu, and Justice and Peace Commission of Gulu Archdiocese, 2002.

Roper, S., and L. Barria, 'State Cooperation and International Criminal Court Bargaining Influence in the Arrest and the Surrender of Suspects', *Leiden Journal of International Law*, 22, 2008, pp. 457–6.

Rosenberg, S., 'How Did the ICC Trial of Laurent Gbagbo Impact the Elections in Côte d'Ivoire?', Democracy in Africa blog, 13 November 2015, http://democracyinafrica.org/how-did-the-icc-trial-of-laurent-gbagbo-impact-the-elections-in-cote-divoire/.

Ross, S., 'A Rebel's Escape – an LRA Commander Tells his Story', Justice in Conflict blog, 31 July 2013, https://justiceinconflict.org/2013/07/31/a-rebels-escape-an-lra-commander-tells-his-story/.

Roth, K., 'Africa Attacks the International Criminal Court', *New York Review of Books*, 6 February 2014.

Rothwell, J., 'Darfur Conflict: "Hundreds of Children Gassed to Death since January by Government in Sudan"', *Daily Telegraph*, 29 September 2016, www.telegraph.co.uk/news/2016/09/29/darfur-conflict-sudanese-government-has-gassed-hundreds-of-child/.

Rowell, A., 'Former Tory PR Advises Kenyan Facing Hague Trial', *Independent*, 13 October 2012, www.independent.co.uk/news/uk/politics/former-tory-pr-advises-kenyan-facing-hague-trial-8210442.html.

Rubbers, B. and E. Gallez, 'Why Do Congolese People Go to Court? A Qualitative Study of Litigants' Experience of Two Justice of the Peace Courts in Lubumbashi', *Journal of Legal Pluralism and Unofficial Law*, 44, 66, 2012, pp. 79–108.

Rwanda Demobilisation and Reintegration Commission, 'Demobilisation', http://demobrwanda.gov.rw/.

Schabas, W., *An Introduction to the International Criminal Court* (5th edition), Cambridge University Press, 2017.

'The Banality of International Justice', *Journal of International Criminal Justice*, 11, 2013, pp. 545–51.

'Prosecutorial Discretion v. Judicial Activism at the International Criminal Court', *Journal of International Criminal Justice*, 6, 2008, pp. 731–61.

Scharf, M., 'The Amnesty Exception to the Jurisdiction of the International Criminal Court', *Cornell International Law Journal*, 32, 1999, pp. 507–27.

Schiff, B., *Building the International Criminal Court*, Cambridge Univerisity Press, 2008.

Schmitt, P., 'France, Africa and the ICC: The Neocolonialist Critique and the Crisis of Institutional Legitimacy', in K. Clarke, A. Knottnerus and E. de Volder (eds.), *Africa and the ICC: Perceptions of Justice*, Cambridge University Press, pp. 138–43.

Schomerus, M., 'Even Eating You Can Bite Your Tongue: Dynamics and Challenges of the Juba Peace Talks with the Lord's Resistance Army', Ph.D. thesis, London School of Economics and Political Science, 2012.

'"They Forget What They Came For": Uganda's Army in Sudan', *Journal of Eastern African Studies*, 6, 1, 2012, pp. 124–53.

Seils, P. and M. Wierda, 'The International Criminal Court and Conflict Mediation', International Center for Transitional Justice, Occasional Paper Series, June 2005.

Sekhon, N., 'Complementarity and Postcoloniality', *Emory International Law Journal*, 27, 2013, pp. 799–828.

Servant, J.-C., 'Briefing: Kikuyus Muscle in on Security and Politics: Kenya's Righteous Youth Militia', *Review of African Political Economy*, 34, 113, September 2007, pp. 521–6.

Shklar, J., *Legalism: Law, Morals, and Political Trials*, Harvard University Press, 1964.

Sikkink, K., 'The Age of Accountability: The Rise of Individual Criminal Accountability', in F. Lessa and L. Payne (eds.), *Amnesty in the Age of Human Rights Accountability: Comparative and International Perspectives*, Cambridge University Press, 2012, pp. 19–41.

Silk, J., 'Caring at a Distance', *Philosophy and Geography*, 1, 2, 1998, pp. 165–82.

Simonse, S., W. Verkoren and G. Junne, 'NGO Involvement in the Juba Peace Talks: The Role and Dilemmas of IKV Pax Christi', in T. Allen and K. Vlassenroot (eds.), *The Lord's Resistance Army: Myth and Reality*, Zed Books, 2011 pp. 223–40.

Simpson, G., *Law, War and Crime: War Crimes Trials and the Reinvention of International Law*, Polity, 2007.

Slosson, M., 'ICC Prosecutor Courts Hollywood with Invisible Children', Reuters, 1 April 2012, www.reuters.com/article/2012/04/01/us-kony-campaign-hollywood-idUSBRE8300JZ20120401.

Sluiter, G., 'The Problematic Absence of Subpoena Powers at the ICC', *New Criminal Law Review*, 12, 2009, pp. 590–608.

Smirl, L., *Spaces of Aid: How Cars, Compounds and Hotels Shape Humanitarianism*, University of Chicago Press, 2015.

Smith, D., 'Hunting The Terminator: Congo Continues Search for Bosco Ntaganda', *Guardian*, 28 November 2012, www.theguardian.com/world/2012/nov/28/terminator-search-bosco-ntaganda-congo.

'ICC Prosecutor Shelves Darfur War Crimes Probe', *Guardian*, 14 December 2014, www.theguardian.com/world/2014/dec/14/icc-darfur-war-crimes-fatou-bensouda-sudan.

'New Chief Prosecutor Defends International Criminal Court', *Guardian*, 23 May 2012, www.theguardian.com/law/2012/may/23/chief-prosecutor-international-criminal-court?newsfeed=true.

Smith, P., 'Interview: Luis Moreno Ocampo, ICC Prosecutor', *The Africa Report*, 21 September 2009, www.theafricareport.com/News-Analysis/interview-luis-moreno-ocampo-icc-prosecutor.html.

Snyder, J. and L. Vinjamuri, 'Trials and Errors: Principle and Pragmatism in Strategies of International Justice', *International Security*, 28, 3, Winter 2003/4, pp. 5–44.

Social Science Research Council, 'Consolidating the Peace: Closing the M23 Chapter', paper prepared on behalf of the DRC Affinity Group, December 2014.

Sriram, C., 'Justice as Peace? Liberal Peacebuilding and Strategies of Transitional Justice', *Global Security*, 21, 4, 2007, pp. 579–91.

Sriram, C. and S. Brown, 'Kenya in the Shadow of the ICC: Complementarity, Gravity and Impact', *International Criminal Law Review*, 12, 2, 2012, pp. 219–44.

Stahn, C., 'Introduction: Bridge over Troubled Waters?', in C. Stahn and M. El Zeidy (eds.), *The International Criminal Court and Complementarity*, vol. I, Cambridge University Press, 2011, pp. 1–18.

Stahn, C. (ed.), *The Law and Practice of the International Criminal Court*, Oxford University Press, 2014.

Stearns, J., 'Strongman of the Eastern DRC: A Profile of General Bosco Ntaganda', Rift Valley Institute, 12 March 2013.

Stephen, C., 'Gaddafi son Saif al-Islam Freed by Libyan Militia', *Guardian*, 11 June 2017, www.theguardian.com/world/2017/jun/11/gaddafi-son-saif-al-islam-freed-by-libyan-militia.

Straus, S., *The Order of Genocide: Race, Power, and War in Rwanda*, Cornell University Press, 2006.

Struett, M., *The Politics of Constructing the International Criminal Court: NGOs, Discourse, and Agency*, Palgrave Macmillan, 2008.

Tait, D., 'Remote and Intimate Justice: Challenges and Paradoxes for Courts of the Future', paper presented at the 2004 Australasian Law Reform Agencies Conference, Wellington, 16 April 2004.

Tallgren, I., 'We Did It? The Vertigo of Law and Everyday Life at the Diplomatic Conference on the Establishment of an International Criminal Court', *Leiden Journal of International Law*, 12, 13, 1999, pp. 683–707.

Taylor, M., 'Game on between Uganda's Former Liberation Allies', International Crisis Group, 7 October 2015, http://blog.crisisgroup.org/africa/uganda/2015/10/07/game-on-between-ugandas-former-liberation-war-allies/.

Tedeschini, M., 'Complementarity in Practice: The ICC's Inconsistent Approach in the Gaddafi and al-Senussi Admissibility Decisions', *Amsterdam Law Forum*, 7, 1, 2015, pp. 76–97.

Teitel, R., *Globalizing Transitional Justice: Contemporary Essays*, Oxford University Press, 2014.

'Global Transitional Justice', Project on Human Rights, Global Justice & Democracy, Working Paper No. 8, Spring 2010.

Humanity's Law, Oxford University Press, 2013.

Tejan-Cole, A., 'The Complementary and Conflicting Relationship between the Special Court for Sierra Leone and the Truth and Reconciliation Commission', *Yale Human Rights and Development Journal*, 6, 1, 2014, pp. 139–59.

Thapa, S., 'LGBT Uganda Today Continue to Face Danger despite Nullification of Anti-Homosexuality Act', Human Rights Campaign, 30 September 2015, www.hrc.org/blog/lgbt-ugandans-continue-to-face-danger-despite-nullification-of-anti-homosex.

Thoms, O., J. Ron and R. Paris, 'State-Level Effects of Transitional Justice: What Do We Know?', *International Journal of Transitional Justice*, 4, 3, 2010, pp. 329–54.

Titeca, K., 'The Spiritual Order of the LRA', in T. Allen and K. Vlassenroot (eds.), *The Lord's Resistance Army: Myth and Reality*, Zed Books, 2010, pp. 59–73.

Titeca, K. and T. Costeur, 'An LRA for Everyone: How Different Actors Frame the Lord's Resistance Army', *African Affairs*, 114, 454, 2015, pp. 92–114.

Tomuschat, C., 'The Legacy of Nuremberg', *Journal of International Criminal Justice*, 4, 2006, pp. 830–44.

Trahan, J., 'A Complementarity Challenge Gone Awry: The ICC and the Libya Warrants', *Opinio Juris*, 30 August 2015, http://opiniojuris.org/2015/09/04/guest-post-a-complementarity-challenge-gone-awry-the-icc-and-the-libya-warrants/.

Tran, M., 'Ugandan Rebel Leader Fails to Sign Peace Deal', *Guardian*, 11 April 2008, www.theguardian.com/world/2008/apr/11/uganda.

Trapani A., 'Complementarity in the Congo: The Direct Application of the Rome Statute in the Military Courts of the DRC', DOMAC Project, DOMAC Paper 11, November 2011.

Trial Watch, 'Yves Mandro Kahwa Panga', last modified 14 June 2016, https://trialinternational.org/latest-post/yves-mandro-kahwa-panga/.

Uganda Human Rights Commission, 'Workshop Report: Implications of the International Criminal Court Investigations on Human Rights and the Peace Process in Uganda', 5 October 2004.

Ullrich, L., 'Beyond the "Global/Local Divide": Local Intermediaries, Victims and the Justice Contestations of the International Criminal Court', *Journal of International Criminal Justice*, 14, 3, 2016, pp. 543–68.

United Nations, 'Statute of the International Criminal Tribunal for Rwanda', 1995.

United Nations High Commissioner for Refugees, '2014 Democratic Republic of the Congo Operations Profile', copy on file with author.

United Nations Human Rights Council, 'Report of the Independent, International Commission of Inquiry on Côte d'Ivoire', 6 June 2011.

United Nations Joint Human Rights Office, 'Report of the United Nations Joint Human Rights Office on Serious Human Rights Violations Committed by Members of the Congolese Defense and Security Forces in Kinshasa in the Democratic Republic of Congo between 26 November and 25 December 2011', March 2012.

United Nations Mission in the Democratic Republic of Congo, 'Human Rights Monthly Assessment: March 2008', 14 May 2008.

United Nations News Centre, 'Security Council Urges DR of Congo to Meet Next June's Election Deadline', 7 November 2005, https://reliefweb.int/report/democratic-republic-congo/security-council-urges-dr-congo-meet-next-junes-election-deadline.

United Nations Office for the Coordination of Humanitarian Affairs, 'Consolidated Appeal for Uganda 2006', 30 November 2005.

United Nations Office of the High Commissioner for Human Rights, 'Rule-of-Law Tools for Post-Conflict States: Amnesties', 2009.

United Nations Security Council, 'Meetings Coverage: State Cooperation with International Criminal Court Vital to Ensure Justice for Victims of Atrocity Crimes in Libya, Prosecutor Tells Security Council', 8 May 2017.

'Reports of the Secretary-General on the Sudan and South Sudan', 12 December 2014.

United States Congress, 'Democratic Republic of the Congo Relief, Security, and Democracy Promotion Act', 16 December 2005, www.govtrack.us/congress/bills/109/s2125.

United States Department of State, 'War Crimes Reward Program', www.state.gov/j/gcj/wcrp/.

United States House of Representatives, 'Resolution Expressing Support for Robust Efforts by the United States to See Joseph Kony, the Leader of the Lord's Resistance Army, and his Top Commanders Brought to Justice and the Group's Atrocities Permanently Ended', 3 March 2012, http://royce.house.gov/uploadedfiles/mcgovern_royce_res_spotlights_kony_and_lra_3.13.12.pdf.

van den Berg, S., 'Defence Tactics Exposed in Ongwen Case at ICC', International Justice Tribune, 6 December 2016, www.justicetribune.com/blog/defence-tactics-exposed-ongwen-case-icc.

Verweijen, J., 'The Disconcerting Popularity of Popular In/justice in the Fizi/ Uvira Region, Eastern Democratic Republic of the Congo', *International Journal on Minority and Group Rights*, 22, 2015, pp. 335–59.

Vilmer, J.-B., 'The African Union and the International Criminal Court: Counteracting the Crisis', *International Affairs*, 92, 6, 2016, pp. 1319–42.

Vines, A., 'Does the International Criminal Court Help to End Conflict or Exacerbate It?', *Guardian*, 22 February 2016, www.theguardian.com/ global-development/2016/feb/22/international-criminal-court-help-to-end-conflict-or-exacerbate-it.

Vinjamuri, L., 'Deterrence, Democracy and the Pursuit of International Justice', *Ethics & International Affairs*, 24, 2, 2010, pp. 191–211.

'Is the International Criminal Court Following the Flag in Mali?', Political Violence@a Glance blog, 22 January 2013, https://politicalviolenceataglance .org/2013/01/22/is-the-international-criminal-court-following-the-flag-in-mali/.

Vinck, P. and P. Pham, 'Searching for Lasting Peace: Population-Based Survey on Perceptions and Attitudes about Peace, Security and Justice in Eastern Democratic Republic of the Congo', Harvard Humanitarian Initiative and UNDP, 2014.

Waddell, N. and P. Clark (eds.), *Courting Conflict: Justice, Peace and the ICC in Africa*, Royal African Society, 2008.

(eds.), *Peace, Justice and the ICC in Africa*, Royal African Society, 2007, www.lse.ac.uk/international-development/Assets/Documents/PDFs/csrc-background-papers/Peace-Justice-and-the-ICC-series-report.pdf.

Wakabi, W., 'Another 777 Victims to Participate in Bemba Trial', International Justice Monitor, 14 November 2012, www.ijmonitor.org/ 2012/11/another-777-victims-to-participate-in-bemba-trial/.

'Challenges of Holding Ntaganda's Trial in Congo', International Justice Monitor, 20 March 2015, www.ijmonitor.org/2015/03/challenges-of-holding-ntagandas-trial-in-congo/.

Waldorf, L., 'Mass Justice for Mass Atrocity: Rethinking Local Justice as Transitional Justice', *Temple Law Review*, 1, 55, 2006, pp. 1–80.

Weatherall, T., 'The Evolution of "Hibernation" at the International Criminal Court: How the World Misunderstood Prosecutor Bensouda's Darfur Announcement', *American Society of International Law* online series, 20, 10, 2016, www.asil.org/insights/volume/20/issue/10/evolution-hibernation-international-criminal-court-how-world.

Weiner, A., 'Prudent Politics: The International Criminal Court, International Relations and Prosecutorial Independence', *Washington University Global Studies Law Review*, 12, 2013, pp. 545–62.

Weissman, F., 'Humanitarian Aid and the International Criminal Court: Grounds for Divorce', Centre de Réflexion sur l'Action et les Savoirs Humanitaires (CRASH), Médecins sans Frontières, July 2009, www .msf-crash.org/sites/default/files/2017-06/7d9b-fw-2009-humanitarian-aid-and-international-criminal-court-grounds-for-divorce.-_fr-art-p._.pdf.

Whiting, A., 'Dynamic Investigative Practice at the International Criminal Court', *Law and Contemporary Problems*, 76, 3/4, 2013, pp. 163–89.

'Finding Strength within Constraints', International Criminal Justice Today project, American Bar Association-International Criminal Court, 23 November 2016.

Whiting, A., 'The Significance of the ICC's First Guilty Plea', Just Security blog, 23 August 2016, www.justsecurity.org/32516/significance-iccs-guilty-plea/.

Whitlock, C., 'US-Trained Congolese Troops Committed Rapes and Other Atrocities, UN Says', *Washington Post*, 13 May 2013, www.washington post.com/world/national-security/us-trained-congolese-troops-committed-rapes-and-other-atrocities-un-says/2013/05/13/9781dd88-bbfe-11e2-a31d-a41b2414d001_story.html.

Wikileaks, 'Ambassador DiCarlo Meets with International Criminal Court President Song', 19 May 2009, https://wikileaks.org/plusd/cables/09USUNNEWYORK519_a.html.

Wilkerson, M. and F. Nyakairu, 'Museveni Offers Kony Amnesty', *Daily Monitor*, 5 July 2006, www.allafrica.com/stories/200607051328.html.

Willems, R., *Security and Hybridity after Armed Conflict: The Dynamics of Security Provision in Post-Civil War States*, Routledge, 2015.

Wing, S., 'Mali: Politics of a Crisis', *African Affairs*, 112, 448, 2013, pp. 476–85.

Wilson, R., 'Through the Lens of International Criminal Law: Comprehending the African Context of Crimes at the International Criminal Court', *Studies in Ethnicity and Nationalism*, 11, 1, 2011, pp. 106–15.

Young, T., 'A Project to Be Realised: Global Liberalism and Contemporary Africa', *Millennium: Journal of International Studies*, 24, 3, 1995, pp. 527–46.

Zongwe, D., F. Butedi and P. Clément, '*The Legal System of the Democratic Republic of the Congo (DRC): Overview and Research*', Hauser Global Law School Program, January/February 2015.

Index